Privatization Amidst Poverty

Contemporary Challenges in Latin American Political Economy

Privatization Amidst Poverty

Contemporary Challenges in Latin American Political Economy

Edited by

Jorge A. Lawton

DISTRIBUTED BY

LYNNE RIENNER PUBLISHERS

1800 30TH ST., SUITE 314, BOULDER, CO 80301
TEL: 303-444-6684 · FAX: 303-444-0824

The mission of the North-South Center is to promote better relations and serve as a catalyst for change among the United States, Canada, and the nations of Latin America and the Caribbean by advancing knowledge and understanding of the major political, social, economic, and cultural issues affecting the nations and peoples of the Western Hemisphere.

Permissions to reprint the following have been granted:

Atwood, J. Brian. 1993. *Statement of Principles on Participatory Development.* U.S. Agency for International Development Bureau for Legislative and Public Affairs. Speech delivered by U.S. AID Director J. Brian Atwood, Nov. 16, 1993.

Reprinted by permission of *International Economic Insights.* Feinberg, Richard E. 1992. "Latin America: Back on the Screen." III (July/August, 4): 3-6.

Reprinted by permission of The Brookings Institution. Graham, Carol. 1991. *From Emergency Employment to Social Investment: Alleviating Poverty in Chile.* Washington, D.C.: The Brookings Institution.

Reprinted by permission of The Brookings Institution. Lustig, Nora. 1992. "Mexico: The Social Costs of Adjustment." *Mexico: The Remaking of an Economy.* Washington, D.C.: The Brookings Institution.

Reprinted by permission of Sage Publications, Inc. Pastor, Robert. 1994. "The U.S. and the Caribbean: The Power of the Whirlpool." *ANNALS of the American Academy of Political and Social Sciences* 533 (May)

"Percussion of the Sea," photographed on the cover, is a steel painted with acrylic work of Puerto Rican sculptor Luis Torruella, who has exhibited at the World's Fair in Seville, Spain; Costa Rica; the United States; Moscow; and Puerto Rico. Mr. Torruella is represented by Galerie Botello, Plaza las Americas, San Juan, Puerto Rico.

Library of Congress Cataloging-in-Publication Data

Privatization amidst poverty :   contemporary challenges in Latin Ameri-
   can political economy /   edited by Jorge A. Lawton.
          p   cm.
   Includes bibliographical references and index.
   ISBN 0-935501-95-9
   1. Poverty — Latin America. 2. Structural adjustment (Economic policy) —
Latin America. 3. Privatization — Latin America.
   I. Lawton. Jorge A.
   HC130.P8P75 1995   94-33740
   338.98—dc20   CIP

Printed in the United States of America
99 98 97 96 95 6 5 4 3 2 1

Dedication

This book is dedicated to my father, G. Albert Lawton, entrepreneur and man of ethics, vigorous in his eighth decade, and to Eliana Corona of Chile, who has quietly shown through professional competence and compassion, together with personal courage, how fully life can be celebrated.

Contents

Acknowledgments ix

Introduction xiii
Jorge A. Lawton

Strategy

Sustaining and Consolidating Latin America's Recovery 1
Richard E. Feinberg

The Dilemmas of Development:
A Latin American Perspective 9
Richard D. Fletcher

Conceptualizing Development:
Moving Beyond Linear Northern Perspectives 15
Jorge A. Lawton

Key Case Studies

Economic Liberalization and Political Instability:
The Venezuelan Experience 39
Moisés Naim

Mexico: The Social Costs of Adjustment 69
Nora Lustig

Privatizing the Economies:
Lessons from the Chilean Experience 111
Felipe Larraín B.

From Emergency Employment to Social Investment:
Alleviating Poverty in Chile 121
Carol Graham

Political and Economic Reform in Argentina and Brazil:
Contrasting Priorities, Contrasting Success 163
Margaret Sarles

Argentina's Progress from Insolvency to Recovery 179
Richard S. Newfarmer

**Public Policies in Conflict: Structural Adjustment
Versus Alternative Development in Bolivia** 193
Kevin Healy

Critical Issues and Themes

Poverty, the Environment, and Women in the Work Force 211
Marguerite S. Berger

**Development Banks, NAFTA,
and the Enterprise for the Americas Initiative** 221
Muni Figueres de Jiménez

**The Evolving Concept of Environment
and Sustainable Development** 227
Barbara J. Bramble

The U.S. and the Caribbean: The Power of the Whirlpool 235
Robert A. Pastor

**The Evolving Japanese Perspective on the
North American Free Trade Agreement** 251
Kanako Yamaoka

Appendices

Expanding Trade and Creating American Jobs 259
Bill Clinton

Statement on the Signing of NAFTA 275
Bill Clinton

Statement of Principles on Participatory Development 277
J. Brian Atwood

Contributors 283

Index 287

Acknowledgments

That the process of privatization would bring with it multiple social costs, some temporary but others much longer and more difficult to address, was apparent in theory at the outset of this ambitious project. In organizing the original seminar presentations, we anticipated thematic, policy strategic, and key case study dimensions of this broad phenomenon. But we also chose to keep a close eye on the reality of the hemisphere's dramatic economic and social transitions, thereby significantly enlarging and extending our original conception but, we believe, enriching and strengthening the final volume.

The analytical process has thus covered an unusually long road — incorporating many unfolding events and worked on by many hands. The embryo of this volume was originated by the editor as part of the Latin American and Caribbean seminar series of the Southern Center for International Studies (SCIS), now with more than a quarter of a century's tradition in hosting international fora and fostering education on a broad range of global issues. We thank Peter White, SCIS president, and Julia White, vice president and moving force behind the SCIS video educational series. We extend particular gratitude to the editor's colleague and sage partner throughout the original seminar organization, fund-raising, hosting, and transcription process, Cedric Suzman, SCIS vice president and director of educational programs. As additional collaborators were invited and continual updating by the editor was required, Cedric's patience was exemplary.

Further thanks go to successive staff at The Southern Center: to Parke Kennedy, the current affairs library director, and her successor in preparing the hard copy of the transcripts, Marcia Hoinville, to the ever upbeat Patsy Conn until we lost her to further studies in Australia, and especially, throughout SCIS' involvement, to the efficient, good-humored, and thoroughly southern SCIS program associate, Rhonda Geiger.

The original financial support for the project came from the Inter-American Development Bank (IDB) and the assistance of IDB's external affairs and speakers bureau representative, Judith Melamud; also from the

North-South Center of the University of Miami, headed by Ambassador Ambler H. Moss, Jr., who participated as moderator and intellectual catalyst at one of the seminar sessions; from The Katherine John Murphy Foundation through its executive board; and from The South-North Communications Group in the form of months of the general editor's time, as the project passed through its many successive stages.

Evident gratitude goes to each of the colleagues whose original seminar presentations gave impetus to the book: Marguerite Berger, Morris Blachman, Barbara Bramble, Muni Figueres, Richard Fletcher, Robert Pastor, Margaret Sarles, and Kanako Yamaoka.

During the entire first phase of the project, the reality of events continuing to unfold helped make us acutely aware of how the entire volume would be strengthened if we incorporated further key country case studies, soliciting authors who had participated directly in the privatization negotiating process, others with the critical view of close observers of the process, and some focusing on the strategic skills and errors of the process's decisionmakers.

Specifically, we thank Felipe Larraín, consultant/participant from The World Bank in the case of the very distinct second round (mid-1980s) of Chile's highly conditioned privatization; and Richard Newfarmer, then senior economist at The World Bank for Argentina. The editor is particularly grateful to the former governor of Caracas and adroit former chair of the U.N. Security Council, Diego Arria, for recommending the work of Moisés Naim, former Venezuelan minister of state and prolific writer/analyst. We thank Carol Graham for her study of Chile's special public employment projects for those unemployed, officially classified as falling into "extreme poverty"; and to Kevin "Benito" Healy, clearly committed for more than a decade and a half to working side by side with Bolivia's peasant majority, for the series of drafts analyzing not only their welfare, but also his critical analysis of the observed effects on their lives of IMF and U.S. administrations' structural adjustment policies.

Richard Feinberg, drawing on his rich personal experience, not in any way on his official role as senior National Security Council advisor on Latin American affairs to President Clinton, managed to add a hemispheric perspective to those he denominates the "technipols," in reference to the current generation of cabinet-level advisors to key Latin American presidents and the ensuing effects on the widespread governmental disposition toward privatization.

Finally, editorial decisions had to be made with regard to the thorny case of Mexico. We turned to the precise scholarship of Nora Lustig in order to be able to lay the foundation for understanding Mexico's profound present crisis.

Her carefully documented samples of the effects of Mexico's structural adjustment on household purchasing power illuminate the initial social costs incurred.

We know at present, in mid-1995, that Mexico has entered into a broad social, economic, and political crisis. We also know that this is one case clearly demonstrating the wider social, financial, and legal ramifications of the economic transition occurring throughout the hemisphere and beyond. Since the dramatic devaluation of the peso at the end of 1994 by the incoming Zedillo administration, the Banco de México has acknowledged slightly over a 100 percent loss of purchasing power in the first five months of 1995 alone.

Labor-intensive, small and medium-scale Mexican firms and their employees have become the victims of the current scramble for survival. Banco de México statistics for the same five-month period acknowledge an unemployment and severe underemployment level of more than 58 percent of the economically active work force.

At this point, overall morale is inevitably affected, since no one can authoritatively say how long it will take Mexico to raise and sustain production levels of the surviving firms. How far into this vast unemployed force will retraining programs reach? What proportion of Mexico's firms will be able to take advantage of the "opening to the world market"?

While such widespread unemployment and loss of purchasing power hits Mexican workers, the inevitable increase in theft and violent crime is growing. Corruption up to the highest levels continues to be uncovered, not only in the Russian and many of the Central European market transitions, but also in too many of the Latin American cases.

Instantaneous international communication networks add an international dimension of possible "contagion" from "national crises" like Mexico's. While the U.S. Treasury moved quickly to transfer emergency capital into Mexico, investors in other countries watched anxiously. The Argentine presidential campaign process proceeded, with the mid-May re-election of the aggressively pro-privatization Carlos Saúl Menem, despite Argentine government statistics showing an unemployment rate officially exceeding 12 percent and full knowledge of Mexico's current crisis.

These cases are cited as vivid examples of how the solid analyses laid out in the various country and thematic studies will be indispensable for an understanding of the multiple dimensions of the privatization process that are continuing to emerge. A newly vigilant and creative state must also emerge if such broad market transformations are to benefit the majority.

Various colleagues have offered valuable critiques. We thank especially Marc Lindenberg, Richard Weisskoff, David C. Bruce, Henry Esposito, Richard Newfarmer, Michael Wooller, Carolyn Boyd Hatcher, and Pierre Ferrari, among others. Paula Bevington generously gave of her editing skills, breathing new life and, we trust, bringing greater clarity to a significant portion of the text.

We want to thank the publisher, the North-South Center, whose capable editorial and publications staff is headed by Richard Downes, director of communications. Jayne Weisblatt, editor, copy edited the chapters; Diane Duys, editorial assistant, proofread and entered corrections; Stephanie True Moss, publications designer, designed and formatted the text of the book and created the index; and Mary Mapes, publications director, coordinated production and designed the cover from the photograph of Luis Torruella's striking sculpture, "Percussion of the Sea." One person deserves unlimited respect and gratitude for the constancy of her support, encouragement, and confidence in the quality of the project. She grasped the importance of the successive phases and the time-consuming additional chapters in strengthening the final product. This is Kathleen Hamman, officially the North-South Center's editorial director, who, in practice, became the true "madrina" of *Privatization Amidst Poverty*. She worked closely with the general editor in coordinating the book, managing to keep in touch, whether he was on the East or West coasts, in the Caribbean, and, particularly, when nearly inaccessible during the international embargo in Haiti. Ms. Hamman understood the balance between the editor's decision to add new analysts while updating earlier chapters and the pragmatic need to complete each piece for the final mosaic to take form.

Finally, we extend our thanks to the distinguished individuals who have taken their time to read and endorse the lessons contained in this work: Dr. Johnnetta B. Cole, Dr. James W. Fowler, Dr. Marc M. Lindenberg, the Honorable Michael Manley, and the Honorable Andrew Young.

Each author, of course, assumes responsibility for his or her own contribution and the editor for the volume as a whole.

Jorge A. Lawton, editor

Introduction

Reach of the Market

Jorge A. Lawton

The essays in this volume break new ground. They analyze the economic rationale for the radical market reforms sweeping the hemisphere, but they also probe the real social effects of these same market mechanisms. From different vantage points, the authors ask what effects the new market and a revamped state will have on the lives of the poor. Up to an estimated three-quarters of the Western Hemisphere's population still experience some degree of malnutrition, and half (more than 222 million people) live in poverty.[1] This is the reality within which adjustment and privatizations are taking place.

While most of the contributors to this volume consider a market-oriented economy necessary for development, none would consider it sufficient. Their optimism over the renewed economic growth in the hemisphere is tempered by an acute awareness of its fragility and of the millions who still remain outside the circle of its benefits. Many traditional economists still tout the goal of "growth," not concerning themselves with who benefits from the growth. The contributors to this volume, however, are well aware that for vast numbers of the hemisphere's unemployed and underemployed, the contemporary phenomenon of measuring a country's success by its gross domestic product (GDP) still translates for them as "growth with unemployment."

Privatization Amidst Poverty: Contemporary Challenges in Latin American Political Economy enters into the challenging realm of political economy. What the market contributes is vital; no less vital is the range of political economy concerns — from "social context" to "decision-making access" to "opportunities for equity" — concerns that lie beyond the reach of conventional economics and the market itself. Thus, this volume sets out to analyze not only the performance of economic adjustment in the abstract but also its social costs and its impact in practice.

It is well known that the fundamental economic adjustment policies being implemented throughout the hemisphere were adopted in the wake of the "lost decade" of the 1980s. As Latin America's economies suffered stagnation, a body of "new poor" were created. Dysfunctional economies, beset by low productivity, crippling debt, hyperinflation, chronic undertaxation, and an obsolete protective tariff system were subjected to market "rationalization."

Bloated state monopolies were privatized under formulas varying from country to country and case to case. Top-heavy labor oligarchies in Argentina and elsewhere found themselves stripped of their traditional privileges. They and the former state monopolies were made to follow the competitive market path. Yet those not equipped for such a change, once displaced, only added to the sections of citizens below the poverty line.

At the same time, as elections and the early stages of democratization returned, many new or renewed citizen groups demanded that those responsible for the series of privatization sales, from the heads of state on down, be held accountable. Charges of rampant corruption were levied against those at the highest levels. In Brazil and Venezuela, for example, investigations into corruption led to the 1993 removal, under threat of impeachment, of the elected presidents. While these painful corruption investigations gave longer term hope for some level of future accountability, in the short term, only cynicism grew. The exposure of official corruption in country after country confirmed a popular Latin American perception that there had long been two different economic systems operating under two different sets of rules: one for "them," a small elite, and the other for "us," the largely disenfranchised majority. If so, where then was "our incentive" to try to compete on such an uneven playing field?

Outside Latin America, the Western Hemisphere's "era of economic adjustment" and series of privatizations have been heralded with nearly unbridled praise. At home, the "transition process" of adjustment has been recognized as far less smooth, as the most vulnerable societal sectors have been trapped with even fewer resources than before. Freed from hyperinflation — the indirect taxation of the old era — they do not yet have the means to compete in the new. Most have been cut off from their prior gauze-thin safety nets before gaining access to new credit mechanisms.

In the meantime, who will provide for primary health care and basic public education? How will corrections for gender imbalance and ecological disregard be built into the new systems? What will be the attributes of a revamped state? How can market and state work efficiently — and equitably — together? What can be identified as the "cardinal sins" of privatization, and what are some of the specific corrective actions the state needs to carry out?[2]

Now that the concept of income distribution has finally become accepted as a goal of mainstream development doctrine, a new generation of staff economists is rediscovering the hemisphere's extremes of income concentration. We are reminded that today, years after Brazil's "economic miracle," for example, the wealthiest 20 percent receive 26 times the income of the poorest 20 percent.[3]

We know that, historically, many of this hemisphere's societies never passed through any redistributive social revolution after independence, not even the middle class one of the North's industrial revolution. One consequence is the glaring absence of "intermediary institutions."

In "developed economies" it is precisely these mediating information and service networks that tend to act both as early warning systems and shock absorbers. Often these networks can point out alternatives for their constituents well before the onset of adverse economic adjustments, or knowing they will be adversely affected, at least they can broker concessions.

Latin American countries' entry into international competition in an ever more integrated world capitalist economy may be a given, but early success cannot be presumed. Dismantling the import substitution and other protective tariff barriers Latin America has grown accustomed to may be overdue, but the transition is not an easy one. Until the composition of Latin American exports evolves, disadvantageous international terms of trade will remain a reality.

The transition's "social costs" are not mute; rising voices of exclusion are all around us. Prison riots in Argentina, food riots in Venezuela, hunger and legions of street children in Brazil, the 1994 and 1995 "Zapatista" indigenous uprising in Chiapas — all make it abundantly clear that even, or especially, with the new market reforms, ever greater numbers see themselves as beyond the benefits of the market, stuck in poverty with the way out still not visible.

Contributors, Scope, and Content

The fifteen analysts contributing to this volume represent recognized excellence in their own specialties. Here, however, they demonstrate a willingness to go beyond the confines of traditional economic or political inquiry. The operative premise binding the individual chapters is a simple one: for an interdisciplinary problem — such as development — there must be interdisciplinary analysis.

Thus, these essays bring the rigor of analytic theory to the messy world of reality. We are not satisfied with how "under ideal conditions" market forces "should interact," but rather, we are interested in observing the real costs and lessons from adjustment policies in practice.

Many of the analysts have directly witnessed — from varying perspectives, as World Bank or Inter-American Development Bank senior officers, advisors to grass-roots community organizations, or state ministers — the challenges in practice of economic adjustment, differing phases of privatization, and the acute effects on already struggling populations.

One of the authors analyzes the increasing importance and impoverishment of women in "development," while another explores the role of active environmental planning occurring along with economic adjustment. They come from throughout the hemisphere and beyond. In addition to U.S. citizens with years of direct experience abroad, the authors include a Venezuelan, an Argentine, a Chilean, a Costa Rican, a Jamaican, and to appreciate Japan's perception of NAFTA, a Japanese economist.

The book is organized into three sections: strategies for development, six key case studies, and critical issues to be confronted.

Richard Feinberg opens the first section with the question of sustainability of the hemisphere's market-oriented reforms. He stresses the need to confront potentially derailing shocks, whether from inflation fears, capital shortage, limited export capacity, or human and institutional limitations. Feinberg sees the chronic human limitations of underdevelopment as being partially overcome by the emergence of a new breed of government technocrats, "technopols," who are sensitive to the technical management of reforms as well as to the need to build supportive political coalitions.

Subsequent essays underscore how each case of adjustment and privatization differs, not only from country to country but also from phase to phase, under evolving conditions in the same country. Inclusive conditionality, applied in Chile's mid-1980s privatizations, was adopted as one of the lessons learned from the exclusive and failed mid-1970s privatizations. A clear and coherent overall development strategy must leave ample room for such variations.

Richard Fletcher and Jorge Lawton, respectively, examine traditional "southern" and "northern" strategies of development, each offering their own critiques and alternative principles.

Six key case studies follow. Former Venezuelan Minister of State, Moisés Naim, points out that his country shared the same increase of market influence and diminishing of the state being experienced from the mid-1980s throughout the hemisphere. Fundamental market reforms in Chile and Mexico preceded those in Venezuela; yet by the early 1990s the reaction was most intense in Venezuela, and, according to Naim, led to "massive riots, unprecedented inflation and recession, two military revolts, the deterioration of public services to the verge of collapse, and the ouster of President Carlos Andrés Pérez."

Analyzing the Venezuelan trauma, Naim cites Antonio Gramsci's observation that, "The ancient is dying and the new has yet to be born. In this interlude, monsters are bred." to describe the depth of Venezuela's transformation. He challenges President Ramón J. Velázquez's new government's, and indirectly the hemisphere's other market reform programs', capacity to convince their citizens "to abandon their lynching mood..." and to acquire a "deeper sense of shared burdens and shared destiny."

Naim warns that all the reforming countries, although more intense in Venezuela's case, had best heed the similarly "explosive mix" of "high expectations, incompetent public organizations, [...] exaggerated state intervention, and the collapse of an institutional setting based on economic, political, and social conditions that had ceased to exist."

Nora Lustig assesses the impact of Mexico's adjustment process on living standards for the Mexican people. With characteristic technical precision, Lustig elucidates how the adjustment process will have a pronounced effect on real incomes. This real income drop occurs if, as happened in Mexico's case, policies directed at expenditure switching (from tradable goods to goods that cannot be traded in world markets), in addition to policies directed simply at expenditure reduction, have a contractional effect on the economy. Mexico followed one common switching policy via nominal devaluation of domestic currency. Both earned (pretax) and total real wages are shown to fall with the adjustment process. Lustig specifies that this fall came from a level of previous Mexican living conditions in the late 1970s, when "41 percent of 1977 sampled households had total earnings below the prevailing minimum wage, ...or poverty line, ...then equal to $120 per month." In 1979, nearly one quarter of Mexico's population, "almost nineteen million people, ...suffered from malnutrition," and in 1978, "an estimated 45 percent of the population ...was not receiving health care coverage." The 1980 census estimated that "50.1 percent of Mexican households had no running water ...and 25 percent did not have electricity."

Relevant to the central concern of this volume of essays, Lustig reminds us how "the international rules of the game give labor and capital asymmetrical treatment." She explains how the weight of Mexico's adjustment process was borne unequally and how "the wealthy could always protect, and even expand, their wealth far more easily than the rest of society by simply transferring their assets abroad." This allowed them to protect their wealth "from the negative impact of devaluations and inflation on the real value of assets, while often earning huge capital gains."

Two conclusions from Lustig's analysis of the Mexican case strengthen our understanding of the overall effects of the adjustment process: "The crisis ...left Mexico with a relatively impoverished middle class, an increasing number of poor households, and the poor worse off than before." This damage was especially clear for those of the urban poor and rural and urban middle sectors most reliant on wage income. Lustig adds the caveat, "Although the middle ranges lost relatively more than the bottom of the population, one should be aware that even a minimal decline in the income of the poor can have devastating effects...." Lustig concludes with the sober warning that economic growth alone may be ineffective in cutting back hardcore poverty. Her analysis shows that if the per capita income of Mexico's bottom 10 percent were to grow steadily by Mexico's former post-war annual average of 3 percent, it would take them "about sixteen years to reach an income level equal to the extreme poverty line." Or, if growing at the 1988-1990 rate of 1 percent, "the waiting period would be almost forty-seven years ...[to be able] to buy only the necessary food intake." Thus, "equity-oriented reforms will have to be implemented, combining "immediate relief with productivity-enhancing policies."

The precipitous decline in the value of the peso at the end of 1994 and into 1995 and the shock of high-level political assassinations and subsequent investigations have prompted Mexican President Zedillo to say that "for many months" Mexicans would encounter considerably increased suffering.

At the same time, the Mexican crisis has revealed the heightened interdependency of the hemisphere. Indeed, there are not only fears of a "contagion effect" on countries such as Brazil and Argentina, but also questioning in the broader international community — Japan as well as Europe — of whether Mexico and the hemisphere possess the financial sophistication to cope with new trade demands.

Felipe Larraín participated in the two distinct rounds of adjustment and privatizations in Chile, the first from 1974-1978 and the second in 1985. Larrain warns that each process of privatization, anywhere in the world, will necessarily differ from others. But he offers useful insights into the lessons learned from Chile's first round, as well as the fresh conditions and adaptive forms employed in Chile's second round. The first round of privatizations and adjustment occurred primarily in 1975, a year when Chile "was facing the worst depression since the early thirties. National savings were at a low, the domestic capital markets were at a very primitive phase," and credit was restricted to very few hands. In addition to further concentrating wealth, Larrain adds that the first round also "had a negative effect on both savings and investment."

Chile's second round of privatizations in 1985 followed a very different set of formulas. Critical distinctions were made among traditional capitalism, in which individual investors would buy shares through the market; institutional capitalism, in which private pension funds were allowed to purchase limited shares through the market; and labor capitalism, in which workers were offered access to their severance funds and other incentives in order to become stockholders.

A variant of the third formula of "popular capitalism" was devised in the 1985 round when Chile divested its two largest banks and many of its savings and loan institutions. This time the required down payment was limited to only 5 percent, with the remainder available via a subsidized government loan. Credit subsidies and tax break incentives applied only to individuals, who then faced strict maximum stock ownership limits.

Unfortunately, the very adaptability of the formulas for the second round to Chilean national circumstances of the time led to charges that the rules of the game were subject to change as the process evolved. Larraín cites as second round successes: 1) the significant dissemination of property, 2) the access of workers to company ownership, and 3) the solid financial position with which the privatized new firms started off.

Carol Graham provides extensive data to examine the "other side" of the "Chilean miracle," or the Chilean military government's approach toward poverty and extreme poverty. Former President Patricio Aylwin, when referring to the extent of overall poverty at the beginning of his term of office (1989-1994), estimated that approximately five million persons, or 40 percent of the Chilean population, were living in poverty. Of the five million in poverty, over three million (nearly one third of the country) in 1985 were found to be condemned to "extreme poverty," defined as having a monthly income insufficient to meet basic subsistence needs. The Chilean government targeted its anti-poverty measures toward the poorest 10 percent, or the lowest third even of those defined to be in extreme poverty. For this poorest of the poor, Graham shows that some progress was made in nutrition, preventive health care, and primary education but points out that any progress there came "partly at the expense of other social needs such as housing, curative health care, and advanced education." She then cites further studies showing that the "Chilean miracle" did not reduce overall poverty: "In 1987 as many as 2.1 million workers, over half the labor force, lacked access to social security" [which they had enjoyed prior to 1973]."

Margaret Sarles tackles the entangled economic reform and political democratization processes in post-dictatorial Brazil and Argentina. She identifies reasons why the process rapidly became derailed in Brazil, while at least initially in Argentina the reformers developed a constituency for the adjustment process. Sarles contrasts the hyperinflation and strong party support facing President Carlos Menem in Argentina against the lower inflation levels and lack of any coherent political organization in [former President] Fernando Collor de Mello's case in Brazil. The leadership for privatization measures in Brazil under Collor de Mello was tentative and "tepid," while in Argentina Menem quickly used his political capital to organize tax and other fiscal reforms and to privatize state companies ranging from "airlines, telecommunications, railways, power, and oil concessions

...[to] even industries controlled by the military — petrochemicals, steel and munitions."

Sarles also argues that some private Argentine decisionmakers showed a remarkable capacity to adapt. When the adjustment process induced a recession, some formerly highly protected domestic manufacturers turned to export promotion. In order to reduce the import costs of their inputs, the same Argentine manufacturers, acting out of a revised self-interest, lent their weight to implementation of tariff reform and trade liberalization. Sarles adds that the Menem reform policies "brought inflation down to international levels and led to three years of economic expansion and substantial reductions in absolute poverty."

In contrast, Brazil's economic reform process failed abjectly during the tempestuous three years between President Collor's March 1990 inauguration and his December 1992 removal by impeachment. When Collor began his term, he "froze savings accounts, declared a moratorium of internal debt payments, posted 'for sale' signs on 188 government companies, ...set a preliminary target of dismissing from eighty thousand to seven hundred thousand national government workers, ...[and] abolished the linkage between wage increases and the inflation rate (indexation)."

After this reformist burst and some initial success at trade liberalization and export promotion, Collor's program became more and more bogged down. "Inflation crept back up steadily through 1990, and GDP fell by 4 percent [before] Collor tried a second adjustment plan in February 1991." The Brazilian Congress overwhelmingly rejected this program in August 1991.

Collor had virtually no congressional or state-to-state support, nor did he ever succeed in developing a national consensus to back basic reforms. By the end of 1990, what few elements of the reform process Collor had not already spoiled by ineptness, corruption, and political isolation were countered by the effect of the state governors organizing against him. Prodded by the governors, Congress reimposed indexation in December 1990. At the same time, various governors, backed by their increased powers from the 1988 Constitution, substantially increased public spending.

Collor's successor, Vice-President Itamar Franco, issued an executive decree to centralize in the presidency all subsequent privatization decisions. Paralleling the Mexican and Chilean approach, Franco then linked social welfare directly to any privatizations. He authorized for workers the right "to participate in setting auction prices, provide for retraining programs, and directly allocate some of the profits of privatization to health, education, and scientific and technological projects."

After Franco, President Fernando Henrique Cardoso explicitly asserted that in 1995 and beyond, the policy of privatizations would be pursued even more broadly and aggressively.

Richard Newfarmer provides revealing insights into the myriad structural and administrative reforms undertaken in Argentina since Carlos Menem's assumption of office in July 1989. At the end of the 1980s, Argentina's economy was plagued with chronic hyperinflation (200 percent monthly) driven by an entrenched maze of subsidies and a severe public deficit, deep recession, acute capital flight, savings and investment at half the rates of the previous decade, and Central Bank liquid reserves approaching zero — in sum, an economy on the brink of insolvency. Argentina's comprehensive reforms encompassed the legal framework, key institutions, and public policy. The reforms' immediate costs, overall rationale, and end purpose were repeatedly communicated to the population at large, already stung by hyperinflation. The pillars of the reforms centered on 1) revenue mobilization — a fundamental overhaul of the quantity and quality of the federal tax system; 2) a lowering of public expenditures through sharp reduction in public employment, privatizations, and fiscal decentralization; and 3) a restructuring of domestic and foreign liabilities.

Kevin Healy, focusing on Bolivia, posits that there is an inherent and disturbing conflict between two major public policies: structural adjustment and anti-narcotics. The World Bank and The International Monetary Fund chose Bolivia to implement a "radical, free market adjustment policy" as a "quasi-official doctrine of economic recovery and sustainable development for Third World countries." However, Healy argues that this official adjustment policy works to "increase coca-cocaine expansion ..., which, in turn, undermines the success of the U.S.-Bolivia drug policy."

On the premise that "without peasant development [42 percent of the population] in Bolivia, national development is a myth," Healy recommends that the Clinton administration move away from its endorsement of the structural adjustment policy for Boliva in favor of a "mix of state intervention and open markets" in order to support "peasant purchasing power, income and employment."

As an economist specializing in the role of women in development, Marguerite Berger offers a plethora of information. Problems include falling but still high birthrates, high risks of death in childbirth, low literacy and education levels, lower earnings than men for similar work, and less political clout than men. Latin American women's participation in the labor force, while lower than the 40 percent in the United States, has doubled from 15 percent to 30 percent over the past three decades and continues to rise at rates "between 3 percent to 6 percent per year in the past two decades, double the growth rate for men."

Parallel to the economic adjustment process, Berger points out "an invisible adjustment process within households ...[having to] produce [items] in their homes that they previously were able to buy, substituting for services such as health care, education, and other social services, and providing food in groups." Berger notes that structural changes toward a greater service sector, more light assembly operations, and more agricultural exports (packaging phase especially) have also brought an increasing demand for female labor. In the urban informal sectors, another area with a high concentration of women, labor laws are often not enforced affecting women in "street vending, home-based manufacturing shops for shoes and clothing, and informal restaurants." Small-scale agriculture is another sector where, increasingly, women participate.

Berger recommends improvements in health care services and basic infrastructure, especially in the areas of clean, safe water for cooking and heating and adequate sanitation facilities. Training and credit for micro enterprises, child development and day care, and strengthening women's grass-roots and community organizations are also among the series of practical policy suggestions raised by Berger to halt the increasing impoverishment of women in the hemisphere.

Muni Figueres de Jiménez examines the economic transition occurring in the hemisphere from the point of view of trade reform and social fund management by regional development banks. Her departure point comes in mid-1991 with the Bush administration's Enterprise for the Americas Initiative (EAI). Figueres perceives the larger task for the hemisphere as democracy building and "extending economic content to that democracy, both so that living conditions will improve and so that democratic systems can then be consolidated ...[or]...reforming an economy that in turn transforms the society."

Figueres conceives of the development banks as a "'fulcrum' between programs such as the EAI and the countries that would carry out the series of changes contemplated in the Initiative." Signs that regional institutions such as The Inter-American Development Bank (IDB) may be adapting to this fulcrum role are already visible. The IDB's ambitious 1993 "Forum on Social Reform and Poverty," the sixty-five essays resulting from that forum,[4] and the modification of the Banco Interamericano de Desarrollo (BID)'s internal structure to include a commitment to various social issues such as "governance" and "women in development" are further examples.

Figueres adds that Latin American and Caribbean countries are watching how NAFTA develops with "extreme caution," as the "outcome may well serve as a model for what they will have to negotiate." She points out that a new kind of hemispheric reality is evolving, whose tendency "seems to be toward the formation of a hemispheric economic unity." Figueres concludes by asking if, as Latin America withdraws its protective barriers, there will be "symmetrical liberalization of sensitive industries within the United States and Canada" in this process, for which the "social cost is immensely high."

Barbara Bramble analyzes the difficult environmental/economic interface, focusing over the past decade on "projects funded by multilateral development banks that had severe detrimental environmental and social impacts on local people."

As the director of International Programs for the National Wildlife Federation (NWF), Bramble recounts how she and other colleagues reached out to the people who had been directly affected by these projects, particularly Brazilian indigenous groups and rubber tappers, and brought representatives of these groups to the United States to tell the story of how they had been hurt, sometimes displaced, directly to the people making the development decisions in the banks, as well as in the U.S. Congress and the Department of the Treasury.

As a result, access to key decisionmakers improved from one visit to the next. But also, the witnesses, "seemingly powerless, isolated, unimportant people, whose low status enabled the authorities to foist such projects off on them, suddenly went home as international celebrities." This in turn allowed some of their proposals for alternative development projects to be listened to by their own governments, rather than the proposals imposed from the outside.

An ongoing concern, articulated by Bramble and taken up by the NWF, is responsibility for the effects on the environment of the hemisphere's growing free trade. "Who is going to be responsible for the negative environmental effects — water pollution, soil erosion, and toxic waste dumps — affecting people's health and the potential for future development?" Many free trade advocates are not going to pay for poverty reduction programs because they believe all social problems will be solved by the creation of a free market. She argues that trade itself is not the goal; the goal is creating sustainable livelihoods while improving the quality of people's lives. Free trade should be seen as a means toward achieving that goal.

Bramble later responds to her own question stating, "The NWF is asking that a small percentage of NAFTA's resources be devoted specifically to cleaning up the resultant pollution or be directed for use in Mexico by environmental agencies for capacity building, regulatory equipment, standard setting, and enforcement of rules and regulations."

Robert Pastor examines U.S. policy toward the Caribbean by dividing the twentieth century into three periods: the protectorate era (1898-1933), the Good Neighbor Policy (1933-1953), and the Cold War (1953-1990). Pastor's theory postulates U.S. involvement in the Caribbean as a "whirlpool pattern

xxiv
Privatization Amidst Poverty

of intensive involvement followed by disinterest" and suggests that within this pattern, "security considerations have remained paramount." The United States in all three periods of this century has become involved only when threatened by the possibility that other more powerful nations would forge a relationship in the Caribbean and use their foothold as a base to attack or harass the United States. As Pastor states, "Although the history of U.S. relations with the Caribbean is replete with examples of America's drive to extract resources, uproot seemingly alien ideologies, implant a political philosophy, or prescribe an economic orthodoxy, this whirlpool pattern suggests that the dominant motive has been U.S. security."

After surveying the history of U.S.-Caribbean relations, Pastor expresses his belief that the end of the Cold War presents an opportunity for the United States and the nations of the Caribbean "to swim free of the whirlpool that has captured the entire region since the turn of the century." The United States needs to develop "a collective defense of democracy and a social safety net for the poor people in the countries of the region" that will "assist the process of development and the pursuit of social justice."

Japanese analyst Kanako Yamaoka contributes the view of NAFTA as seen from Tokyo. Discussing the vital importance to Japan of exports and the U.S. market, the growing importance of Mexican and Latin American trade, as well as the difficult debate over manufacturing rules of origin, Yamaoka succinctly summarizes the Japanese view of NAFTA as one of "interest and suspicion."

Throughout this volume, the needs for efficiency and growth via some form of economic adjustment are discussed and analyzed. But, as can now be appreciated, the contributors also address equity and the majority's basic needs. Jean-Bertrand Aristide has expressed the goal for Haiti, the hemisphere's most wretched case, as movement from "misery to poverty with dignity." The UNDP's *Human Development Report 1994* succinctly summarizes the "paradigm of sustainable human development [as one which] values human life for itself."[5]

Our premise in this volume is that for adjustment programs to benefit people, and not the reverse, these programs must be analyzed and carried out in a context of holistic and participatory development. The search for vigorous and humane economies amidst gnawing poverty is an ongoing journey. In this volume, we hope to clarify a few more steps along the road.

Notes

1. Richard Weisskoff, 1993, "Basic Human Needs and the Democratic Process in Latin America," *North-South Issues* 2(2):1, North-South Center, University of Miami.

2. On the basis of the approximately 1400 privatizations carried out chiefly in Latin America between 1980 and 1991, the UNDP lists the following as the "seven sins of privatization": 1) maximizing revenue without creating a competitive environment, 2) replacing public monopolies with private ones, 3) using non-transparent and arbitrary procedures, 4) using the proceeds to finance budget deficits, 5) simultaneously crowding the financial markets with public borrowings, 6) making false promises to labor, and 7) privatizing without building a political consensus (UNDP, 1993, *Human Development Report* [New York: Oxford University Press, 5]).

The same report does not hesitate to argue that "the state needs to regulate and correct [when markets do not produce a desirable outcome]. This would include protecting competition through anti-monopoly laws, consumers through regulations on product standards, workers through adequate and well-enforced labor legislation, and such vulnerable groups as children and the elderly. It would also include protecting the environment, by banning certain types of pollution and ensuring that polluters pay" (UNDP, 1993, 4).

3. UNDP, 1993, 17.

4. *Reforma Social y Pobreza, Hacia una agenda integrada de desarrollo,* 1993, Banco Interamericano de Desarrollo (BID) y Programa de las Naciones Unidas para el Desarrollo (PNUD), 227. Washington, D.C., and New York.

5. UNDP, 1994, *Human Development Report* (New York: Oxford University Press, 13).

Strategy

Sustaining and Consolidating Latin America's Recovery

Richard E. Feinberg

Latin America, despite some continuing downside political risks, is on track to become a dynamic growth region in the 1990s. This remarkable turnabout from the debt-induced depression of the 1980s results from the region's nearly unanimous embrace of market-oriented economic fundamentals, the boost to regional free trade with the passage of NAFTA, and to the rise of a new breed of government technocrats — "technopols" — who are determined to make the reforms endure. However, that positive progress could be abruptly derailed by the failure to build supportive political coalitions and by other domestic and external shocks.

Latin America is turning around. After a decade of massive resource outflows, astronomical hyperinflation, and shrinking incomes, the region is regaining lost ground. Per capita gross domestic product (GDP) is expanding, prices are stabilizing, and investors are returning. One indication of the region's better health: foreign exchange reserves have doubled in the last two years.

In comparison to its debt-ridden depression of the 1980s, Latin America looks red hot today. The economies of the region are indeed heating up, but

A previous version of this article was published in *International Economic Insights*, (July/August 1992). Reprinted by permission from *International Economic Insights*, "Latin America: Back on the Screen" by Richard E. Feinberg, vol. III number 4, pages 3-6. The views expressed here are solely those of the author and do not necessarily reflect the policies or views of the Inter-American Dialogue or the U.S. government.

Since February 1993, Richard E. Feinberg has been special assistant to the President and senior director, Inter-American Affairs, National Security Council. Prior to assuming this position, Dr. Feinberg was president of the Inter-American Dialogue and executive vice president and director of studies at the Overseas Development Council.

so far most growth rates are lukewarm — and are likely to remain tepid over the medium run. Constrained by inflation fears and capital shortages, Latin America is unlikely to enjoy the spectacular 8 to 10 percent annual growth racked up by the Asian Tigers [Republic of Korea, Taiwan, Singapore, and Hong Kong] during their boom years.

Indeed, there are still notable downside risks. The Mexican and Chilean economic reforms appear solidly on course, but Argentina and Venezuela could still be derailed, and Brazil — the hemisphere's big disappointment — is lagging badly. Also worrisome is the precariousness of governance: Latin American politics are much less volatile than a decade or two ago, but democracy is still not firmly rooted. Nasty surprises are certainly possible.

These caveats notwithstanding, the new optimism and self-confidence gripping much of Latin America are well grounded in fundamentals. Overall, the region is now governed by better economic policies, smarter policymakers, and consensual democratic politics.

The Progress of Reform

The more buoyant mood in Latin America reflects, first and foremost, progress in macroeconomic management. In the hemisphere's celebrated star performers, Mexico and Chile, inflation has fallen to under 20 percent. In Venezuela, the corrective inflationary bubble of 85 percent in 1988 is now history, although prices continue to rise by 30 percent per annum.

Overall in the region, consumer prices, which soared by an earthshaking 1000 percent per year from 1988-1990, climbed by 200 percent in 1991. In 1992, Argentina experienced magnificent price stability, leaving Brazil as the only major economy still with triple-digit inflation.

Inflation is subsiding, but it is far from slain. Years of rising prices have built a strong inertial bias into the system, and rational people remain averse to holding money balances in domestic currencies. Moreover, tight monetary policies, by forcing up interest rates that add to the costs of business, are themselves an inflationary impulse. There remains the danger of another round of currency devaluations, which fuel inflation by increasing the costs of tradeables.

Fiscal Correction

However, the chief underlying cause of the great Latin American inflations — fiscal deficits — has been substantially corrected. Central government deficits, which averaged nearly 7 percent of GDP from 1981-1988, were slashed to 2.3 percent during 1989-1991. However painful, this progress has been vital to restoring macroeconomic balance.

Moreover, the severe fiscal crises of the 1980s had the salutary effect of forcing governments to sanitize public finances. Throughout the hemisphere, special-interest subsidies to consumers and producers are being deleted, many costly state-owned enterprises are being privatized, and bloated civil service rolls are being trimmed and reorganized (although much remains to be done to strengthen the public sector). Tax codes and collection systems are also being modernized and computerized. Increasingly, the more efficient states are shifting expenditures toward badly needed physical infrastructure and human capital formation (education, health, nutrition).

External Adjustment

The picture of the external accounts is also much brighter. In the early 1980s, two adverse external shocks jolted Latin America's balance of payments — a spike in interest rates and the flight of commercial lenders. Now, in a dramatic reversal, the region is the beneficiary of two favorable shocks — the dip in global interest rates and renewed acceptance on international capital markets.

Consequently, the region's debt service burden has become less onerous. Interest payments due sopped up only 22 percent of exports of goods and services in 1991, down from 36 percent during 1983-1986. Chile's improvement is most dramatic, its interest ratio having fallen to 15 percent.

At the same time, international capital has rediscovered Latin America. Gross private inflows jumped from $13 billion in 1990 to over $40 billion in 1991 and [were predicted to] skyrocket further [in 1992], according to Solomon Brothers.[1]

Some of these flows are merely seeking quick returns from the region's high real interest rates, but some investors are also expressing confidence in the region's future. Foreign as well as domestic investors (in some cases drawing on the earnings of their international portfolios, often derogatorily labeled "flight capital") are rushing to acquire equity shares in the booming stock markets, purchase international bond offerings, or finance imports of capital and consumer goods.

The combination of lighter debt service and massive capital inflows has enabled the region to enjoy an import surge while simultaneously beefing up foreign reserves. Even besieged Peru, with its virulent guerrilla insurgency, has watched capital inflows finance consumer imports and augment the wealth of its central bank.

Trade Reform

The rapid adjustment demanded by the sudden onslaught of the debt crisis in the early 1980s could only be accomplished through import suppression. Now, Latin America is seeking a healthier external equilibrium through export promotion. To spur exports while increasing overall economic efficiency and lowering domestic prices, governments have been unilaterally dismantling their highly protectionist trade regimes. Many have abolished quantitative restrictions and are dramatically lowering trade barriers. Argentina has cut its average tariff from 43 percent to 9 percent, Colombia from 37 percent to 14 percent, and Venezuela from 35 percent to 10 percent. Brazil's progress, albeit more tentative, still represents a definite break with the past.

Additional trade liberalization is occurring within the revitalized subregional trade zones. The Central American Common Market, the Caribbean Common Market, the Andean Pact, and MERCOSUR (Brazil, Argentina, Uruguay, and Paraguay) are all setting ambitious targets for market openings. Even if some dates slip, the enthusiasm for freer trade — with contiguous neighbors and the rest of the world — is a shift of historic proportions.

The Politics of Economic Change

The emphasis on exports is part of what Enrique Iglesias, the president of the Inter-American Development Bank, refers to as the region's "silent revolution" in economic philosophy. A key reason for the new optimism about Latin America is the coming to power of a generation of well trained and politically adept social scientists — individuals such as Pedro Aspe, Domingo Cavallo, and Alejandro Foxley, finance ministers of Mexico, Argentina, and Chile, respectively.[2] These men share a desire to integrate their nations into global commodity and financial markets. As idealists, they are driven by intellectual convictions that often place them in opposition to powerful vested interests. But they enjoy the support of their respective presidents, whom they serve essentially as prime ministers and, potentially, as future heirs.

These technocrats in government — *technopols,* if you will — are assisted by committed economists who share common language and values, enabling them to design comprehensive strategies and to assure their implementation through the staffing of key government agencies. The exception that proves the rule is Brazil: in part because of his government's incoherence and alleged corruption, former President Fernando Collor de Mello was unable to assemble an equivalent team, allowing the Brazilian economy to continue to flounder.

Less interested in national sovereignty than in sound economic policy, the *technopols* favor free trade areas as a way of locking in their rationalist policies and foreclosing backsliding by their successors. They are well plugged into international networks and work closely with the Bretton Woods institutions. They negotiate as equals with the International Monetary Fund and the World Bank staff, extracting finance and advice as befits their programmatic needs. Indeed, the *technopols* have an edge over these foreign advisors — their superior feel for local politics and institutions.

Building Governing Coalitions

A winning political coalition is essential to the *technopols'* success. The Salinas Mexican team built a triumphant coalition by creating a successful pro-reform export sector. Alejandro Foxley persuaded a suspicious business elite to join his middle-class base. But in Venezuela, Miguel Rodríguez and his aloof president, Carlos Andrés Pérez, failed to hammer together a political foundation to sustain economic reform — an oversight that became all too apparent from the February 1992 coup attempt that registered widespread popular support and culminated in the 1993 impeachment of President Pérez. The lesson of the Venezuelan case is clear: economic reformers must also possess an integrated political strategy if their programs are to endure. In particular, *technopols* and their political associates must overcome widespread doubts about their fairness and compassion and strive hard to communicate their purposes to civil society.

More broadly, economic reformers must work to fortify emergent democratic processes, which hold the best hope for continuity in economic policy. In earlier years, Latin America's highly polarized politics produced frequent swings in basic economic policies, causing ruinous discontinuities. Today, however, the end of the Cold War has accelerated a depolarization of politics and an acceptance of such basic norms as private property and the rule of law, thus making democratic bargaining possible. In this more tolerant environment, economic advance and democratic opening can be compatible.

The *technopols* are Latin America's best and brightest. If they listen carefully to the neediest sectors and build domestic political support, maintain the backing of the international financial community (private and official), and lock in their policies through free-trade accords, they will succeed in remaking the hemisphere in their own image. However, there are numerous downside risks.

The Capital Market Roller Coaster

The volatility of international capital markets continues to batter Latin America. The recent inflow of capital has relaxed balance of payments constraints but also pushed up exchange rates. If sustained, this currency appreciation will be a disincentive to exports and could undermine the *technopols'* entire outward-oriented development strategy.

To prevent capital movements from swamping trade policy, Latin American governments are searching for ways to stem the financial inflow without undermining confidence in the capital markets that they have worked so hard to earn. Central bankers are employing their entire repertoire, including lower interest rates, higher reserve requirements on foreign deposits, and the sterilization of inflows. To slow the increase in reserves, Chile has liberalized capital outflows and reduced tariffs. (Always heterodox, Colombia has resorted to subsidies to keep exports competitive.) Nevertheless, capital continues to flow into the region at rates which may not be sustainable.

Nor is the debt problem definitively behind us. Debt service ratios are indeed lighter — so long as global interest rates remain low. In fact, the ratio of the debt stock to exports in 1991 was 263 percent — uncomfortably near the crisis levels of the early 1980s.[3] Should international interest rates rise and short-term flows reverse, the region could once again experience a negative net transfer of resources.

The Influence of the U.S. Electorate

Another imaginable external shock — this one manmade — would have arisen with a defeat of the North America Free Trade Agreement (NAFTA). Economic models suggest that while the short-term impact would have been modest, the potential longer term destabilization of investor confidence could have been far more serious. Furthermore, the shock waves from an anti-NAFTA vote would have been felt well beyond Mexico, since it is the preeminent leader and hence test case for economic reform. In the decisive vote for NAFTA on November 17, 1993, the people of the United States through their representatives have acted to bolster economic progress in Latin America.

The devastation wrought by hyperinflation has weakened the appeal of irresponsible populism, but poverty and inequality remain potent prods to irrational politics. Now that the pressing exigencies of financial stabilization are largely behind governments, they will need to turn their attention to the badly neglected social agenda.

The Re-emergent Social Agenda

Poverty increased in Latin America in both relative and absolute terms during the 1980s. The proportion of the poor rose from 41 percent to 44 percent of the population, leaving over 180 million people without basic necessities, according to UN definitions. The redress of these injustices is required not only on ethical grounds; the political durability of economic reforms depends on it. Furthermore, the region's future international competitiveness hinges on the productivity of its labor force, which in turn is a function of the quality of social services.

In sum, the sustainability of recovery depends upon the region's ability to inject more sustainability into its international financial accounts, to negotiate trade agreements, and to build more equitable and democratic societies. These are not impossible tasks.

Why Not Miracles?

Forecasters, both official and private, are virtually unanimous in predicting a return to growth rates in the 4 to 5 percent range through the 1990s, assuming that the *technopols* triumph and policy reform endures. Why the moderation? Why not foresee a surge to Asian-style growth rates?

The major constraints on the Latin American rebound are these:

- **Inflation fears.** Central banks will try to keep a tight lid on monetary emissions, in order not to reignite inflationary expectations. And if GDP growth is too rapid, capacity bottlenecks will place upward pressure on prices.

- **Capital shortage.** Investment rates jumped from 19 percent in 1990 to an estimated 21 percent of GDP in 1991, but [in 1992 were] still far short of the 25 to 30 percent rates sustained in Asia.[4] Pent-up consumer demand will hold down domestic savings rates. Long-term capital inflows may fill some but certainly not all of the investment gap.

- **Export capacity.** Better incentives and further free-trade pacts like NAFTA should stimulate export growth. Most forecasters project real export growth in the respectable but not spectacular 5 to 7 percent range, on the assumptions that governments are unwilling or unable to restrain consumption growth entirely and that investment does not surge.

- **Human and institutional limitations.** Managers will need time to learn to function in a more competitive environment, and dilapidated educational systems must be overhauled if they are to graduate technologically literate workers. At the same time, the new public sector must become more selective and expert in its chosen tasks.

Certainly, modest but sustainable growth is far superior to the boom-and-bust syndrome that has too often plagued Latin America. In fact, the Asian Tigers achieved accelerated growth rates only after periods of gradual expansion. But if Latin America can attain and sustain a temperate recovery through the mid-1990s while incorporating broader sectors into the benefits of the economic mainstream, it may have laid the foundation for its own "miracle" by the opening of the next millennium.

Notes

1. Gross private inflows for 1992: 62 billion. Gross private inflows for 1993: 54.4 billion. Source: Solomon Brothers.

2. Information is current. Foxley left office in March 1994.

3. Ratio of debt stock to imports for 1992: 294 percent. Ratio of debt stock to imports for 1993: 293 percent. Source: *Preliminary Overview of the Economy of Latin America and the Caribbean,* ECLAC.

4. Investment percentage of GDP for the region: 1992: 19.5 percent. Source: The World Bank (Additional data is pending).

The Dilemmas of Development: A Latin American Perspective

Richard D. Fletcher

This review of the current situation in Latin America will attempt to point out the dilemma facing Latin America today and illustrate why the choices are acutely difficult.

The most important factor to recognize is that throughout the 1980s, appropriately termed "The Lost Decade," the Latin American region suffered economic stagnation. Never before had the region experienced such a phenomenon. Extremely diverse, with a population of close to 500 million and over $1 trillion in gross domestic product (GDP), the region as a whole grew vigorously during the thirty years following World War II. Latin America's economies expanded at close to 6 percent per year; the region's GDP more than quadrupled between 1950 and 1980.

Not only did the region experience tremendous growth during this period, it also underwent several major transformations. Industries developed, and social indicators improved so much that people began to take for granted that development would occur as a natural course of events. Then, beginning in the early 1980s, there was a decade during which the region stagnated. This stagnation, after so many years of growth, came as a shock. Incomes that had been expected to double during the 1980s did not grow at all. This caused tremendous damage.

Regional loss of income has had the severest impact on the poor. Poverty and social conditions have worsened. There has been widespread malnutrition and a recurrence of several diseases, such as cholera, which were thought to have been eradicated. Some of this damage will be lasting.

Richard D. Fletcher is deputy manager, Plans and Programs Department, Inter-American Development Bank and former minister of State and Planning, Jamaica.

An example of a continuing, pervasive social problem is lack of education or the availability of only poor quality education. Generally, the young people of Latin America are not getting the quality or level of education that they need. Education has value not just for its own sake. An educated population is also an important factor of production. The labor force that Latin America will rely on to produce goods and services in the twenty-first century is already in school. The deterioration in the quality of education these students are receiving will affect the ability of Latin American nations to compete and to produce quality goods and services in this next century.

Why did this period of stagnation occur? This has been the subject of much debate in Latin America. It is important to identify two extreme explanations which have emerged.

One extreme explanation, very popular with people who come from the same sort of political background as I do, blames stagnation on imperialism. They believe that the world economic order is unfair, with the cards stacked against the people of the Third World. This, they argue, and the crushing burden of debt have worked to increase the exploitation of the South by the North.

This explanation works very well as a political platform, and many of us have made our livings as proponents of this idea. However, there are some very serious flaws with this rationale. Within Latin America and the Caribbean, some countries managed to do quite well during the 1980s — Colombia, Barbados, and the Bahamas, for example. And in East Asia, there are countries that have done amazingly well: Korea, Taiwan, Singapore, Hong Kong — the famous Four Tigers — as well as Indonesia and Malaysia. Thus, the explanation that puts all the blame on outside imperialist forces is not convincing.

Another extreme explanation for recent poor economic performance in the region places all the blame on the Latin American countries, pointing to incompetent, corrupt governments and their bad policies. Mismanagement is cited as the reason for high levels of capital flight from Latin America to Switzerland and North America. Latin Americans are said to have no one to blame but themselves.

The model of industrialization through import substitution also comes in for heavy criticism. This economic strategy is associated with the Argentine economist Raúl Prebish, the early head of the UN Economic Commission for Latin America (ECLA), based in Santiago, Chile. Basically, the model advocated that the Latin American countries develop their economies by closing off domestic markets to imports and using domestic purchasing power to form their own industries. The idea was that by protecting the domestic markets, they would protect nascent industries, and their economies would grow and diversify.

The conventional wisdom today is that this policy failed. Quite frankly, I disagree. The import substitution policy was a spectacular success for thirty years. Between 1950 and 1980, the Latin American economies grew at an average of 6 percent per year. Vast industrial transformations took place. Brazil, for example, developed an automobile industry that was capable of exporting to North America. Brazil even became a major exporter of armaments in that competitive world.

During those thirty years there were tremendous social improvements throughout Latin America: illiteracy was halved, infant mortality declined by more than 60 percent, and life expectancy grew by 30 percent. In some countries — Argentina, Costa Rica, Barbados, Cuba, and a few others — life expectancy and infant mortality rates approached levels comparable to those in North America and Europe. The import substitution model did not fail; instead, it thrived for some time.

However, by the 1980s, the model no longer worked. It had exhausted its possibilities. When Latin American societies needed to pursue other strategies for development, they were unable to do so precisely because the import substitution model had functioned so successfully. It had created very powerful vested interests whose narrow viewpoints benefited from the maintenance of the outmoded strategy.

What should have happened? The next step should have been to move from the inward focus developing industry to export-led growth, a focus outward on development capacity. This transition should have been made by the Latin American economies in the late 1960s or the early 1970s. Those that made the transition, the countries of the Far East, Malaysia, Thailand, and others, did exceedingly well in the 1980s. Admittedly, these countries did not have to contend with impediments represented by interests with a tremendous stake in the maintenance of the import substitution industrialization strategy.

The central dilemma for Latin America in the 1990s comes down to this: How can Latin America avoid policies that perpetuate the stagnation of the 1980s? The answer may seem obvious. These countries have seen what did not work for them in the 1980s and what did work elsewhere, so the choice should be very clear.

But is it that clear? First, there is no guarantee that what worked for East Asia in the 1980s will work for Latin America in the 1990s. The import substitution model worked well in the 1950s, 1960s, and 1970s, but it was a disaster in the 1980s. Success in one period of time does not guarantee enduring success. Continuous success requires doing the right thing at the right time.

There also are many who say that while export-led growth worked in East Asia, we cannot all be exporters. What works for East Asia will not necessarily work for Latin America, due to distinct cultural traditions and other differences. There is much skepticism and questioning as to whether export-led growth is the appropriate strategy for Latin America. The appropriate direction to take now depends on what world we will confront in the mid-1990s and beyond.

This is the heart of the dilemma. We don't know what sort of world we will be facing for the rest of the 1990s. Will it be a world like the 1980s, with further openings for trade, or will it be a world like the 1970s, with oil prices skyrocketing and commodity prices booming? We don't have a crystal ball, but we do know some things with a fair degree of certainty.

First, the end of the Cold War and the superpower conflict is going to have a profound political and economic impact. It remains to be seen what form a peace dividend will eventually take, but I believe it will result in a much greater degree of confidence in world society and a greater willingness both to open up markets and to integrate the world economy more tightly. There will be less defensive posturing on the part of the United States and Europe. Countries will be willing to take greater risks in terms of opening up their markets.

Second, in Latin America there has been a gradual reduction in the debt crisis. The debt was a major financial and even greater psychological block to development. In my opinion, one of the reasons for Latin America's stagnation in the 1980s was the amount of attention allocated to coping with the debt crisis. The debt crisis distracted attention from more important and positive aspects of development. Now the Brady Plan has created a formula for approaching the debt problem that actually reduces its impact on the Latin American countries.

Third, former President George Bush declared his plan for future U.S.-Latin American relations with The Enterprise for the Americas Initiative, which envisions a free trade zone throughout the Western Hemisphere, beginning with the North American Free Trade Agreement, details of which are under discussion by the Clinton administration with Canada and Mexico and under legislative review by each party to the Agreement.

Finally, we must recognize that these political developments are occurring in combination with an overwhelmingly powerful technological force, the information or communication revolution, that creates a world of instantaneous transactions. People no longer need to communicate by letter or by telegram when facsimile and computer modem are faster. Capital moves across boundaries freely, and people's skills are exported while they stay at home.

These developments mean that international boundaries have become irrelevant to economic development. Economic nationalism is becoming obsolete. In this context, success in the 1990s depends on the ability of countries to compete in a global market. Nations no longer can adopt defensive postures, trying to insulate themselves behind their own economic boundaries. The old ideal of "Fortress Latin America" is no longer viable.

If competition in the global marketplace is the key to success in the 1990s, how will Latin America fare? A recent book by Michael Porter, *The Competitive Advantage of Nations,* maintains that there is no such thing as a competitive nation, *only competitive firms or competitive individuals* (1990). A competitive nation is merely one in which competitive firms choose to locate their activities.

This choice of location will no longer be based on nationality. American firms do not need to choose to locate in the United States; they can operate in Mexico, Africa, Asia, or wherever they want. This is occurring even with Japanese firms. Japanese automobile manufacturers located in the United States are considering Mexico; they have also opened plants in Malaysia and Colombia. If a nation wants to be competitive, it has to create the conditions to attract competitive firms, whether those firms originate inside that country or elsewhere.

This is the dilemma facing Latin America. For thirty years, a whole set of structures and institutions created a situation in which firms have relied on protection, patronage, and privilege for success. Patronage and privilege were provided by interventionist state governments working in close collaboration with the business communities.

Looking to the future, it is clear that this will not be the formula for competing successfully in the world economy. In Latin America, the major dilemma of development in the 1990s involves making the decision to open up markets for competition. Latin America now must be ready to endure the pain and difficulty that this process will entail. The time has come for Latin America to develop the capability to compete successfully in the global marketplace of the next century.

References

Porter, Michael E. 1990. *The Competitive Advantage of Nations.* New York: MacMillan.

Conceptualizing Development: Moving Beyond Linear Northern Perspectives

Jorge A. Lawton

W ho determines what development is? Simplistic and damaging stereotypes have long permeated the conventional discourse in the so-called
"developed" North about the causes and cures of underdevelopment elsewhere.[1] Traditionally, as seen from the North, the complex human process of
development in its varied social, political, psychological, and cultural dimensions too often was reduced to a series of strictly economic indicators —
socially undifferentiated and ethnocentric.

This study will first analyze some of the general characteristics of the
northern stereotype of development; second, it will examine whether or not
these same characteristics were present in long-term U.S. hemispheric
initiatives evolving since the beginning of the century; third, it will question
to what degree, during the Cold War, U.S. aid officials and U.S. theorists
believed in this stereotype, designing U.S. aid programs around it; finally, it
will offer some fundamental principles for an alternative development
strategy: an integration of human rights and development, a strategy that is
global, participatory, accountable, and sustainable.

The Development Stereotype

M ost strategies for development of the South that emanated from the North
have taken for granted that the northern world is rich and the South, with
its denser population living in backward or underdeveloped economies, is
poor.

Jorge A. Lawton is director of The South-North Group and Human Rights and
Human Development Fellow at Emory University's Center for Ethics in Public
Policy and the Professions.

Worldwide, the gap between North and South is widening in terms of indices such as real gross domestic product (GDP) per capita, mean years of schooling, overall enrollment, and fertility. The gap has narrowed in terms of other indices such as life expectancy, under-five mortality, daily caloric intake, and adult literacy.[2] Even these indices represent national aggregates primarily for cross-national comparison. They fail to illustrate the considerable disparities among subregions, urban and rural areas, ethnic groups, genders, and diverse social sectors within each country.

If the daunting task for the South to emerge from poverty, to overcome underdevelopment, is ever to be successful, the process must become a shared responsibility. Internally, it needs to be shared by the poor countries' private and public sectors and across class lines by workers and managers. Externally, the agenda must be advanced by both North and South.

In the North, development strategies for the South are shaped by the North's own economic needs and policies, by the evolving rules and prescriptions of the World Bank and other international financial institutions, and by the detached attitudes often conceived and discussed by donors.

Growth rates for production of national goods and services, rates of inflation and national savings, monetary supply, balance-of-payments accounts for foreign trade, foreign exchange reserves, levels of foreign debt and debt servicing, and inevitably, estimated income per capita — undifferentiated by gender or social class income — traditionally were cited as the ultimate macro indicators of development or underdevelopment. Only as much more disaggregated data were consciously and painstakingly gathered has it become possible to document the social disparities, and, where there is sufficient political will, to redesign the original development strategies. As Khadija Haq stated in his foreword to the report of the third conference on human development:

> ...After the Keynesian revolution, economists moved from policy making at the micro level to the macro level, from disaggregates to aggregates. The tools of analysis commonly used are [gross national product] GNP, savings and investments, exports and imports, and the whole structure of national accounts. This second stage...took us from the market economy to national accounts....But we missed the third stage..., a macro framework for analyzing societies in human terms: poverty profiles, evaluations of the way people live, a study of the distribution of income among different levels and classes of people, etc. We need to know how the development process has affected human development both quantitatively and qualitatively in order to obtain a true picture of the benefits that societies are supposed to derive from development.[3]

The terms of discourse in themselves are euphemistic. Code words, such as "developing," were applied indiscriminately in polite development jargon even to those wretched, but not so uncommon cases as Latin America in the 1980s, where development was in fact resulting in stagnation or even economic and social regression. In that lost decade, the reality of development in Latin America and the Caribbean was an overall increase in the number of poor in every country and regionally an increase of people in poverty by nearly 70 million, reaching 222 million people or some 50.5 percent of the overall population.[4]

Further, the stereotypical view of development was unidisciplinary. The fundamental interrelationship among sustainable economic development, economic and social rights, and institutional (public and private) vibrancy or decay, not being easily measurable, was not considered relevant in the narrow, conventional views of northern economists specializing in development. The original terms of the economic development discourse in the North minimized the interaction of the cultural and psychological factors of development with the central economic formulae. Margaret Anstee and John R. Mathiason observe in their paper from the Budapest conference:

> There is a general lack of tools in policy analysis that would permit examination of the qualitative dimension of human behavior, meaning the values and attitudes which underlie economic and social choices and which are either taken for granted or ignored. This also embraces social structure, class, group and status, which in many respects underpin the economic structure. More importantly, the cognitive structure of people, the way in which people think, cannot be easily assessed. Ironically, it is probably a central assumption of most policy prescriptions that either people make economic choices rationally in terms of economic return, or that they inevitably respond in certain ways to stimuli.[5]

Too often, the most prominent economic development policy planners in the United States and other northern countries projected the only experience they knew — northern-led, post-industrial revolution, capitalist growth — onto pre-industrial revolution, internally distorted, and institutionally stunted Third World societies. The development process was presumed, consciously or unconsciously, to be singular and linear: if only "they" could manage to catch up with "us." If the impoverished southern economies would follow the successful model of the North, then they too could enjoy the fruits of development.

Walt Rostow, President Lyndon Johnson's White House adviser, referred to the critical point in this imitative process as economic "take-off." The aeronautical analogy suggests that once in flight, the previously underdeveloped economy would soar above and beyond its earlier earthbound backwardness. The aerodynamics of relatively even distribution and balance were minimized, and the refueling needs for sustained targeted annual growth rates were largely overlooked.

Analysts tended to disregard the larger context of a single world system in which both North and South, rich and poor simultaneously play diverse roles and bear critical relationships to each other. Thus, the relational dimension of underdevelopment — whether or how the underproduction/ underdevelopment of the South was in any functional way related to the overproduction/development of the North — often was dismissed as rhetoric or ignored entirely in the policy circles of the North.

Few among the prominent northern development opinion makers appeared to appreciate how some dominant models of development, while modernizing, in practice could prolong the South's dependency on the North, aggravating the growing North-South dissonance or the equally severe income disparities within individual societies. They simply and simplistically believed that "world poverty could be conquered by economic growth."[6]

Despite the reality of these often growing disparities, development thinkers clung to a presumption of trickle down betterment. Failing to focus on the relational dimension, mainstream northern development counsels liked to predict that greater total income, generated through higher levels of worldwide production, would gradually diffuse itself, or trickle down from North to South. They postulated that over time some of the newly created wealth within the South would spill over from its concentration in the higher income brackets to the newly created middle income sectors, and eventually from there on down to the poor majority.

Similarly, a modicum of the economic surplus from urban centers was expected eventually to seep outward toward remote rural areas. The inward migration patterns far in excess of urban employment capacities, so familiar to Third World reality today, were not part of the smooth trickle-down and trickle-out original scenarios. Victor Tokman asserts that even statistical evidence failed to shake the trickle-down conviction:

> The warning voices raised in the 1970s that a significant and growing number of people were being left out of the modern sector and forced into low-productivity, badly paid activities went generally unheeded, save for some academic interest. The traditional belief in the trickle-down strategy, reinforced by the high economic dyna-mism registered by the Latin American region in the previous decade, prevented this concern from reaching the decision-making levels, despite the fact that information available for 1970-1980 showed that the informal sector's share in the total work force had grown from 16.9 to 19.3 percent, while the accelerated creation of

modern sector jobs had only managed to reduce the proportion of informal sector jobs in the urban centers from 19.6 to 18.7 percent.[7]

Social class relations in patterns of ownership, accumulation, distinct modes of production, and internal distortion in terms of both access to and benefits from decision making, when considered at all, were looked upon as the unintentionally uneven results of development, not as possible contributing factors to that unevenness. In their place, Adam Smith's invisible hand of the market was expected to bring supply and demand into balance, and at times, even to explain the skewed distribution of goods, services, wealth, and income as the result of irrational economic modeling.

Growth was seen to depend heavily on savings. Since only the relatively affluent minority could afford to save, policies of distribution, or of movement toward equity, would have to wait until sufficient growth had been achieved. The fact that the same elites[8] who benefited from the early stages of modernization would use their initial advantage to consolidate the established disequality drew little attention. They would be on guard to see that subsequent access for the vast majority would become far less, not more, likely. Any eventual democratic political institutionalization, in turn, would have to coexist with this ever less equitable economic order.

Early northern economic development theory made little or no attempt to integrate the aggregate indices of economic measurement already referred to with the less easily quantifiable social indices. Social indices would include conditions such as fertility, migration, and mortality rates, caloric intake and nutritional levels, and estimates of the purchasing power of minimum-wage families to determine how many did or did not have access to a balanced diet, potable water, electricity, housing, basic schooling, and health care, both preventive and emergency reactive. Geoffrey Kay blames neoclassical economic theory, at least in part, for this mindset: "It asserts the existence of a universal economic problem, *scarcity*...which turns neoclassical economics into an exclusively quantitative analysis."[9]

Anstee and Mathiason comment on the same problem:

The statistical series used for analysis describe a quantitative world, but the problems to be analyzed may rather be qualitative, and the information at our disposal does not assist us in looking at that factor. For example, it is known that the differences between men and women are significant for economic development, but the process of assembling empirical information on this is only beginning.[10]

Great strides have been made in recent years with indices such as the UNDP's "HDI" (United Nations Development Programme's human development index), including three key components: longevity, knowledge, and income.[11] It is also (according to Anstee and Mathiason) "gender-sensitive," adjusted for income distribution, adjusted over time and, for five countries for purposes of illustration, disaggregated for subgroups within the countries.[12]

Clearly, if development strategy, North or South, is dependent on broad national statistics and not on data broken down across income sectors, it is a hobbled strategy in its very essence for any society. The distortion it provokes increases in Third World regions like Latin America and sub-Saharan Africa, where the core defining characteristics include high income concentration, pervasive poverty, and limited social mobility.

The relatively recent and evolving analysis of national income and other common macro statistics in deciles by age, gender, race, individual income, schooling, occupational training, workplace organization (hierarchical and individualistic or shared responsibility of small interdisciplinary production teams), access to and participation in local decision making, literacy, rural/urban migration, and population breakdown has offered us new resources for the design of development strategies. Vast improvement in availability and method of computation and analysis of statistical data now makes it relatively simple to refine some of the conceptual generalizations of the past.

For example, data for price sampling over time of a popular basket of basic necessities can be compared with the purchasing power held by minimum wage workers. This appraisal allows a much more meaningful measurement of the cost of public policies, such as the economic adjustment programs throughout Latin America today, on common people's lives.

Differing concepts of development will determine differing methodologies. There is no methodological impediment to tracking how much and what kind of development is occurring. It is, however, crucial to understand that the people living and working in the South, the poor majorities, are the real subjects of development. As Haq observes,

> We have begun to focus on basic human needs, the question of poverty profiles, and the situation of the bottom 40 percent of society often bypassed by development. We have started to measure the costs of adjustment not only in terms of lost output but also in terms of lost lives, lost human potential. We have finally begun to accept the axiom that human welfare is the ultimate end of development, not GNP figures, which are only convenient aggregates.[13]

When awareness of development for whom is understood, it becomes clear why development by whom, or the relative degree of access to national decision makers, is important.

Once analysis identifies the discriminatory, but true, character of uneven development in practice, it comes much closer to precision and more socially useful than the deceivingly inclusive macro indicators of the past such as national income per capita.

Statistical targeting of the least benefited can fall into numerous population subcategories, such as elderly, rural women, pre-school urban children, or the so-called middle sectors income deciles. When these categories are used for proportional comparison of one's share to the other's, an x-ray of the grim but real face of development emerges. Beyond analysis, it also can become an integral tool for policy adjustment, where there is the political will to do so, even in predominantly market-oriented developing societies.

The likelihood for political will for such distributive adjustments to be present depends in turn on how democratic the social and political structure is, or relatively how much access the poor majorities have to policy design. Increased precision of analysis does not, by itself, necessarily lead to effective policies designed to reduce income disparities and the overall condition of poverty. Expression of self-interest is likely to be far more effective. Thus, the human rights conditions favoring mobilization and participation of previously excluded sectors are vital.

In extreme cases, an authoritarian government may deem it in its own longer-term self-interest to enact policies targeting the most abject subsector of poverty, lest overall social control be lost. This is the case of the Chilean government in the mid- to late 1970s and 1980s, when it targeted the poorest of the poor in emergency employment and public works programs.[14]

The Depth of the Problem

Richard Fletcher's companion essay in this volume[15] discusses evolving development strategies as seen from the South. Fletcher argues that Latin America's import-substitution policy (ISI) worked very well indeed for the three decades from 1950 to 1980. But, he adds, its very success created "very powerful vested interests whose narrow points of view benefited from the maintenance of the outmoded strategy."[16]

The hemisphere's challenge throughout the 1990s and beyond, Fletcher posits, will be to move beyond the structures that allow firms to rely on "protection, patronage, and privilege" and endure the pain that comes with opening up markets and entering into the next century's global marketplace.[17]

Fletcher asserts that part of the challenge for any broad, genuine development lies within the South. It will be necessary to break the monopoly of "powerful vested interests" who function with "narrow [and outmoded] points of view." We have seen here how both the thinking and institutions in the North also fundamentally influence the choice of development strategy eventually taken in the South.

In the particular case of development in this hemisphere, it is important to identify the roots and setting of traditional U.S. views of development. The power disparity of the United States ensures that the U.S. development mindset disproportionately influences the choice of strategies. It is not enough to stimulate development initiatives from previously disenfranchised communities in the South without overcoming resistance in the North toward locally based, southern-centered, alternative development strategies.

To appreciate the depth and persistence of the traditional, linear development perspective, it is important to understand 1) how and when these stereotypes first emerged; 2) what relationship, if any, their conceptualization bore to the evolving perceptions of how foreign economic policy toward the hemisphere could best represent U.S. interests; and 3) how both later manifested themselves in the official development mindset during the Cold War.

Earliest U.S. Hemispheric Interests

A dispassionate review of U.S. hemispheric policy in this century must consider two central variables motivating and defining U.S. interests. At the most basic level, one arises from the normal profit motive of U.S. business or economic interests. The other derives from a hegemonic power's fundamental insecurity — its fear of forces of change, or even potential change, in the existing order. From within the United States, the latter is euphemistically referred to as the nation's security interests.

Proprietary U.S. rhetoric about *its* hemisphere can be traced to the Monroe Doctrine's blunt warning to European powers in 1823 that the United States would not welcome any outside intervention in its hemisphere. Not until after 1895, however, did the United States manage unilaterally to assert its presence in one country after another, especially throughout the greater Caribbean Basin, converting its rhetoric into reality.

By 1898, as the Spanish-American War drew to a close, Puerto Rico and Cuba fell like ripe pears from Spain's grasp into the outstretched hands of the United States. Both the worst fears of Jose Martí, Cuba's proud independence leader killed earlier in the war against Spain, and the most extravagant U.S. expressions of self-interest toward Cuba were realized in the Platt Amendment. Presented by U.S. Senator Orville Platt (although written by Secretary of War Elihu Root) in March 1901, this convenient piece of legislation awarded the United States the right to intervene in Cuba's internal affairs whenever the United States deemed intervention necessary.

By 1903, Teddy Roosevelt's Rough Riders and U.S. naval forces had no difficulty in assuring the success of the Panamanian revolt against Colombia, thereby securing terms for the canal lease, similar to the 1898 lease of the Guantánamo naval base in Cuba "in perpetuity."

Shortly after, in a December 1904 message to Congress, President Theodore Roosevelt announced his corollary to the Monroe Doctrine. On this basis, in February 1905, the U.S. government moved to set up customs houses, first in the Dominican Republic and later in Haiti, Nicaragua, and elsewhere. Through this mechanism, the U.S. government became directly involved in collecting Dominican and other customs receipts and managing those countries' finances.

The U.S.-run customs houses purposely signaled an economic *Pax Americana,* sending a clear warning to European creditors and extra-hemispheric powers: the United States could and would intervene in the internal affairs of other hemispheric nations. The Europeans would, therefore, be wise to stay out.

Thus, the United States gradually established its own system of economic and political hegemony in the hemisphere. This privileged position flowed easily from the reality of U.S. hemispheric asymmetry and the unwillingness after 1895 of any major foreign power, even Great Britain, to check or counter the new U.S. hegemony.

Theodore Roosevelt, William Howard Taft, Woodrow Wilson, and their presidential successors encouraged significant increases in U.S. hemispheric investments. Extra-hemispheric loans were replaced with loans from U.S. banks. Capital from these loans was often channeled toward development activities. These development activities consisted of an outward oriented network of highways, railroads, and port facilities serving the rapidly growing U.S. investments in extractive industries.

As other authors have pointed out,[18] the U.S. hegemony implied an imposed homeostasis; i.e., so long as the behavior of the newly subordinate parties remained within the limits prescribed by the dominant power, rule by direct force was neither needed nor invoked.

Cold War Development

The U.S. hemispheric hegemony, established early in the century, gradually began to be perceived from Washington not as a temporary dominance but as a natural, even necessary order. Official development initiatives assumed a much higher profile in the era ushered in after World War II. During the subsequent Cold War, to one degree or another, these initiatives, and, more fundamentally, the hegemonic impulse underlying them, were rationalized through the rhetoric of anti-communism. Kay remarks:

> As a result of war-time experience when communists had played a leading role in anti-fascist and anti-Nazi liberation movements and had in fact seized state power in some countries — China and Yugoslavia — and had only been prevented from doing the same in others by massive economic and military intervention — Greece, Turkey, Korea, Indo-China and even France and Italy — it is hardly

surprising that the nationalist movements in the underdeveloped world were viewed with suspicion in the West.[19]

In a classic study published over twenty years ago,[20] Robert Packenham, a U.S. scholar with field experience in Brazil, rigorously examines the development views of U.S. aid officials (and, in parallel, the theories of development held by his fellow U.S. social science scholars) over the first two decades of the Cold War (1947-1968). While not pretending in any way to summarize Packenham's nearly 400 compact pages here, a few of his findings are particularly relevant to this discussion.

Packenham states early on that "aggregate annual rates of economic growth *declined* in underdeveloped countries from 1950 to 1966," and that the "income gap between rich and poor countries *widened*."[21]

As precedents for the U.S. post-war development doctrines toward the Third World and their goals, Packenham cites the influence of the largely successful experience of the European Recovery Program. Its "main approach was economic....The United States provided aid; the economies revived; Communist parties did not come to power;...by and large...stability and democracy were the political results...."[22]

Packenham makes several revealing points regarding the relative unanimity of attitude and development goals between U.S. development officials' doctrines and mainstream U.S. social scientists' theories. Describing the evolution in his own thinking about this practitioner/theorist relationship before and after his research, Packenham states,

> Whereas I used to be moderately optimistic about the contributions that social science theories could make to policy and policymakers, I am now struck by the similarities between doctrines and theories and the relative poverty of the theories....Whereas I earlier argued that the [economic] means needed to be strengthened, I now believe that the overambitiousness of the goals constituted a more serious flaw.[23]

Donald Devine came to the same conclusion, as explained in his analysis of surveys carried out between 1936 and 1970: a striking consistency obtains between the values and beliefs shared by U.S. officials and U.S. scholars.[24]

Interestingly enough, many of the crucial premises underlying the type of development sought for the Third World, not clearly articulated in the official discourse, Devine nevertheless found embedded in the same underlying U.S. political culture.

What were some of the goals sought by U.S. development officials in the Cold War period? Packenham's research, like that of Samuel Huntington,[25] showed that both these officials as well as the preponderance of U.S. social scientists defined their goals for development to be "stable, nonradical, constitutional, and, if possible, peaceful and pro-American polities."[26]

The theorists were found to be "more ideological than they were generally perceived to be, or conceded themselves to be during the period, and their ideology, like that of the officials, was strongly affected by the style and substance of the Cold War."[27] The development ideas of both officials and theorists, Packenham described as "sometimes appropriate, but very often naive, ethnocentric, and rigid."[28]

Three main approaches, or policy means, toward development are isolated in the 1947 to 1968 period studied. Packenham calls these three approaches the "economic," the "security" (or Cold War), and the "explicitly democratic." The first sought to promote growth of per capita gross domestic product and other conventional economic measures in order to lead to overall political and social development. The second, prevalent in the Dwight Eisenhower and Lyndon Johnson years, viewed aid as a narrowly defined Cold War tool. The third, least common and "least influential doctrine," Packenham locates in the Latin American policy of the John F. Kennedy administration in 1962 and 1963, and after 1966 when the U.S. Congress amended the Foreign Assistance Act to include Title IX ("Utilization of Democratic Institutions in Development").

Packenham summarizes four kinds of beliefs about development that he found most Americans, officials and academicians, regardless of political party or political administration, *grosso modo*, to hold and follow:

1. Change and development are easy.
2. All good things go together.
3. Radicalism and revolution are bad.
4. Distributing power is more important than accumulating power.[29]

Packenham traces the development-is-easy belief to a projection of the exceptionally easy historical process experienced by the dominant white culture in U.S. history. "Protected from external conflicts, with high agricultural productivity and a low ratio of men to the land...and industrialization [that was] relatively easy and breathtakingly quick" helped "foster the assumption, scarcely conscious, that change and development were easy everywhere."[30]

A corollary of this easy thesis is the immediatist thesis, expressed by former World Bank President Eugene Black in 1969, referring to U.S. tendencies toward development as "a desire for quick results and a tendency to oversimplify."[31]

This critique was shared by the authors of the Pearson Report, referring to the damaging and naive expectations of "instant development."[32]

The second tenet, that all good things go together, has been succinctly referred to by Samuel Huntington as the U.S. belief in a "pleasant conjuncture of blessings," laying a necessarily positive and direct correlation between economic, political, and social indices of development, that in the example of social reform

> in some circumstances...may reduce tensions and encourage peaceful rather than violent change. In other circumstances, however, reform may well exacerbate tensions, precipitate violence, and be a catalyst of, rather than a substitute for, revolution.[33]

Even the consummate insider — the court historian of the Kennedy years, Arthur M. Schlesinger, Jr. — acknowledged that their Charles River approach had a "certain blandness," making Third World development appear "a little too easy and continuous," even representing "a very American effort to persuade the developing countries to base their revolutions on Locke rather than Marx...."[34]

Examples of the third U.S. belief that radicalism and revolution are bad are abundant throughout the 1947 to 1968 early Cold War period and beyond. U.S. anti-communism informed Cold War foreign policy and its U.S. Agency for International Development (AID) doctrines. Its realization may be most prominent in President Lyndon Johnson's policies toward Vietnam and Latin America.

Explanations for the pervasiveness of "anti-communism" and "anti-radicalism" for a country that is fond of harkening back to its own egalitarian revolution lie in the historical reality that the United States was "born equal; it needed no profound social revolution to become so."[35] Or, in other words, "it is the absence of the experience of social revolution which is at the heart of the American dilemma."[36]

Was this third strain absent from U.S. policy during the Kennedy years? Packenham argues persuasively that

> the differences between the Johnson and Kennedy years were mainly those of style, personality, and emphasis, rather than overt doctrines. Many of the permanent bureaucrats in AID and the Department of State who served under both presidents maintained largely the same doctrines after November 1963 as before.[37]

But if presidential style and personality are no substitute for bureaucratic doctrine, they do matter. Various historians have given President Kennedy credit for evolving and learning. Both Sorensen and Schlesinger cite Kennedy's frequent reference, first enunciated publicly in November 1961, to the inherent limits of U.S. influence in the world:

> We must face the fact that the United States is neither omnipotent nor omniscient — that we are only 6 percent of the world's population — that we cannot impose our will upon the other 94 percent of mankind — that we cannot right every wrong or reverse each adversary — and that there cannot be an American solution to every problem.[38]

The final tenet put forward by Packenham to identify the central beliefs of U.S. officials toward development, that distributing power is more important than accumulating power, is the least persuasive and the least insightful of the four when applied to the historical record.

There is no flaw in his assertion that among the central questions posed by U.S. officials in their assessments of Third World regimes are 1) "How is power distributed?" and 2) "How much [central] power exists?" This thesis posits that "Americans pay more attention to how power is distributed [separation of powers and pluralistic institutions] than to the amount of power."[39]

Here, the central argument that Americans feel uncomfortable with dictatorial, power-centering regimes, or conversely that they "tend strongly to prefer" that development occur through "popular participation [and] within pluralistic political systems,"[40] even if true as an idealistic preference or U.S. comfort level, in practice provides very little consolation to victims of anti-communist regimes supported by the United States, nor is it likely to console or convince citizens of those authoritarian "mobilization regimes," staunchly opposed by the United States, even where the concentration of power (usually for radical or reformist ends) does not necessarily connote limiting popular participation.

One need not look far for examples of the above in this hemisphere. U.S. opposition to Jacobo Arbenz in Guatemala, Juan Bosch in the Dominican Republic, Cheddi Jagan in Guyana, João Goulart in Brazil, Salvador Allende in Chile and, conversely, U.S. support for the power-centralizing authoritarian regimes overthrowing them, however "uncomfortable" at times, is a matter of record.

President Kennedy gives us a very clear example of U.S. priorities among conflicting preferences in his succinct review of U.S. policy options toward the Dominican Republic following the May 1961 assassination of Raphael Trujillo:

> There are three possibilities in descending order of preference: a decent democratic regime, a continuation of the Trujillo regime, or a Castro regime. We ought to aim at the first [decent democracy], but we really can't renounce the second [continuation of Trujillo] until we are sure that we can avoid the third [another Fidel Castro].[41]

Post-Cold War Development Strategy

A key strategic question confronting hemispheric development in the 1990s is, then, what happens to the U.S. development aid position after the Cold War? Does the Cold War's unbending stand against radical or reformist forces of change continue despite the new world context? We have seen how the elastic standard of anti-communism served to define and encourage a reactive policy. In what ways will that policy change now that the Cold War has given way to ethnic and other conflicts? Does the fact that we can trace many of the same characteristics in the earliest years of the century convey any implication of the depth of these attitudes?

In *The Liberal Tradition in America: An Interpretation of American Political Thought Since the Revolution*,[42] Louis Hartz sheds further light on mainstream U.S. political culture. He points out how the U.S. liberal tradition, on a world scale, actually represents rather conservative political thought. He goes on to probe this phenomenon, referred to as U.S. "exceptionalism," or how the formative nation-building process in the United States' own case, for historical and geopolitical reasons, was exceptional. For the United States, the early nation-building process was far less conflictive than for most other northern nations, and certainly far less conflictive than today's formative social processes in Third World countries.

Most Americans, Hartz argues, are unaware of this exceptionalism. Nor are they aware of just how influential this relatively conservative, if unspoken, ideology — what he calls the "liberal tradition" — has been in forming a U.S. mindset. By extension, this mindset has led, on an official level, to a tacit but persistent expectation that the development process in other countries will be northern-inspired, economics-driven, linear, relatively easy and quick. On an experiential level, however, examples abound that grossly uneven development has tended to be the norm rather than the exception. In the fall of 1994 *The New York Times* reported that

> Indeed, for all the benefits of Latin America's new economics — the revamping of industry, the new jobs, the controlling of inflation, the stabilization of currencies, and the relatively stable process of democracy — millions of people have been left out....Economic growth has been highly uneven. The new wealth has flowed mostly to the rich....New jobs tend to be either short-term, low-paying construction jobs or highly paid managerial jobs....*Poverty is even likely to increase slightly.* As of 1986, 37 percent of the region's families were living in poverty; by 2000, the [UN] economists say, the figure will be 38 percent, or 192 million people.[43]

Principles Informing an Alternative Approach

If, despite islands of progress, poverty persists as the daily reality for vast numbers throughout the Third World, and if it is quite clear that the 1980s in this hemisphere, the lost decade, resulted in stagnation, where are we beginning to look for alternatives? If the adjustment and privatization processes are proving to be no more than part of the way out, what else is needed?

The literature on lessons of development and approaches to development has proliferated in the past thirty years. Some of it is helpful.[44] New approaches to development seem to appear and reappear in predictable cycles, starting early in the century with Manifest Destiny and Pax Americana, moving after World War II to reconstruction and development modeled on the Bretton Woods System, the Marshall Plan, and the Truman Doctrine post-war development blueprints; the Alliance for Progress and other development with reform initiatives of the Kennedy years; the Vietnam era's nation-building literature and programs; the early 1970s' reaction to the growth with poverty 1960s' experience[45] and, more recently, the renaissance of democratization and governance studies, together with the many rounds of task force meetings on the reorganization and reorientation of AID held in the first year of the Bill Clinton administration.[46]

Yet despite the proliferation of new principles, old practices are slow to die.[47] For our purposes, it is enough to realize that just as there have been no simplistic formulae in the linear, stereotypical models, nor any proven panaceas, so there is no single, neat, alternative methodology for development. But, increasingly, we can identify certain interrelated core principles.

1. Genuinely human and sustainable development cannot be an exclusively statist nor an individualistic enterprise. The initiative must come from below, at the local scale and community level through the slow, internal process of consciousness-raising and articulation of needs.

2. Beginning with the most fundamental local decision makers, there must be full and transparent individual and group accountability at all levels for the process and the results of decisions taken.

3. A particular market-state partnership must be designed in each case — supporting and supplementing those areas where the market is incapable of satisfying local needs by itself.

4. Linkages between sectors must be established. We have learned that development cannot be reduced to a linear economic formula. We must also commit to a conscious linking and coordination of economic, political, social, psychological, and cultural needs and values.

5. Sustainability depends upon participation, which in turn depends on both the climate of full respect for human rights and the community self-interest, as identified by the local participants engaging in their own planning process.

6. A combination of individual rights ("individuization," not hyper-individualism) with a community and needs-based approach to development should be affirmed. At the same time, the inherent limits of legal positivism and its self-limitation to individual rights need to be recognized.

7. Participation in development cannot be confined to an intended participation in the eventual benefits (outcome) alone, but must start with access to and participation in the local design and decision-making process (inputs).

8. Explore and further coordinate the natural and necessary links between human rights, electoral process strengthening, democratization, and participatory development.

9. The first item of business for outside experts is to learn to listen. It is for the local community, not the outsiders, to articulate what together, from the point of view of their own culture, they see as priorities.

10. Even with local community initiative, intermediaries must be able to communicate their needs to the state, to sources of capital and credit, and eventually, to outside markets.

11. Specialized non-governmental organizations (NGOs) — being neither part of the official state apparatus nor acting as private individuals — will have a role to play as intermediaries, as advisers, and in representation of community grass roots groups. The NGOs must be held to the same rigorous standards and principles listed above, and limited in scale from the temptation of big money projects, or else they too will become new instances of the same damaging, stereotypical top-down development attitudes.

12. Community-based, micro credit alternatives for traditionally exclusive bank lending and repayment criteria need to be sought.

13. Utilize and further refine the broader development indicators, such as the Overseas Development Council's Quality of Life Index (QLI), the UNDP's HDI (Human Development Index), and the now commonplace (after years of inadmissibility) Income Distribution indicators, not only the abbreviated or summary gini coefficient, but preferably a clear breakdown of income shares (top and bottom percentiles) to shares of population, and where desired, methodology such as the Lorenz curve for plotting those shares in seeking urban/rural or cross-country comparisons.[48]

14. Sensitivity from the outset of a development planning process to gender participation, impact of plans on indigenous people and the ecology,

and preference for policy means and mechanisms that reinforce decentralization and ongoing grass roots participation must be fostered.

15. Support for an ethos that believes in and fully expresses each local culture's creative capacity, together with support from inside and outside capital and technical expertise, is needed to design and sustain its own development strategy.

The above principles would represent some of the working tenets informing an alternative, participatory, bottom-up process of development, focused, as the UNDP *Human Development* annual reports flatly state, on "people-centered development." It is an alternative, holistic process both deceptively fundamental and consistently violated.

In no way do these alternative development principles deny the catalytic role of the market, but they would insist upon democratizing the market by beginning at and from the bottom, providing access to capital and to technical expertise for small-scale, community-level developers.

There are no "quick fixes." Mindsets, both North and South, need to be fundamentally adjusted. The United Nations 20-20 proposal, wherein 20 percent of industrial country aid and 20 percent of underdeveloped countries' budgets are allocated to human priority expenditures, as discussed in Copenhagen at the March 1995 social conference, would be a start. But the fundamental underlying causes of poverty, so often denied, uncomfortable and challenging as they are, must be put on the table.

Northern or outside technical aid personnel — while maximizing genuine incentives — and seeking to harmonize scale with absorbtive capacity, still must co-design realistic "exit strategies" before plunging in to "develop others."

Such an alternative approach to human-centered development violates the culture of some veteran development managers, whether they are from national agencies, international financial institutions, or their local counterparts. They all, north and south, will have to learn how, in practice, to let go of long-held illusions of control and face rigorous accountability.

Without learning to let go, the mantra-like seeking of "sustainable development" will degenerate to hollow cliché. Through applying such alternative principles, there is a possibility that over the long term global poverty and underdevelopment, which have increased both absolutely and relatively over the past decades, could be consistently reduced. Will we allow ourselves the opportunity to let those who ultimately know best about their own lives participate in this common effort?

Notes

1. By "North" or "Northern-led development," we are referring to obsolete strategies emanating primarily from the advanced industrialized economies, where one-fifth of the world's population receives over four-fifths of the world's income and uses 70 percent of world energy. Globally, in 1960, the richest 20 percent received 30 times the income of the poorest 20 percent; by 1991, this disparity had doubled (*Human Development Report,* 1994, 35). We are not arguing here for a sterile confrontation between "North and South," but for a genuinely collaborative effort involving the market, the state, and workers' strategies between North and South and also from South to South for what has become a global problem.

2. UNDP, *Human Development Report 1993* (New York: Oxford University Press, 1993), "Indicators," 147-149.

3. Khadija Haq and Uner Kirdar, *Managing Human Development* (Islamabad: North-South Roundtable, 1958), xii.

4. Richard Weisskoff, "Basic Human Needs and the Democratic Process in Latin America," *North-South Issues,* Vol. II, No. 2, (1993), 1.

5. Margaret J. Anstee and John R. Mathiason in Haq and Kirdar, 1958, 37.

6. Charles K. Wilber, *The Political Economy of Development and Underdevelopment* (New York: Random House, Inc., 1988), preface.

7. Victor E. Tokman in Haq and Kirdar, 1958, 67.

8. Theodore H. White's observation in *In Search of History* (New York: Warner Books, 1979, 304) about the Marshall Plan has a poignant parallel here: "Generally, those who benefited first from our money were the poorest, the neediest, the most hungry; but those who benefited longest and most were some of the most unlovely and greedy men of Europe."

9. Geoffrey Kay, *Development and Underdevelopment: A Marxist Analysis* (New York: St. Martin's Press, 1975), 4-5.

10. Anstee and Mathiason in Haq and Kirdar, 1958, 37.

11. UNDP, 1993, Technical Note #1, 100: "Longevity is measured by life expectancy at birth as the sole unadjusted indicator. Knowledge is measured by two educational stock variables: adult literacy and mean years of schooling [weighted two-thirds/one-third]....For income, the HDI is based on the premise of diminishing returns from income for human development using an explicit formulation for the diminishing return....The higher the income relative to the poverty level, the more sharply the diminishing returns affect the contribution of income to human development."

12. UNDP, 1993, 101-103.

13. Haq and Kirdar, 1958, x.

14. See Carol Graham's chapter on Chile in this volume.

15. Fletcher, this volume.

16. Fletcher, this volume.

17. Fletcher, this volume.

18. See, for example, Jorge Domínguez, "The U.S. Impact on Cuban Internal Politics and Economics, 1902-1958: From Imperialism to Hegemony," paper delivered to the 1976 meeting of the American Political Science Association, Chicago, Il.

19. Kay, 1975, 3.

20. Robert A. Packenham, *Liberal America and the Third World, Political Development Ideas in Foreign Aid and Social Science* (Princeton, N.J.: Princeton University Press, 1973).

21. Packenham, 1973, 8-9, emphasis added; see also Barbara Ward, J. D. Runnalls, and Lenore D'Anjou, eds., *The Widening Gap: Development in the 1970s* (New York: Columbia University Press, 1971).

22. Packenham, 1973, 8.

23. Packenham, 1973, xvii.

24. Donald Devine, *The Political Culture of the United States: The Influence of Member Values on Regime Maintenance* (Boston: Little, Brown, 1972).

25. Samuel P. Huntington, *Political Order in Changing Societies* (New Haven, Conn.: Yale University Press, 1968).

26. Packenham, 1973, 6.

27. Packenham, 1973, 6-7.

28. Packenham, 1973, 4.

29. Packenham, 1973, 20.

30. Packenham, 1973, 113.

31. "A Message from Eugene R. Black," Pamphlet (Washington, D.C.: Overseas Development Council, April 1969).

32. Lester B. Pearson, Chair, *Report of the Commission on International Development* (New York: Praeger, 1969), 41.

33. Huntington, 1968, 5-7.

34. Arthur M. Schlesinger, Jr., *A Thousand Days: John F. Kennedy in the White House* (Boston: Houghton Mifflin, 1965), 588-589.

35. Packenham, 1973, 135.

36. Carl N. Degler, "The American Past: An Unsuspected Obstacle in Foreign Affairs," *The American Scholar*, 32, 2, Spring 1963, 192.

37. Packenham, 1973, 98.

38. Theodore C. Sorensen, *Kennedy* (New York: Bantam, 1966), 601-602 and Schlesinger, 1965, 596 and 615.

39. Packenham, 1973, 153.

40. Packenham, 1973, 153.

41. Schlesinger, 1965, 769.

42. Louis Hartz, *The Liberal Tradition in America: An Interpretation of American Political Thought Since the Revolution* (New York: Harcourt, Brace and World, 1955).

43. Nathaniel C. Nash, "Latin Economic Speedup Leaves Poor in the Dust," *The New York Times*, 1994, September 7, A1, A7.

44. IBRD, *World Development 1990, 1991, 1992, 1993*; UNDP, *Human Development 1991, 1992, 1993*; J. Black, *Development in Theory and Practice* (Boulder, Colo.: Westview, 1991); Robert Maguire, *Bottom Up Development: Haiti* (Rosslyn, Va.: The Inter-American Foundation, 1981); William M. Dyal, Jr., *The Know How* (introduction) (Arlington, Va.: The Inter-American Foundation, 1977, reprint 1986); Patrick Breslin, *Development and Dignity* (Arlington, Va.: The Inter-American Foundation, 1987); Paulo Freire, *Pedagogy of the Oppressed* (New York: Herder and Perder, 1970); James Grant, "Development, The End of Trickle Down?", *Foreign Policy*, #12, Fall, 1973; Elliott R. Morss and Victoria A. Morss, *U.S. Foreign Aid — An Assessment of New and Traditional Strategies* (Boulder, Colo.: Westview, 1982); Theodore W. Schultz, *Investing in People — The Economics of Population Quality* (Berkeley: University of California Press, 1980).

45. See, for example, James Grant, 1973, and his opening statement that "a major rethinking of development concepts is taking place...."

46. See J. Brian Atwood, "Statement of Principles on Participatory Development," internal AID document adopted on November 16, 1993.

47. Amartya Sen, writing on page 48 in Wilber, 1988, asserts that refining data distributionally does not go far enough: "Recently the focus has shifted somewhat from growth of *total incomes* to the *distribution of incomes*....I would argue that 'income' itself provides an inadequate basis for analyzing a person's entitlements. Income gives the means of buying things....Even if there are no schools in the village and no hospitals nearby, the income of the villager can still be increased by adding to his purchasing power over the goods that are available in the market. But this rise in income may not be able to deal at all adequately with his entitlement to education or medical treatment....The entitlement to live, say, in a malaria-free environment is not a matter of purchase with income in any significant way."

48. UNICEF sets a 1995 deadline for improvement in data collection: "As a minimum, all nations should produce annual statistics on basic indicators of social progress — under five mortality, child malnutrition, primary school completion, adult literacy, and family planning. Statistics on economic growth, on inflation and interest rates, are now used on a regular basis by all serious media and have become part of informed political and public debate in almost all nations. They are one of the principal means by which politicians are held accountable in democratic systems. If progress toward meeting minimum human needs is to be given more priority, then similar use must be made of annual statistics which show what percentages of a nation's children are adequately nourished, or are immunized, or are enrolled in school, or have access to clean water and basic health care. It is particularly important that improved systems for collecting data on human well-being should be put in place before the World Summit on Social Development in 1995." Peter Adamson (general editor), *The Progress of Nations 1993* (New York: UNICEF House, 1993), 5.

References

Adamson, Peter (ed.). 1993. *The Progress of Nations 1993*. New York: UNICEF House.

Atwood, J. Brian. 1993. "Statement of Principles on Participatory Development." Internal U.S. AID document adopted on November 16. Washington, D.C.

Black, Eugene R. 1969. "A Message from Eugene R. Black." Pamphlet. Washington, D.C.: Overseas Development Council, April.

Black, J. 1991. *Development in Theory and Practice*. Boulder, Colo.: Westview Press.

Breslin, Patrick. 1987. *Development and Dignity*. Arlington, Va.: The Inter-American Foundation.

Degler, Carl N. 1963. "The American Past: An Unsuspected Obstacle in Foreign Affairs," *The American Scholar*, 32,2,Spring.

Devine, Donald. 1972. *The Political Culture of the United States: The Influence of Member Values on Regime Maintenance*. Boston: Little, Brown.

Domínguez, Jorge. 1976. "The U.S. Impact on Cuban Internal Politics and Economics, 1902-1958: From Imperialism to Hegemony." Paper delivered at the American Political Science Association, Chicago.

Dyal, William M., Jr. 1986[1977]. *The Know How*. Arlington, Va.: The Inter-American Foundation.

Freire, Paulo. 1970. *Pedagogy of the Oppressed*. New York: Herder and Herder.

Grant, James. 1973. "Development, The End of Trickle Down?" *Foreign Policy*, 12, Fall.

Haq, Khadija, and Uner Kirdar. 1958. *Managing Human Development*. Islamabad: North-South Roundtable.

Hartz, Louis. 1955. *The Liberal Tradition in America: An Interpretation of American Political Thought Since the Revolution*. New York: Harcourt, Brace and World.

Huntington, Samuel P. 1968. *Political Order in Changing Societies*. New Haven, Conn.: Yale University Press.

IBRD. *World Development 1990, 1991, 1992, 1993*.

Kay, Geoffrey. 1975. *Development and Underdevelopment: A Marxist Analysis*. New York: St. Martin's Press.

Maguire, Robert. 1981. *Bottom Up Development: Haiti*. Rosslyn, Va.: The Inter-American Foundation.

Morss, Elliott R., and Victoria A. Morss. 1982. *U.S. Foreign Aid — An Assessment of New and Traditional Strategies*. Boulder, Colo.: Westview Press.

Nash, Nathaniel C. 1994. "Latin Economic Speedup Leaves Poor in the Dust," *The New York Times,* September 7.

Packenham, Robert A. 1973. *Liberal America and the Third World, Political Development Ideas in Foreign Aid and Social Science*. Princeton, N.J.: Princeton University Press.

Pearson, Lester B. 1969. *Report of the Commission on International Development.* New York: Praeger.

Schlesinger, Arthur M., Jr. 1965. *A Thousand Days: John F. Kennedy in the White House.* Boston: Houghton Mifflin.

Schultz, Theodore W. 1980. *Investing in People — The Economics of Population Quality.* Berkeley: University of California Press.

Sorensen, Theodore C. 1966. *Kennedy.* New York: Bantam.

UNDP. 1994. *Human Development Report 1994.* New York: Oxford University Press.

UNDP. 1993. *Human Development Report 1993.* New York: Oxford University Press.

UNDP. 1992. *Human Development Report 1992.* New York: Oxford University Press.

UNDP. 1991. *Human Development Report 1991.* New York: Oxford University Press.

Ward, Barbara, J.D. Runnalls, and Lenore D'Anjou (eds.). 1971. *The Widening Gap: Development in the 1970s.* New York: Columbia University Press.

Weisskoff, Richard. 1993. "Basic Human Needs and the Democratic Process in Latin America," *North-South Issues*, II,2.

White, Theodore H. 1979. *In Search of History.* New York: Warner Books.

Wilber, Charles K. 1988. *The Political Economy of Development and Underdevelopment.* New York: Random House, Inc.

Key Case Studies

Economic Liberalization and Political Instability: The Venezuelan Experience

Moisés Naim

In these days, when so many countries are grappling with the transition to a market economy, Venezuela's experience with economic reforms offers many useful lessons. The privileged conditions under which market reforms were launched, and the extreme political turbulence the country experienced, highlight many paradoxes that accompany economic liberalization. Venezuela used to be a happy anomaly in a region plagued by military dictatorships, economic debacles, and political turmoil. It boasted one of the oldest democracies in Latin America, and its huge oil revenues made it very prosperous and politically stable.

In 1989, Carlos Andrés Pérez began his presidency. He had already been president during the 1970s, when oil prices quadrupled and the living standards and expectations of Venezuelans also rose dramatically. This time, in contrast to the policies of his previous government, Pérez launched a surprising set of radical, market-oriented reforms. His new approach was attuned to the country's dire international and economic realities. But it was grossly out of sync with popular expectations bred by decades of pervasive state intervention subsidized by oil. Three weeks after his inauguration, the most violent riots in decades erupted over a rise in bus fares. That year the country experienced its highest inflation ever and its largest drop in economic activity. Nonetheless, the government kept its reforms.

Moisés Naim is a senior associate at the Carnegie Endowment in Washington, D.C.

This paper is based on the author's book, *Paper Tigers and Minotaurs: The Politics of Venezuela's Economic Reforms,* Washington, D.C.: The Carnegie Endowment, 1993.

In some ways, the policy changes paid off very rapidly. Unbearable macroeconomic distortions were corrected, and in 1990 the economy began to grow at impressive rates. From 1990 to 1993 Venezuela had one of the fastest-growing economies in the world. Social safety nets for the poor were implemented, and the stock market boomed, as did foreign investment and new exports. Money-losing state-owned enterprises began to be privatized, and international debt was renegotiated. Unemployment declined at a fast pace; inflation also declined, though much more slowly. Political power was decentralized from the capital to states. Direct elections for state governors and mayors were held for the first time in 1989.

At the same time, however, an ugly sentiment of hostility against politicians and public officials took hold of the country. None of the outcomes that so pleased government officials, the International Monetary Fund (IMF), and foreign investors seemed to matter much to average Venezuelans. Frequent public protests in 1991 were the preamble to two army revolts in 1992. While the coups failed, they led to a powerful political backlash against Pérez and his policies. Calls for his ouster became common, accompanied by a somber mood about Venezuela's future even though only a few months before Venezuela had been a showcase for successful development. Finally, in May 1993, Pérez's political adversaries succeeded in forcing him out of office to face trial on corruption charges.

If these are the consequences of market-oriented reforms in a country that had everything going for it, what can other countries in Latin America or in other regions expect from essentially the same policy changes? Can critics of these reforms rest their case on Venezuela's experience? The answer is no. Pérez and his government can be justly blamed for important political mistakes and gross oversights. Many technical aspects of the reforms are worth debating, but Venezuela's turmoil is essentially the result of a legacy of high expectations, incompetent public organizations wrecked by the abuses of many years of exaggerated state intervention, and the collapse of an institutional setting based on economic, political, and social conditions that have ceased to exist. All reforming countries are being affected by this explosive mix. For this reason, it is of vital importance to derive appropriate lessons about the political effects of economic reforms.

The purpose of this chapter is to provide an overview of the Venezuelan experience and highlight some of its most salient implications in terms of the politics of economic liberalization.

Venezuela's Recent Economic Trajectory

The Venezuelan economy since the 1920s can be summed up in a word: oil. Taxes from oil sales provide more than 70 percent of total government revenue, and oil exports generate more than 80 percent of the country's total foreign exchange.[1]

Beginning in the 1920s, oil exploitation in Venezuela sparked the fastest urbanization on the continent and removed the government's incentive to develop other revenue sources. This trend continued through the 1950s, when the newly democratic government adopted an import substitution program aimed at diversifying the industrial base.

Venezuela was the last of the large economies of Latin America to initiate comprehensive state-led efforts to industrialize. When it did, it achieved impressive results.[2] Economic growth was high in the 1950s and 1960s; inflation was low, and foreign investment was strong, especially in oil and iron ore (see figures 1 and 2). Prior to the mid-1970s, oil prices were not very high, and there were occasional grumblings about deteriorating terms of trade. Nonetheless, oil provided a substantial, steady source of fiscal solvency and foreign earnings.

On the other hand, Venezuela's deep dependence on the oil market made the economy extremely vulnerable to disruption. By the mid-1970s, with oil prices rising from $2 to $14 a barrel and higher, the influx of foreign exchange proved almost impossible to manage and invest wisely.

Growth remained at 6.8 percent, and inflation stayed at a relatively low 6.6 percent during the explosion of oil prices following the first oil "shock" in the mid-1970s. Still, an unprecedented accumulation of reserves — $9 billion in 1976, and over $11 billion in 1981 after the second oil "shock" — gave rise to all manner of illusions, unrealistic expectations, and consequently, policy mistakes.[3]

Thus, when oil prices declined, bringing down income, public expenditures and investment outlays failed to subside. In some years government spending increased even when its income declined precipitously. *On average, since 1970 oil revenues have varied from one year to the next by an amount equivalent to 6 percent of the gross domestic product (GDP)* — a wildly unmanageable fluctuation. But the construction of steel mills, dams, and highways could not be interrupted to take into account lower oil prices and their impact on the government's income. Readily available foreign debt therefore became the preferred means of cushioning the macroeconomic jolts caused by this reeling pattern of fiscal income. Starting at about $2 billion in

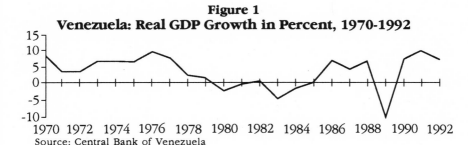

Figure 1
Venezuela: Real GDP Growth in Percent, 1970-1992

Source: Central Bank of Venezuela

Privatization Amidst Poverty

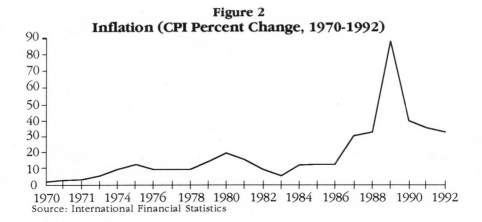

Figure 2
Inflation (CPI Percent Change, 1970-1992)

Source: International Financial Statistics

1973, by 1982 Venezuela owed $35 billion to foreign banks. (Even after continuous servicing, several reschedulings, and renegotiations, this debt was still about $30 billion in the mid-1980s.)

The steady income from oil had allowed the state continually to forestall measures to increase economic productivity. Tariff hikes, import quotas, price controls, massive undirected subsidies, and tax loopholes had deepened the underlying structural inefficiencies of state intervention in industry.

Despite decades of enormous public spending on programs ostensibly for social purposes, the large majority of Venezuelans were poorer in the 1980s than they were in the mid-1970s. Real GDP in 1985 was 25 percent lower than it had been just seven years earlier. Per capita income that year was almost 15 percent lower than in 1973, when oil revenues had first begun to grow. Moreover, throughout the 1980s income distribution grew ever more inequitable. Since 1981 the number of people living below the poverty line rose steadily, from 32 percent in 1982 to an estimated 53 percent by 1989. At the end of that period, 22 percent of households lacked the income to cover the cost of a minimum daily food intake, up from 10 percent who lacked such income at the beginning.[4]

Capital flight also accelerated since 1978, when enormous incentives not to hold local currency were created as byproducts of government economic policies. Estimates of the foreign assets privately held by Venezuelans abroad at the end of the 1980s range from $50 to $80 billion. At the same time, by the mid-1980s the government devoted almost 70 percent of its export revenues to servicing of foreign debt.

After Mexico defaulted on its huge foreign debt in August 1982, precipitating a crisis that had been building for some time, the Venezuelan public sector was unable to borrow abroad. Having lost its only instrument for managing its external imbalances, it was forced to innovate.

In 1983 the government of President Luis Herrera Campins (of the Christian Democratic party) established controls on foreign exchange in an attempt to curb a process that threatened to drain the country's reserves. Known as RECADI (*Regimen de Cambios Diferenciales* — multiple rate regime), this exchange rate regime, which was maintained until the end of 1980s, only compounded economic maladies and became a magnet for corruption. Each year the government estimated the amount of foreign exchange available and allotted quotas to each sector (sometimes even to individual importers) using criteria that frequently changed and were greatly influenced by the moods, interests, and political considerations of government officials and their party bosses. This measure and other government controls created not only massive social inequities and economic inefficiencies but also a highly profitable business for political, business, media, and labor elites. Except for tightening state controls — on prices, interest rates, imports, exports, private investment, exchange rates, merchandising, and international financial transactions — the government implemented no other policy changes.

While the situation steadily eroded, new local and foreign private investment grew scarce, and social services deteriorated. In the second half of the 1980s, the government of President Jaime Lusinchi (of *Acción Democrática*) further postponed a policy redirection and, like its predecessor, resorted to tighter government control of the economy to deal with a constantly deteriorating situation. International reserves were depleted in order to avoid highly unpopular policy reforms. Hence, while government revenue from oil declined 30 percent in 1986 because of a sharp price drop, public spending increased by 10 percent (see figures 3 and 4).

Moreover, since a presidential election was scheduled for December 1988, the government, despite a sharp decrease in revenues, permitted major expansions in credit and foreign exchange so that in 1988 the economy grew almost 5 percent. It was therefore with great surprise that Venezuelans heard their new government disclose that foreign currency reserves were severely depleted, that the fiscal deficit of 1988 had exceeded 9 percent of GDP, that the current account had registered its largest deficit in history, and that most prices, from interest rates to eggs, and from medicine to bus fares, were artificially low and impossible to sustain.

1989: Near Collapse

Carlos Andrés Pérez won the December 1988 election with 54.6 percent of the vote, surpassing his main opponent, Eduardo Fernández (a Christian Democrat), by a significant margin. Nonetheless, his political party, *Acción Democrática*, did not fare as well, losing its majorities in both houses of Congress and in many local governments. Pérez's inauguration took place before an unprecedented number of world leaders, attesting to the interna-

Figure 3
International Oil Prices in U.S. Dollars

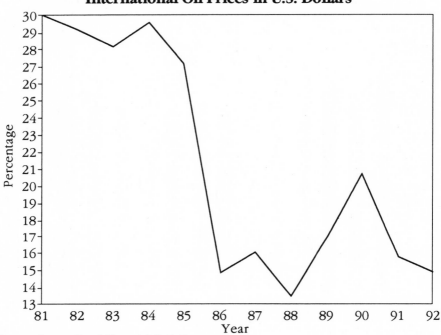

Source: International Financial Statistics

tional solidarity he enjoyed at the time. The honeymoon ended just three weeks later, on Monday, 27 February, when the people of Caracas and three other major cities took to the streets in a rampage of rioting and looting.

The three days of civil turmoil left three hundred Venezuelans dead. Such violence was unprecedented; not even at the height of the Castro-inspired guerrilla war in the turbulent 1960s had so much violent civil disobedience occurred. These riots erupted spontaneously; no organization induced people to protest. Workers living in the outskirts of Caracas had been surprised by a substantial increase in bus fares. The government had approved an increase in fares, but the independent bus owner-operators decided to charge more, feeling that the hike was not enough to cover their cost increases over several previous months.[5]

A more subtle factor fundamental to the riots was the social tension that had been building over an extended period prior to Pérez's inauguration. During the latter part of 1988 and on into early 1989, Venezuelans were experiencing the worst shortage of consumer goods ever. Over the years, protection and subsidies for infant industries had fostered a highly concen-

Figure 4
Government Revenue from Oil

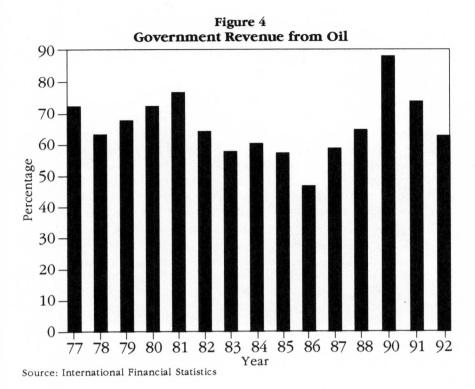

Source: International Financial Statistics

trated ownership structure, with a small number of large firms coordinating their pricing and investment decisions. The lack of price competition, foreign or domestic, justified the Ministry of Industry's intervention regarding an immense, administratively overwhelming array of products and services. However, the procedure by which the Ministry of Industry set prices was a technical and administrative fiction, the result of instructions from the government or political party. Lax monetary policy and a 93 percent devaluation of the bolivar in 1986, aimed at restoring equilibrium, had inevitably added to already powerful inflationary pressures. Given election expectations, the government attempted a general price freeze for most of 1988, when government decision-makers were half-jokingly told to get ready for their "x-ray exam" — don't move, hold your breath, and wait.

Consequently, expectations of price increases, artificially low interest rates, and expansionary election-year fiscal policies had fueled demand, but a full set of disincentives and bottlenecks constrained an adequate supply response. Venezuela, whose poorest citizens had been accustomed to comparatively easy access to staples and consumer goods, experienced strict rationing, long lines, and months of anxiety.

These difficulties, of course, were the concrete expression of deeper structural problems in the economy. Debt crises, lower oil revenues, changing international circumstances, and misguided domestic reactions to these circumstances crippled the economy. Venezuela's macroeconomic distortions and lack of international competitiveness became increasingly difficult to sustain. Cheap foreign exchange made non-oil exports overpriced and provided a powerful incentive for both flight capital and imports. Most goods were subject to high tariffs and strict quotas, and the cost disadvantages of mandatory licensing and duties as high as 940 percent impaired imports by increasing the cost of inputs needed to export. Exporters also had to contend with underfunded and inefficient support infrastructure.

Some importers sought special permission from the Ministry of Industry, which could dispense waivers on quota limits. The net result was that by 1988, Venezuela, with only 4 percent of the region's population, accounted for more than 10 percent of the entire region's imports, while exports other than oil and aluminum remained insignificant. Persistently high import bills depleted reserves to critical levels. At the end of 1988, with the current account registering a $6 billion deficit, the country had lost half of its net reserves.

Government finances also were in crisis. Public revenues from oil crumbled from $1,700 per head in 1981 to $382 in 1992. Still, Venezuelans were convinced that the problem, if any, lay on the spending side and not in the size and composition of public revenues. So successive governments, faced with lower oil revenues and declining productivity in other sectors, and incapable of generating new sources of income, cut spending in areas where the political effects were not so visible. This produced schools with teachers but without water or chalkboards, universities without laboratories, government offices without telephones or typewriters, and public services without maintenance funds.

Not surprisingly, no serious attempt at tax reform had been made in Venezuela for decades — so in 1992, non-oil revenues were a mere 5.6 percent of GDP. In contrast, Chilean, Mexican, and Argentinean tax receipts were approximately 20 percent of GDP, and in industrialized countries, between 30 and 40 percent. The government, having avoided charging consumers world prices for fuel and natural gas, was foregoing revenues amounting to 10 percent of the budget and 1 percent of GDP — as much as is allocated to health care.[6]

Additionally, the Ministry of Public Finance had for more than a decade concentrated almost exclusively on renegotiation of foreign debt and administration of the foreign exchange regime. Thus, capacity actually to manage the country's public finance, collect taxes, or oversee the financial sector was practically nonexistent. At the same time, the state had created conditions that made it especially vulnerable to the massive losses of state-owned enterprises and to its misdirected budget outlays.

Government policies and external events had also precipitated a steep fall in incomes. During the "lost decade" of the 1980s, income per capita throughout Latin America dropped an average of 9.4 percent; in Venezuela, it dropped 20 percent. Poverty in Venezuela reflected this trend, as the drop in incomes affected urban areas most: By 1984, 56 percent of the total urban population resided in slums.

For more than 30 years the government had spent 10 to 15 percent of GDP on so-called "social programs to remedy poverty." But in 1988, Venezuela's infant mortality was 200 percent higher than Jamaica's, 80 percent higher than Chile's, and 30 percent higher than Panama's. In addition, no other country in the region spent more per student than Venezuela, yet illiteracy, school enrollment, repetition, and dropout rates were among the worst in the region. Social service agencies, captured by powerful unions, had their capacity to deliver services severely impaired.[7]

Pérez's Turnaround

By election time in 1989, Venezuela was in obvious economic danger, operating with an increasingly isolated and grossly inefficient economy at the brink of hyperinflation. Under these conditions, the Pérez government launched *El Gran Viraje* ("The Great Turnaround"). The first sign that Pérez would go beyond vague promises came with his surprise appointments to key ministries: They were a group of relatively young, foreign trained, politically inexperienced professionals with no party affiliations. Most were academics or respected managers in the private sector; for many, these appointments were their first public-sector jobs. These technocrats added to the capacity of the state and increased its autonomy. Unfortunately, their lack of political skills, bureaucratic experience, and public appeal would create problems down the road.

Notwithstanding, Pérez also included in his cabinet individuals who, while longstanding members of *Acción Democrática*, were appointed because of the president's own calculations and needs rather than the specific requests of the party hierarchy. In some cases he gave prominent roles to individuals well known for their association with the policies his administration was trying to dismantle. Pérez allowed them to pursue policies that were inconsistent with the overall direction of the government's programs, although he systematically turned back the attempts of some of his ministers to derail reforms. These inconsistencies meant that, after Congress, the cabinet became the most important source of delays and distortions in the reforms.

Among its reforms, the Pérez government eliminated RECADI and established the free convertibility of the currency with a single exchange rate for all transactions, freed practically all prices, liberalized imports and exports, and deregulated entire sectors of economic activity. It also defined an ambitious privatization program and a social policy directly targeting the most vulnerable groups of society. This targeted subsidy replaced the politically sensitive, but highly inequitable and no longer affordable general price subsidies that the population had enjoyed for years.

The administration implemented most of these changes with dizzying speed. Within weeks of taking office, it implemented many of the measures that did not require congressional approval, such as price liberalization, trade reform, and the freeing of the exchange and interest rates. It also increased rates for electricity, water, telephone, gasoline, public transportation, and most other public services. Immediately thereafter, the local currency — *the bolívar* — underwent a 170 percent devaluation, and interest rates climbed from 13 percent to more than 40 percent.

The administration eliminated non-tariff barriers on 94 percent of manufactured imports, did away with special permits for exports, and lowered average tariffs over four years from 35 percent to 10 percent by 1992. It followed through on yearly tariff reduction rounds and gained Venezuela's entry into the GATT. The authorities also secured funding from the IMF, the World Bank, and the Inter-American Development Bank. At the same time, the government renegotiated the foreign debt, thus lowering annual interest payments, and secured a seven-year grace period on payments of the principal.[8] Then, to close the yawning gap in the budget, the administration put legislation before Congress proposing a completely different income tax system and a value-added tax.

On the social front, the artificial prices of the past left the majority of the poor vulnerable to new policies aimed at correcting such distortions. To compensate, the ratio of social-sector spending was increased from 11 percent in 1989 to 16 percent in 1990 and 22 percent in 1992. Unemployment compensation and other measures were initiated to assist laid-off workers. The government also began free maternal and child health programs, reaching 69 percent of a target population of 3.6 million primary school students.

The government set about reforming itself as well. The president was the catalyst in the process that led in December 1989 to the first direct elections of governors (previously appointees) and other state and local officials, including mayors. A reform was passed providing for the election of members of Congress by name instead of by party-determined list, albeit with provisions for parties to appoint some members. Later, it became clear that these political reforms did not sufficiently compensate for the extremely cynical perception Venezuelans had of the government, its reforms, and politicians in general.

Figure 5
Unemployment, 1988-1991 (Percentage of labor force)

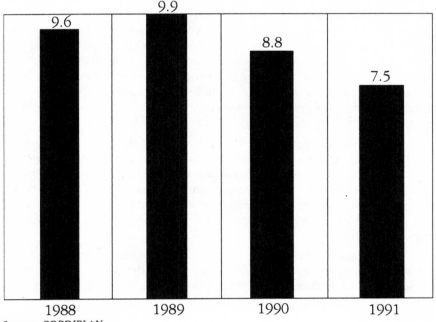

Source: CORDIPLAN

The Consequences

These policies brought on what may have been the most severe income adjustments of any country in Latin America.[9] Inflation for 1989 ran at more than 80 percent, as prices sprang back from two years of artificial repression and major increases in the cost of utilities, raw materials, intermediate products, and all services — from insurance policies to transportation costs — as well as higher interest rates and a devalued currency. Unemployment figures showed a negligible increase after the reforms were introduced, from 9.6 percent to about 10 percent, but concealed the fact that thousands lost higher-paying jobs, taking pay cuts of as much as one-half (see figure 5). Personal disposable income shrank by an overwhelming 14 percent in 1989.[10] Real salaries declined by 11 percent, bringing their decade-long total decline to 45 percent.[11] The real income of urban workers — who constitute 90 percent of the work force — dropped below its 1980 level.[12] Helped along by the added oil revenues in local currency produced by the devaluation, the public sector deficit did shrink from 9.3 percent to 1.3 percent of GDP, but the budget nevertheless was 10 percent smaller in real terms.

Social reaction against the new policies was very violent. Although no further major riots or violent clashes materialized, localized protests erupted constantly throughout 1990 and 1991. The massive outburst of violence at the outset of the changes had been traumatic because of the uncontained mayhem, loss of life, and property damage. Many grocery stores were pillaged and had to be closed. Small stores located in poorer sections had a hard time reopening and many never did, which made essential items unavailable for months afterwards. A related jump in personal crime also created a source of unease. Still, this initial stage of low intensity, but constant, public protests would contrast starkly with the two coup attempts and the more frequent demonstrations of the last years of the Pérez government.

Interestingly, the population's unhappiness with the overall situation was not assuaged by the positive macroeconomic results induced by the new policies. In fact, the new policies yielded results very quickly. After an 8.3 percent drop in output in 1989, the economy grew at 6.5 percent in 1990 and 10.4 percent in 1991, the highest rate the economy had ever experienced and one of the highest rates in the world.[13] In 1992, the economy continued to grow by 7.3 percent.

In contrast to the experience of many developing economies, the presence of oil revenues meant that the adjustment did not become as overly constrained by the external environment as was common in other countries.[14] Quite the contrary, external factors — oil prices boosted by the Gulf War, for instance — played a large part in the 1991 growth and were a positive influence in debt renegotiation. Nevertheless, in keeping with a recurrent pattern, what followed the sudden increase in oil income was an even steeper decline — a trend successive Venezuelan governments have always failed to recognize — and in 1992 oil-GDP contracted by 1.9 percent. Yet, for the first time in many years, growth was sustained by the non-oil components of the economy, notably manufacturing and services.

Non-traditional exports also had an impressive initial surge in response to the reforms. Non-petroleum exports increased 49 percent in 1989 and 15 percent in 1990.

There was a bit of bad fortune in the following years, when a sharp decline in the international price of aluminum, a product which accounts for a substantial share of Venezuela's non-oil exports, led to an export revenue decline (see figure 6). On balance, the rapid growth rate of private-sector exports was not sustainable beyond the initial two years, since the expansion of the domestic market offset the incentive to seek new export opportunities, while uncertainty about the stability of the reforms inhibited new investments needed to restructure firms for international competition. Also, many years of inward-oriented protectionism has left a legacy of laws, regulations, institu-

Figure 6
Total Exports

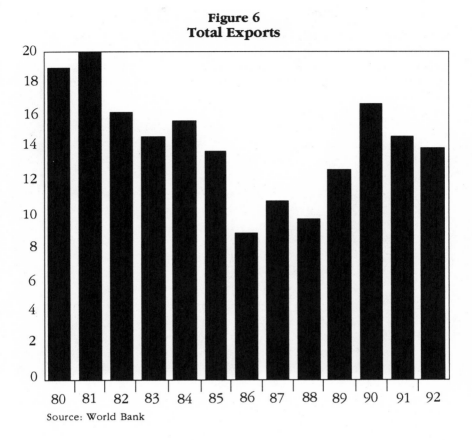

Source: World Bank

tions, and even attitudes that create an anti-export bias in the economy which will take much longer to eradicate.

Of more significance, renewed investor confidence produced an important rebound in foreign capital inflows. Venezuela, with its immense potential, formerly had such an unwelcoming regime for foreign investment that it was ahead only of Bolivia as the Andean region country with the least amount of foreign investment. Economic reforms, debt renegotiation, and the myriad untapped opportunities offered by the country now created a boom in foreign investment (see figure 7). In addition, while in February 1989 an investor could buy one dollar of Venezuelan debt for twenty-seven cents, in 1991 the cost had risen to around seventy cents. At the end of 1991, both the government and private Venezuelan corporations had considerable success placing new debt instruments in international financial markets.

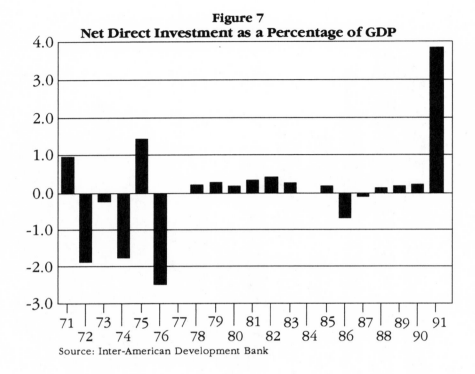

Figure 7
Net Direct Investment as a Percentage of GDP

Source: Inter-American Development Bank

The reforms were also very successful in correcting imbalances in the external sector. The current account went from a $6 billion deficit in 1988 to a surplus of $2 billion in 1989, $8 billion in 1990, and $2.6 billion in 1991. These conditions allowed the country's gross international reserves to double in that period (see figure 8). In 1992, the current account deteriorated again to a $3.7 billion deficit as imports surged past flat export sales by more than 20 percent to reach their highest level in many years. This less comfortable position could continue into the future as a consequence of liberalized imports, a decline in oil prices, and delays in eliminating the many obstacles that still impair the expansion of exports.

The new policies spared the country its first episode of hyperinflation. Without the drastic corrections, inflation in 1989 would have soared well above the 80 percent level it reached. The price level declined after 1989, but stabilized around a still-high 30 percent range. Two main factors accounted for the failure of efforts to bring inflation down below 30 percent. The first, of course, was poor coordination of fiscal and monetary policies and failure to secure a more permanent fiscal balance. The second was the combination of expectations within highly concentrated marketing and distribution chan-

Figure 8
Change in International Reserves

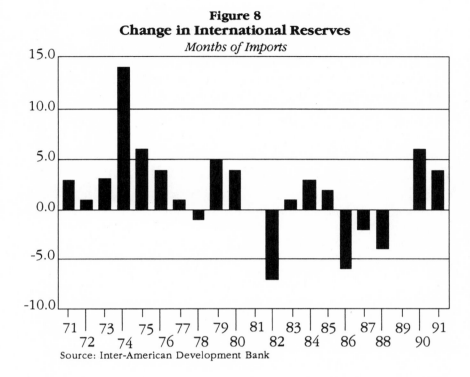

Months of Imports

Source: Inter-American Development Bank

nels. The industrial promotion schemes of the past had allowed subsidized manufacturers to develop their own marketing and distribution networks; so any new imports made available by a more liberal trade regime were distributed through tightly held channels and priced to prop up suppliers' profits.[15] The Venezuelan case shows that in some sectors, it takes a rather long time for trade liberalization to have a substantial impact on domestic competition and inflation.

While prices came down after the initial shock of reform, inflation continued to erode the living conditions of the poor. In order to buffer some of the social impact of the reforms, the government had designed an ambitious program of direct subsidies and other initiatives to provide a social safety net. Unfortunately, too many years of abuse had weakened the state to the point that most agencies could not adequately perform the tasks for which they had been created.

The Sources of Political Instability

Understanding the circumstances that brought about Venezuela's political turmoil sheds light on the political challenges of managing large-scale economic change. This turmoil was produced by several forces acting simultaneously — among them, internal problems and deep divisions within the armed forces, political effects of inevitable but highly unpopular economic reforms, the media's role in amplifying instability, and oligopolistic wars that erupted among private sector groups. An even more basic cause of the nation's political instability was the institutional devastation of the state; the profound deterioration of public institutions had rendered the state incapable of responding adequately to the many demands of the moment.

The Military:
The Consequences of a Truncated Pyramid

The situation within the armed forces was a logical extension of prevailing conditions within the country, the state, and the economy. Certain longstanding trends had eaten away at the mission and the ethos of the Venezuelan armed forces. First, for many years, the rigor of the promotion system had been gradually relaxed. This permitted the number of senior officers to increase at a much faster pace than the number of positions available. This trend accelerated in the 1980s and systematically undermined the hierarchical pyramid on which military organization relies. In effect, each year, more and more generals occupied posts that just a few years earlier had customarily been assigned to captains. Too many generals and admirals were chasing too few real jobs within the armed forces, putting the promotion system under great strain. Individual merit very quickly ceased to be the overriding condition for promotion and career advancement. The need to have friends and mentors within and without the armed forces became as important as having the necessary qualifications. This stimulated strong rivalries between individuals and the small informal groups or "clans" to which they belonged. Therefore, significant pressure existed for aspiring officers, their mentors, and proteges to block or even sabotage the career advances of rivals.

Adding to the comparative weight of factors unrelated to individual merit was a law mandating congressional approval for all promotions to the rank of colonel and general. Although originally envisioned as a healthy check by civil society on the military, the law became an instrument of politicization and barely concealed partisanship, and an incentive for the discrediting tactics that rival officers and their clans commonly employed against each other.

Under these circumstances, the interservice rivalries that in all armed forces shape military organizational behavior acquired a far more divisive role. Not only did competition for budgets, resources, and career opportunities develop among the army, the navy, and the air force; it mushroomed within each branch as well. Competition was intensified by the fiscal crises of the 1980s, when military budgets were tightened and foreign exchange for arms procurement and maintenance became harder to secure. Moreover, between

1980 and 1988, the number of military personnel nearly doubled (from forty-one thousand to seventy-one thousand men) as the economy worsened and the military offered one of the few employment options for many poor Venezuelans. Also as a consequence of the fiscal crisis, the portion of the military budget allocated to foreign exchange grew increasingly larger as the daily needs of soldiers and junior officers went unmet. While major outlays were made to purchase U.S. F-16 fighter planes, sophisticated French tanks, and Italian warships, soldiers had to get by with insufficient supplies of boots, uniforms, housing, and other basics. Officers' salaries declined so much that they could no longer afford cars or even adequate housing. In 1991, the monthly net salary of a lieutenant was the equivalent of two hundred dollars. It became common for several junior officers and their families to share a single apartment in poor *barrios*. This created resentment toward senior officers, who were increasingly isolated from their subordinates and interested almost exclusively in the economics of procurement and the politics of promotion.

The lack of cohesion between junior officers and their superiors was also exacerbated by generational differences. While junior officers had ample opportunities to complement their military education with professional studies at home and abroad, this was not the case for older officers. These were part of the cohort of officers whose academic training in the mid-1960s had been cut short by troop call-ups for the war against the leftist guerrillas. All this contributed greatly to the tension and mistrust between senior officers and their subordinates, adding to erosion of discipline and organizational fragmentation.

Finally, two traits common to all public-sector organizations in Venezuela also affected the armed forces: rapid turnover and lack of clear, stable organizational goals. The average tenure of the minister of defense (who has always been a senior military officer) has been one year. When that year is up, the minister normally reaches retirement age and has to step down both from government and from active military duty. Such regular turnover is a source of instability, politicking, and inefficiency within the armed forces, and it greatly hampers sustained efforts at institutional and organizational development. Another source of instability is rapidly changing domestic and international conditions, which have caused confusion regarding the precise role of the armed forces in a country with the geopolitical, social, and economic characteristics of Venezuela. This confusion has prevented the emergence of a unified and shared vision, an essential component for maintaining a common sense of direction within a complex organization. As a result of these trends within the armed forces, central authority and control became increasingly difficult to maintain.

The Economy:
Record Growth Does Not Buy Political Stability

A s discussed above, the Venezuelan economy reacted very fast and very favorably to the adjustments of 1989. In 1990 it entered a high-growth phase that at least temporarily appeared to be immune to the profound political shocks that later shattered investor confidence in the country.

The country's admirable macroeconomic performance created great enthusiasm among businessmen, government officials, and foreign investors. This was not the case, however, among local politicians, journalists, and the majority of the population, who by and large remained unimpressed by the statistics and highly critical of the government's economic policies. Often, the government's critics were cast-offs of the previous system —the individuals and groups that had lost privileges and power under the new scheme. But there were other, disinterested observers who also expressed serious misgivings, and there was general dissatisfaction among the population. Inflation had become firmly lodged at 30 percent annually and continued to eat away at the buying power of the poor and middle classes, remaining a prime source of social friction. While in 1991 real salaries increased for the first time in many years, they still lagged behind the needs and expectations created by decades of an artificially maintained economy. Also, while food consumption was growing, the share of family budgets going to food and basic necessities reached new highs — bringing to an all-time low the income families could devote to other expenditures that had been a customary part of their consumption patterns (figure 9 shows net per capita income).

Frustration over rising prices was further amplified by the slow pace of government efforts to target special social programs directly to the poor. Although massive, inefficient subsidies can be done away with almost instantaneously, building the institutions required to deliver assistance to highly vulnerable populations takes much longer. As all countries undergoing major structural reforms are discovering, social safety nets are much easier to design than to implement. Other basic state-run services — health, housing, education, and urban transportation — had also been drastically curtailed by a decade of fiscal crises and mismanagement. The economic adjustment process and ineffective or delayed government actions made this situation worse. The condition of public services was a constant source of anger toward the government, and those affected tended to dismiss any claims of macroeconomic advances. Hospitals that failed to function; an unreliable and insufficient water supply system; a bus system incapable of bringing urban workers back and forth to their jobs; a school system in shambles — these realities devastated government popularity. Additionally, unprecedented levels of street crime and the government's apparent failure to handle the personal safety crisis provoked a strong outcry against the administration from all quarters.

Figure 9
Per Capita Income

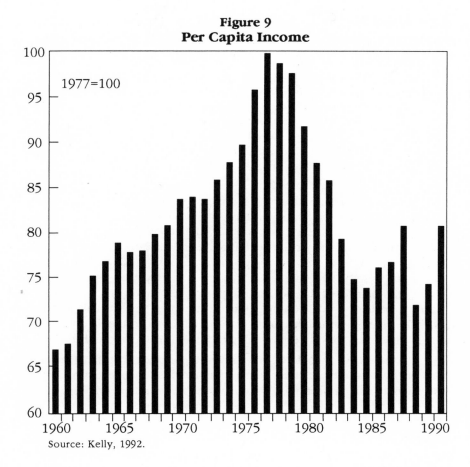

Source: Kelly, 1992.

News of a solid balance of payments or of world record-setting levels of economic growth did little to mollify the negative attitudes born of such tangible public problems. The widely held perception that no explicit effort was being made to rectify the profoundly inequitable distribution of income and wealth that years of demagogic and ill-conceived government intervention had spawned served to reinforce these attitudes. Fortunes were being made in the soaring stock market; previously banned luxury imports filled shopping malls, and those privileged few with savings safely and profitably deposited in foreign banks flaunted their wealth. The great majority of the population thus became convinced that reforms unduly benefited a small group of businessmen, speculators, and politicians at the expense of society at large. Aggravating this sense of inequity was the enormous wealth that a small elite had been allowed to accumulate under the previous policies. The Venezuelan rich tend to be as ostentatious as their counterparts everywhere and provided daily proof that economic reforms did not affect their living standards. That the burden of paying for the mistakes of the past was not being shared equally by everyone became all too apparent.

The government repetitively insisted that hardships imposed by the new economic policies were unavoidable. It also contended that the social costs of reforms were much lower than the social cost of not implementing corrections — that is, hyperinflation and its ravaging consequences. The government correctly argued that any attempt at forcing the rich to bring back the fortunes they kept well hidden abroad was bound to fail and that it would only hamper the voluntary repatriation that was beginning to take place, spurred by new investment opportunities.

While these may have been valid points, they were based in counterfactual arguments that relied on hypothetical possibilities to which most Venezuelans could relate neither intellectually nor through their personal history. The country had never experienced anything like the circumstances it was going through, far less the ordeals of hyperinflation. Day-to-day hardships and frustrations were neither remote nor hypothetical; they were perceived as the direct consequences of the actions of a government that was not trusted. The economic malaise — which public opinion attributed to politicians in general and to the Pérez government in particular — contributed to a social and political ferment that exacerbated the instability prompted by the aborted coups.

Nevertheless, it would be misguided to conclude that the state of the economy was the fundamental force underlying the Venezuelan political and institutional crisis. In fact, the economy was rapidly recovering and serious macroeconomic imbalances were being cured, but far more had been expected since the economic program replaced an all-encompassing, state-centered approach that had held sway for decades. In effect, the economic stabilization program had to fulfill political and ideological functions for which it was neither designed nor suited.[16] Furthermore, in the eyes of public opinion, the new economic policies were the cause of the operational collapse of public services and social service delivery agencies (though these had been neglected or exploited for years).

At the same time, though the economic crisis was far from over, the economy was rapidly becoming an instrument of political stability, as small but influential social groups gradually started to support the new market-oriented approach, and results became more apparent. But while the economy tended to stabilize, social and political systems exhibited a disarray that overwhelmed all else and eventually came to affect the economy as well.

The Political Economy of Corruption

Corruption became the lightning rod that attracted the anger and frustration of all segments of society. It had existed and flourished ever since oil wealth had endowed the state with massive resources to distribute with little oversight or accountability. During the second Pérez administration, however, it acquired an unprecedented political significance.

Government corruption mainly originates in three kinds of activities: the sale of public assets, the procurement of goods and services, and the state's intervention in the economy. The more the state intervenes, the greater the opportunities for profitable collusion between government officials and those who can benefit from biased public decisions. Transactions in which the government is either the seller (as in all privatization) or the buyer (as in all procurement activities) are susceptible to influence from bribes and kickbacks.

From this perspective, and in contrast to the dominant perception, corruption must have greatly diminished during the Pérez government in comparison to what it had been in the past. This is principally because with the elimination of most government controls (on prices, the exchange rate, interest rates, imports and exports, credits, and so forth) the possibility for government officials to weight decisions in favor of a specific individual or firm was greatly diminished. Furthermore, all major decisions related to privatization (even the hiring of consultants and financial advisers) were arrived at through open international auctions accessible to all interested parties. Also, the Pérez administration had to operate under an unprecedentedly vigorous degree of scrutiny from the media and most organized societal groups. This scrutiny was bound to have had some impact on curbing the excesses of the public sector, which had an enormous propensity for corruption bred by many years of opportunity and impunity. This state of affairs had resulted from the lack of effective controls, the practical nonexistence of an honest judicial system, and the actions of the mass media, which, under the old economic regime, had been much more tolerant given their own dependency on the government's goodwill for their profitability.

The traditional tolerance for corruption which the general public had exhibited for decades practically disappeared. It mattered little to the public that the potential for corruption had been undermined by the new policies. There are at least three reasons for this paradox.

First, the bulk of the population harbored two deeply ingrained beliefs: that Venezuela was a very rich country and that it was impoverished by the corruption and thievery of the rich and powerful. Instead of blaming macroeconomic mismanagement, sharply reduced oil revenues, or incompetence, people blamed the country's economic crisis on corruption. With the unprecedented daily economic tribulations, the concept of corruption took on a concrete and personal meaning as opposed to the abstract problem of political ethics and economic power it had been in the past. Second, while the government denounced the corruption that pervaded the economic schemes it was dismantling, it did little to bring those suspected of unethical practices to justice. This fueled the perception that the government was soft to the point of complicity.

Third, the media echoed the frustrations of the population and heightened them, becoming more than ever active and audacious in disclosing and denouncing corruption and bringing it to the forefront of any discussion of government and public policy. This vigilance and outspokenness stood in sharp contrast to the verdicts of the courts; in almost all cases, those accused were found innocent or were able to flee the country. Corruption and its economic and political consequences created the classic scenario where anger and hunger combine to create an inflammable political and social mixture.

The Conglomerates Go to War

That entrenched private conglomerates would fight any government attempt forcing greater competition on them was to be expected. In fact, the deregulation of the economy and elimination of government rules stifling competition became yet another source of their opposition to the Pérez government. An effect which no one anticipated, however, and which proved far more destabilizing than business groups' resistance to reforms, was the warfare that broke out among the groups. The competition induced by reforms spurred large conglomerates into an all-out war with one another for control of newly created opportunities in the economy. An already besieged government found itself in the middle of these battles. (In accordance with the longstanding practice of big business in many Latin American countries, these battles were fought more in the political arena than in the marketplace.)

In a state-centered economy, many years of pervasive government intervention create market structures in which competition is dormant and oligopolistic behavior prevalent. Collusion and tactics to exclude actual or potential rivals become the core of firms' business strategies. Eventually a precarious equilibrium between the existing corporations is reached whereby each group avoids intruding in the others' activities. The balance is periodically upset, and ruinous battles ensue. Government decisions or other factors may alter business conditions in a given sector, triggering a series of moves and countermoves by the dominant groups in the sector.

In Venezuela, surviving the threats of a constantly changing policy environment and the predatory moves of rivals was difficult without having access to politicians and policymakers and the means to influence them. Maintaining close ties with union leaders who could oppose or promote a specific government decision in the name of the working class became a frequently utilized tactic. Another was to employ journalists as highly paid consultants to write or broadcast targeted news items about competitors or influence government decisions through the media. In fact, during the first years of the Pérez administration the longstanding tendency of industrial and financial conglomerates to diversify their holdings to include media companies intensified greatly. Banks and other financial firms bought newspapers and radio stations, paying sums that could never be justified by the profits these businesses could turn on their own.

When market-oriented reforms and deregulation increased domestic and foreign competition, the arrangements, pacts, and other agreements among conglomerates broke down. In certain cases, this pushed some of the large conglomerates into a competitive frenzy in which they used every weapon at their disposal, including government officials, politicians, journalists, union leaders, and intelligence gatherers, to try to ruin their rivals or to gain a dominant position in a given industry.

The deregulation of the financial sector of the stock market, privatization, the takeover of existing firms in alliance with foreign investors, and countless other opportunities opened the door for new competition among business groups. While their politically based tactical weapons may lose their effectiveness in the long run and may even come to be abandoned, they continued to play a major role as tools to support the conglomerates' business strategies during the transition. The added complexity, disinformation, and instability such behavior injected into an already turbulent and confusing political environment was considerable.

In many instances the government found itself in the middle of these wars. Typically, each side would exert great pressures to get the government to act in its behalf. When the government did not, articles, editorials, and even purported news items appeared in the media, showing how the government had been bought by one or the other of the groups in the dispute. This pattern added to the perception of generalized corruption.

Illusory Institutions: The Weakness of the State and the Parties

No single factor contributed as much to the political instability following the attempted coups as the weakness of the state. The Venezuelan state had often been accused of being too rich by virtue of its oil revenues, too large on account of its ownership of an array of firms, or too powerful because of its role in most aspects of economic and social life. Paradoxically, however, having all these attributes enormously weakened the state, minimizing the reliability of its institutions and its capacity to perform its basic functions with a modicum of efficiency.

The demands on the state have been propelled not only by population growth and rising expectations; the policy approach that prevailed for three decades continuously expanded the scope of state action. As the public sector was burdened with added functions and responsibilities, the deterioration of its performance accelerated. Chronic fiscal crises made it impossible to sustain the appropriate funding levels required for expanded public functions. An underpaid and poorly trained civil service plagued by turnover, corruption, congestion, and politicization severely eroded the capacity of public agencies to do their jobs.

The state was weakened by the number of policies it had to formulate, implement, finance, and monitor; it was also weakened by the approach it took in defining the nature of these policies. With few exceptions, each new policy initiative required a public bureaucracy to implement it, and this normally implied an inordinate amount of discretion on the part of civil servants. This bureaucratic approach created fertile conditions for corruption. It also paid off handsomely those particular interest groups that centered their efforts on forcing or persuading bureaucrats and politicians to make decisions and grant concessions in their favor. This again diminished the state's autonomy, further eroding its function.

It followed logically that, over time, the state became ever more focused on responding to the pressures, needs, and requests of influential groups and individuals. This decreased its capacity to implement policies and make decisions aimed at serving the population as a whole. The state, and in particular the executive branch, came to depend for survival on the political support of those specific groups that benefited from their policies. Dependence on narrow segments of society inhibited the development of mechanisms that might have enabled the state to build the broad political support needed to win approval of policies benefiting the general public at the expense of small but well-organized special interests.

Ironically, by choosing an economic policy aimed at transferring to the market important decisions that had been the traditional province of government officials, a very weak state deliberately made itself weaker. All at once, the power that had accompanied the capacity to allocate foreign exchange, set prices, import or bar a specific product, assign or withhold a social subsidy was surrendered. The government suddenly had nothing to give the influential groups and individuals who had supported all recent administrations in exchange for privileged access to special favors.

The Media Barons Take Over

The mass media proved to be another destabilizing factor spawned by the government's abdication of power over economic decisions. Like most other private firms, newspapers, television stations, and radio networks usually were owned by diversified conglomerates with business interests in different sectors. As such, they had been critically dependent on government decisions under the previous economic scheme.

Freedom of expression had long been a central tenet of democratic political life in Venezuela, and every government had been extremely sensitive to criticisms in this domain. In general, both print and electronic media demonstrated a somewhat adversarial attitude toward the government. Nonetheless, easily discernible limits beyond which owners and editors never ventured to criticize government gave evidence of a tacit understanding. This implicit inhibition was abandoned with economic reforms, and the mass media acquired an unprecedented vehemence in their attacks against the government, reporting and amplifying with a vengeance their strident opposition to it. Several forces pushed the media to adopt this belligerent stance.

The mood of the country was undoubtedly one of anger toward government policies and the impunity of corrupt individuals. The media had not created these deeply negative attitudes. This was a social reality that became a basic element of any domestic news coverage. The demand for scapegoats was high, and in the atmosphere of intensified competition the media, like other businesses, competed fiercely to satisfy their customers. A second factor was the typical propensity of the mass media in democratic societies to develop adversarial relationships with those in power. Moreover, media conglomerates engaged in oligopolistic warfare, with all its consequences, and some media owners continued to press the government for special concessions. If the government acquiesced, the rival oligopolies retaliated against it through the media they controlled. If the government denied a concession, the spurned party took aim. In all cases, some aspect of government — not necessarily related to the specific demand — was severely criticized.

In addition, and for a variety of reasons, journalists tended strongly to oppose the economic reform program. Their training made them suspicious and distrustful of the market, and as a group, they belonged to a socioeconomic stratum — lower middle-class professionals — that was hard hit by inflation and declining living standards. As a profession, they also suffered from the countrywide neglect of economic education, making it difficult for them to understand, and no less to report, the nature, purposes, and consequences of the government's economic actions. Government spokespersons shared similar limitations, restricting the development of an effective information strategy that might at least have partially offset the effect of journalists' and media owners' opposition.

The government systematically failed to recognize that under these circumstances, an effective communication strategy had to be one of its top priorities. Instead, a decimated government continued to handle public information with the same assumptions, institutions, and attitudes it had inherited. It ignored the reality that it had cut itself off from the instruments on which previous governments usually relied to keep media owners and journalists from holding it hostage to their interests. In the past, the possibility of using the subtle but powerful influence arising from its many economic decisions allowed the government to neglect the development of a reliable capacity to inform the public and explain its decisions. Such an institutional capacity would not have prevented the political turmoil that emerged, but it would have been a dramatic improvement over the reality of a mute, unexplaining government trying to bring about fundamental societal change.

Conclusions

Chile and Mexico began the transition toward economies less centered around the state earlier than most other Latin American countries. In the rest of the region economic reforms began after the mid-1980s, and by the early 1990s all the Latin American countries were in the throes of the process of liberalizing trade, privatizing state-owned enterprises, deregulating entire sectors of the economy, fighting fiscal deficits, and hoping that their private sectors could compete in world markets. The pace and scope of reforms varied from country to country, but in all of them, the direction of the changes was the same — more control by the market and less by the state.

Venezuela seemed to be well positioned to undertake this transition, so the extraordinarily traumatic reactions and consequences caught the government and most observers by surprise. After all, Argentina under Carlos Ménem, Colombia under César Gaviria, and several countries in Central America had pursued roughly similar reforms without incurring such enormous political costs as beset Venezuela's government. Many of the same destabilizing forces that surfaced in Venezuela are bound to have been present in other countries as well. It seems, however, that they were neutralized by other conditions, lacked the same intensity, or are still brewing under the surface and will eventually become more apparent. It may also well be the case that hyperinflation, military dictatorships, and wars had inoculated these countries' populations with a dose of tolerance for the immediate effects of the reforms which Venezuelans, having been spared these experiences, lacked. A comparative analysis of the reasons why political instability surged with such intensity in Venezuela and not in other countries is beyond the scope of this chapter. This analysis focused instead on the many factors that converged to generate the inflammable social and political atmosphere that threatened South America's longest continuous democracy.

In the early 1990s Venezuela's democracy was able to survive many difficult economic and political shocks — massive riots, unprecedented inflation and recession, two military revolts, the deterioration of public services to the verge of collapse, and the ouster of President Carlos Andrés Pérez and his replacement by the interim government of President Ramón J. Velázquez. At the same time, political liberalization and decentralization provided important anchors for democracy at times when the legitimacy of most traditional political actors practically disappeared.

Antonio Gramsci many years ago wrote: "The ancient is dying and the new has yet to be born. In this interlude, monsters are bred." Venezuela is experiencing the agonies of a country in the midst of a profound transformation. In this interlude monsters have, indeed, been bred. Venezuela has abandoned its previous social, political, and economic system, without having yet adopted a new one. In addition, many other forces that bolster economic modernization and the deepening of democracy have also been unleashed.

The country's main challenge will be to maintain the gains in economic and political modernization made during the Pérez government while restoring the country's stability. A competitive market economy, the recovery of living standards, and an effective fight against poverty require the rehabilitation of the state. A more effective state cannot be built when democracy is at risk and the government is literally under fire. To have the chance to restore crucial capacities to the state, and to have some degree of political stability, Pérez's successors will have to persuade Venezuelans to abandon their lynching mood. They will also have to align their expectations with present realities and convince Venezuelans that protesting about the past is not sufficient to assure a better future. Only by inspiring Venezuelans and by providing a deeper sense of shared burdens and shared destiny will governments during the 1990s be able to tame the monsters that have been bred in this interlude.

Notes

1. Unless otherwise indicated, the sources for the statistics used in this chapter are the Central Bank of Venezuela annual reports and reports issued by OCEI, the Central Office for Statistics and Informatics. Also used were several World Bank reports (1990, 1991a, 1991b, 1991c, 1991d, 1993b), as well as the IMF's *International Financial Statistics.*

2. For an interesting review of Venezuela's macroeconomic evolution in the twentieth century, see Escobar 1984, Hausmann 1990a, Frances 1990.

3. Gelb and Bourguignon 1988, and Hausmann 1991b, articulate the problems which lead to a pattern of government investments incapable of adapting to oil market cycles.

4. Morley 1993; World Bank 1991a and 1993a; Cline and Conninge 1992.

5. For a detailed analysis of the factors that determined the riots, see Naim 1993, 31-34.

6. See Torres 1993.

7. Morley 1993. The problem during the Pérez years was not a decline in resources allocated to the safety net, but the breakdown in service and strikes brought on by public sector unions' blockade of intra-agency reforms in such critical areas as health and education.

8. For an analysis of Venezuela's debt renegotiation utilizing game theory, see Gueron 1992.

9. See Morley 1992.

10. See Palma 1990.

11. Hausmann 1990b and 1991a offers a comprehensive review and analysis of the macroeconomic dynamics of this adjustment process. For the impact on the labor market and the social situation, see Márquez 1992.

12. See Morley 1993, 4.

13. Just prior to the first coup attempt, Venezuela's 10 percent GDP growth made it the world's fastest growing economy. It surpassed the performance of economic power-houses like Singapore (6.5 percent), Malaysia (8.6 percent), Thailand (7.9 percent), and Indonesia (7 percent). Its expansion of output far exceeded the major industrial countries' average (2 percent) and Latin America's as a whole (2.6 percent). See World Bank 1992, 2.

14. See Taylor 1993.

15. From mid-1989 to mid-1991, consumer prices increased 82 percent while the wholesale price index rose 47 percent. See Cline and Conninge 1992, 24.

16. For further discussion of this point, see Naim 1992, 84.

References

Central Bank of Venezuela. 1960 to 1992. *Informe Anual.* Caracas: Banco de Venezuela.

Cline, William R., and Jonathan Conninge. 1992. *Venezuela: Economic Strategy and Prospects.* Washington, D.C.: Inter-American Development Bank.

COPRE. 1993. *Un Proyecto Nacional para la Venezuela de 2000.* Caracas: COPRE (Presidential Commission on State Reform).

Escobar, G. 1984. "El Laberinto de la Economía." In *El Caso Venezuela: Una Illusión de Armonía,* eds. Moisés Naim and Ramón Piñango. Caracas: Ediciones IESA.

Frances, Antonio. 1990. *Venezuela Posible.* Caracas: Ediciones IESA.

Gelb, Alan, ed. 1988. *Oil Windfalls: Blessing or Curse?* Oxford: Oxford University Press.

Gelb, Alan, and François Bourguignon. 1988. "Venezuela: Absorption Without Growth." In *Oil Windfalls: Blessing or Curse?,* ed. Alan Gelb. Oxford: Oxford University Press.

Gueron, Eva. 1992. "Las Estructuras de Negociación en la Renegociación de la Deuda Externa de Venezuela." Caracas: Instituto de Estudios Políticos, Universidad Central de Venezuela. Mimeo.

Hausmann, Ricardo. 1990a. *Shocks Externos y Ajuste Macroeconómico.* Caracas: Banco Central de Venezuela.

Hausmann, Ricardo. 1990b. "The Big Bang Approach to Macro Balance in Venezuela." Paper presented at the World Bank's Economic Development Institute senior policy seminar, Latin America: Facing the Challenge of Adjustment and Growth, held at IESA, Caracas.

Hausmann, Ricardo. 1991a. "Adoption, Management, and Abandonment of Multiple Exchange Rate Regimes with Import Controls: The Case of Venezuela." Paper presented at the tenth Latin American meeting of the Econometric Society, Punta del Este, Uruguay.

Hausmann, Ricardo. 1991b. "Dealing with Negative Oil Shocks: The Venezuelan Experience in the Eighties." Paper presented at the Conference on Temporary Trade Shocks held at St. Anthony's College, Oxford University.

International Monetary Fund. 1970 to 1992. *International Financial Statistics.* Washington, D.C.: International Monetary Fund.

Kelly, Janet. 1992. "Venezuela: The Question of Inefficiency and Inequality." Paper presented at the conference, Lessons of the Venezuelan Experience, Woodrow Wilson Center and American University, October, Washington, D.C.

Márquez, Gustavo. 1992. "Poverty and Social Policies in Venezuela." Paper presented at the Brookings Institution and Inter-American Dialogue conference, Poverty and Inequality in Latin America, July, Washington, D.C.

Morley, Samuel. 1993. "Poverty and Adjustment in Venezuela." Washington, D.C.: Inter-American Bank. Working Paper Series 124.

Naim, Moisés. 1992. "The Launching of Radical Policy Changes: The Venezuelan Experience." In *Venezuela in the Wake of Radical Policy Reform*, ed. Joseph Tulchin. Boulder, Colo.: Lynne Rienner Publishers.

Naim, Moisés. 1993. *Paper Tigers and Minotaurs: The Politics of Venezuela's Economic Reforms.* Washington, D.C.: The Carnegie Endowment for International Peace.

Naim, Moisés, and Ramón Piñango, eds. 1984. *El Caso Venezuela: Una Ilusión de Armonía.* Caracas: Ediciones IESA.

OCEI. 1970 to 1992. *Encuesta de Hogares.* Caracas: OCEI (Central Office of Statistics and Informatics).

OCEI. 1970 to 1992. *Encuesta Industrial.* Caracas: OCEI.

Palma, Pedro Agustín. 1990. "Una Nueva Política Económica en Venezuela." Paper presented at the seminar, Venezuela: Development Options for the 1990s, held in September at the Latinamerika Instituet, Stockholm University.

Taylor, Lance, ed. 1993. *The Rocky Road to Reform.* In press.

Torres, Gerver. 1993. "La Economía que Podemos Construir." In *Un Proyecto Nacional para la Venezuela de 2000* by COPRE. Caracas: COPRE (Presidential Commission on State Reform).

Tulchin, Joseph, ed. 1992. *Venezuela in the Wake of Radical Reform.* Boulder, Colo.: Lynne Rienner Publishers.

World Bank. 1990. *Venezuela: A Review of the 1990-1993 Public Sector Investment Programs.* Washington, D.C.: World Bank. Report no. 8588-VE.

World Bank. 1991a. *Venezuela Poverty Study: From Generalized Subsidies to Targeted Programs.* Washington, D.C.: World Bank. Report no. 9114-VE.

World Bank. 1991b. *Venezuela: Public Administration Study.* Washington, D.C.: World Bank. Report no. 8972.

World Bank. 1991c. *The Challenge of Development: World Development Report 1991.* New York: Oxford University Press.

World Bank. 1991d. *Venezuela: Industrial Sector Report.* Washington, D.C.: World Bank. Report no. 9028-VE.

World Bank. 1992. *Global Economic Prospects and the Developing Countries.* Washington, D.C.: World Bank. March.

World Bank. 1993a. *Poverty and Income Distribution in Latin America: The Story of the 1980s.* Washington, D.C.: World Bank. Report no. 11266-LAC.

World Bank. 1993b. *Venezuela: Oil and Exchange Rates.* Washington, D.C.: World Bank. Report no. 10481-VE.

Mexico:
The Social Costs of Adjustment

Nora Lustig

Foreword

The process of adjustment that followed the 1982 balance of payments crisis in Mexico produced considerable economic hardship for the Mexican people. To the extent that the fall in living standards reflected the fact that the previous expansionary policies were unsustainable, some may argue that the costs of adjustment were inevitable, since people had been living "beyond their means." However, adverse external conditions, such as the worsening of the terms of trade and lack of adequate external credit, caused the recovery in Mexico to be slow despite large internal efforts to restore equilibrium.

This paper covers the impact of Mexico's adjustment process on living standards until early 1991. Between that time and 1993, there have been no dramatic changes. The tendency observed since 1989 for average real wages to rise in real terms has continued, and so has public spending in the social sectors. The latter rose to nearly 50 percent of total non-interest government spending in 1992. Average per capita growth rates, however, have been modest, increasing the difficulty of reducing poverty in the short term.

Adjustment, Living Standards, and Income Distribution

Following a standard theoretical distinction, an adjustment process can be separated into two kinds of mechanisms: 1) those directed at expenditure reduction and 2) those directed at expenditure switching from tradable goods

---

This chapter was originally published as Chapter 3 in *Mexico: The Remaking of an Economy*, by Nora Lustig, published by the Brookings Institution in October 1992. The period covered in the book ends in mid-1991.

to goods that cannot be traded in world markets. When a country faces a long-lasting external shock in its terms of trade, and external credit becomes so tight that a previous expansionary policy is unsustainable, these two mechanisms come into play to restore equilibrium both in the domestic market and in the balance of payments.[1] These mechanisms will come into play either in an "orderly" manner by explicit policy decisions, or in a "disorderly" manner by inflation, or, more likely, in some combination of both.[2]

Switching policies are supposed to increase output of tradables and reduce their consumption, while expenditure reduction policies are supposed to reduce consumption of both tradables and nontradables. The most commonly used switching device is nominal devaluation of the domestic currency. The standard expenditure reduction is cutback of the fiscal deficit. Both mechanisms affect real incomes and their distribution between wages and profits; if switching and expenditure-reduction mechanisms have a contractional effect on the economy, as they did in Mexico, their impact on real incomes will be more pronounced.

This analysis follows a distinction some authors make among *earned* income (pretax), *disposable* income (earned income minus taxes plus transfers), *social* income (value of services provided by government nontransfer expenditure), and *total* income (the sum of disposable and social income).[3] A devaluation of the currency (switching policy) changes the pattern of earned income and its distribution. Under the most plausible assumptions, devaluation will result in a fall in real earned wages[4] that is more pronounced the less responsive domestic supply is to relative price changes. A cut in the fiscal deficit (expenditure reduction policy) results in a fall in the earned wage, the social wage, and the disposable wage, and thus in the total real wage. Several mechanisms cause this fall. First, a reduction of the fiscal deficit in the short run results in a drop in aggregate demand and thus in output. Labor demand slackens, and therefore real earned wages will tend to fall. Second, the fiscal deficit is usually reduced through a combination of tax increases and elimination of subsidies, which reduces disposable incomes. Third, fiscal cutbacks are achieved by a reduction of nontransfer expenditures (such as social spending), which reduces both the social wage and often earned wages because expenditures are reduced by cutting the wages of governmental employees. In addition, public investment cutbacks may reduce future earned and social income.

Thus, adjustment does cause earned and total real wages to fall. The fall in real wages is higher when structural rigidities are more widespread (for example, when imported machinery or raw materials cannot easily be replaced with domestic production), and, above all, when adverse external conditions are more persistent, because these circumstances will entail a greater fall in output and aggregate expenditures and thus total earned income.[5] In addition, the more "stubborn" inflation is, the more pronounced is the fall in real wages in the transition from a high-inflation equilibrium to a low one.[6] Switching policies may result in a rise in earned profits, but social and disposable profits can fall. However, this process refers to domestic profits alone. Profits earned by nationals will tend to rise as they receive interest or dividends on capital invested abroad.

The adjustment process also entails changes in domestic relative prices associated with switching and expenditure-reducing mechanisms. A change particularly relevant for Mexico is the evolution of the terms of trade between agriculture and the rest of the economy. The reason for this is that a high proportion of the poorest households (the bottom 20 percent) in Mexico are engaged in agricultural activities, and a high proportion of those engaged in agriculture are concentrated among the lower income-deciles (Table 1).[7] The available data for Mexico do not allow us to trace the effect of adjustment on the neatly defined categories mentioned above for a number of reasons. First, for example, no information exists on aggregate profits. Mexican National Accounts pool together all non-wage income including mixed incomes, and in particular the wages imputed to the self-employed. As a result, part of this income category should be classified as wages. Second, there are no data on disposable income disaggregated into wage and non-wage income, nor on personal disposable income even at an aggregate level. Third, the evolution of real social income is measured by real social spending, that is, nominal social spending deflated by the implicit gross domestic product (GDP) price deflator. This "real" social spending, however, may not be an accurate measure of "real" output in the social sectors.[8] Finally, the trend in real incomes captures not only the impact of market forces on factor payments, but also the evolution of general consumption subsidies as captured by the consumer price index.

In addition, to obtain an accurate picture of the impact of adjustment costs on poverty and the distribution of household income, one would ideally have access to two household income and expenditure surveys (with a record of pre- and after tax income), one before and one after adjustment. Unfortunately, such information is not available except for aggregate tabulations. The only available survey with information at the household level was conducted in 1984, two years after the crisis started; a second one, conducted in 1989, still had not been made public at the time this book was completed.[9] In the absence of such information, the analysis of who bore the cost of adjustment must be inferred from the behavior of other variables such as wages, agricultural incomes, and the known characteristics of poor households.

Data limitations notwithstanding, enough information exists to make an initial assessment of the impact of adjustment on living standards. On the basis of the available information, the following questions are addressed: What happened to real wage and non-wage incomes? How did agricultural indicators perform? What was the evolution of employment and unemployment? What was the impact of fiscal cuts on social expenditures? Were social services affected by declining resources? Which sectors of the population were most affected by declining incomes? In addition to income, other indicators of welfare are examined — including infant mortality rates, causes of death and disease, years of schooling, and school dropouts — and their performance is also analyzed.

Living Conditions before the Crisis

The fall in Mexico's living standards since 1992 occurred when large segments of the Mexican population were already living under precarious conditions. Despite remarkable growth and governmental efforts to improve living conditions in the post-World War II era, by the end of the 1970s poverty was pervasive, and the levels of education and public health were in need of substantial improvement.

According to the 1977 Income and Expenditure Survey, approximately 41 percent of sampled households had total earnings below the prevailing minimum wage (in 1977 equal to $120 a month), considered at the time an acceptable poverty line.[10] Small landowners and landless peasants in rural areas and those employed in the so-called informal sector in urban areas (especially those in commerce and personal services) seem to have made up the bulk of poor households.[11]

Although per capita supply of calories and proteins was sufficient to meet nutritional standards (had food availability been uniform), in 1979 the National Institute of Nutrition reported that almost 19 million people, 13 million of whom lived in rural areas, suffered from malnutrition.[12] The estimated rate of infant mortality in 1981 was 51.3 per 1,000.[13] Infants of low birth weight constituted 12 percent of the total — high compared with similar countries having lower per capita income levels, such as Colombia and Panama. In addition, between 1979 and 1983 Mexico's rate of low birth weight infants was higher than the estimated average of 10.1 percent for all of Latin America.[14] Avitaminosis and other nutrition-related problems were the sixth most frequent cause of infant mortality.[15]

In 1978 an estimated 45 percent of the population, a substantial proportion of which was made up of the rural poor, was not receiving health care coverage from private sources because of cost, nor from any of the institutions providing free or quasi-free care.[16] Illiteracy was approximately 17 percent in the early 1980s, a substantial improvement over the approximately 26.5 percent figure in 1970.[17] In the early 1980s, however, approximately 22 million Mexicans still were either illiterate or had not finished primary school, and average schooling in 1980-1981 was 5.4 years (Table 11).[18] According to the 1980 census, 50.1 percent of Mexican households had no running water, and 32 percent used the kitchen as the bedroom.[19] It was also estimated that 25 percent of Mexican households did not have electricity.[20]

Trends in Earned Real Incomes since 1982

An analysis of the broad trends in earned real incomes — disaggregated into wage income, non-wage income, and incomes in agriculture — is presented below. For reasons mentioned previously, it was not possible to measure the evolution of pure factor returns; therefore, some combination of them was used.

Wage Income

The mechanisms involved in the adjustment process resulted in a fall in real wages.[21] As shown in Table 2, the fall of real wages per worker was drastic: between 40 and 50 percent in the period 1983-1988, with the sharpest declines occurring during 1983 and 1986, the two years of deepest economic contraction. The total wage bill fell by a similar amount (Table 2). The behavior of wage income is the combined result of the evolution of the real wage and employment. Available indicators show that the decline of wage income is a result of contracting real wages, not of reduced employment. According to the Mexican National Accounts, employment rose an average of 0.4 percent a year between 1983 and 1988 (Table 3).[22]

The data on real wages show some interesting patterns (Table 2). For instance, between 1983 and 1988 the wage contraction in *maquiladoras* was lower than in the rest of the economy. Wages in the formal industrial sector also contracted less than those in other sectors, except for *maquiladoras*. However, employment in this sector declined (Table 3). It is also important to note that the minimum wage is not always a reliable indicator of wage performance; for example, in 1989 the minimum wage contracted, whereas all the other wages increased.[23]

Given the large contraction of real wages, one wonders whether some policy decisions subjected wages to an unwarranted decline, that is, a fall beyond what was required to restore equilibrium in the economy, even with the prevailing external conditions.[24] This is an important question. Such an analysis would shed light on whether some of the measures undertaken — or not undertaken — by policymakers to restore equilibrium and curb inflation placed an unnecessary burden on wage earners.[25]

It is questionable, first, whether an earlier application of incomes policy would have reduced some of the wage losses linked to stabilization and adjustment. The results of the Economic Solidarity Pact (Mexico's anti-inflation program introduced at the end of 1987) seem to support the idea that stabilization programs combining fiscal and monetary restraint with incomes policy have a lower negative impact on wages, perhaps because they reduce part of the loss caused by accelerating inflation. Second, one may question whether policies directed toward improving the relationship between business and government (that is, an early-on reprivatization of the banking system) may have resulted in higher investment levels and precluded part of the contraction in wages. Lastly, one may question whether Mexico's labor law, which makes layoffs difficult or expensive, may have produced a greater contraction of the real wage than would have prevailed under more flexible employment practices. The good side of Mexican labor laws, however, has probably meant that unemployment remained relatively low even in times of severe output contraction (Table 3). Further research on all these subjects is needed.

At first it seems puzzling that it was possible to inflict such wage cuts without provoking widespread political or social unrest and countless strikes.[26] One possible reason is that though wages were heavily cut, the cuts did not affect household incomes to the same extent because many households received income from other sources besides wages, and non-wage income declined substantially less. Data on real per capita consumption support this interpretation. Private consumption per capita declined cumulatively by 11.1 percent between 1983 and 1988, whereas real wage income dropped 41.5 percent during the same period (Table 2). This seems to indicate that Mexican households must have received income from other sources besides wages, or were using their savings. The lack of resistance to wage cuts can also be explained by the government's long-standing control of the labor movement, exercised through a remarkable combination of coercion and cooptation ever since the 1930s.

Non-wage Income

In contrast to wage income, which declined on average 8.2 percent a year from 1983 to 1988, non-wage income declined only 1.2 percent a year (Table 4). This resulted in a sharp increase in the share of non-wage income in total income (wage plus non-wage), which rose from 60 percent in 1981 to 71.5 percent in 1988. The behavior of non-wage income — in contrast to wage income — perhaps reflects the fact that prices of goods and services, excluding those produced by the public sector and those subject to price control regimes (including services performed by the self-employed), were more "freely" set than wages.

Part of the better non-wage performance is accounted for by rising profits in the modern sector of the economy. Though there are no estimates of profit rates, the profit margin (as a proportion of total sales) rose in most manufacturing sectors during 1982-1987.[27] It would be a mistake to believe, however, that all non-wage income is profits, rents, or interest income that accrues only to the wealthy. The non-wage category includes income of the poor peasants or small shop owners, as well as that of wealthy modern businessmen. Non-wage income is an important share of the total income of the poor and the wealthy; it is also a smaller part of the income of the middle sectors. For example, the bottom 10 percent of Mexican households derive one-third of their income from wages, with the other two-thirds more or less equally distributed between nonmonetary income (for example, home-consumed crops and imputed housing costs) and non-wage monetary income (Table 5). Given the behavior of per capita consumption described earlier, part of the non-wage income must go to other income groups besides the wealthy.

Incomes in Agriculture

Because most of the very poor in Mexico are engaged in agricultural activities (Table 1), it is important to analyze the evolution of wage and non-wage income in agriculture as well as of the output and price of corn — the basic peasant crop — during the adjustment period. Table 6 records the evolution of specific variables for agriculture and for all sectors combined. Several things should be noted. First, agriculture seems to have a life of its own in terms of output performance; it does not follow the general pattern. For example, during the severe economy-wide contraction in 1983, agricultural output grew. Conversely, while the rest of the economy was set on a recovery path in 1988-1989, agriculture experienced a severe setback.

During the first stabilization program, from 1983 to 1985, agricultural output and employment fared better than the overall economy. Real wages in agriculture fell less than aggregate real wages (Table 4). Non-wage income in agriculture rose, while non-wage income in the nonagricultural sector contracted (Table 4). Better prices for agricultural goods and unusually favorable weather conditions may explain this performance. Real devaluations and attempts to align agricultural prices with world prices contributed to an improvement in agricultural prices, and the on-farm price of corn was no exception (Table 6). Because most poor peasants are corn growers[28] and most of the corn is grown by poor peasants,[29] poor rural households may have suffered less during this crunch than their urban counterparts.

This result is confirmed by findings of another author, who conducted interviews in mid-1985 concerning the employment conditions in rural areas.[30] In all but one of Mexico's midsection states, farmers complained of labor shortages. In several areas wages offered to rural workers were well above the minimum wage. Labor shortages apparently stemmed from migration to the United States. In addition, the author found a virtual absence of return migration from urban areas, despite cuts in urban wages.

This favorable pattern for agriculture reversed itself in 1986, when output in the sector contracted (Table 6). In addition, from 1987 on, and especially in 1988 and 1989, agriculture's performance was worse than that of the economy as a whole (Table 6).[31] Bad weather conditions and a deterioration in agricultural prices might explain this downturn. A reduction in agricultural subsidies and credit, as well as an absence of new investment, further explain the decline.[32] During 1988-1989, agricultural prices may have lagged behind as a result of the Economic Solidarity Pact, which clamped down on agricultural prices more than others.[33]

The evolution of corn output and prices, as well as of wage and non-wage agricultural income, indicates that economic hardship in agriculture must have been severe for the period 1988-1989 (Table 6). This suggests that during the period of the pact, in 1988-1989, just when the rest of the economic outlook appeared promising, the poorest population suffered a deterioration in living standards. The 1990 data show an improvement in agricultural output and prices (Table 6), and hence the incomes of the rural poor may have also recovered. The absence of data at the household level does not allow further analysis.

Unemployment and Employment Patterns

The initial sharp deceleration in aggregate output growth in 1983 was accompanied by an approximately 50 percent increase in the open urban unemployment rate (Table 3). However, despite lagging economic performance and continuous additions to the economically active population, estimated at close to one million a year,[34] the unemployment rate during the 1980s soon descended to levels below those during the oil boom (Table 3).

This at first surprising result might be explained by the downward flexibility of Mexican real wages, as discussed earlier. The large decline in real wages, on the one hand, allowed firms to keep labor costs in check while facing declining demand without reducing employment; on the other hand, it allowed the government to reduce total expenditures without resorting to widespread layoffs. Moreover, those who did not remain employed as wage earners in the formal sector[35] were likely to be willing to work in the informal sector for lower pay or as non-remunerated family labor.[36] In a country like Mexico with no unemployment insurance benefits, it is not surprising that people will accept working at lower quality jobs rather than be unemployed. To be unemployed is a luxury that most Mexicans cannot afford.

The urban open unemployment rates seem too low when compared with the aggregate "implicit" unemployment rate, measured by the ratio of total work places divided by the economically active population. Implicit unemployment was 11.4 percent in 1980 and 20.3 percent in 1985.[37] This discrepancy arises because the two statistics measure different things. For implicit unemployment, the National Accounts measure the labor posts required to produce a certain amount of output (with a given technology).

Urban employment statistics are calculated as the difference between the economically active population and those people who were employed for at least one hour during the week of reference, including those who worked for no remuneration (among whom are family members who work for no explicit payment). Thus, the definition of employment embedded in open unemployment statistics includes all the cases of "precarious" employment, whereas the National Accounts' definition does not. In practice, for example, one labor post can be occupied by more than one person. The difference in the performance of the two indicators perhaps can be interpreted as a rough estimate of the evolution of "underemployment."[38]

The shift in the employment structure according to occupational category illustrates a deterioration in employment conditions. The proportion of wage earners in the urban labor force fell from 83.4 percent in 1982 to 76.2 percent in 1985, whereas the number of self-employed increased from 12.1 to 15 percent and unpaid family workers from 2.1 to 4.6 percent.[39] Thereafter, the proportion of wage earners continued to decline, though at a much slower rate, about 1 percentage point annually until 1989.[40] Between 1980 and 1988, employment in services (characteristic of informal employment) as a proportion of total employment increased slightly, whereas the proportion in agriculture hardly changed and in industry declined, especially in construction. The changes have been 1 percentage point or less in one direction or the other.[41] The rise in the proportion of self-employed and of employment in services is consistent with the idea that during the adjustment process informal employment rose. The income obtained from informal employment was probably able to compensate partly for the dramatic decline in wage income from formal employment within households.[42]

Social Income: The Evolution of Public Spending on Social Sectors

An essential component of the Mexican stabilization programs was a reduction in the public deficit. The government's efforts in this direction were significant: The fiscal deficit went from equal to 16.9 percent of GDP in 1982 to a fiscal surplus in 1992. Increasing public revenues and reducing government expenditures made the decline in the fiscal deficit possible. Such a policy meant higher prices for publicly produced goods and services and higher tax rates, as well as cuts in public investment, subsidies, and other public expenditures.

Total government spending declined by 6.8 percent cumulatively from 1983 to 1988 (Table 7).[43] However, the external debt servicing component could not be reduced because its magnitude was largely dependent on factors beyond the government's direct control. As real interest rates continued to be relatively high and the initial stock of debt was large, public expenditures allocated primarily for domestic and external debt servicing (nonprogrammable spending) rose 29.6 percent between 1983 and 1988 (Table 7). Thus, to comply with required fiscal goals, all other noninterest expenditure categories, including social expenditures, had to be reduced. The share of all noninterest expenditures (the so-called programmable expenditures) in total government spending went from about 80 percent in 1980-1981 to 54.3 percent on average from 1983 to 1988 (Table 7).

Social spending, comprising primarily expenditures on education and health,[44] contracted by 33.1 percent between 1983 and 1988 (Table 7). Social spending was cut more than total programmable spending; as a whole, then, at the beginning of the crisis the government did not shift programmable spending in favor of the social sectors.[45] As a result, the ratio of social spending to programmable expenditures declined from 31.2 percent in 1981 to 28 percent in 1983. The tendency began to reverse itself in 1985. However, the sharpest reversal occurred from 1989 on, and in 1990 the ratio reached 37.6 percent. The Mexican economy began to recover in 1989, and in 1990 domestic interest rates began to fall sharply. Coupled with the Salinas government's commitment to improve social conditions, this explains the absolute and relative recovery of social spending.

Education and health expenditures constitute about 85 percent of social outlays. Expenditures in both areas contracted from 1983 to 1988. Spending on education fell by 29.6 percent, and spending on health by 23.3 percent. Education and health expenditures then were reduced by less than total social spending, leaving the sharpest cuts to be made in other social programs. Whether this change in the composition of expenditures within social spending was desirable is unclear. More detailed research is needed to determine the complete and definitive social impact of the reallocation of social expenditures. Some cuts, such as the programs implemented by Coordinación General del Plan Nacional de Zonas Deprimidas y Grupos Marginados (COPLAMAR), probably hurt the very poor.

This discussion is subject to one important caveat. To convert expenditures into real constant pesos, expenditure categories were divided by the implicit GDP deflator rather than by a sector-specific deflator because of the unavailability of the latter. But the decline in government social spending may well be a reflection of lower wage outlays in those sectors rather than a reduction in "output" of the government services.[46] To correct this bias, at least partially, resource availability — physical and human — in health and education is measured in the next section.

Resource Availability in Education and Health

Though spending in public education contracted significantly, some key indicators of the resources available in the sector show improvement. For example, student-per-teacher and student-per-school ratios for total and primary school decreased (Table 8).[47] However, part of this improvement may be due to the decline in school enrollment rather than to an improvement in resources. Unfortunately, this information could not be verified.

Nonetheless, even if the improvement in indicators is due partly to an enrollment below desirable levels, per capita human and physical resources were not subjected to reductions anywhere near those indicated by the drop in education expenditures. Therefore, most of the decline in expenditures must be attributable to using the "wrong" price deflator. Instead of the implicit GDP deflator, a sector-specific deflator should have been used. The reduction in education spending, then, primarily reflects the drop in real wages of education employees and investment in the sector. It also might reelect a cut in the availability of school material and in the maintenance of existing facilities. The impact of such drops on the quality of education regrettably cannot yet be assessed. Over time the teaching profession may absorb less-qualified and less-motivated people, something that must affect the quality of education.

Per capita medical units, beds, and doctors per capita available in the "formal" health sector deteriorated between 1983 and 1988 (Table 9). That is, the quality health care services provided by agencies that cover only those who contribute through the social security system probably worsened during adjustment. For example, medical units, hospital beds, and doctors per covered member of the Mexican Institute of Social Insurance (IMSS) declined on average since 1983 (Table 9). The Health and Social Security Institute for State Employees (ISSSTE), a separate health organization that only covers government employees, has faced similar declines in beds and units. These institutions covered, respectively, 41.8 percent and 8.8 percent of the total Mexican population on average between 1982 and 1989 (Table 9).

The deterioration of IMSS and ISSSTE per-member physical and human resources in health may have resulted from sudden increases in the number of people who joined the social security health care sector in 1984, 1985, and 1987 (Table 9). This is particularly true in the case of IMSS, which covers private sector employees. Some believe this to be the result of more people who previously used private doctors and hospitals needing access to medical service through social insurance schemes because of decreasing incomes.

To estimate per capita health resources in the Ministry of Health, the institution that provides health care to the poorest sectors of the population, is unfortunately very difficult, because there are no accurate estimates of the population the Ministry serves. Nonetheless, there is no indication of a reduction in total resources. Thus, if one assumes that the population served by the Ministry is the difference between the total and that covered by ISSSTE and IMSS, then the resources per capita in the Health Ministry must have improved.

Food Subsidies: From General to Targeted

To reduce public expenditures, the government began eliminating general food subsidies,[48] replacing some of them with targeted subsidies available to consumers through the public sector's food distribution chain, CONASUPO (National Commission for Popular Subsistence). Beginning in 1984 the government eliminated the general subsidy for corn tortillas, the staple of the popular diet, and introduced a two-price system whereby CONASUPO stores would sell a cheaper tortilla.[49] In April 1986 the government launched a "tortilla-stamp" program that distributed coupons which could be exchanged for tortillas at a discounted price.[50] In early 1991 CONASUPO introduced a card distributed among the urban poor, who are entitled to one kilo of free tortillas a day.[51] In addition, the general subsidies on beans, cooking oil, bread, and eggs were also gradually eliminated during the 1980s.

Total spending on general food subsidies distributed through the CONASUPO system declined in real terms. This decline resulted from a shift away from the generalized subsidy scheme, in which all consumers had equal access to the subsidized price, to the more targeted schemes, in which only a select number of consumers benefited. However, expenditures on targeted subsidies rose in 1988 and 1989 as a result of the Pact, though remaining below the level of spending in 1983.

Although justifiable from a fiscal point of view, targeting probably meant that substantial portions of the population — whose incomes were declining, and who were far from well-to-do — no longer enjoyed access to subsidies. Second, some general food subsidies were not replaced by targeted programs.[52] Poor urban households consequently may have suffered from the resulting increases in food prices. The relative cost of a basic diet for a standard four-member family helps to illustrate the impact of these price increases. As a percentage of the minimum wage, the cost of the basic food basket rose from 30 percent in 1982 to over 50 percent in 1986.[53] This increase occurred as minimum wages declined (Table 2).

Moreover, based on the results of a study that estimated the impact of lower prices on several consumption goods,[54] it can be argued that general price subsidies on corn, corn derivatives, beans, bread, rice, noodles, cooking oil, and eggs are justified from an equity point of view — that is, a higher proportion of the subsidy accrues to the poor.[55] In practice, general price subsidies have not been replaced by targeted subsidies on a one-to-one basis, and so the transfers received by poor families in the form of food subsidies have declined. In this sense, the elimination of some of the general food subsidies may have increased poverty.

Social Indicators: Nutrition and Health, Education, and Incidence of Crime

The effect of declining incomes and changes in the food subsidy program on consumption and nutritional levels has not been estimated. Surveys completed by the National Consumers Institute (INCO) in Mexico City provide information on the possible impact of declining income levels on family diet. The results of the first survey,[56] compiled between March and June 1983, demonstrated that the majority of families with incomes lower than twice the minimum wage experienced a decrease in consumption of all food products except tortillas.[57] In addition, there was clearly a substitution away from animal proteins.[58] The results of a second survey, conducted between January and August 1985, were similar except that a relatively smaller percentage of households continued to experience a decrease in food consumption.[59]

The countrywide infant mortality rate continued to decline between 1982 and 1989 (Table 10).[60] Some indicators, however, reveal a deterioration in health standards. For instance, infant and preschool mortality caused by avitaminosis and other nutritional deficiencies increased from 1982 onward after years of steady decline (Table 10).[61] The infant mortality rate probably could have improved more rapidly had nutritional conditions not deteriorated.[62]

Other indicators confirm a pattern of worsening nutritional conditions. The ISSSTE recorded an increase in the number of infants from birth to age one suffering from slow fetal growth and malnutrition, both in absolute terms and in proportion to total diseases. Children suffering from these ailments represented 8.5 percent of the total number of diseased children in 1981. The percentage increased to 10.3 percent in 1982, 10.6 percent in 1983, and 11.7 percent in 1984.[63]

With regard to education, after 1982 the proportion of each level of graduates who entered the subsequent educational level declined — that is, relatively more children were either dropping out of school, particularly after finishing junior high or high school, or postponing their entry into the next level, probably because they entered the work force (Table 11, "coverage for demand" statistics).[64] This may explain why the average schooling years of the population during the 1980s improved by one year, whereas the improvement between 1970 and 1980 equaled two years (Table 11). It may also imply a delay in the development of skills, marked by a decline in the proportion of students advancing from one educational level to the next beyond primary school.

The percentage of children enrolled in primary school as a ratio of children in the relevant age group continued to rise (Table 11, "coverage for demand"). Dropout rates from primary school continued to decline through 1987 (Table 11). But further disaggregation shows that dropout rates improved for urban children only; in rural zones the dropout rate rose by almost 3 percent, from 7.2 percent in 1981 to 10 percent in 1987-1988.[65]

Nationwide statistics on crime are not readily available. There is, however, a fairly complete record for the Federal District. According to this record, the number of reported robberies jumped from 40,800 in 1981 to 73,500 in 1983, and to 101,600 in 1987. In 1989 robberies were back at 71,600, still considerably above the average for the oil boom years: 38,300 a year between 1978 and 1981. Other crimes did not rise significantly.[66] As real income in the city contracted, more people attempted to bridge the gap by taking someone else's income.

Household Survival Strategies

The discussion above shows that wages declined quite dramatically during the 1980s. However, although wages declined drastically, households' total income probably fell by a lesser amount. As shown in Table 2, the decline in per capita consumption was considerably less than in wages, so the fall in total income for the average household was most likely less drastic than the wage drop. As income from wages declined, one would expect to see that individual members of households worked more hours in the same job; that they sought additional income-generating activities, perhaps informally as non-wage earners; and that more members of households joined the work force.

Though no record of such a process exists at the national level, evidence from micro-level studies of rural villages and urban households indicates that in rural and urban areas, the poor, as well as the middle-income sectors, sharpened and expanded their strategies for economic survival.[67] At the household level, families intensified their work efforts and redirected expenditure patterns. For example, male household heads contributed a larger proportion of their income to the household budget, and families could no longer use the "extra" income to improve on their physical or human capital or to have a hedge against emergencies.[68] More hours were dedicated to working and diversifying sources of income. The hardships imposed by the crisis and adjustment policies, therefore, should not be measured simply by declines in income but also in relation to changes in quality of life, such as length of the work week and hours available for leisure and rest.[69]

In addition, there is evidence that migration to the United States increased. Remittances probably continued to be an important potential source of income for some rural and urban families, and information from anthropological studies indicates that an increasing number of workers viewed migration to the North — to the United States — as their best alternative.[70] As evidence of this, the number of alien apprehensions averaged 1,260,855 a year for 1981-1986, up 50 percent from the average for 1971-1980.[71]

Who Bore the Costs and to What Extent?

The question of who bore the costs of the crisis is of particular relevance in a country like Mexico, where concentration of income is high and poverty is widespread. Table 12 shows that income concentration at the top 10 percent of the population was high for all years studied. The data show some redistribution from the top to the middle sectors between 1963 and 1977 and a further small decrease in inequality between 1977 and 1984. However, this result should be viewed with caution; an accurate comparison is not possible because the surveys are not strictly comparable. Moreover, the 1984 survey indicates that income disparities were still striking: Average per capita income at the top decile was 25 times greater than at the lowest decile (Table 1).[72]

The incidence of poverty in Mexico has also been high, though declining over time. Based on survey data, it has been found that the incidence of "extreme" poverty was 69.5 percent in 1963, 56.7 percent in 1968, 34 percent in 1977, and 29.9 percent in 1984.[73] In another study, which selects a different poverty line, the incidence of extreme poverty in Mexico in 1968 was 12 percent.[74]

Despite the lack of consensus in determining the level of poverty at a particular point in time, the available empirical evidence suggests that between 1963 and 1977, poverty was diminishing.[75]

Using my own estimates, I find that in 1984 the proportion of extremely poor households was somewhere between 11.2 and 14.7 percent.[76] The extreme poor are predominately rural and agricultural households. But in the third and fourth deciles, the majority of households still living in poverty are urban and nonagricultural. Even though most of the poorest households are rural, 27.5 percent of the lowest decile (more or less equivalent to the extreme poor) are urban (Table 1).

Compared with the rest of the population, the households of the extreme poor have more self-employed heads of household and fewer who are wage earners.[77] In terms of income sources, the extreme poor seem to derive almost one-third of their income from "profits" (Table 5). Nonmonetary income is important to the extreme poor, accounting for another third of their total income. Income derived from wages constitutes the final third of income. Wage income becomes increasingly — though not monotonically — important from deciles 2 to 7, at which point its share begins to decline, albeit slightly.

The characteristics of the population by income level provide some hints about how the social costs of the crisis may have been distributed. First, because most of the extremely poor work in agriculture and derive about two-thirds of their income from non-wage sources (Tables 1 and 5), the absolute and relative impact of adjustment on poverty depends on the performance of agricultural output and prices, and, to a lesser extent, agricultural wages. Second, given that wages are the principal source of income for the middle ranges (Table 5), the fate of these groups will be largely tied to changes in wages.

Because wage income contracted far more than did non-wage income during the 1980s, it would appear that the middle-income ranges suffered to a greater degree than those at either the bottom or the top. This is confirmed by the comparison of the size distribution of income between 1984 and 1989 presented in Table 12. While the bottom 40 percent lost 1.4 percentage points of total income, the "middle" 50 percent lost 3.7 percentage points. However, because agricultural wage and non-wage income deteriorated substantially from 1986 on (Table 6), the rural poor may have endured sharp declines in living standards between 1986 and 1989.

Although the middle ranges lost relatively more than the bottom of the population, one should be aware that even a minimal decline in the income of the poor can have devastating effects on a household's present and future welfare. Also, households located in the middle range of the distribution are far from being "middle-class" families by the standards of advanced industrial countries. Those at the bottom of the middle range include many of the poor living in urban areas, where prices of goods are higher (Table 1). One result that should be underscored is the sharp rise in inequality observed in this period. This is best illustrated by the rise in the concentration of income in the top 10 percent, whose share increased by 5.1 percentage points between 1984 and 1989 (Table 12).

Concluding Remarks

The analysis and the data presented lead to several conclusions. Despite a drastic decline in real wages, many Mexican households were able to avoid comparable drops in total income and per capita consumption by working additional hours, seeking new income-generating activities, and sending more family members into the work force. In rural and urban areas, the poor and the middle-income sectors sharpened and expanded their strategies for economic survival. Families worked harder and spent more carefully, struggling to maintain their standard of living despite hardships imposed by the crisis and by adjustment policies. Migration to the United States appears to have increased, as remittances continued to be an important source of income for some families.

The consequences of the crisis were not borne equally by all social groups. The wealthy could always protect, and even expand, their wealth far more easily than the rest of society by simply transferring their assets abroad. For example, capital flight has been estimated at between $22.1 billion and $35.7 billion between 1977 and 1987, depending on the method of calculation.[78] Those without savings — the majority of the population — did not have a similar option.

The international rules of the game give labor and capital asymmetrical treatment. Whereas capital can always find a safe-haven country, labor cannot freely enter other countries. This arrangement allowed Mexican asset owners substantially to avoid the cost of adjustment in the 1980s by protecting their wealth from the negative impact of devaluations and inflation on the real value of assets, while often earning huge capital gains. Those who possessed no wealth enjoyed no equivalent escape mechanism to avoid the adjustment cost. Becoming an illegal worker in the United States and accepting lower wages than legal workers was probably the best safety valve available.

Besides this dichotomy between the fate of the wealthy and that of the rest, the data on income distribution indicate that households in the middle range bore a higher share of the costs. The middle-range families, which include some of the urban poor and the rural and urban middle sectors, were apparently hurt by their reliance on wage income. The rural poor are likely to have been badly hurt from 1986 on, given their reliance on agricultural output and prices. The crisis and its aftermath have probably left Mexico with a relatively impoverished middle class, an increasing number of poor households, and the poor worse off than before.

Economic growth alone may be ineffective in reducing hard-core poverty. If the per capita income of the bottom 10 percent in 1984 (Table 1) grew steadily by 3 percent a year, the average growth rate of Mexico's per capita GDP in the postwar period, it would still take this group about sixteen years to reach an income level equal to the extreme poverty line (about $50 per capita per quarter). If the income of the lowest decile were to grow at the average 1988-1990 per capita GDP growth rate, about 1 percent a year, the waiting period would be almost forty-seven years. In the end, this still would provide only enough income to buy the necessary food intake.[79]

This underscores the fact that implementing equity-oriented reforms is the principal task ahead. These reforms will have to combine immediate relief with productivity-enhancing policies.[80] The Salinas administration made the alleviation of poverty a major objective — at least in its political discourse — and on December 2, 1988, the day after Salinas assumed office, launched a program called PRONASOL (Programa Nacional de Solidaridad).[81] However, more time and information are required to judge its effectiveness in reducing poverty.

Table 1
Demographic Characteristics of Households, Intra- and Interdecile, Third Quarter, 1984
Percent unless otherwise specified

Household Decile[2]	Average per capita income[3]	Intradecile[1]				Interdecile[1]				Household size	Ratio of income earners to household size	Ratio of members under 12 to household size
		Rural	Urban	Agri-culture	Nonagri-culture	Rural	Urban	Agri-culture	Nonagri-culture			
I	6,190.1	72.5	27.5	66.6	33.4	20.9	4.2	22.7	4.7	7.0	23.2	45.2
II	10,680.6	58.1	41.9	51.9	48.1	16.7	6.4	17.7	6.8	6.6	26.3	42.2
III	14,295.8	47.6	52.4	44.8	55.2	13.7	8.0	15.3	7.8	6.0	29.7	36.8
IV	18,651.4	35.6	64.4	31.8	68.2	10.2	9.9	10.8	9.7	5.5	34.0	31.3
V	23,573.9	37.7	62.3	29.8	70.2	10.8	9.6	10.2	9.9	5.2	34.1	30.9
VI	29,649.8	30.1	69.9	17.1	82.9	8.7	10.7	5.8	11.7	4.8	37.5	27.3
VII	38,051.9	17.4	82.6	11.7	88.3	5.0	12.7	4.0	12.5	4.6	41.6	24.3
VIII	48,753.1	18.1	81.9	13.4	86.6	5.2	12.6	4.6	12.3	4.1	48.1	21.7
IX	68,621.9	17.0	83.0	14.2	85.8	4.9	12.7	4.7	12.2	3.8	52.7	19.7
X	151,588.0	13.8	86.2	12.4	87.6	4.0	13.2	4.2	12.4	3.1	60.7	12.6
TOTAL	41,005.6	34.8	65.2	29.4	70.6	100.0	100.0	100.0	100.0	5.1	38.8	29.2
RURAL	25,451.4	–	–	–	–	–	–	–	–	5.3	35.7	32.5
URBAN	49,303.5	–	–	–	–	–	–	–	–	4.9	40.4	27.4

Source: Author's calculations based on data from Instituto Nacional de Estadística, Geografía e Informática (INEGI), *Encuestra nacional de ingresos y gastos de los hogares, tercer trimestre de 1984* (Mexico City, 1989).

[1] Proportion of total households within group.

[2] The total number of households is 14,988,551. Households are ranked by total per capita income.

[3] Pesos per quarter, June 1984 pesos. Income includes monetary and nonmonetary income. Dollar figures can be obtained by dividing the figures in pesos by the June 1984 exchange rate, which was equal to 185.19 pesos per dollar.

Table 2

Evolution of Real Wages and Per Capita Private Consumption

1981 - 1990

Annual rates of change of yearly averages in percent

	1981	1982	1983	1984	1985	1986	1987	1988	1989	1990 (prelim)	Average 1983-88	Cumulative Change 1983-88	Average 1983-85	Average 1986-87
Total Wage Income (a)(*)	11.3	-5.4	-24.7	-2.8	2.0	-10.7	-2.0	-8.3	5.9	3.0	-8.2	-40.0	-9.2	-6.4
Wage Income Per Worker (b)	4.8	-5.1	-22.9	-5.0	-0.2	-9.4	-3.0	-9.1	4.6	1.9	-8.6	-41.5	-9.9	-6.2
Wages in Maquiladoras (c) (*)	-0.4	8.5	-20.1	-2.0	-0.6	-2.2	1.7	-4.4	6.3	0.4	-4.9	-26.0	-8.0	-0.2
Wages in Maquiladoras (Blue-Collar Only)(d)(*)	-0.6	4.6	-21.9	-3.5	-2.7	-6.2	-1.2	-5.9	16.6	-3.9	-7.2	-36.0	-9.8	-3.7
Wages as registered by IMSS (e) Total	n.a.	n.a.	n.a.	-1.8	0.7	-7.5	-9.9	-5.9	6.6	-0.7	n.a.	n.a.	n.a.	-8.7
Total (Dec/Dec)	n.a.	n.a.	-25.0	-6.2	-1.8	10.1	5.0	-35.1	9.3	0.7	-10.4	-48.2	-11.6	7.5
With < 10 Workplaces	n.a.	n.a.	n.a.	3.4	-0.2	-2.4	-14.3	-9.9	3.8	0.0	n.a.	n.a.	n.a.	-8.6
With > 300 Workplaces	n.a.	n.a.	n.a.	-4.3	0.4	-9.2	-7.6	-4.8	4.8	-1.6	n.a.	n.a.	n.a.	-8.4
Wages Quoted by Industrial Survey (f)	5.0	0.1	-24.1	-6.8	1.1	-6.9	-6.5	-0.5	8.9	n.a.	-7.7	-38.0	-10.6	-6.7
Minimum Wage (g)	1.0	-0.1	-21.9	-9.0	-1.2	-10.5	-6.3	-12.7	-6.6	-9.1	-10.5	-48.5	-11.1	-8.4
Wages to Government Employees Per Worker(h)(*)	5.4	-2.6	-28.0	-5.8	0.3	-14.0	0.6	-8.4	7.1	n.a.	-9.8	-46.1	-12.0	-7.0
Private Consumption Per Capita (i)	4.9	-4.8	-7.4	1.1	1.5	-4.6	-2.2	0.3	4.5	4.0	-1.9	-11.1	-1.7	-3.4

Table 2 *(continued)*
Evolution of Real Wages and Per Capita Private Consumption
1981 - 1990

n.a. Not available.

(*) Real figures are calculated using the CPI from the Banco de Mexico, "Indicadores Económicos," Resumen, p. f (Mexico, February 1990). The 1991 index was calculated using the average annual change in consumer prices as reported by Banco de Mexico, "The Mexican Economy 1991: Economic and Financial Developments in 1990, Policies for 1991," Table 28, p.204 (Mexico City 1990). All price indices are converted to base 1980=100.

(a) Total Wage Income - Source: The figures for 1980 to 1986 are from the Comisión Nacional de los Salarios Mínimos, "Compendio de Indicadores de Empleo y Salarios," (Mexico, December 1989), Table 4.6, p.135. The figures for 1987 to 1990 are from the Instituto Nacional de Estadística, Geografía e Informática (INEGI), unpublished document.

(b) Total Wage Income Per Workplace - Source for Workplace: The figures for 1980 to 1986 are from the Comisión Nacional de los Salarios Mínimos, "Compendio de Indicadores de Empleo y Salarios," (Mexico, December 1989), Table 2.6, p.67. The figures for 1987 to 1990 are from the Instituto Nacional de Estadística Geografía e Informática (INEGI).

(c) Maquiladoras - Source: The Comisión Nacional de los Salarios Mínimos, "Compendio de Indicadores de Empleo y Salarios," p. 180 (Mexico (December 1989) Table 4.16, p. 132 (Sept. 1991).

(d) Maquiladoras (Blue-Collar Only) - Source: Nominal wage figures are from Salinas de Gortari "Segundo Informe de Gobierno: 1991-Anexo," p. 336 (Mexico, 1991).

(e) Wages as registered by IMSS (Instituto Mexicano del Seguro Social) - Source: The Comisión Nacional de los Salarios Mínimos, "Compendio de Indicadores de Empleo y Salarios," pp.127-8 (Mexico, December 1989) and p.122 (Mexico, Sept. 1991). Data on wages are averages from bimonthly observations and are deflated by the Consumer Price Index in (*). The missing 1987 October observation is estimated as the August-December average. The 1983 yearly average, used to estimate the rate of growth for 1984, is constructed as the Dec.1982-Dec.1983 average. The Total (Dec/Dec) is the real change in the IMSS wage from December of any one year to December of the following year.

(f) Wages/Industrial Survey - Source: The Comisión Nacional de los Salarios Mínimos, "Compendio de Indicadores de Empleo y Salarios," pp. 157-160 (Mexico, December 1989) and p.122 (Mexico, Sept. 1991). Figures for 1989 are preliminary.

(g) Minimum Wage - Source: The figures for 1980 to 1986 are from the Comisión Nacional de los Salarios Mínimos, "Salarios Compendio Estadístico," Table 5A, pp. 25-27, (Mexico, December 1986). The figures for 1987 to 1990 are respectively from Banco de Mexico, "Informe Anual," p.119 (1987), p.136 (1988), p.138 p.139 (1990).

(h) Wages/Government Employees - Source: Carlos Salinas de Gortari, "Tercer Informe de Gobierno: 1991, Anexo" p. 145 (Mexico,1991).

(i) Private Consumption Per Capita - Source: For the 1980 to 1984 figures the Instituto Nacional de Estadística Geografía e Informática (INEGI), "Sistema de Cuentas Nacionales de México 1980-1986: Tomo I, Resumen General," Tables 66-69, pp. 118, 120, 123, 126 and 129 (Mexico, 1988). The 1985 figure is from INEGI, "Sistema de Cuentas Nacionales de Mexico 1985-1988: Tomo I, Resumen General," Table 60, p. 80 (Mexico 1990). The 1986 to 1987 figures are from INEGI, "Sistema de Cuentas Nacionales de Mexico 1986-1989: Tomo I - Resumen General," Tables 60-63 (Mexico, 1991). The 1988-1991 figures are from Macro Asesoría Económica, S.C., "Macro Perspectivas: Diagnóstico y Perspectivas de la Economía Mexicana," Table V.1, p.22 (July-September 1992). The population figures are calculated using growth rates from Manuel Odorica, "Las cifras preliminares del censo," which appeared in "Demos: Carta Demográfica Sobre Mexico," pp.4-6 (1990).

Table 3
Employment and Unemployment
1981-1990

| | Annual rate of change in percent | | | | | | | | | | Average | | |
	1981	1982	1983	1984	1985	1986	1987	1988	1989	1990 (prelim)	1983-88	1983-85	1986-87
Employment (a) *	6.3	-0.3	-2.3	2.3	2.2	-1.4	1.1	0.9	1.3	1.1	0.4	0.7	-0.2
Agriculture and Cattle	2.8	-3.3	4.2	1.1	2.6	-2.5	1.5	2.5	-2.1	-4.6	1.6	2.6	-0.5
Mining	7.2	5.8	0.4	4.2	4.0	-0.4	5.0	2.4	-1.6	2.8	2.6	2.9	2.3
Manufacturing	4.8	-2.0	-7.1	2.1	3.2	-1.9	1.1	0.1	2.5	0.6	-0.5	-0.7	-0.4
Construction	16.7	-2.6	-19.2	6.7	3.5	-3.3	0.4	0.3	11.8	13.1	-2.3	-3.8	-1.5
Electricity	6.2	4.7	1.1	3.3	5.3	2.0	3.0	2.5	2.1	4.2	2.9	3.2	2.5
Commerce	6.4	0.9	-2.7	1.8	0.6	-1.2	1.4	1.5	2.8	3.0	0.2	-0.1	0.1
Transport	7.5	6.7	-4.5	1.6	2.3	0.6	2.4	-2.4	-0.4	5.0	-0.1	-0.3	1.5
Financial Services	9.7	10.4	2.6	6.6	0.9	0.2	1.6	1.7	0.5	1.6	2.3	3.3	0.9
Personal Services	6.3	1.4	-0.1	2.3	1.8	-0.4	0.2	-0.2	0.6	1.0	0.6	1.3	-0.1
Employment Monthly Industrial Survey (b) *	5.5	-2.4	-9.6	-1.0	2.3	-4.0	-3.4	–	2.4	0.0	–	-2.9	-3.7
Urban Open Unemployment (percent)(c)	4.2	4.2	6.3	5.7	4.3	4.3	3.9	3.5	3.0	2.8	4.7	5.4	4.1

* Percentage Change
(a) Source: The figures for the years 1980 to 1986 are from the Instituto Nacional de Estadística, Geografía e Informática (INEGI), "Sistema de Cuentas Nacionales de Mexico: 1986-1989 - Tomo I, Resumen General," (Mexico, 1991). The figures from 1987-1990 are from the Dirección de Contabilidad Nacional y Estadísticas Económicas (SICNEB), Instituto Nacional de Estadísticas Geografía e Informática (INEGI), internal document.
(b) Source: Comisión Nacional de los Salarios Mínimos, "Compendio de Indicadores de Empleo y Salarios, No. 2," Table 2.8, pp.74-77 (Mexico, December 1989). The figures up to 1987 refer to a sample of 1,157 establishments encompassing 57 classes of economic activity. The figures for 1988 and and 1989 refer to a sample of 3,218 establishments encompassing 129 classes of economic activity. Therefore, the 1988 rate cannot be calculated because the figures for 1987 and 1988 are not comparable. The rates for 1990 and 1991 are from Macro Asesoria Económica, S.C., "Macro Perspectivas," p.26, April-June 1992, Year 5.
(c) Source for 1981-1988: Macro Asesoria Económica, "Realidad Económica de Mexico: 1991" table 15, p.427 (Mexico 1990). For 1989 and 1991, "GEA Económico", No. 12, March 12, 1992, p.5.
(d) Source: Comisión Nacional de los Salarios Mínimos, "Compendio de Indicadores de Empleo y Salarios, No. 2," Table 1.1, p. 27 and Table 2.6, p.67 (Mexico, December 1989). Implicit unemployment is defined as one minus the ratio of total employment (note (a)) to economically active population. The figures for total employment are from p. 67, and the figures for the economically active population are from p.27. The 11.4 percent figure is for 1980.

Table 4
Wage and Non-Wage Income
1981 - 1990

Annual rates of change and shares in percent

	1981	1982	1983	1984	1985	1986	1987	1988	1989	1990	Cumulative			
											Average 1983-88	Change 1983-88	Average 1983-85	Average 1986-87
All Sectors (a)														
Wage Income	11.3	-5.4	-24.7	-2.8	2.0	-10.7	-2.0	-8.3	5.9	3.0	-8.2	-40.0	-9.2	-6.4
Non-Wage Income	4.8	2.0	1.7	0.3	-2.0	-7.5	4.6	-3.8	8.0	7.4	-1.2	-6.9	0.0	-1.6
Share of Non-Wage Income in Total Income	60.0	61.8	68.6	69.2	68.4	69.1	70.5	71.5	71.9	72.7	69.5	–	68.7	69.8
Agriculture (b)														
Wage Income	10.0	-12.7	-13.2	-3.8	3.0	-2.0	-5.6	-12.6	-6.7	-8.6	-5.9	-30.5	-4.9	-3.8
Non-Wage Income	5.9	-8.9	-2.0	14.1	9.0	-8.0	-2.2	-15.7	8.9	13.4	-1.3	-7.6	6.8	-5.1
Share of Non-Wage Income in Total Income	73.9	74.7	77.0	79.8	80.7	79.8	80.3	79.8	82.3	85.2	79.6	–	79.2	80.0
Non-Agricultural (b)														
Wage Income	11.4	-5.0	-25.3	-2.7	2.0	-11.2	-1.7	-8.0	6.8	3.7	-8.3	-40.5	-9.5	-6.6
Non-Wage Income	4.7	3.3	2.1	-1.1	-3.3	-7.4	5.5	-2.4	7.8	6.7	-1.2	-6.9	-0.8	-1.1
Share of Non-Wage Income in Total Income	58.6	60.6	67.8	68.1	67.0	67.9	69.4	70.7	70.9	71.5	68.5	–	67.6	68.7

(a) Source: The figures for 1980-1984 are from the Instituto Nacional de Estadistica Geografia e Informática (INEGI), "Sistema de Cuentas Nacionales de Mexico 1980-1986: Tomo I, Resumen General," Tables 43, p. 90 (Mexico, 1988). The figures for 1985-86 are from INEGI "Sistema de Cuentas Nacionales de Mexico 1985-1988: Tomo I, Resumen General," Tables 37, p. 63 (Mexico 1991). The figures from 1987 to 1990 are from the Instituto Nacional de Estadistica, Geografia e Informática (INEGI), unpublished document (received by fax from Maria Eugenia Gomez Luna, Director of National Accounts, INEGI).

(b) Source: The figures for 1980-1984 are from the Instituto Nacional de Estadistica Geografia e Informática (INEGI), "Sistema de Cuentas Nacionales de Mexico 1980-1986: Tomo I, Resumen General," Tables 30-37, pp. 77-84 (Mexico, 1988). The figures for 1985 from INEGI "Sistema de Cuentas Nacionales de Mexico 1985-1988: Tomo I, Resumen General," Tables 24-25, p. 57 (Mexico, 1990). The figures for 1986 are from INEGI, "Sistema de Cuentas Nacionales de Mexico 1986-1989: Tomo I - Resumen General," Table 2, Mexico, 1991). The figures from 1987 to 1990 are from the Instituto Nacional de Estadistica, Geografia e Informática (INEGI), unpublished document. The sector categories used here from INEGI are defined as follows. Agriculture: agriculture, cattle raising, forestry and fishing. Non-Agricultural: industrial manufacturing; construction; electricity; gas and water; trade, restaurants and hotels; transportation, warehousing and communications; financial services, insurance and real estate; and community, social and personal services. Real figures were derived using using the Consumer Price Index where 1980=100, from the Banco de Mexico, "The Mexican Economy: 1991," Table 28, p. 204 (Mexico, 1991).

Table 5
Distribution of Total Household Income by Source, Third Quarter, 1984[1]

Percent unless otherwise specified

Household Decile[2]	Average per capita income[3]	Non-monetary	Wages and salaries	Profits	Rents	Cooperatives	Transfers	Other	Total
I	6,190.1	30.3	33.2	28.4	0.1	0.2	7.7	0.0	100.0
II	10,680.6	22.8	46.0	23.1	0.6	0.3	7.2	0.0	100.0
III	14,295.8	21.9	41.2	29.0	0.2	0.2	7.5	0.0	100.0
IV	18,651.4	21.1	45.0	24.8	1.1	0.1	7.8	0.0	100.0
V	23,573.9	21.3	46.5	24.5	1.2	0.1	6.5	0.0	100.0
VI	29,649.8	20.5	49.3	19.3	1.3	0.4	9.1	0.1	100.0
VII	38,051.9	22.6	52.4	16.8	1.2	0.0	7.0	0.0	100.0
VIII	48,753.1	27.0	47.2	16.7	2.3	0.0	6.6	0.2	100.0
IX	68,621.9	24.3	46.0	18.8	3.5	0.4	6.7	0.3	100.0
X	151,588.0	21.6	43.3	20.4	5.0	0.2	9.0	0.6	100.0
TOTAL	41,005.6	23.3	45.0	22.2	1.7	0.2	7.5	0.1	100.0
RURAL	25,451.4	26.9	32.3	31.1	1.0	0.3	8.1	0.1	100.0
URBAN	49,303.5	21.4	51.7	17.4	2.0	0.1	7.2	0.1	100.0

Source: Author's calculations based on data from INEGI, *Encuesta nacional de ingresos y gastos de los hogares, tercer trimestre de 1984*.
[1]The number in each entry is the intradecile proportion of total households within group.
[2]The total number of households is 14,988,551. Households are ranked by total per capita income.
[3]Pesos per quarter, June 1984 pesos. Income includes monetary and nonmonetary income.

Table 6
Evolution of the Agricultural Sector, 1981 - 1990
Annual rate of change and shares in percent

	1981	1982	1983	1984	1985	1986	1987	1988	1989	1990 (prelim)	Cumulative 1983-88	Average Change 1983-88	Average 1983-85	Average 1986-87
GDP in Agriculture (a)	6.1	-2.0	2.0	2.7	3.8	-2.7	1.4	-3.2	-3.3	7.4	0.6	3.8	2.8	-0.7
GDP in All Sectors (b)	8.8	-0.6	-4.2	3.6	2.6	-3.8	1.7	1.3	3.3	4.4	0.2	1.0	0.6	-1.0
Total Wage Income in Agriculture(c)	10.0	-12.7	-13.2	-3.8	3.0	-2.0	-5.6	-12.6	-6.7	-8.6	-5.9	-30.5	-4.9	-3.8
Total Wage Income in All Sectors(c)	11.3	-5.4	-24.7	-2.8	2.0	-10.7	-2.0	-8.3	5.9	3.0	-8.2	-40.0	-9.2	-6.4
Wages Income per Worker in Agriculture (c,d)	7.0	-9.7	-16.7	-4.9	0.3	0.5	-7.0	-14.8	-4.7	-4.1	-7.3	-36.7	-7.4	-3.3
Wages Income per Worker in All Sectors (c,d)	4.8	-5.1	-22.9	-5.0	-0.2	-9.4	-3.0	-9.1	4.6	1.9	-8.6	-41.5	-9.9	-6.2
Employment-Agriculture (e)	2.8	-3.3	4.2	1.1	2.6	-2.5	1.5	2.5	-2.1	-4.6	1.6	9.8	2.6	-0.5
Employment-All Sectors (e)	6.3	-0.3	-2.3	2.3	2.2	-1.4	1.1	0.9	1.3	1.1	0.4	2.7	0.7	-0.2
Share of Agricultural Employment in Total Employment (e)	27.0	26.2	28.0	27.7	27.8	27.5	27.6	28.1	27.1	25.6	27.8	-	27.8	27.5
On-Farm Real Price of Corn (f)	7.7	-6.9	2.7	4.3	-4.6	-7.0	-9.8	-0.9	n.a.	n.a.	-2.7	-15.0	0.7	-8.4
Corn Production (g)	17.6	-26.0	22.5	-3.0	10.3	-16.9	-1.0	-8.7	3.3	33.7	-0.3	-1.6	9.4	-9.3
Non-Wage Income in Agriculture(c)	5.9	-8.9	-2.0	14.1	9.0	-8.0	-2.2	-15.7	8.9	13.4	-1.3	-7.6	6.8	-5.1
Non-Wage Income in All Sectors (c)	4.8	2.0	1.7	0.3	-2.0	-7.5	4.6	-3.8	8.0	7.4	-1.2	-6.9	0.0	-1.6
Share of Non-Wage Income in Agriculture (c)	73.9	74.7	77.0	79.8	80.7	79.8	80.3	79.8	82.3	85.2	79.6	-	79.2	80.0
Share of Non-Wage Income All Sectors (c)	60.0	61.8	68.6	69.2	68.4	69.1	70.5	71.5	71.9	72.7	69.5	-	68.7	69.8

n.a. Figures not available.

(a) Source: The figures for 1980 to 1984 are from the Instituto Nacional de Estadística Geografía e Informática (INEGI), "Sistema de Cuentas Nacionales de México 1980-1986: Tomo I, Resumen General," Table 91, p. 194 (México, 1988). The figures for 1985 to 1987 are from INEGI, "Sistema de Cuentas Nacionales de México 1985-1988: Tomo I, Resumen General," Table 79, p. 118 (México, 1990). The 1988 to 1990 figures are from INEGI, unpublished mimeo (March 1992).

(b) Source: Same as Table II.4.   (c) Source: Same as Table III.3.   (d) Source: Same as Table III.1.   (e) Source: Same as Table III.2.

(f) Source: CONASUPO (the National Commission of Popular Subsistence), cited by Kirsten Appendini, "La política Alimentaria y Restructuración Económica en México," Table 9, Appendix K, (UNRISD/El Colegio de México, 1991-unpublished).

(g) Source: From the Secretaría de Agricultura y Recursos Hidrálicos, in Carlos Salinas de Gortari, "Tercer Informe de Gobierno," p. 211 (México, 1991).

Table 7
Social Spending: Total, Education and Health, 1980 - 1990
Annual real rate of change and shares in percent

	1980	1981	1982	1983	1984	1985	1986	1987	1988	1989	1990	Average 1983-88	Cumulative Change 1983-88	Average 1983-85	Average 1986-87
Total Government Spending(a)	–	27.8	16.7	-10.8	-0.3	-1.7	6.9	6.9	-6.6	-13.9	-3.8	-1.2	-6.8	-4.4	6.9
Total "Non-Interest"** Spending (a)	–	23.4	-8.9	-15.7	5.7	-5.5	-6.7	-4.7	-5.4	-6.7	6.5	-5.6	-29.2	-5.6	-5.7
Total "Interest"** Spending (a)	–	47.8	114.6	-3.0	-8.9	4.5	26.9	19.5	-7.6	-20.4	-14.5	4.4	29.6	-2.6	23.1
Share of "Non-Interest"** Spending in Total Spending (%)(a)	82.1	79.3	61.9	58.5	62.1	59.7	52.1	46.4	47.0	51.0	56.4	54.3	–	60.1	49.3
Social Spending (b)	–	24.1	-1.3	-30.1	4.3	6.3	-8.1	-4.9	-1.1	3.6	12.9	-6.5	-33.1	-8.2	-6.5
Per Capita Social Spending(b,d)	–	21.2	-3.5	-31.5	2.1	4.3	-9.7	-6.7	-2.7	1.8	11.1	-8.2	-40.2	-10.0	-8.2
Share of Social Spending in Total "Non-Interest"** Spending (b)	31.0	31.2	33.8	28.0	27.6	31.1	30.7	30.6	32.0	35.5	37.6	30.0	–	28.9	30.6
Social Spending on Education(b)	–	25.1	3.9	-29.9	7.5	2.9	-11.7	2.2	0.6	2.1	10.1	-5.7	-29.6	-8.1	-5.0
Share of Educational Spending in Social Spending (b)	38.9	39.2	41.2	41.3	42.6	41.2	39.6	42.6	43.4	42.7	41.7	41.8	–	41.7	41.1
Share of Educational Spending in GDP (b,c)	3.1	3.6	3.8	2.8	2.9	2.9	2.6	2.6	2.6	2.6	2.7	2.7	–	2.8	2.6
Social Spending on Health (b)	–	13.9	-0.6	-21.1	-4.2	2.8	2.9	-7.7	3.8	9.3	13.9	-4.3	-23.3	-8.0	-2.5
Share of Health Spending in Social Spending (b)	43.6	40.0	45.5	41.8	41.8	40.4	45.3	44.0	46.2	48.7	49.2	43.9	–	42.6	44.6
Share of Health Spending in GDP (b,c)	3.5	3.7	3.0	2.8	2.8	2.8	3.0	2.7	2.8	3.0	3.2	2.9	–	2.9	2.9

Table 7 *(continued)*
Social Spending: Total, Education and Health, 1980 - 1990
Annual real rate of change and shares in percent

Note: Real figures were calculated using implicit GDP deflators from the Banco de México, "The Mexican Economy: 1991," Table 6, p.180 (México, 1991).

- "Non-Interest" spending is "programmable" spending and "Interest" spending is "non-programmable" spending.

(a) Source: The figures for "total spending," "total 'non-interest' spending" and "total 'interest' spending" are from Carlos Salinas de Gortari, "Tercer Informe de Gobierno: 1991-Anexo," p. 153 (México, 1991).

(b) Source: The figures for "total social spending" and "social spending by sector" are from Carlos Salinas de Gortari, "Tercer Informe de Gobierno: 1991-Anexo," p. 157 (México, 1991).

(c) GDP Source: The figures for 1980 to 1984 are from the Instituto Nacional de Estadística Geografía e Informática (INEGI), "Sistema de Cuentas Nacionales de México 1980-1986: Tomo I, Resumen General," Table 46, p. 93 (México, 1988). The figure for 1985 is from INEGI, "Sistema de Cuentas Nacionales de México 1985-1988: Tomo I, Resumen General," Table 34, p. 62 (México, 1990). The 1986 to 1989 figures are from INEGI, "Sistema de Cuentas Nacionales de México 1986-1989: Tomo I - Resumen General," (México, 1991). The preliminary 1990 figure is from the Banco de México, "The Mexican Economy: 1991," Tables 4 and 10 on pp. 178 and 184 (México, 1991).

(d) Population Source: Yearly levels are calculated using growth rates from Manuel Ordorica, "Las cifras preliminares del censo," which appeared in "Demos: Carta Demográfica Sobre México," pp. 4-6 (1990). Ordorica provides yearly growth rates for the 1980-1990 decade and cites the 11th population census preliminary figure for total population in 1990, estimated to be 81.1 million.

Table 8
Educational Resources, Total and Primary School
1980/81 - 1991/92
in percent

	80/81	81/82	82/83	83/84	84/85	85/86	86/87	87/88	88/89	89/90	90/91	91/92 (e)	Average 83/83- 88/89	Average 83/84- 85/86	Average 86/87- 87/88	Average 88/89- 90/91
Rate of Change of Matriculated Students - Total	6.6	5.6	4.5	3.3	1.2	2.0	0.7	0.0	0.0	-0.9	-0.5	2.5	1.2	2.2	0.4	-0.5
Students Per Teacher Ratio - Total	28.5	27.7	27.1	26.6	25.6	24.8	24.2	23.9	23.3	22.9	22.5	22.8	24.7	25.7	24.1	22.9
Students Per School Ratio - Total	206.1	201.5	194.9	190.2	188.5	183.0	172.0	170.5	165.3	163.7	156.9	155.1	178.3	187.3	171.3	161.9
Rate of Change of Matriculated Students - Primary School	3.8	2.1	1.6	1.0	-1.0	-0.6	-0.9	-1.5	-0.8	-1.1	-0.6	1.3	-0.6	-0.2	-1.2	-0.8
Students Per Teacher Ratio - Primary School	39.1	37.5	36.6	35.9	34.8	33.6	32.8	31.9	31.3	31.1	30.5	30.6	33.4	34.8	32.4	31.0
Students Per School Ratio - Primary School	192.9	196.4	195.4	194.9	199.8	197.2	187.3	185.3	180.2	179.7	175.0	173.8	190.8	197.3	186.3	178.3
Free Textbooks Per Student Ratio - Primary School	4.8	4.9	5.2	5.4	5.4	5.4	4.9	5.0	4.8	5.0	5.1	5.1	5.2	5.4	5.0	5.0

Source: Salinas de Gortari, Carlos. "Tercer Informe de Gobierno: 1991 - Anexo," pp. 345, 346 and 349 (Mexico, 1991).

(e) The figures for 1991/92 are estimates.

Table 9
Health Resources, 1980 - 1991
Ratios and annual rates of change in percent

IMSS (a)	1980	1981	1982	1983	1984	1985	1986	1987	1988	1989	1990	1991 (est.)	Average 1983-88	1983-85	1986-87
Population Covered (Thousands)	24125.0	26916.0	26885.0	26977.0	29388.0	31529.0	31062.0	34336.0	35066.0	37213.0	38575.0	38117.0	31393.0	29298.0	32699.0
	14.9	11.6	-0.1	0.3	8.9	7.3	-1.5	10.5	2.1	6.1	3.7	-1.2	4.5	5.5	4.4
As a Ratio of the Total Population (b)	36.4	39.6	38.6	37.9	40.4	42.5	41.1	44.6	44.8	46.7	47.6	43.9	41.9	40.3	42.8
Medical Units Per Thousand	0.050	0.054	0.056	0.057	0.049	0.046	0.047	0.043	0.044	0.042	0.042	0.043	0.048	0.051	0.045
		8.5	3.9	0.8	-13.4	-7.5	4.1	-8.3	0.9	-4.2	-1.1	2.5	-4.1	-6.9	-2.3
Beds Per Thousand	1.142	1.041	1.095	1.095	1.007	0.851	0.865	0.776	0.747	0.715	0.711	0.721	0.89	0.98	0.82
		-8.8	5.1	0.0	-8.1	-15.5	1.6	-10.2	-3.8	-4.2	-0.5	1.4	-6.2	-8.1	-4.5
Doctors Per Thousand	0.975	0.955	0.931	1.007	0.758	0.760	0.769	0.725	0.750	0.714	0.719	0.786	0.79	0.84	0.75
		-2.0	-2.5	8.1	-24.7	0.2	1.2	-5.7	3.3	-4.7	0.6	9.3	-3.6	-6.6	-2.3
Nurses Per Thousand	1.71	1.66	1.68	1.81	1.72	1.74	1.77	1.66	1.70	1.74	1.70	1.81	1.73	1.76	1.71
		-2.9	1.7	7.2	-4.5	1.0	1.5	-5.9	2.2	2.5	-2.5	6.4	0.2	1.1	-2.3
Ratio of Nurses to Doctors (c)	1.7	1.7	1.8	1.8	2.3	2.3	2.3	2.3	2.3	2.4	2.4	2.3	2.20	2.12	2.29

Table 9 *(continued)*
Health Resources, 1980 - 1991
Ratios and annual rates of change in percent

ISSSTE

	1980	1981	1982	1983	1984	1985	1986	1987	1988	1989	1990	1991 (est.)	Average 1983-88	Average 1983-85	Average 1986-87
Population Covered (Thousands)	49850.0	5319.3	5467.8	5611.0	6080.4	6447.9	6957.3	7356.6	7415.1	7844.5	8302.4	8509.7	6644.7	6046.4	7157.0
	2.2	6.7	2.8	2.6	8.4	6.0	7.9	5.7	0.8	5.8	5.8	2.5	5.2	5.6	6.8
As a Ratio of the Total Population (b)	7.5	7.8	7.8	7.9	8.4	8.7	9.2	9.6	9.5	9.8	10.2	n.a.	8.9	8.3	9.4
Medical Units Per Thousand	0.2	0.2	0.2	0.2	0.2	0.2	0.2	0.1	0.2	0.1	0.1	0.1	0.2	0.2	0.2
		-3.8	0.3	-2.1	-3.4	-4.0	-5.8	-5.4	3.1	-4.9	-3.9	-1.6	-3.0	-3.2	-5.6
Beds Per Thousand	1.066	0.988	1.002	1.001	1.009	0.951	0.884	0.837	0.830	0.781	0.770	0.755	0.884	1.0	0.9
		-7.3	1.4	-0.1	0.8	-5.7	-7.1	-5.3	-0.8	-5.8	-1.4	-2.0	-3.1	-1.7	-6.2
Doctors Per Thousand	1.510	1.515	1.666	1.623	1.674	1.619	1.616	1.507	1.640	1.521	1.503	1.580	1.6	1.6	1.6
		0.4	10.0	-2.6	3.1	-3.3	-0.2	-6.7	8.8	-7.3	-1.2	5.1	-0.3	-1.0	-3.5
Nurses Per Thousand	1.6	1.7	2.0	2.0	2.2	2.1	1.8	1.9	2.1	2.0	2.0	2.0	2.0	2.1	1.9
		4.3	17.9	-1.4	11.6	-3.5	-13.0	2.8	9.3	-3.2	-0.9	3.9	0.6	2.0	-5.4
Ratio of Nurses to Doctors (c)	1.1	1.1	1.2	1.2	1.3	1.3	1.1	1.2	1.3	1.3	1.3	1.3	1.2	1.3	1.2

(a) Source: Salinas de Gortari, Carlos. "Tercer Informe de Gobierno: 1991-Anexo," pp. 370-371, 376-379, 381, 386, and 390 (México, 1991). Doctors are those in direct contact with patients. Beds are the number of registered beds (censables).

(b) Population Source: Yearly levels are calculated using growth rates from Manuel Ordorica, "Las cifras preliminares del censo," which appeared in "Demos: Carta Demográfica Sobre México," pp. 4-6 (1990). Ordorica provides yearly growth rates for the 1980-1990 decade and cites the 11th population census preliminary figure for total population in 1990, estimated to be 81.1 million.

(c) The recommended ratio of nurses to doctors is three. See Cruz Rivero, et al. UNICEF, p. 16.

Privatization Amidst Poverty

Table 10
Social Indicators in Health
1980 - 1989

	1980	1981	1982	1983	1984	1985	1986	1987	1988	1989	Average 1983-88	Average 1983-85	Average 1986-87
Infant Mortality Rate (Per 1000 Births)(a)	53.1	51.3	49.6	48.0	46.4	44.8	43.4	42.0	40.6	39.3	44.2	46.4	42.7
Death Caused by Nutritional Deficiencies as a % of Total Infant Mortality (b)	1.0	1.1	1.5	1.5	1.7	2.0	2.1	2.9	5.2	n.a.	2.6	1.7	2.5
Death Caused by Nutritional Deficiencies as a % of Total Pre-School Mortality (b)	1.5	1.6	1.8	2.4	2.7	2.9	3.0	5.3	9.1	n.a.	4.2	2.7	4.2

n.a. The figures are not available.
(a) Source: Consejo Nacional de Población (CONAPO), "Proyecciones de la Población de Mexico: 1980-2025," (Mexico, November 1989).
(b) Source: Carlos Salinas de Gortari, "Tercer Informe de Gobierno: 1991-Anexo," pp. 367 and 368 (Mexico, 1991).

Table 11
Social Indicators in Education
1970/71 and 1980/81 - 1991/92

	70/71	80/81	81/82	82/83	83/84	84/85	85/86	86/87	87/88	88/89	89/90	90/91	91/92 (e)	Average 83/84-88/89	Average 83/84-85/86	Average 86/87-87/88
Average Schooling of the Population 15 Years or Older (# Years)(a)	3.4	5.4	5.6	5.7	5.8	5.9	6.0	6.1	6.2	6.3	6.3	6.4	6.4	6.1	5.9	6.2
Average Schooling of the Population 15 Years or Older (% Change)(a)	n.a.	4.7 (*)	3.7	1.8	1.8	1.7	1.7	1.7	1.6	1.6	0.0	1.6	0.0	1.7	1.7	1.7
Coverage for Demand for Schooling-Total (%)(a)	51.7	58.7	60.6	62.0	62.9	62.7	62.9	62.5	61.8	61.2	60.1	59.4	59.1	62.3	62.8	62.2
Coverage for Demand for Primary School (%)(a)	78.4	91.4	92.5	93.5	95.4	98.0	98.0	98.0	98.0	98.0	98.0	98.0	98.0	97.6	97.1	98.0
Coverage for Demand for Junior High School (%)(a)	62.2	82.0	86.8	86.2	85.4	82.9	84.4	83.7	83.0	83.2	82.4	82.3	82.4	83.9	84.2	83.4
Coverage for Demand for High School (%)(a)	69.7	68.8	69.6	66.5	65.6	66.5	64.0	59.2	59.4	59.8	60.2	61.0	61.6	62.7	65.4	59.3
Coverage for Demand for Higher Levels or University (%)(a)	n.a.	88.6	82.1	84.6	78.5	70.0	77.4	63.7	63.8	57.7	62.0	64.4	66.0	69.5	75.3	63.7
Drop-out Rates (b) Primary School (%)	n.a.	7.2	6.9	6.0	5.7	6.4	5.4	5.3	5.9	5.3	5.7	5.3	5.0	5.7	5.8	5.6
Junior High School (%)	n.a.	10.5	9.6	10.3	8.9	9.8	7.9	9.3	9.1	9.1	10.0	9.5	9.1	9.3	8.9	9.2
High School (%)	n.a.	12.4	15.5	15.7	16.2	16.3	16.3	18.4	15.1	16.3	18.5	16.4	16.0	16.6	16.3	16.7

(e)The figures for 1991/92 are preliminary.
(a) Source: Carlos Salinas de Gortari, "Tercer Informe de Gobierno: 1991 - Anexo," p. 357 (Mexico, 1991).
(b) Source: Carlos Salinas de Gortari, "Tercer Informe de Gobierno: 1991 - Anexo," p. 354 (Mexico, 1991). The drop-out rate includes those students who had registered for a year of school and had not finished that same year, or who had not registered for the next course.
(*) The rate is the estimated annual rate of increase over the decade 1970-1980.
n.a. not available.

Table 12
Income Distribution in Mexico 1963, 1968, 1977, 1984, 1989
Percentage of total household income
Percentile Groups of Households

	40 lowest	50 intermediate	10 highest	Total
1963	10.2	47.6	42.2	100.0
1968	11.2	48.8	40.0	100.0
1977	10.4	52.8	36.8	100.0
1984	14.3	52.9	32.8	100.0
1989	12.9	49.2	37.9	100.0

Source: For 1963, 1968, and 1977, Oscar Altimir, "La pobreza en América Latina: Un examen de conceptos y datos," Revista de la CEPAL, No. 13, (1981), Table 8, p. 90. For 1984, INEGI, "Encuesta Nacional de Ingresos y Gastos de los Hogares, Tercer Trimestre de 1984," Instituto Nacional de Estadística, Geografía e Informática, 1989, Mexico City, Table 4, p. 20. For 1989, INEGI, "Encuesta Nacional de Ingresos y Gastos de los Hogares 1989, Transacciones Económicas, Ingresos y Gastos de los Hogares," Instituto Nacional de Estadística, Geografía e Informática, 1992, Mexico City, Table 1 (no page number).

Notes

1. For an exposition of these mechanisms, see, for example, W. M. Corden, *Inflation, Exchange Rates, and the World Economy: Lectures on International Monetary Economics* (University of Chicago Press, 1977), chaps. 1, 2; and François Bourguignon, Jaime de Melo, and Christian Morrisson, "Poverty and Income Distribution during Adjustment: Issues and Evidence from the OECD Project," *World Development* 19 (November 1991): 1485-1508.

2. In general, real life situations lie somewhere in between, because governments may be unable to produce a smooth adjustment even with carefully engineered policies.

3. See, for example, Corden, *Inflation, Exchange Rates, and the World Economy*, 28-29.

4. See, for example, Corden, 26-28; Rudiger Dornbusch, *Open Economy Macroeconomics* (Basic Books, 1980), 73-74; and Lance Taylor, *Structuralist Macroeconomics: Applicable Models for the Third World*, (Basic Books, 1983), 25-27.

5. For an analytical discussion of these issues, see Joshua Aizenman and Marcelo Selowsky, "Costly Adjustment and Limited Borrowing," *International Economic Journal* 5 (Summer 1991): 17-38.

6. Real wages can be flexible in the downward direction even if money wages are not, so long as the rise in money wages falls below that of the general price level.

7. Instituto Nacional de Estadística, Geografía e Informática (INEGI), *Encuesta nacional de ingresos y gastos de los hogares, tercer trimestre de 1984* (Mexico City, 1989).

8. One way out of this is to analyze the evolution of physical and human resources per capita in the health and education sectors.

9. See INEGI, *Encuesta nacional de ingresos y gastos, 1984*; and INEGI, *Encuesta nacional de ingresos y gastos de los hogares 1989, transacciones económicas* (Mexico City, 1992).

10. Coordinación General del Sistema Nacional de Información, *Encuesta nacional de ingresos y gastos de los hogares 1977: Primera observación* (Mexico City, Secretaría de Programación y Presupuesto, August 1979), 79 (Table P2.3). For a compilation of these data, see Nora Lustig, "Distribución del ingreso y consumo de alimentos: estructura, tendencias y requerimentos redistributivos a nivel regional," *Demografía y Economía* 16, no. 2 (1982): 111, Table 2. For the minimum wage in pesos, see Lustig, 112, Table 3. For the dollar exchange rate, see Macro Asesoría, *Realidad económica de Mexico, 1991* (Mexico City, 1990), 445.

11. Nora Lustig, "Distribución del ingreso y consumo de alimentos," 115, Table 5.

12. Poder Ejecutivo Federal, *Plan global de desarrollo, 1980-82* (Mexico City), 199. Mexico's total population was 66.9 million in 1980. See INEGI, *Estadísticas históricas de México*, vol. 1 (Mexico City, August 1985), 33.

13. See Table 11. Mexico's rate is higher than those of other countries with lower per capita income levels (such as Malaysia and Paraguay). UNICEF, *Estado mundial de la infancia* (Madrid: Siglo Veintiuno de España, 1984, 1986).

14. UNICEF, *Estado mundial de la infancia*, 1986, 120, 135. Low birth weight is one indication of the prevalence of malnutrition.

15. Miguel de la Madrid, *Cuarto informe de gobierno: Anexo* (Mexico City, 1986), 316.

16. Coordinación General del Plan Nacional de Zonas Deprimidas y Grupos Marginados (COPLAMAR), *Necesidades esenciales en México: Situación actual y perspectivas al año 2000*, vol. 4 (Mexico City: Siglo Veintiuno, 1982), 172-75.

17. UNICEF, *Estado mundial de la infancia*, 1986, 139.

18. Jorge Padua, *Educación, industrialización y progreso técnico en México* (Mexico City: El Colegio de México, 1984), 105 and Table 10.

19. Centro de Investigación para el Desarollo (CIDAC), *Vivienda y estabilidad política* (Mexico City: Editorial Diana, 1991), 16.

20. Coordinación General del Plan Nacional de Zonas Deprimadas y Grupos Marginados (COPLAMAR), *Necesidades esenciales en México*, vol. 3 (Mexico City: Siglo Veintiuno, 1982), 57.

21. There was *no* decline in nominal wages. Real wages declined as nominal wages rose at a slower pace than the general price level.

22. The definition of *employment* used by the National Accounts is of workposts, that is, the number of laborers needed to produce a certain level of output given some labor-to-output coefficients. It is an indirect estimate of employment.

23. The other wages included in table 2 measure actual wage performance, whereas the minimum is a legal convention.

24. One author, for example, suggests that other paths are possible though perhaps difficult to implement. See Raúl Ramos Tercero, "La caída de los salários reales y las transferencias al exterior: Una interpretación inspirada por la experiencia mexicana, 1982-1987" (Mexico City, n.d.).

25. Some authors go as far as to state that real wages did not need to decline at all if a different policy direction had been taken. For example, David Barkin suggests that crisis management in Mexico should be equivalent to managing a "war economy." His recommended solution is for Mexico to raise grain prices substantially and pass "a decree to double the 1990 minimum wage." See Barkin, *Distorted Development: Mexico in the World Economy*, (Boulder, Colo.: Westview Press, 1990), 115-23. In another study, using a computable general equilibrium (CGE) model of the Mexican economy, Irma Adelman and J. Edward Taylor found that abandoning what they call the "wage-repression strategy" would result in higher growth rates, a more equal distribution of income, a lower fiscal deficit, and a just slightly worsened trade balance. See Adelman and Taylor, "Is Structural Adjustment with a Human Face Possible? The Case of Mexico," *Journal of Developmental Studies* 26 (April 1990): 387-407. For all their humanitarian appeal, the recommendations of these authors may not be based on solid analytical ground. If the decision were to absorb external shocks internally, a rise in nominal wages would result in higher inflation, increased capital flight, and a deeper economic decline. If the decision were *not* to absorb shocks internally, then keeping

real wages from falling would depend on the impact of a debt moratorium on private investors' behavior and the availability of other sources of foreign exchange. Adelman and Taylor's results probably follow from their assumptions about the determinants of output (primarily demand-driven) and the behavior of expectations. In real life, countries that tried to apply policies analogous to those they recommend found themselves in deep trouble — for example, Perú after the 1986 "heterodox shock" and Brazil after the "Cruzado Plan."

26. The number of strikes did rise compared to prior years, but the increase seems modest when compared with the size of wage cuts. In 1982 the number of strikes rose by over sixfold to 675. However, the number fell in 1983 to 230, even though real wages declined by 25 percent; there was an upsurge with the 1986 oil shock, when the number reached 312. Thereafter the numbers fell to pre-crisis levels. Carlos Salinas de Gortari, *Segundo informe de gobierno: Anexo* (Mexico City, 1990), 334.

27. Alain Ize, "Trade Liberalization, Stabilization, and Growth: Some Notes on the Mexican Experience," Working Paper 90/15 (International Monetary Fund, March 1990), 6, Table 1.

28. CEPAL, *Economía campesina y agricultura empresarial: Tipología de productores del agro mexicano* (Mexico City: Siglo Veintiuno, 1982), 152, Table 17.

29. Kirsten Appendini, "De la milpa a los tortibonos: La reestructuración de la política alimentaria en México," Instituto de Investigaciones de las Naciones Unidas para el Desarrollo Social (UNRISD), June 1991, 69-70.

30. Peter Gregory, "The Mexican Labor Market in the Economic Crisis and Lessons of the Past," in *Mexico's Economic Policy: Past, Present and Future*, William E. Cole, ed., Socioeconomic Research Series (Knoxville, Tenn.: Center for Business and Economic Research, November 1987), 57.

31. Appendini, "De la milpa a los tortibonos," 64-66.

32. Appendini, "De la milpa a los tortibonos," 75-76.

33. Appendini, "De la milpa a los tortibonos," 84-85.

34. *Compendio de indicadores de empleo y salarios* (Mexico City: Comisión Nacional de los Salarios Mínimos, 1989), p. 27.

35. There is evidence that formal sector employment declined. Gregory, "The Mexican Labor Market in the Economic Crisis," 56.

36. The percentage of wage earners in total employment fell between 1982 and 1989. The percentage of family workers without remuneration in three major urban centers increased between 1982 and 1985, then held steady afterward. Of the three urban centers, only in Mexico City was there an increase in the percentage of self-employed workers between 1982 and 1985. Between 1985 and 1989, the average percentage of self-employed workers in sixteen urban areas rose. See Nora Lustig, "Economic Crisis and Living Standards," 56, Table 9; and *Compendio de indicadores*, 99-100.

37. The implicit unemployment rate was calculated as the ratio between total employment and the economically active population (EAP). Figures for total employment are from *Compendio de indicadores*, 27, Table 1.1. The figure for EAP is a linear extrapolation from the 1980 and 1985 figures; see *Compendio de indicadores*, 67, Table 2.6.

38. The concept of underemployment is always difficult to define. It refers to the fact that people are employed in activities with very low productivity levels and pay.

39. Gregory, "The Mexican Labor Market in the Economic Crisis," 55.

40. *Compendio de indicadores*, 99-100.

41. *Compendio de indicadores*, 67.

42. An indirect indicator of this is that real private consumption per capita declined by substantially less than real wages (Table 2).

43. Total government spending here refers to the sum of the so-called programmable plus nonprogrammable expenditures. For a definition, see Table 7.

44. Social expenditures also include spending on two categories known as "solidarity" and "urban development."

45. This was not the case every year, but it was particularly true in 1983.

46. This means that actual changes in government services may differ from those reflected by the numbers in the text, and also that trends among the various expenditure categories cannot be compared. In particular, sector-specific deflators for programmable and nonprogramable expenditures are probably different.

47. Some of the yearly changes in the student-per-school ratios cannot easily be explained. See, for example, the sharp decline between 1985-1986 and 1986-1987, a shift that may be more indicative of the poor quality of education statistics in Mexico than of any actual changes.

48. The general food subsidies covered bread, tortillas, beans, eggs, milk, and cooking oil. Their final price was set by the government, and producers were provided with subsidized inputs. For a description of the subsidy schemes and how they changed, see Antonio Martín del Campo and Rosendo Calderón Tinoco, "Restructuración de los subsidios a productos básicos y la modernización de CONASUPO," in Carlos Bazdresch, Nisso Bucay, and Nora Lustig, eds., *Mexico: Auge, crisis y ajuste* (Mexico City: Fondo de Cultura Económica, forthcoming).

49. Martín del Campo and Tinoco, "Restructuración de los subsidios," 43.

50. Martín del Campo and Tinoco, "Restructuración de los subsidios," 44.

51. Author's interview with CONASUPO official, December 1991.

52. Martín del Campo and Tinoco, "Restructuración de los subsidios," 24-33.

53. For a description of the author's methodology in this calculation, see Lustig, "Economic Crisis and Living Standards," 38.

54. Pascual García Alba and Jaime Serra Puche, *Causas y efectos de la crisis económica en México* (Mexico City: El Colegio de México, 1983), 104-7, Table 23.

55. This is so because the consumption of these items is more concentrated at the lower level of the income scale. In contrast, the general subsidy on gasoline is strikingly regressive.

56. Instituto Nacional del Consumidor (INCO), "100 días en el consumo familiar," Mexico City, 1983.

57. Jacobo Schatan, "Nutrición y crisis en México," paper presented at the Fifth Seminar on Third World Agricultural Economics, UNAM, Mexico City, November 11-15, 1985, 47.

58. Schatan, "Nutrición y crisis en México," 51.

59. Schatan, "Nutrición y crisis en México," 52.

60. It has been observed that the impact of an economic crisis is usually not reflected in average indicators and that its effect on health becomes obvious only over the long run. See, for example, a classic study on the effects of the Great Depression on health: G. St. J. Perrott and Selwyn D. Collins, "Sickness among the Depression Poor," *American Journal of Public Health* 24 (February 1934): 101-7.

61. Carlos Salinas de Gortari, *Tercer informe de gobierno: Anexo* (Mexico City, 1991), 367-68.

62. To establish this would require a more careful analysis, however. An increase in the death rate due to nutritional deficiencies may be a consequence of a decrease in a substitute cause, such as intestinal diseases. Nonetheless, data show that deaths associated with both causes declined steadily through the 1970s. However, in the 1980s deaths caused by "intestinal diseases" fell, while those caused by "nutritional deficiencies" rose in both absolute and relative terms. See Salinas de Gortari, 1991, *Tercer informe de gobierno: Anexo*. Even so, statistics on causes of death may be subject to large measurement errors, and thus one should read the trends presented in Table 10 with caution.

63. Miguel de la Madrid, *Tercer informe de gobierno: Salud y seguridad social*, vol. 16 (Mexico City, 1985), 417-18.

64. These trends should be treated cautiously. There are some oscillations in the yearly figures that are difficult to explain and may be the result of measurement errors.

65. Fernando Valerio, "Fiscal Shock, Wage Compression and Structural Reform: Mexican Adjustment and Educational Policy in the 1980s," Innocenti Occasional Papers, Economic Policy Series, Fiscal Policy and the Poor (UNICEF, June 1991), 26.

66. Salinas de Gortari, *Segundo informe de gobierno*, 118.

67. Merilee S. Grindle, "The Response to Austerity: Political and Economic Strategies of Mexico's Rural Poor," in William L. Canek, ed., *Lost Promises: Debt, Austerity, and Development in Latin America* (Boulder, Colo.: Westview Press, 1989), 190-215; and Mercedes González de la Rocha, "Economic Crisis, Domestic Reorganisation and Women's Work in Guadalajara, Mexico," *Bulletin of Latin American Research* 7, no. 2 (1988): 207-23.

68. González de la Rocha, "Economic Crisis," 219-20.

69. González de la Rocha mentions that the people she interviewed were more tired, worked more, and were more anxious about their future. González de la Rocha, "Economic Crisis," 220.

70. This was recorded by Grindle in her study of three rural Mexican villages; see Grindle, "The Response to Austerity," 199-205. For a discussion of undocumented migration to the United States, see Frank D. Bean, Barry Edmonston, and Jeffrey S. Passel, eds., *Undocumented Migration to the United IRCA and the Experience of the 1980s* (Washington: Urban Institute Press, 1990).

71. Apprehensions peaked in 1986 at 1,767,400 and slowed to 1,099, 165 on average for 1987-1988, probably as a result of the Immigration Reform and Control Act of 1986 (IRCA). Georges Vernez and David Ronfeldt, "The Current Situation in Mexican Immigration," *Science* 251 (March 8, 1991): 1190.

72. The Gini coefficient for households was estimated at .4384 and for individuals at .4881. See Table 15 in Nora Lustig, "The Incidence of Poverty in Mexico, 1984: An Empirical Analysis" (Brookings, October 1990).

73. Enrique Hernández-Laos, "Medición de la intensidad de la pobreza y de la pobreza extrema en México," *Investigación Económica* 49, no. 191 (1990): 282. According to Hernández-Laos, the extremely poor were those households or individuals whose income fell below a minimum consumption basket, which includes food and nonfood items.

74. Oscar Altimir, "The Extent of Poverty in Latin America," Working Paper 522 (World Bank, 1982), 82. Poor households are those whose income falls below a minimum food consumption basket.

75. In addition to Hernández-Laos, Joel Bergsman has presented evidence of diminishing poverty during this period. See Bergsman, "La distribución del ingreso y la pobreza en México," in *Distribución del ingreso en México: Ensayos*, vol. 1 (Mexico City: Banco de México, 1982), 224, Table 5.

76. The poverty lines used to calculate the proportion of extremely poor households were $50.60 and $56.50 per quarter, respectively. The first poverty line is proposed in Santiago Levy, "Poverty Alleviation in Mexico," Policy, Research, and External Affairs Working Paper 679, no. 42 (World Bank, May 1991), 28, and 24A-24B, Table 2. The second poverty line is proposed by CEPAL, "Magnitud de la pobreza en América Latina en los años ochenta," no. 533 (May 31, 1990), 46, Table 9. For a description of my method of poverty estimation, see Lustig, "Incidence of Poverty," 18-20. I converted the peso-dominated lines of Levy and CEPAL to June 1984 U.S. dollars.

77. Lustig, "Incidence of Poverty," Table 21. Of those who are wage earners, a large proportion work in agriculture. It is interesting to note that the fraction of employers, especially small employers, does not differ greatly between the lowest deciles and the ninth decile. The poor employers are probably peasants or small shopkeepers who may hire workers who are also poor to help with tasks. Most of the heads of household who are agricultural workers belong to the lowest deciles: 78 percent of them are in the lower 50 percent of households. See Lustig, "Incidence of Poverty," Table 27.

78. The lower estimate excludes interest earned on foreign assets from capital-flight estimates. For more details, see Nora Lustig, "Dollar Waves: Mexico's Experience with Capital Flight and Repatriation," *International Economy* 5 (November-December 1991): 67-71.

79. By definition the extreme poverty line is the total cost of a food basket required to cover minimum caloric and protein needs.

80. For a discussion of policy options and their advantages and disadvantages, see Levy, "Poverty Alleviation in Mexico," 45-71.

81. *Programa nacional de solidaridad: La solidaridad en el desarrollo nacional* (Mexico City: Secretaría de Programación y Presupuesto, September 1991), 3.

References

Adelman, Irma, and J. Edward Taylor. 1990. "Is Structural Adjustment with a Human Face Possible? The Case of Mexico." *Journal of Developmental Studies* 26 (April): 387-407.

Altimir, Oscar. 1982. "The Extent of Poverty in Latin America," Working Paper 522. World Bank.

Appendini, Kirsten. 1991. "De la milpa a los tortibonos: La reestructuración de la política alimentaria en México." Mexico City: Instituto de Investigaciones de las Naciones Unidas para el Desarrollo Social.

Barkin, David. 1990. *Distorted Development: Mexico in the World Economy.* Boulder, Colo.: Westview Press.

Bean, Frank D., Barry Edmonston, and Jeffrey S. Passel, eds. 1990. *Undocumented Migration to the United States: IRCA and the Experience of the 1980s.* Washington, D.C.: Urban Institute Press.

Bergsman, Joel. 1982. "La distribución del ingreso y la pobreza en México." In vol. 1 of *Distribución del ingreso en México: Ensayos.* Mexico City: Banco de México.

Bourguignon, François, Jaime de Melo, and Christian Morrisson. 1991. "Poverty and Income Distribution during Adjustment: Issues and Evidence from the OECD Project." *World Development* 19 (November): 1485-1508.

Centro de Investigación para el Desarollo (CIDAC). 1991. *Vivienda y estabilidad política.* Mexico City: Editorial Diana.

CEPAL. 1982. *Economía campesina y agricultura empresarial: Tipología de productores del agro mexicano.* Mexico City: Siglo Veintiuno.

CEPAL. 1990. "Magnitud de la pobreza en América Latina en los años ochenta," No. 3 (May 31).

Compendio de indicadores de empleo y salarios. 1989. Mexico City: Comisión Nacional de los Salarios Mínimos.

Coordinación General del Sistema Nacional de Información. 1979. *Encuesta nacional de ingresos y gastos de los hogares 1977: Primera observación.* Mexico City: Secretaría de Programación y Presupuesto.

Coordinación General del Plan Nacional de Zonas Deprimidas y Grupos Marginados (COPLAMAR). 1982. *Necesidades esenciales en México: Situación actual y perspectivas al año 2000.* Vols. 4. Mexico City: Siglo Veintiuno.

Corden, W.M. 1977. *Inflation, Exchange Rates, and the World Economy: Lectures on International Monetary Economics.* Chicago: University of Chicago Press.

de la Madrid, Miguel. 1985. *Tercer informe de gobierno: Salud y seguridad social.* Vol. 16. Mexico City.

de la Madrid, Miguel. 1986. *Cuarto informe de gobierno: Anexo.* Mexico City.

Dornbusch, Rudiger. 1980. *Open Economy Macroeconomics*. Basic Books.

García Alba, Pascual, and Jaime Serra Puche. 1983. *Causas y efectos de la crisis económica en México*. Mexico City: El Colegio de México.

González de la Rocha, Mercedes. 1988. "Economic Crisis, Domestic Reorganisation, and Women's Work in Guadalajara, Mexico." *Bulletin of Latin American Research* 7 (2): 207-23.

Gregory, Peter. 1987. "The Mexican Labor Market in the Economic Crisis and Lessons of the Past." In *Mexico's Economic Policy: Past, Present and Future*, ed. William E. Cole. Socioeconomic Research Series. Knoxville, Tenn.: Center for Business and Economic Research.

Grindle, Merilee S. 1989. "The Response to Austerity: Political and Economic Strategies of Mexico's Rural Poor." In *Lost Promises: Debt, Austerity, and Development in Latin America*, ed. William L. Canek, 190-215. Boulder, Colo.: Westview Press.

Hernández-Laos, Enrique. 1990. "Medición de la intensidad de la pobreza y de la pobreza extrema en México." *Investigación Económica* 49 (191).

Instituto Nacional del Consumidor (INCO). 1983. "100 días en el consumo familiar." Mexico City.

Instituto Nacional de Estadística, Geografía e Informática (INEGI). 1985. *Estadísticas históricas de México*. Vol. 1. Mexico City.

Instituto Nacional de Estadística, Geografía e Informática (INEGI). 1989. *Encuesta nacional de ingresos y gastos de los hogares, tercer trimestre de 1984*. Mexico City.

Instituto Nacional de Estadística, Geografía e Informática (INEGI). 1992a. *Encuesta nacional de ingresos y gastos, 1984*. Mexico City.

Instituto Nacional de Estadística, Geografía e Informática (INEGI). 1992b. *Encuesta nacional de ingresos y gastos de los hogares 1989, transacciones económicas*. Mexico City.

Ize, Alain. 1990. "Trade Liberalization, Stabilization, and Growth: Some Notes on the Mexican Experience." Working Paper 90/15 (March). International Monetary Fund.

Levy, Santiago. 1991. "Poverty Alleviation in Mexico," Policy, Research, and External Affairs Working Paper 679, no. 42 (May). World Bank.

Lustig, Nora. 1982. "Distribución del ingreso y consumo de alimentos: estructura, tendencias y requerimentos redistributvios a nivel regional." *Demografía y Economía* 16 (2).

Lustig, Nora. 1990. "The Incidence of Poverty in Mexico, 1984: An Empirical Analysis." Brookings Institute.

Lustig, Nora. 1991. "Dollar Waves: Mexico's Experience with Capital Flight and Repatriation." *International Economy* 5 (November-December): 67-71.

Macro Asesoría. 1990. *Realidad económica de Mexico, 1991*. Mexico City.

Martín del Campo, Antonio, and Rosendo Calderón Tinoco. 1992. "Restructuración de los subsidios a productos básicos y la modernización de CONASUPO." In *Mexico: Auge, Crisis y Ajuste*, eds. Carlos Bazdresch, Nisso Bucay, and Nora Lustig. Mexico City: Fondo de Cultura Económica.

Padua, Jorge. 1984. *Educación, industrialización y progreso técnico en México.* Mexico City: El Colegio de México.

Perrott, G. St. J., and Selwyn D. Collins. 1934. "Sickness among the Depression Poor." *American Journal of Public Health* 24 (February): 101-7.

Poder Ejecutivo Federal. N.d. *Plan global de desarrollo, 1980-82.* Mexico City.

Salinas de Gortari, Carlos. 1990. *Segundo informe de gobierno: Anexo.* Mexico City.

Salinas de Gortari, Carlos. 1991. *Tercer informe de gobierno: Anexo.* Mexico City.

Schatan, Jacobo. 1985. "Nutrición y crisis en México." Paper presented at the Fifth Seminar on Third World Agricultural Economics, UNAM, in Mexico City, 11-15 November.

Secretaría de Programación y Presupuesto. 1991. Programa nacional de solidaridad: La solidaridad en el desarrollo nacional. Mexico City.

Taylor, Lance. 1983. *Structuralist Macroeconomics: Applicable Models for the Third World.* Basic Books.

Tercero, Raúl Ramos. N.d. "La caída de los salários reales y las transferencias al exterior: Una interpretación inspirada por la experiencia mexicana, 1982-1987." Mexico City.

UNICEF. 1984. *Estado mundial de la infancia.* Madrid: Siglo Veintiuno de España.

Valerio, Fernando. 1991. "Fiscal Shock, Wage Compression and Structural Reform: Mexican Adjustment and Educational Policy in the 1980s." Innocenti Occasional Papers, Economic Policy Series, Fiscal Policy and the Poor. UNICEF.

Vernez, Georges, and David Ronfeldt. 1991. "The Current Situation in Mexican Immigration." *Science* 251 (8 March).

Privatizing the Economies: Lessons from the Chilean Experience

Felipe Larraín B.

Nationalization, not privatization, was the course of economic policy in many countries of Latin America during the late 1960s and early 1970s. A wave of nationalizations followed the 1968 military coup in Peru. The new government of General Juan Velasco quickly expropriated the oil sector, the telephone company, foreign-owned banks, public utilities, and the largest copper producer. In nearby Chile, the socialist government of the Unidad Popular (1970-1973) carried out a massive program of nationalizations in agriculture, banking, industry, and mining. Venezuela nationalized foreign-owned oil companies in 1976, during the first administration of Carlos Andrés Pérez. As recently as 1982, the Mexican government nationalized all banks. Those were the times when the private sector — and multinationals in particular — came under heavy attack from many quarters in Latin America.

Privatization: Across Geographical and Ideological Boundaries

Times have changed dramatically since then. Today, privatization is the buzzword in Latin America, Eastern Europe, the former Soviet Union, and elsewhere. In Latin America, privatization started out as an isolated attempt by Chile in the mid-1970s, mostly as a response to a massive round of nationalizations in the early 1970s. A new round of privatization was launched

Felipe Larraín B. is professor of economics at the Universidad Católica de Chile. He has worked as economic advisor to several governments in North America, Latin America, and the Caribbean and has been a consultant to the IDB, the IMF, the UN, and the World Bank. He has published over fifty articles and seven books in Latin America, the United States, and Europe.

in Chile in 1985, but once again it was, by and large, an isolated event. By the end of the decade, however, the trend had become widespread in Latin America. Several new governments realized that the state had become overextended and that spreading itself too thinly prevented adequate performance of its primary responsibilities. Political and economic collapse of the old regimes in Eastern Europe also helped to underline the shortcomings of the state as entrepreneur.

Quite significantly, privatization has jumped over ideological boundaries. A few years ago, it was considered a patrimony of the right. Today, it is applied as well by the left. Clearly, the cases of Felipe Gonzalez's Spain and François Miterrand's France have served as inspirations to the more flexible minds in Latin America's left, and the fact that privatization is so widely accepted across the political spectrum helps the process itself. Investors are keen to notice that wide acceptance signals no future reversal of the process after a change in government. At the same time, local economies are undergoing profound economic liberalization. This makes investments safer and stimulates both the repatriation of local capital held abroad and the interest of foreign investors.

Many long-held beliefs have disappeared in this process. Only a few years ago, for example, it would have been unthinkable to privatize the state airline, long a symbol of nationalistic pride. Even less palatable would have been selling one to foreign investors. Argentina, Mexico, and earlier, Chile did swallow nationalism and privatized the airlines. It was also widely thought that public utilities could not be privatized because they often are natural monopolies. But telephone companies are already in private hands in Argentina, Chile, and Mexico, and electric companies (doing both generation and distribution) have been privatized in Chile and Argentina. The key to a successful privatization of utilities is appropriate regulation, especially regarding their tariff rates.

Privatization corresponds to a general worldwide trend and also to the process of structural adjustment that many economies of Latin America are now undergoing. As stressed above, it is not the result of ideology (as many said of the Chilean process of the 1970s). Indeed, in some countries, it is the result of outright necessity. The case of Argentina — one of the most aggressive recent privatizers — is perhaps one of the most evident, and its motivation is eminently practical. The Argentine public sector simply does not have the resources necessary to maintain normal operations in many state companies. With a foreign debt that it could not pay and domestic liabilities that were unilaterally rescheduled by the government, the public sector lacked access to credit markets. Consequently, investment and maintenance levels were cut so much that productive capacity actually declined in the mid- to late 1980s. The result was a major deterioration in public services.

To reap the fruits of privatization, however, it is necessary to do it right. While there is no unique model for privatizing, there are important lessons to be learned from the experiences of some countries that have been through this process. Chile, as the first country in the region to go through a major privatization program, offers interesting insights for other would-be privatizers.

The First Round of Privatization in Chile: 1974-1978

The Chilean military government that took power in September 1973 decided to transfer to the private sector most of the assets that had come under state control in the previous administration, as part of an overall effort to restructure the public sector. This was the primary motivation of the privatization program that took place mostly between 1974 and 1978, and especially in 1975.[1] The means of divesting state-controlled assets and the extent of the program varied depending on the economic sector.

The principal actions the government took in the *agricultural sector* were the regularization of property rights for the new owners of expropriated land, the return of land to previous owners, and the sale of farms at auction. These actions involved relatively short and simple administrative procedures in 95 percent of cases. The previous owners who recovered all or part of their land in this way had to renounce any indemnification or further claims on the government. In about 5 percent of cases, the former landowners undertook legal action, with varying degrees of success after long judicial confrontations.

Close to 10 million hectares had been expropriated during the process of land reform, most of it in 1970-1973. About 3 million of these were now assigned to new owners, another 3 million were recovered by their previous owners, and the rest were either sold to the private sector or remained with the Corporación de Reforma Agraria (CORA). The fastest action involved the restitution of property to owners when legal expropriation had not occurred; most of this was completed in 1974.

One important effect of the land reform was a major redistribution of wealth. Even after the return of land, the former landowners still suffered an estimated patrimonial loss of approximately US$800 million to $1 billion in 1974, given that the compensation they received amounted to only 10 percent of the commercial value of the property. The net transfer received by new owners is estimated to have been on the order of $500 to $800 million.

In *mining*, nationalization of big companies was an irreversible process, and the government retained the big mines under state control. The only privatization carried out within the mining sector involved some small mines auctioned by the National Mining Enterprise (ENAMI). The total value of this process was insignificant when compared to the parallel privatization processes in agriculture, industry, and banking.

Firms in the so-called "social area" of *industry*, those intervened with by the previous government (but not legally nationalized), were rapidly returned to their owners. To receive their properties, those owners had to renounce any further legal claims against the state, as was the case in agriculture. This process moved very quickly: By the end of 1974, 202 of the 259 firms were back in the hands of their owners.

Another important aspect of this privatization was the sale of assets owned by the Chilean Development Corporation (CORFO). This corporation set its policy to privatize companies through public auctions in early 1974. Any individual or entity, either national or foreign, could participate. A down payment of between 10 and 20 percent was required, with the rest payable in quarterly installments. The remaining debt carried an annual real interest rate that fluctuated between 8 and 12 percent and had to be guaranteed by real assets amounting to 150 percent of the value of the debt. Thus, the normal mechanism for privatization was an open bid. In cases where CORFO considered the offers to be insufficient, it entered into direct negotiations. The post-1974 reprivatization of banks and industrial properties in the hands of CORFO followed very similar procedures.

Privatization did not affect the biggest companies in the mining, energy, and service sectors, which remained in the public domain. The state also retained Banco del Estado, a commercial bank that had traditionally been part of the public sector, as it had an important role in national currency operations. CORFO sold most of its banking shares and a significant part of its industrial properties in 1975, the year of an unprecedented crash in economic activity, with the gross domestic product (GDP) falling by almost 13 percent.

The First Round of Privatization, 1974-1978: An Overall Assessment

The value of assets sold by the government was about $1.2 billion, mainly from the sale of industrial properties and commercial banks. A vast majority of the almost two hundred firms privatized were transferred to the Chilean private sector. By 1980, only forty-three public enterprises were left. Government's share in GDP had declined from about 40 percent in 1973 to a still-considerable 24 percent of GDP in 1981, since the most important public firms had remained in state hands — especially in the communications, mining, and utility sectors.

Several other points can be made about this privatization process:

1. The regularization of private assets in which the Unidad Popular government had intervened or simply taken over was accomplished quickly

in both agriculture and industry, with the bulk of the transfers completed in 1974. This process provoked little controversy, as it seemed clear the property that had been illegally acquired needed to be returned to its owners.

2. Although there was an established procedure for public auctions for the privatization of CORFO's property, the timing of the sales was very inappropriate. Most privatizations were carried out in 1975, when Chile was facing the worst depression since the early 1930s. National savings were at a low, the domestic capital markets were at a very primitive phase of development, and the overwhelming majority of credit was either controlled by the state or a few private groups.

3. The way in which firms were generally sold, with a 10 to 20 percent down payment and the rest as credit provided directly by CORFO, does not appear satisfactory. The newly privatized firms started out with a too-high debt/equity ratio that rendered their financial position extremely unstable. When the economic depression of 1982-1983 occurred and interest rates rose, many firms went bankrupt.

4. Little care was taken during this process to disseminate property. A limit was established in 1974 on the proportion of bank equity agents could own — 1.5 percent for individuals and 3.0 percent for corporations — but this restriction was easily bypassed and was soon abolished. Sales made through open bids ended up concentrating property in the few groups with access to foreign credit, which eventually became big conglomerates. The process typically started with a highly leveraged purchase of a financial company from CORFO, which was then used to bid on other industrial companies subsequently sold by the state. Through this procedure, groups with very small capital bases managed to control large volumes of assets. Other methods that would have resulted in greater dissemination of property, such as the sale of small packages of shares through the stock market or directly through CORFO, were not tried.

5. Whether public assets were sold very cheaply in the privatization process, with consequent damage to public finances, has been a controversial issue. Foxley (1983), for example, has calculated that firms were sold at about 30 percent less than their net worth. The fact that the biggest part of privatization occurred at the time of a major depression in 1975 gives a basis to this conclusion. However, Hachette and Luders (1987) have concluded that the prices paid for the privatized companies turned out to be relatively high.[2] In support of this argument, it seems that the prices paid reflected, to some extent, the competition to control the existing assets of the country. Since the down payment was a small fraction of the value of the purchase and CORFO was financing the loan, only a relatively small amount of money was required to gain control of auctioned firms.

6. The evidence indicates that the privatization process had a negative effect on both savings and investment. On the one hand, the bidding process favored a small group of agents, and, given the low level of development of financial markets, did not provide incentives for private savings, while the revenues from privatization were not invested in cash-flow-producing assets. On the other hand, public investment fell dramatically as the divestitures occurred (Hachette and Luders 1987).

The Second Round of Privatization, 1985–1989

As a result of the intervention and closure of financial institutions in early 1983, a large volume of assets accrued or returned to public hands, including the two largest private banks, the two biggest administrators of pension funds (AFPs), and several other companies related to the banks. A variety of new formulas were used to privatize these companies, the so-called "odd" sector of the economy. The procedure used and the timing of the process improved considerably over the earlier privatization process.

"Popular capitalism" was used to divest the two largest banks and a significant portion of the two biggest AFPs. Sales required a down payment of only 5 percent, with the balance provided in the form of a subsidized loan from the government to the buyer (with companies capitalized on 100 percent of the sale). The incentives (the credit subsidy and a tax break) applied only to individuals, who also faced strict maximum limits on stock ownership in each firm. Open sales through the stock exchange and auctions to select groups of investors were also used, but 100 percent down payment was required in these cases.

In a development totally unrelated to the financial crisis, the government also privatized many state firms that remained in its hands after the first privatization round. The objective here was not to regularize property in the odd sector but simply to reduce the size of the state.

Several means were used to privatize these companies. Private pension funds were allowed to purchase limited quantities of shares through the stock market, the so-called "institutional capitalism." Workers were given important incentives to become stockholders in the privatizing firms, such as access to their severance funds to pay for the shares ("labor capitalism"). Individual investors bought shares through the stock market or participated in the bidding processes ("traditional capitalism").

Several important state firms became private in this process, including the telephone and telecommunications companies, electricity generation and distribution firms, and the national airline. More time will still be needed ultimately to assess the performance of the newly private companies, but results so far have been generally encouraging. Also, returns on investment for new owners have been quite good, especially in energy distribution firms.

Some concerns have arisen about this second privatization round regarding changes in the program as the process evolved, the privatization of natural (though regulated) monopolies, and the subsidization of foreign investors. Nonetheless, the program has already scored important successes. It has provided a large dissemination of property in the privatized firms, the access of workers to ownership in the companies, and the solid financial position with which newly private firms started.

How to Privatize?

While privatization is now a worldwide trend, one should stop well short of thinking that there is a unique way to carry it out. The Chilean process can provide useful lessons for other countries in Latin America and elsewhere, where a significant private market already exists. Privatization in Eastern Europe and the former Soviet Union, however, is a totally distinct phenomenon, for which the same procedure that Chile used rather successfully in its second round should not be recommended. In most countries of Eastern Europe and the former Soviet Union, the state owns over 90 percent of industrial capital. Private markets are tiny and only recently emerging, and stock markets are only starting to be organized. Moreover, placing a value on state firms is a highly cumbersome task. Thus, a quick, free distribution of shares in many state firms would have to play a major role in the process, a procedure that would not be recommended for Latin America.

Notes

1.   Related debts from the purchase of government property, however, were not finally extinguished until 1982.

2.   Ten years after the privatization, in all but one of the firms they studied, the return on investment was lower than that of a short-term bank deposit.

References

Foxley, Alejandro. 1983. *Latin American Experiments in Neoconservative Economics*. Berkeley: University of California Press.

Hachette, Dominique, and Rolf Luders. 1987. *Aspects of the Privatization Process: The Case of Chile 1974-1985*. Mimeograph. (April). Washington, D.C.: The World Bank.

Larraín, Felipe. 1991. "Public Sector Behavior in a Highly Indebted Country: The Contrasting Chilean Experience." *In The Public Sector and the Latin American Crises*, eds. F. Larraín and M. Selowsky. San Francisco: ICS Press.

From Emergency Employment to Social Investment: Alleviating Poverty in Chile

Carol Graham

During the recent transition to democracy in Chile, the extent of present-day poverty and appropriate government anti-poverty policy were among the most heated and divisive issues. As in the debate over human rights violations, at issue in the diagnosis are both the extent and the severity of the problem, with ideology playing a major role in positions taken. Even more controversial than the disagreement over the measurement of poverty is the question of fundamental principles underlying the design of social welfare policy needed to attack poverty.

Proponents of neoliberal economic thought see poverty as a direct result of individuals' inability to participate in the market economy, arguing that poverty can be eliminated by meeting basic needs. Most others define poverty and its causes much more broadly, taking into account socioeconomic structural and cultural factors. While these concepts are not necessarily totally at odds with each other, the resulting policy prescriptions tend to conflict.

Another reason for the divisiveness of the debate on poverty in Chile is the nature of the regime which began to implement the dramatic economic structural reform process. Chile's steady growth rates, low inflation, and liberal trade and investment regimes are now looked upon as models for the rest of Latin America. Its political legacy, however, presents a paradox.

Carol Graham is a visiting fellow in the Vice Presidency for Human Resources at the World Bank and professorial lecturer in Latin American Studies at Johns Hopkins University School of Advanced International Studies.

This chapter is a slightly revised version of a Brookings Institution occasional paper, published originally as Carol Graham, 1991, *From Emergency Employment to Social Investment: Alleviating Poverty in Chile* (Washington, D.C.: The Brookings Institution).

121

On September 11, 1973, the Chilean armed forces, led by General Augusto Pinochet, broke with a long tradition of democratic government by ousting Socialist President Salvador Allende in a bloody coup. When Pinochet intervened, Chile's economy and polity were in chaos, suffering from hyperinflation, rampant strikes, shortages of basic goods, and political stalemate. The Allende government was crippled by lack of coherence within its governing socialist coalition and antagonistic and increasingly violent behavior by extremists of the right and of the left.

The virulently anticommunist Pinochet regime launched a radical reorientation in economic policy and adopted the neoliberal economic philosophy of Milton Friedman and the "Chicago school" as of 1975.

The Pinochet regime also freed itself of political constraints and the rule of law by suppressing all forces of organized opposition (banning opposition political parties and labor unions), while decreeing a series of market-oriented reforms. In the short term these measures dramatically increased unemployment, cut back social welfare benefits for all but the very poorest groups, and induced severe recession as well as unrestricted competition from foreign trade. Although the long-term economic results have been quite positive for different sectors, many of those Chileans eventually benefiting view this progress as having been achieved at the cost of seventeen years of repressive dictatorship and unconstrained human rights abuses, as well as the dismantling of one of the most progressive and comprehensive social welfare structures on the continent.

In October 1988, Chile, by its 1980 constitution, was required to submit General Pinochet's continued rule to a national plebiscite, leading to his defeat. In December 1989, Patricio Aylwin, the centrist head of a coalition of Christian and Social Democrats, won the presidency in the first open democratic Chilean election since President Allende's September 1970 victory. General Pinochet stayed on as commander in chief of the armed forces. Not surprisingly, the return of electoral politics generated increased debate on Chile's economic policy. People asked about ongoing poverty and on how — or whether — to reform Chile's social welfare structure.

Chile's active state role in social welfare policy dates back at least to the 1920s; it was substantially expanded during the presidencies of Christian Democrat Eduardo Frei (1964–1970) and Socialist Allende (1970–1973). The military government that seized power in 1973 took a dramatically different approach, focusing on increasing basic services for the poorest of the poor, while drastically cutting state involvement in social welfare provision for the rest of society.

The post-1973 military government was remarkably successful at protecting the social welfare of the very poorest 10 percent during a time of severe economic crisis and sharply curtailed fiscal expenditures. Despite overall reductions in per capita social welfare expenditures, total spending for the poorest decile (10 percent) increased, and indicators such as infant mortality continued to improve overall (see table 1).[1] In addition, many of the poorest who had been excluded from benefits under the previous system were reached for the first time. This record is particularly notable compared with that of most of Chile's neighbors.[2]

Table 1
Infant Mortality in Chile, Selected Years, 1920-1989
Deaths per 1,000 live births

Year	Rate	Year	Rate
1920	>250.0	1972	72.7
1952	104.0	1974	65.2
1955	116.0	1976	56.6
1960	120.3	1978	40.1
1962	109.2	1980	33.0
1965	95.4	1988	20.0
1970	82.2	1989	19.0

Sources: Dagmar Raczynski and Cesar Oyarzo, "¿Por qué Cae La Tasa de Mortalidad Infantil en Chile en Los Años 70?" Documento de Trabajo (Santiago: CIEPLAN, August 1981): and World Bank, *World Development Report 1990* (Washington, World Bank, 1990).

Success for the poorest of the poor was achieved at a cost to the slightly less poor and working class. The Pinochet regime slashed services to the working and middle class, something that few democratic governments could, or would, have attempted. Many more people than the very poorest, even those still at the margin of the poverty line, for example, lost access to critical services such as health insurance. Furthermore, the military's radical new policy could never have been implemented without the preexisting social safety network and experienced and efficient ministries in the health and education sectors.

The shift in approach to social welfare policy, and the authoritarian manner in which it was implemented, redefined social services from citizens' rights to state subsidies only for those who could not provide for themselves, giving the use of state services a social stigma. Because of this approach, combined with the authoritarian nature of the military government, critics dismissed the regime's policies as *paternalistic* and palliative. Those same critics often overlook the military regime's progress in alleviating extreme poverty.

Now, with the benefit of hindsight, it is possible to examine the successes and failures of the regime's social welfare policy in a more objective manner. The military regime's record may be relevant for other countries seeking to protect the poorest at a time of severe economic crisis or structural change. At the same time, its lessons, like its achievements, are limited by the extent to which the military's political control objectives accompanied its policies for poverty alleviation.

Although its policies for the poor were constrained by its authoritarian nature and goals, the military regime's attempt to devote a larger proportion of social expenditure to the groups that traditionally were at the margin of state benefits is still worthy of attention (Vergara 1989, 24). The military's approach to poverty alleviation stemmed from a dual logic. First was the efficient use of limited resources for social welfare; spending was directed at meeting the basic needs of the poorest and most needy. Targeting of state expenditure was in keeping with the military's neoliberal economic philosophy.[3]

However, as the recession deepened and unemployment reached crisis proportions, this limited strategy was broadened to include large-scale emergency employment programs. This was a response to the threat of political destabilization posed by massive unemployment as much as it was an effort to meet basic needs.

This dual logic had contradictory effects on the poor. On the one hand, basic needs were effectively and efficiently attended to, but, on the other, the authoritarian preclusion of autonomous political initiative prevented the poor from participating in solutions to their own problems. This led to alienation and dependency.

The Aylwin government took a very different approach to poverty alleviation, making social policy one of the four main pillars of its governing platform, along with maintenance of macroeconomic equilibrium, integration into the international economy, and fostering investment and long-term growth.[4] The Frei government, elected in December 1993, was expected to continue and even broaden the Alywin government's four pillars. Yet even in the electoral campaign, the Aylwin government made its commitment to maintaining macroeconomic equilibrium very clear and stressed that progress on the social front would be limited by the government's ability to pay for it. Most policy changes were financed by a tax reform passed in the first few months of the government's tenure. Along with a series of other policies introduced in its first two years in power, including a program to improve the quality of education in the thousand or so most disadvantaged primary schools in the country and a large-scale training program for unskilled youth run out of the labor ministry,[5] the government implemented a demand-based social fund, the Fund for Solidarity and Social Investment (FOSIS), to respond to proposals presented by local governments or community organizations. Although the military regime's progress in alleviating extreme poverty provided the Aylwin government a firm basis for a more comprehensive social welfare policy, the authoritarian legacy created substantial barriers at the local and municipal levels to the implementation of a demand-based, decentralized policy. This raises numerous questions about the role of politics in the implementation of policies for the poor. Such issues are particularly difficult to resolve in a context where the political process has been stalled for almost two decades: Many people are participating for the first time and are particularly vulnerable to partisan manipulation. Yet the decentralized, demand-based design of FOSIS gives it an inherent advantage in coping with political issues, as it both builds local participation into its operations and limits the potential for centralized political control. The experience of FOSIS, like that of the military, will provide useful lessons for future efforts to alleviate poverty.

The Extent of Poverty in Chile

There is a substantial amount of debate over the extent of poverty in Chile, with estimates ranging from 15 to 45 percent of the population.[6] The Aylwin campaign referred to 5 million poor — or 40 percent of the population — but some independent sources use lower figures. Pilar Vergara, combining the results of several studies, as well as 1985 figures for government subsidies for the extreme poor, estimated that the population in extreme poverty was 3,197,000 people, or 31 percent of the population.[7] Exact figures aside, poverty remains a prevalent issue (see table 2).

Table 2
Indigent and Poor Households in Santiago,
Selected Years, 1969-1989
Percent

Status	1969	1979	1988	1989
Indigent[a]	8.4	11.7	22.9	14.9
Poor[b]	20.1	24.3	26.8	26.3
Nonpoor	71.5	64.0	50.3	58.8

Sources: Programa de Economía del Trabajo, *Encuestas de Empleo: Santiago* (Santiago, PET, 1990): and Erik Haindl and others, *Gasto Social Efectivo* (Santiago: Universidad Católica, 1989).

a. Family income insufficient to meet basic food needs.

b. Insufficient income to meet other basic needs: a level of income less than twice that of indigence.

Despite the debate over numbers of poor and kinds of poverty, empirical evidence shows improvement in the indicators that most effectively reflect extreme poverty, such as infant mortality and incidence of child malnutrition. According to these indicators, Chile's position vis-à-vis its neighbors improved dramatically between 1975 and 1989 (see table 3).[8] The explanation for this lies in the extensive social welfare system that existed before 1973 and in the military government's efforts to turn that system into a safety net for the extremely poor.

Table 3
Infant Mortality in Selected Latin American Countries,
Selected Years, 1960-1989
Deaths per 1,000 live births

Year	Chile	Peru	Bolivia	Brazil	Mexico
1960	114	163	167	118	91
1965	101	130	160	104	82
1975	79	65	n.a.	n.a.	50
1980	43	88	131	77	56
1985	20	91	117	67	50
1989	19	79	106	59	40

Source: World Bank, *World Development Report,* various years.
n.a. Not available.

In part because the exact numbers are difficult to measure, the results of this process of change are the basis for the ongoing debate on the extent and nature of poverty. Although progress was made in meeting basic needs such as nutrition, preventive health care, and primary education, it was partly at the expense of other social needs such as housing, curative health care, and advanced education. Extreme poverty — defined as the inability to meet basic nutritional needs — was reduced. Poverty — more broadly defined as the inability to meet a variety of needs adequately — was not reduced and may have been exacerbated. Per capita spending on health, education, and housing in 1986 was only 40 percent of the 1970 level, for example (Vergara 1989, 44). Distribution of income became more inequitable.[9] As the majority of new spending was targeted to the poorest and to the financing of the government's special employment programs (discussed below), a large number of beneficiaries of the pre-1973 social welfare system either lost access or had their benefits cut substantially. For example, as many as 2.1 million workers — or over one-half the labor force — lacked access to social security in 1987.[10] Before detailing the military regime's record, therefore, it is necessary briefly to describe the previous system.

Social Services before 1973

A labor code was introduced in Chile as early as 1931; preventive health care was extended to workers' families in 1938; and the Junta Nacional de Auxilio Escolar (National Junta for Student Aid) was set up in 1952 to provide food and other essentials for low-income students. The 1964–1970

Christian Democratic Frei government placed major emphasis on redistribution of income and increased expenditure in all social welfare areas, with a particular focus on social security and education. The 1970–1973 Allende government increased emphasis on redistribution and focused on labor rather than the middle class. Under both administrations, improvements were made in housing, curative medicine, and high school and university education. From 1920 to 1972, social welfare spending grew ten times faster than national income, resulting in a vast coverage by the state's health, education, and social security systems. As a result, even after the Pinochet government made substantial reductions, average social welfare expenditure as a percentage of GNP remained comparable to that of several OECD nations (see table 4).[11]

Table 4
Public Social Expenditure in Selected Countries, 1980
Percent of GNP

Country	Social expenditure	Country	Social expenditure
Latin America		*OECD*	
Costa Rica	18.0	Germany	26.9
Chile	17.3	Canada	22.4
Brazil	11.5	Spain	14.3
Mexico	10.1	United States	16.3
Panama	13.6	France	25.7
Uruguay	13.9	Greece	14.7
Venezuela	10.2	Holland	34.8
Bolivia	6.0	Italy	29.9
Ecuador	6.1	Japan	13.2
El Salvador	6.3	United Kingdom	25.3
Guatemala	4.2	Sweden	22.0

Source: José Pablo Arellano, *Políticas Sociales y Desarrollo: Chile 1924-1984* (Santiago: CIEPLAN, 1985), p. 290.

There was a great deal of room for improvement in Chile's social welfare system, however. The system was not a product of coordinated planning, but rather the result of a decades-long bargaining process that involved various groups of organized workers and the state. Workers in the most vital sectors of the economy, including copper mining and railroads, made the earliest strides and attained the most benefits. Numerous pension and health insurance schemes varied according to industry. The social security system in particular reflected the eclectic process by which it had been formed and the differentiation between economic sectors. Because of this differentiation, the unorganized workers in the poorest sector were to a large extent marginalized from the social welfare system.[12] Two scholars described it in 1974:

> This process has given rise to a number of groups of workers that have a growing and at times conflicting influence. . . . Access by [low-income] groups to social security benefits is very limited, either because they have no way of joining the system, or because their employers fail to pay their share of the contribution, or simply because there is a large amount of discrimination in the granting of benefits. Thus, the social security system. . .in practice only has a redistributive effect internally within the groups of relatively well organized workers who, because they are organized, enjoy higher incomes (Foxley and Muñoz 1974, 31, 39).

Although the social welfare system was extensive and highly developed, particularly in relation to other Latin American countries, it clearly had flaws, the most important being the exclusion of the poorest.[13] The military government set out to restructure the system dramatically, with two overriding goals. The first — a political as well as economic one — was curbing the power of organized labor. The second was targeting the poorest groups as the primary beneficiaries of state involvement in the social welfare arena.

Policies for the Poor under Military Rule

The military regime's application of neoliberal economic philosophy to social welfare policy was a marked departure from the Chilean state's traditional progressive role in income distribution and welfare. The regime viewed poverty as a result of rigidities in the social structure and distortions in the functioning of the market. Overcoming it, therefore, did not require changing the existing economic and social order or direct state intervention in the economy. It was sufficient to identify those groups existing below a basic standard of living and to provide them with the goods and services that they needed to meet that standard (Vergara 1989, 23). The state's role was to provide assistance — in the form of subsidies — for those unable to take care of themselves. Subsidies were not designed to guarantee or enhance equity. Overall state expenditure in the social sector, both as a percentage of GNP and per capita, was initially cut. Although as a percentage of GNP social expenditure returned to its early 1970s level by the early 1980s, in per capita terms it continued to remain below traditional levels (see table 5) (Vergara 1989, 43; Haindl et al. 1989). This was exacerbated by the regime's regressive wage and tax policy. At the same time, social spending on the poorest sectors increased in both relative and absolute terms.

Table 5
Public Social Expenditure in Chile,
Selected Years, 1969-1985

	Expenditure (millions of 1978 pesos)		Percent of
Year	Total	Per capita	GNP
1969	41,551	4,517	18.7
1970	45,330	4,853	19.8
1974	53,592	5,345	16.5
1976	40,293	3,885	16.7
1978	45,137	4,205	16.7
1980	41,968	3,779	16.6
1982	49,031	4,268	22.8
1984	n.a.	n.a.	20.7
1985	n.a.	n.a.	19.5

Source: Alejandro Foxley and Dagmar Raczynski, "Vulnerable Groups and Recessionary Situations: The Case of Children and the Young in Chile," *World Development*, vol. 12 (March 1984), p. 228: and Haindl and others, *Gasto Social Efectivo*. n.a. Not available.

The main thrust of the military's efforts was to increase the efficiency of the social welfare system through effective targeting of the poorest, while at the same time decentralizing the system. The focus on the poorest corrected the system's bias toward formal-sector labor. The targeting process was directed by the National Planning Office (ODEPLAN). Decentralization resulted in the creation of thirteen administrative regions, the creation within ODEPLAN of the Regional Secretariat for Coordination and Planning (SERPLAC), and then a gradual devolution of responsibilities to municipal governments (Castañeda 1990). In theory, decentralization began a process of increasing local government independence, both financial and programmatic, from the central government.[14] Municipalities were responsible for administering a wide array of subsidies targeted at the extremely poor, as well as the government's employment programs (discussed below). Yet because municipalities neither had democratic elections during the military years nor allowed the participation of local groups, they remained a link in a highly centralized chain of command.[15]

A network of subsidies for those in extreme poverty was implemented. Some were continuations or variations of preexisting programs, whose range of coverage was cut to include only the poorest poverty deciles; others were new programs. Eligibility for all programs was determined by a poverty index (social stratification measurement system) called the Ficha (Comités Comunes de Acción Social — CAS). The Ficha, based on household surveys conducted by municipalities, used a variety of criteria to determine a person's position in five poverty deciles. Benefits were supposed to cover deciles 1–3, but in reality usually reached only the first two. The Ficha used a wide range of measures, from ownership of household appliances to education and employment. It was widely criticized because it did not use income levels as a measure. With the economic crises of the 1970s and 1980s, there were many cases of benefits being denied to homeowners who had lost their jobs and were now below the poverty line or being denied to owners of household appliances such as refrigerators and gas stoves which had long since ceased to function (Scholnik and Teitelboim 1988).

Several of the government programs, some preexisting and others new, are worthy of mention. The national complementary feeding program (PNAC), created in 1954, gave universal coverage to all the beneficiaries of the national health system. It provided supplementary food to 80 percent of pregnant and nursing mothers, infants, and preschool children. In 1974 the program was cut back to target only the poorest or malnourished groups. The 1985 socioeconomic characteristics survey (CASEN) showed that the poorest 30 percent received 49.5 percent of PNAC benefits, while the 30 percent at the top of the income scale received only 11 percent. PNAC was largely responsible for continued improvement in infant mortality and malnutrition rates despite the severity of the economic crisis (Vergara 1989).

In 1973 a variety of programs were initiated in preschool care and education. Most notable was the National Association of Child Care Centers (JUNJI). JUNJI provided food, day care, and a monthly subsidy of four thousand pesos per child for children in CAS level 1. This subsidy was a substantial amount for poor families; it equaled 60 percent of the minimum wage. JUNJI were not always well attended, though, for several reasons. Some were cultural, such as an unwillingness to recognize publicly that someone else was taking care of one's children. In other cases, ironically, the material support requirements, such as certain clothing items or minimal payment, precluded the poorest (Vergara 1989). Allowing local participation in program implementation could easily have solved these problems, but such an approach was anathema to the regime's authoritarian political logic.

The school lunch program, created under President Frei in 1964, covered all children from ages six to fourteen. Even with universal coverage, the program cost only 5 percent of the public-sector education budget. The military regime made several attempts to cut eligibility for the program, reducing the number of beneficiaries and the amount of rations (see table 6). The program was restricted to children under 6 and pregnant and nursing mothers, and the caloric content of free milk was increased. Because coverage was no longer universal, the recipients of school lunches were forced to declare their poverty publicly. Despite severe cutbacks in the program, it continued to function reasonably well and maintained equally good coverage in rural as well as urban regions, which is rare in antipoverty programs (Vergara 1989). The program could continue to function despite cutbacks because of its long-term existence, experienced program personnel, and well-established distribution network. The revamping of the feeding programs was part of a broader policy of replacing general food subsidies with targeted nutrition policies; an example was the establishment of the Corporación de Nutrición Infantil (CONIN).

Table 6
School Feeding Programs in Chile, Selected Years
1970-1982

Thousands of meals

Year	Breakfasts	Lunches or dinners
1970	1,301.2	619.2
1973	1,445.6	674.3
1976	769.8	361.0
1979	759.4	294.5
1982	759.0	295.3

Source: Foxley and Raczynski, "Vulnerable Groups and Recessionary Situations," p. 239.

The military regime altered housing policies in a manner similar to the changes in other programs for the poor. State provision of low-cost housing was abandoned in favor of subsidies for the poorest (Vergara 1989, 205). Lots with basic services were provided for homes to be constructed by the recipients. At least half the subsidies leaked to the middle-income population, as the minimum savings ratio required precluded the poorest. In addition, housing subsidies did not cover the total cost of home acquisition or construction, and the poorest often lacked the necessary credit or technical skills. Finally, private-sector construction of low-cost homes resulted in their location in remote regions where it was cheaper to build, which entailed greater travel time and costs for inhabitants, as well as less access to community services.[16] The effects of the housing policies exemplify how the military's approach often served to stigmatize and alienate the poor rather than enhance their potential to participate in society.

The health care and social security systems were also revamped and tilted toward private provision for those who could afford it and state provision for those who could not. In the health sector, primary care for pregnant women, infants, and children was emphasized, with a reduction in expenditure on secondary and tertiary care and a corresponding decline in hospital services. Eligibility for free care was determined by an arbitrary income level cutoff, which left many people in the lower middle-income sector without access to secondary and tertiary care (Castañeda 1990). Preventive care was free. Pregnant women and children under age six received free universal coverage for all care, in contrast to before the reforms, when 90 percent of the entire population had received free care. There were two significant positive elements: the poorest, those without insurance, previously marginalized from the system, were able to attain access; and the system was decentralized, with the administration of health posts delegated to the municipalities (Vergara 1989). In social security, the military introduced a network of assistance pensions to provide minimum benefits for those without access to social security pensions. The disabled and the elderly whose incomes were less than 50 percent of the minimum pension also were eligible (Castañeda 1990).

Even harsh critics of the military regime accept the importance of its achievements in combating extreme poverty (Vergara 1989, 24-25).[17] Unfortunately, the military's authoritarian nature and approach undermined the potential of its policies. The government's narrow and vertical approach to poverty alleviation — providing subsidies rather than investment in human capital — was palliative and encouraged dependence. A segment of the population was publicly stigmatized and became increasingly dependent on the state for subsidies to meet its basic needs.

Emergency Employment Programs

Few programs implemented by the military regime created as much controversy as the emergency employment programs, the minimum employment program (PEM), and the occupational program for heads of household (POJH). Almost all observers agree that the special employment programs were necessary to alleviate the effects of the economic crisis, as Chile's open unemployment rate averaged 18.1 percent between 1974 and 1982 (Stallings and Kaufman 1989). While most observers agree that the programs helped many of the poorest, they also harshly criticize the manner in which the programs were implemented. Nowhere is the contradiction between the vertical approach of authoritarian regime and its efforts to ameliorate poverty more evident than in the PEM-POJH experience.[18] The emergency employment programs consumed large shares both of the central government's social spending and of municipal resources.[19] In 1983, at the height of the economic crisis, PEM and POJH employed close to 500,000 people, or 11 percent of the country's labor force (see table 7).[20]

Table 7
Enrollment in Special Employment Programs in Chile,
1975-1988ᵃ

Thousands

Year	PEM	POJH	PIMO	Others	Total
1975	72.7	—	—	—	72.7
1976	157.8	—	—	—	157.8
1977	173.2	—	—	—	173.2
1978	117.6	—	—	—	117.6
1979	161.5	—	—	—	161.5
1980	203.1	—	—	—	203.1
1981	168.1	—	—	—	168.1
1982	336.5	102.8	—	—	439.2
1983	263.8	221.9	6.8	4.1	496.7
1984	170.9	207.6	13.6	19.1	411.2
1985	105.6	171.4	4.8	48.3	330.1
1986	61.4	122.8	1.0	42.9	228.1
1987	22.2	64.2	12.8ᵇ	5.1ᵇ	104.4
1988	3.5	5.3	11.4ᵇ	1.2ᵇ	21.4

Sources: Data from SERPLAC Metropolitana, Intendencia de Santiago: and PREALC, *Empleos de Emergencia* (Santiago: PREALC, 1988).

a. Monthly averages.
b. Santiago metropolitan region only.

Program History

The military first initiated the minimum employment program in March 1975 as a response to deep economic recession and the resulting high levels of unemployment. The government gave the employment crisis high priority primarily because it posed a threat of political destabilization. The perceived threat was great enough that the government waived its usual fiscal caution and allotted whatever resources were necessary to alleviate the crisis.[21] PEM was initially implemented in an improvisational, reactive manner and provided extremely low-skilled work, such as street and park cleaning. As the crisis dragged on and unemployment increased, the program for heads of household was set up in September 1982 to provide higher-skilled workers with better salaries and to produce more sophisticated public works. By the mid-1980s, as the employment "crisis" became less pressing, and perhaps because the military recognized the limited long-term benefits of the employment programs as well as some of their negative aspects, a few more innovative programs were introduced. The labor-intensive program (PIMO) subsidized private-sector hiring in labor-intensive projects. An expansion program for professionals (PEP) and a national training program for youth were also introduced. As the economy recovered and unemployment was gradually reduced, falling to approximately 6 percent in 1989, the programs were gradually phased out — PEM and POJH by the end of 1988 and PIMO at the end of 1989.

PEM was the largest and longest lasting of the three programs, employing more than 336,000 workers, or 9.2 percent of Chile's labor force, in 1982. It is to date the largest employment program of its kind in Latin America. PEM was intended to provide temporary compensation for laid-off workers in the context of a severe recession. The program paid the equivalent of one-fourth of the minimum wage, usually for a partial day of labor. The minimum monthly wage in Chile in 1987 was approximately 12,500 pesos, or $56, and a monthly minimum family basket was calculated in 1986 at 8,000 pesos (Graham 1990; Scholnik and Teitelboim 1988).

To be eligible to join PEM, workers had to be over eighteen and not be receiving any other form of government compensation. They worked seven hours or less per day, five days a week. The works executed included creating public parks, street cleaning, painting public buildings, and building sanitation facilities in poor areas. The percentage of female workers in PEM grew with time, particularly after the introduction of POJH. Fifty-seven percent of PEM workers had completed basic education, 33 percent had a high school degree, and 5 percent had a higher technical or university degree (Graham 1990).

Along with PEM, POJH was responsible for providing the bulk of employment relief during the crisis years (see table 7). POJH was intended specifically for heads of household and was more sophisticated in design than PEM. To be eligible for POJH, workers had to be unemployed heads of household (not students) between ages eighteen and sixty-five and to have had some stable job or profession before. While works were similar to those of PEM, there were different scales of work and salary according to skill. POJH workers were also paid more than PEM workers, earning approximately 40 percent of the official minimum monthly wage (5,000 pesos, or $36) for full-time work (Graham 1990).

The composition of the POJH work force reflects the different populations targeted. Seventy-four percent of POJH workers were men; 44 percent were between ages twenty-six and thirty-five; and 77 percent were married, widowed, or separated. Education levels in the two programs were similar, however. Fifty-five percent of the POJH workers had a primary education; 37 percent had a high school degree; and 5 percent had a university or higher technical degree. The majority (56 percent) had previously been blue-collar workers (PREALC 1988). Neither PEM or POJH workers had any sort of guarantee of job stability; they were, however, eligible for the free state health care services designated for persons below a certain income level.

PIMO, initiated at the end of 1983, was designed to encourage private-sector involvement in labor-intensive projects. After bidding for projects selected by the central government in conjunction with municipalities, private-sector firms were eligible for a subsidy for each post created. The subsidy could not exceed 20,500 pesos, or $91 monthly, per post. PIMO workers were of various levels, but in general were more skilled than those in the other programs and were salaried rather than subsidized. The disadvantage of PIMO labor was that it was more difficult to target poor groups, in part because most of the works took place in the city and usually required a certain skill level. PIMO cost the government slightly over 28,000 pesos a month per post, while POJH averaged slightly over 6,679 pesos per post created. PIMO generated 25,000 posts at its height in 1987 (Graham 1990).

PEP was created in March 1985 for unemployed professionals, who were employed at a salary of 34,483 pesos, or $157 a month, to meet unfilled needs in state ministries or municipalities. Although the scale of the program was small — approximately 250 people a year — it did at least provide unemployed professionals the opportunity to use their skills and earn a salary more appropriate to their capacity than could have been provided by either PEM or POJH. PEP ran through the end of 1987 (SERPLAC 1990).

The national training program was established in November 1986 to train or prepare workers in special programs for entry into other jobs. The target population was youths between the ages of eighteen and twenty-eight. From November 1986 through March 1987, when the program was phased out, 11,000 workers, primarily from PEM and POJH, completed training programs. The average cost of enrolling a worker in a ninety-day training program was 6,670 pesos. Twenty-five percent of those who enrolled in the programs found private-sector jobs by the end of 1987 (SERPLAC 1990). Given the duration and extensive nature of the special employment programs, the training programs seem to have been an afterthought of limited scale.[22] One can only speculate about the internal logic that generated this shift in approach, albeit a limited one, but the ability to adapt to a changing social and political context was not out of character with the Pinochet regime's record of being sophisticated and efficient as well as repressive.

Administration and Implementation

All the special employment programs were under the jurisdiction of the *intendéncias* (regional administrations) and administered by the municipalities, who chose the works that were implemented. Communal committees were set up for that purpose in each municipality, each composed of the mayor, an urban adviser, the head of communal services for the municipality, three representatives from the communal union of the municipality, and two representatives from other communal groups (Graham 1990). In theory, this implied decentralized program administration that incorporated local participation; this would have been a departure from the typical implementation of aid programs, which are controlled by the center as instruments of patronage in much of Latin America.[23] In practice, it was merely a vertical extension of central government authority. Mayors were appointed rather than elected, as were the representatives of local neighborhood organizations. Thus there was no genuine incorporation of local participation. Differences in implementation between municipalities in implementation primarily depended on the varying degrees of commitment among the mayors to both municipalities and programs.[24]

In theory and in design, the special employment programs in Chile were superior to many of their counterparts or successors in other Latin countries.[25] In practice, however, their potential was severely limited by the authoritarian approach of the Pinochet government, by the ad hoc manner in which the programs were implemented in the early stages, and by the low level of wages paid.[26] Critics came to see PEM as creating a permanent worker underclass and as a means of social control for the Pinochet government, saying, for example, "The PEM as an institution. . .appears mainly as a mechanism of authoritarian control, where negotiations for the right to work and a fair salary are dominated by the threat of hunger and repression" (Ruiz-Tagle and Urmaneta 1984, 5). Even program officials admit that although the nature of the economic crisis dictated giving the employment issue immediate attention, experience was lacking. Thus there was a great deal of improvisation in the early stages of the program. PEM labor was misused at times, as when several hundred workers swept one downtown Santiago street.[27]

Program workers were often used to build projects for the military, such as an Air Force aerodrome,[28] or for the wealthy, such as an access road to the airport for the northern suburbs of Santiago.[29] Even where community improvements were made, the absence of local participation was blatantly obvious. In the municipality of La Cisterna, for example, POJH workers built a huge amphitheater and a football stadium. The amphitheater is currently closed to the public, and the football stadium is leased to a private football company most of the time.[30] The same amount of resources could have been used to create substantial amounts of smaller-scale infrastructure more readily available to the community — such as schools, parks, and small community centers — and more relevant to the workers in the program. Work sometimes entailed extremely heavy labor, for example, carrying rocks from the amphitheater site to the football stadium site. The hundreds of men pushing wheelbarrows full of rocks were described as "a line of worker ants" by the project administrator. Little wonder that worker resentment resulted in a great deal of tension, which exploded at times, as in the attempted burning of the amphitheater in 1986.[31]

Program Effects

Once established, this negative image affected both worker morale and program potential. Workers had little incentive, given the salary levels and lack of opportunity for advancement in the programs. In addition, the misuse of labor, in many cases, was extremely demoralizing. "All prefer to do anything other than to enroll in the famous PEM. . .because it is the worst that there could be, like the ultimate humiliation of the worker" (Politzer 1985, 36). When POJH workers were given the opportunity to create productive infrastructure works or projects that they deemed worthwhile, worker morale increased despite the fact that wages did not.[32]

This negative image had long-term effects on workers. Several private-sector representatives voiced reservations about hiring former PEM and POJH workers, because of the poor working habits and discipline in the program.[33] "But then, often the participation in these programs resulted in deterioration in labor discipline, loss of good working habits, and corruption. After a certain period, all this ends up causing irreparable damage for many workers" (Vergara 1989, 329). Even when improvements were made, such as the differentiation of payment scales in POJH and the introduction of PIMO and the national training program, the programs were not able to shed the negative image that had been created from the start.

The government included emergency employment program workers as employed persons in its statistics, which made a major difference in reported unemployment levels. A difference of over 10 percent in the level of open unemployment obviously had political as well as economic significance. This difference was even greater in poor areas, where unemployment was much higher as was participation in the special employment programs. In some Santiago *poblaciones* (shantytowns) up to 30 percent of the labor force was employed by PEM and POJH.[34] Despite the bad reputation of the programs, they were a major factor in reducing social unrest in the face of unprecedented unemployment levels. Even harsh critics of the programs agree that they alleviated the frustration and alienation that would have occurred had such a large number of unemployed workers remained at home with no foresee-able opportunities for work. In this instance, the opportunity to work, even for an inadequate wage, had some inherent value.[35]

As with all outside interventions or aid programs, the employment programs had unforeseen side effects at the community level. The most notable were the effects on women, who accounted for 75 percent of PEM participants in 1986. PEM was much more popular among women than among men, for several reasons. Because of substantial discrimination against female participation in the formal labor market, PEM often provided women with their first opportunity to earn an income, no matter how minimal. For female-headed households, the opportunity to earn desperately needed income in close proximity to home was often invaluable. For women who were second-income earners, the PEM income provided them with financial independence for the first time. Most PEM work was less physically demanding than that of

POJH. In PEM's latter stages, workers were often organized into productive workshops. Thus women found a new means of social interaction in a context where participating in autonomous organizations was often dangerous. The side effects on male-female relationships, such as an increase in divorces and marital problems, were at times troublesome.[36] These stemmed from two causes. Males lost their role as sole providers for their families, and women's independence increased with their new financial independence.

A Flawed Approach

One of the programs' major flaws resulted more from the military government's approach to poverty than from the nature of the programs themselves. Because the regime narrowly defined poverty as the result of market failure and dismissed broader structural definitions, it made little attempt to link its employment efforts with overall social policies. There was no conception of using the programs as a means to invest in human capital or to increase the capacity of the poor to generate income. Only in 1986, with the formation of the national training program, was a broader vision of the employment programs proposed. At this point it was clearly too little, too late. Considering the amount of resources that were invested in these programs, and their proportionate share of social welfare spending, a valuable opportunity for a long-term investment in human capital was lost.

The programs were phased out as the employment rate improved, because to some extent they were no longer necessary. Yet the programs had also served as an alternative source of employment for the structurally unemployed — those workers (largely youths and women) who are marginalized from formal-sector jobs regardless of the state of the economy. There was a correlation between the programs and the level of unemployment in the mid-1980s (see table 8). The fact that the workers were often stigmatized by working in the programs created even greater barriers to entrance into the formal sector. Underemployment rates and the size of the informal sector remained the same, or grew, in the decade the programs were in place.[37]

Table 8
Labor Participation in Chile, by Employment Category, 1982 and 1987
Numbers in millions

Employment category	October-December 1982		March-May 1987	
	Number	*Percent*	*Number*	*Percent*
Employed	2.539	69.4	3.758	86.5
Unemployed	0.718	19.6	0.420	9.7
Special employment programs	0.404	11.0	0.165	3.8
Total labor force	3.661	100.0	4.343	100.0

Source: PREALC, *Empleos de Emergencia.*

The extent to which short-term relief for the poor gives them the future capacity to help themselves is one of the key measures of success of antipoverty interventions. In the case of PEM and POJH, this clearly was not a consideration. This indicates the extent to which the employment programs were used as a means of political control as well as of alleviating poverty. The military's approach to alleviating poverty was to create a segment of the poor who depended on the state for survival and were publicly stigmatized as the sole users of state-provided employment, health services, and benefits such as school lunches. PEM and POJH, the government's most visible and far-reaching programs to subsidize income, were a central part of this strategy. By joining PEM and POJH, a worker was then eligible for a group of subsidies that, if fully utilized, added up to more than a minimum wage income. Yet this net of subsidies entailed no participation, training, or communal participation in service provision (Vergara 1989, 329).

The government had little interest in sponsoring autonomous community organizations, and indeed PEM and POJH were seen as a means to discourage them. Traditional community organizations — including religious ones — were seen as suspect.[38] Thus those who were most active in community organizations were the least likely to participate in PEM and POJH. Workers were often treated in an authoritarian and deprecating manner; women often suffered sexual abuse by the *capataces* (field supervisors);[39] and workers were sometimes forced to go to Pinochet marches.[40] Control over PEM and POJH labor — and thus over access to desperately needed income and employment — signified substantial power.[41] Demonstrative of the extent to which that power was utilized for political purposes was the aftermath of the first PEM worker protests in 1983, which took place in the context of the antigovernment unrest of that year: Program size and enrollment levels were cut in the communities where protests occurred.[42] While this sort of manipulation of emergency employment workers has occurred in other countries, such as Peru,[43] it created a great deal more resentment in Chile, where workers were more educated, had a history of strong organization, and were more politically conscious than most of their Latin counterparts.

The authoritarian nature of the PEM and POJH programs was perceived at all different levels — observers and critics in the opposition camp, the beneficiaries, and nonparticipants in communities where the programs operated. Opinions range from the confrontation that "the POJH was the greatest misery that the dictatorship could have done for this country" to the assertion that PEM did nothing positive, nothing more than "take a few steps, sweep the street."[44] Informal-sector workers, who may have been earning the same as or even less than POJH income, often expressed pride that they were *not* in PEM and POJH, and that they were their own *patrones* (bosses).[45] What stands out is the overwhelmingly negative impression of the programs, which is confirmed by former program officials themselves. Other countries' experiences with state-sponsored employment have yielded more mixed reactions, particularly among beneficiaries, at least some of whom had a more positive view.[46] In the Chilean case, the reaction was due much more to the authoritarian manner and context in which the programs were implemented than to the design of the programs themselves.

Because the programs were so negatively perceived, and the regime and its municipalities were for the most part not concerned with electoral politics, the programs were rarely used for the purpose of political proselytizing, as has happened in many other countries. Yet this changed somewhat in the period before the 1988 plebiscite. Unlike the traditional party of the right (National Renovation), the pro-Pinochet party (the Independent Democratic Union) was extremely active at the grass-roots level and attempted to politicize the administration of the employment programs. At this point it became virtually impossible for the regime's nonsympathizers to have any role at all in the administration of the programs.[47] Yet the negative image of the employment programs clearly limited their potential for any political payoff. Politics are a much greater factor in the implementation of programs for the poor under democratic government, at both central and local government levels.

In evaluating the effects of the Pinochet government's emergency employment programs and comparing them with policies implemented by the Aylwin government, it is extremely important to note the different economic and political contexts. The emergency employment programs were able to reach a great number of people and mobilize a vast amount of resources very quickly at a time of severe economic crisis. Even extreme critics of the programs admit that they provided necessary — if insufficient — income support at a time of high unemployment and social pressure.[48] Had the crisis been short term in nature, then the programs might have been better suited to popular needs. Because they became semi-permanent institutions and the relative amount of investment in them increased, their lack of basis in a longer-term strategy for social development became more of a liability than it would have been otherwise.

One positive aspect of the programs was that they required work, although not always productive work, in exchange for the subsidy they provided. The most negative perceptions of the programs stemmed from the early stages, when productivity was not taken into account. It was perceived that workers were being denied their right to make a productive contribution to society. This perception remained even when improvements were made. Participants retained some stigma afterwards — of being considered lazy or unreliable, with poor work habits. Despite the drop in the open unemployment rate, many former program workers remained marginalized from formal-sector employment. The high value attributed to productivity as a part of employment is an important lesson for those implementing employment or compensation programs in any setting. The Aylwin government team has clearly incorporated this lesson into the design of its primary policy for the poor. Another extremely important lesson from the military experience that has been incorporated by the Aylwin administration is that however well designed a program may be in technical terms, its potential will be jeopardized if it is implemented in a top-down manner with no input from the beneficiaries.

Policies for the Poor after the Transition

The Aylwin government made no major changes in the structure of the social safety net. The government did take an immediate step to make the tax system more progressive by slightly increasing taxes for the wealthiest sectors, and all the revenue generated by the increase was directed at social sector spending. In addition to policies such as bettering the quality of public education and providing vocational training for unskilled youth, a major innovation for the poor under the Aylwin government was FOSIS. While the program is still in its initial stage and too new to evaluate [at the time the present research was done], it is possible to assert that FOSIS is a marked departure from the previous government's approach to policy toward the poor. At the same time, it builds upon the existing social safety net, which continues to be administered through the relevant ministries, as well as on the relatively strong economic base inherited from the military regime. Finally, it builds on the experience of the military government with a centrally run employment scheme and on the recent experiences of other countries, such as Bolivia, with decentralized social investment funds.

FOSIS is an autonomous fund set up within the planning ministry (MINEPLAN, successor to ODEPLAN), which responds to low-income communities' proposals for social welfare infrastructure and credit and technical support for productive activities, such as microenterprises. FOSIS operates with a small and highly trained staff, which is committed, at least in theory, to nonpartisan management of the program. The proposals, which come from local governments and nongovernmental organizations, must meet specific technical criteria, and the projects usually also entail some sort of voluntary community participation. The demand-based design of the program not only encourages, but also depends upon community participation. Participation by beneficiaries is important in poverty alleviation for two reasons. It is more likely to result in projects appropriate to local needs, and, by legitimizing the participation of the poor in bettering their communities and generating employment, it enhances their capacity to make the difficult progression from poverty to integration into the productive economy.

The creators of FOSIS had, as a starting point, a very different conceptual approach to poverty than did the military regime. Most of them were specialists in either poverty alleviation or employment and had years of experience in either international organizations or respected research institutes in Chile.[49] The designers of FOSIS were as attuned to fiscal constraints and the need for long-term economic viability as their military predecessors, but they were also concerned with helping the poor to overcome the additional barriers that exclude them from the productive economy. In the productive arena this includes access to credit, technology, and training; and in the social welfare arena, this includes projects to better the quality of life in poor communities — projects such as community centers, continuing support for preventive health care, recreational and cultural activities, and training courses for community workers, as well as improved access to information about rights, resources, and services (Flaño 1990).

The structure of FOSIS resembles that of social investment funds in other countries. It has an independent status in the state planning ministry, with the executive director appointed by, and directly accountable to, the president of the republic. Although FOSIS is committed to cooperative work with the sector ministries, this independent status gives it a flexible and heterogeneous character that sectoral ministries do not have. Funds will come from the central government budget and from foreign donors, although initial estimates of foreign donations were far too optimistic. The budget for 1991 is projected at $20 million, but may be substantially less.[50] The staff is small (fewer than one hundred people), highly trained, and deeply committed to the cause of alleviating poverty. In the case of Bolivia's Emergency Social Fund, such a combination proved highly effective.[51] While it is too early to evaluate FOSIS, early indications are that its staff will attempt to operate in an efficient and transparent manner.

FOSIS operates on three basic assumptions. The first is a recognized need for state action to ameliorate the effects of several years of economic adjustment. The second is that this action needs to take place outside the traditional social welfare activities of the state, recognizing the obvious limits of the authoritarian state and the need to incorporate local participation. The third assumption is that the state's approach to alleviating poverty has been limited and inflexible.

The design of FOSIS was heavily influenced by recent international experience with multisectoral development funds. Such funds are an outgrowth of the acknowledgment of limited state resources and a new emphasis on the role of the market in Latin America, as well as a recognition of the need to incorporate local participation and demand in the design of aid or antipoverty programs. They are "a sort of synthesis of the participatory thesis of the more progressive sectors of society with the thesis of the subsidizing nature of the state, propounded by the neoliberals."[52] Applicants must present economically viable social welfare projects that entail community or individual participation and support. Projects must demonstrate post-FOSIS viability. FOSIS can react to the heterogenous and decentralized nature of poverty in a way that is not possible for the state, which has to provide a certain basic and standard level of social welfare. Both areas of FOSIS activity, social development and support for productive enterprises, can be considered an investment in society: the former in health and welfare, and the latter in people's capacity to generate their own income and means of support.

FOSIS has an advantage over similar funds in other countries. Many of these, such as Bolivia's Emergency Social Fund, grow not out of a need to establish a new state role in social assistance, but of a need to establish a starting point where no effective state role existed. They operate outside the sectoral ministries not because the ministries are already filling certain sectoral roles, but because they are not filling any role. In this sense, FOSIS has a unique flexibility to support innovation in productive and social welfare activities, because basic health, education, and other social services for the poor are already available. From a technical standpoint, FOSIS has an opportunity to do exactly what its mission calls for: open a new role for the state in the social welfare.

FOSIS also has a strong base of nongovernmental organizations to rely upon. Unlike Bolivia, where nongovernmental organizations' activity is relatively new and their cooperation with state programs was largely underdeveloped, Chile has a long tradition of nongovernmental organization involvement in social welfare policy and a remarkable number of active nongovernmental organizations and church groups. Decentralization created some opportunities for these groups' participation in health, education, and housing.[53] These opportunities were, of course, limited by political considerations. With the transition to democracy and the introduction of FOSIS, the door was opened for a new stage of collaboration between nongovernmental organizations and the government.

Yet FOSIS also has to deal with the same problems that plague other funds and antipoverty programs in developing countries. One is a function of poverty: The poorest are poorest with respect to voice as well as to resources, and thus are the least organized and able to press their demands in a demand-based aid program. It may be possible to overcome this problem, partially because FOSIS design has already accounted for it. Although it will depend on local demand, FOSIS will also operate with a "poverty map" and will have regional as well as population group targets for its activities. Unlike other Latin countries, Chile has ample information about who the poorest are and where they live. FOSIS will sponsor locally presented projects, but it will also have a bank of its own projects. It will attempt to aid some of the poorest communities in either presenting or executing projects. Although it is unlikely that the most destitute will be direct beneficiaries, some of the poorest communities will probably be reached.

The second obstacle is a function of an authoritarian legacy: Local government is extremely underdeveloped, particularly in the realm that is critical to the success of FOSIS, incorporating local participation and organization. For the first two years of the Aylwin government, mayors were not directly elected; municipal elections were only held on June 30, 1992.

A third obstacle is a function of democratic government and party politics: There is constant pressure to allow partisan or political criteria to enter into program operation at both the local and central government levels. The FOSIS team is determined to operate in a nonpartisan manner, which is a good first step. Yet when the first executive director, Nicolás Flaño, a Christian Democrat, resigned in December 1990 to return to the World Bank, there was substantial delay in the appointment of a successor, Patricio Fernández, also a Christian Democrat. In the multiparty structure of the current government, an appointment such as the FOSIS directorship can create intraparty competition. It controls a great deal of money and has a high visibility among the *pobladores* (shantytown dwellers), so it is very attractive politically. This seems to have already delayed program implementation.[54] Partisan pressure is likely to increase substantially at election time. The date set for municipal elections is precisely the time that FOSIS will begin to generate projects. It will be a challenge to avoid partisan pressure at this point.

The extent to which partisan politics affect FOSIS will also depend largely on local actors and organizations. At the local political level, autonomous pobladores' organizations are usually formed for functional rather than partisan reasons; the role of partisan politics has been minimal to date. Nongovernmental organizations, a key focus of FOSIS activity, are usually oriented to the left, which has already put political pressure on FOSIS from critics on the right.[55] Party politics at the poblador level are far from straightforward and are made even more so by an authoritarian legacy that discouraged any kind of participatory activity or community organization.

Municipalities in Transition

In Chile, as in most Latin American nations, municipal governments have traditionally been largely dependent, both financially and administratively, on the central government.[56] In theory, the military government's municipal reform laws opened the door to decentralized municipal government. The laws established a certain degree of financial and administrative independence for municipalities by allowing them to generate their own resources and hire additional technical and professional personnel; guaranteed certain fiscal transfers to the municipalities; and established the common municipal fund

(Fundo Común Municipal), through which wealthier municipalities transferred resources to poorer ones.[57]

Municipalities became central to the military government's policies for the poor, as they were responsible for designating beneficiaries — through social action committees, with criteria based on the Ficha CAS — and then distributing the subsidies and providing the services. While most of these resources were tied to specific tasks, the municipalities also received lump sums for the implementation of the special employment programs and were given almost total freedom to design and implement the projects.[58] These resources were by no means insignificant for the municipalities; indeed, there was concern that municipal services would deteriorate after the special employment programs ended, as PEM and POJH labor were often used to make up for shortfalls in municipal personnel (Raczynski and Serrano 1987). PEM and POJH resources at times accounted for 30 to 90 percent of poor municipalities' total budgets (Herrera 1989).

Despite the decentralization legislation and the large amount of unrestricted resources the municipalities had at their disposal, true decentralization never really occurred. Authoritarian central government structures were transmitted down through the municipalities. During most of the Pinochet regime, all mayors were designated by the government. A new municipal law was passed in 1988, which established that the mayors of the fifteen most populous cities would be directly appointed by the central government and the rest would be appointed by the Community Development Council (CODECO) of each municipality. Before the military regime, CODECO members were elected; after the coup, they were designated. Approximately half were private-sector representatives and half were Junta Vecinal (neighborhood organization) leaders and other neighborhood representatives. Functional organizations such as unions and political parties were denied access. Thus in 1988 more than three hundred mayors were appointed by the state for a term of office that went well beyond the 1990 transition to the Aylwin regime. Critics justifiably saw the 1988 municipal "reform" law as an attempt by the Pinochet regime to control the transition to democracy at the local level (Jiménez 1990).

Within the municipalities, the mayors had ultimate authority: they were "mini-Pinochets" of sorts.[59] The allocation of special employment program resources was totally up to the mayor, and indeed the implementation of the programs varied with the personal goals or traits of the mayor.[60] In all cases, however, there was an absence of community development activities. In general, mayors favored large infrastructural activities with high visibility rather than those with a training or social component. The use of PEM and POJH resources to build an amphitheater and football stadium in La Cisterna is a case in point.

The relationship that the municipalities had with the community in carrying out social policy was based on *assistentialism* and dependency. Their role was to identify the people who were in extreme poverty and to channel government subsidies to them. Municipal workers themselves expressed frustration with their situation, which they described as "of an emergency and 'window dressing' nature" and "pure giving and giving" without "training or development" (Raczynski and Serrano 1987). Although municipal reforms had provided the mechanism for a decentralized resource base, they certainly did not do so for a decentralized political base, which would have allowed for participation from below.

FOSIS obviously will operate with a different conception of social policy and with a base in community participation. Yet the structure that it will have to operate in. . .is an amalgamation of old and new. In 1991, Aylwin had appointed the fifteen mayors allotted to the president by the constitution, but all the other remaining mayors — and therefore those in some of the poorest communities — [were] those appointed by the Pinochet regime. The power structure within municipalities remains largely the same. Power remains with the CODECO and ultimately, with the mayor.

Most of the new Junta Vecinales directors are participating in politics for the first time in sixteen years, if not the first time ever, and are dealing with mayors appointed by authoritarian bodies that are hardly accustomed to listening to demands from below. Because mayors are unaccustomed to political opposition, the relationship between opposition Junta Vecinal directors and appointed mayors is often antagonistic and even violent.[61] Thus it is quite difficult to incorporate community participation. In addition, in communities whose mayors are highly political, community organizations that are not of the same political leaning are even more marginalized.[62] As long as this situation remains, FOSIS will often have to bypass or operate outside the municipal realm. Because municipalities have the major responsibility for social policy, this is counterproductive to a coordinated effort to alleviate poverty as well as to the longer-term process of decentralization. Until a reform law is passed and direct elections are held, the transition to democracy at the local level will remain at an impasse, as will the efforts of FOSIS to introduce a new approach to policies for the poor at the municipal level.

Municipal reform was the subject of much debate in the legislature during the Aylwin government and was a prerequisite to holding direct municipal elections. The debate on reform focused on the direct election of mayors; creation of directly elected municipal councils to represent the local population; creation of advisory communal development councils based on functional sectors, including unions and parties; more efficient redistribution of the National Fund for Regional and Municipal Development; expansion of municipal activities to support small-scale enterprises, agriculture and fisheries, and commercial and handicraft activities; expansion of education-related activities, such as programs for youths with drug addiction; and reintroduction of the right of the mayor to appoint officials *de confianza* (personal appointments made outside the permanent bureaucracy).[63] Agreement on municipal reform was finally reached in January 1992.

The main actors in the parliamentary debate over reform were the Party for Democracy (PPD) and the Socialists on the left and the Independent Democratic Union (UDI) on the right. This replicated the party competition occurring at the municipal level. The left has traditionally been very active at the local or grass-roots level. The UDI also had a very active grass-roots level campaign during the 1988 plebiscite and the 1989 elections. There was clearly a desire to maintain UDI supporters in office, many of whom received appointments in exchange for working to create support for Pinochet in the plebiscite. A large majority of the mayors appointed by Pinochet were UDI members.[64] There was a great deal of tension, as UDI mayors asserted that the Aylwin government was denying them resources for political reasons.[65] This situation was an obstacle to coherent municipal government and was also one for the operations of FOSIS until municipal elections were held in June 1992. It is also a symptom of a fundamental issue that remains unresolved in most countries: the role of politics in the allocation of benefits for the poor. It is particularly difficult to resolve in Chile, as the local political system is still in a transitory phase.

Pobladores' Organizations and Other Institutions

Political impasse at the municipal level had a great deal of influence at the most critical local government level: that of the *pobladores* and their neighborhood and functional associations. *Pobladores'* organizations will be key to both democratic municipal government and to the success of FOSIS, which relies on their participation. In the current situation, *pobladores'* organizations remain largely marginalized from municipal government and independent of political parties.

"By concentrating attention on those who are organized one tends to lose sight of the mass who are not" (Lowden 1989). Attempts to reach the disorganized *pobladores* often create tensions, as the diverse and locally oriented interests of the *pobladores* do not necessarily coincide with the "corporatist-oriented" goals of the organizers. Not surprisingly, heterogenous nongovernmental organizations have traditionally had a better record of reaching the disorganized *pobladores* than have formal institutions such as political parties and municipal governments.

The level at which most *pobladores* are directly involved with municipal governments is that of the Juntas Vecinales. Although not all *pobladores* are organized, and indeed most are not, virtually every neighborhood has a Junta

Vecinal.[66] Juntas Vecinales, as well as other groups such as Centros de Madres (Mothers' Centers), were first given legal status by the Frei government.[67] In addition, organizations such as Promoción Popular (Popular Promotion) were set up to encourage and support their activities. These groups grew in number and became increasingly political under the Allende government, some becoming ideological to the detriment of their functional roles. Yet in general they took an increasingly active and cooperative role in promoting the delivery of, or improvements in, services such as health care and housing in conjunction with political parties and state agencies. At this point, opportunities were gradually opening for the poor "to begin to tackle their own social needs in a collective fashion in such fields as literacy programs, public health, construction, vocational training, etc." (Foxley and Muñoz 1974, 21-44).

The nature of the juntas changed substantially with the Pinochet government, as junta directors were appointed rather than elected. Those in the neighborhoods interested in independent community development worked with either nongovernmental organizations or popular economic organizations rather than with the juntas. Junta *dirigentes* (directors) were usually Pinochet loyalists or were paid as PEM-POJH workers to take on neighborhood leadership responsibilities.

After the 1990 transition to democracy, direct elections were held for juntas for the first time in sixteen years. Results were mixed. "Known" dirigentes — those who had previously been appointed — were reelected in many cases, as the communities were not used to making choices or participating in politics.[68] At the same time, independent dirigentes — who were often in direct political opposition to the previously appointed ones — were also elected. The former appointees have an obvious advantage in working with the mayor — also appointed — in most municipalities. The elected dirigentes vary from those who were more militant in their demand-making to those who are much more ignorant about what their rights are vis-à-vis the municipality.[69] The latter group is much more vulnerable to manipulation by the authorities. At the same time, they are much less likely even to know about FOSIS[70] and thus are much more dependent on the municipalities for access to FOSIS projects. In addition, some juntas still in the control of appointed dirigentes are insisting that proposals to FOSIS from the community must go through the junta.[71] Although there may also be cases of newly elected junta leaders attempting to control FOSIS projects, it seems less likely. The appointed dirigentes are used to operating in a top-down manner and are much less comfortable with independent community activity.

The disorganized *pobladores* clearly should be a central focus of FOSIS activities. Their relationship with the juntas and municipalities takes on increased importance because of the lack of intermediary organizations to represent them. Thus the efforts of the juntas and ultimately municipal governments will in the long run be key to their participation in FOSIS projects. Although municipal reform and the direct election of mayors should help this dynamic somewhat, it will take some time before a full transition to democracy is made at the Junta Vecinale level. There is a clear need for civic education, as well as for experience in participatory politics. This is, no doubt, one of the costs of sixteen years of dictatorship. The tradition of vertical decision making and authoritarian politics clearly will affect the ability of FOSIS to operate effectively. In the short term, those communities with active popular organizations outside official local government channels will probably be best positioned to take advantage of the FOSIS mechanism.

Although there are numerous popular organizations, many of which emerged in opposition to the Pinochet government, most, including communal kitchens or popular economic organizations, are functional organizations based on day-to-day survival activities. Only 2 percent of all organized *pobladores* in the Santiago metropolitan region are organized into territorial or coordinating committees with broader political goals (Hardy 1989, 181-82). The resistance of local groups to coordination into larger intermediary organizations is a function of a breach that exists in many Latin American nations between the concerns and problems of the poor and politics at the national level. In Chile this has been exacerbated by a long period of authoritarian rule. Yet these groups are gradually growing in size and importance and in the long term, may play a role in reconstructing the broken ties between private life and public action.

Nowhere is the gap between popular or nongovernmental functional organizations and formal political institutions as evident as in the relationship between *pobladores'* organizations and political parties. Popular organizations in Chile are usually wary and resentful of the challenges to their autonomy posed by political parties (Oxhorn 1989), as the benefits of maintaining their autonomy seem to outweigh the advantages of attaining upward linkages to the state. This distance increased during the Pinochet years, as the ability of parties to provide linkages disappeared altogether and political involvement signified costs in terms of repression as well as trade-offs in terms of autonomy.

Popular economic organizations grow out of a very different tradition than do traditional organized interest groups whose goal is the fulfillment of certain rights — to work, housing, or health care — from the state. There is an incentive in organized interest groups to create a vertical mass structure that can make demands on the state through a coherent top-level leadership. Political parties often play a central role in organizing and directing the action of such groups and mediating with the state. By contrast, popular survival or economic organizations are organized horizontally, as they have little to gain at a level beyond that of the neighborhood. Social networks are more important than unions or confederations. Functional support organizations, not political parties, are the most relevant external group (Razeto et al. 1990). It is hardly surprising that communal self-help organizations are fundamentally less political than the parties.

The complex relationship between grass-roots movements and parties in Chile is not unlike that in other Latin American countries. In Peru, for example, grass-roots movements were key to the victory of the unknown Alberto Fujimori. At the same time, support in these groups is by no means analogous to the organized base of support that a political party represents (Graham 1992). In Bolivia, parties are totally out of touch with grass-roots movements, a phenomenon that has been demonstrated in the growth of support for such antisystem populists, with no party base, as "Compadre" Palenque, who became the first political force in La Paz virtually overnight; and in beer king Max Fernández's recent victory in Sucre (Rivadeneira 1990). The lack of ties is exacerbated in Chile, where the cost of organizing or participating in the political realm was prohibitive for many years.

Thus the role of parties in the *poblaciones* is a marginal one.[72] *Pobladores* have traditionally been excluded from national political society in Chile, as party politics has always had a basis in unions rather than in grass-roots movements. "The sad truth is that in the central committees of the political parties of the left, there is no poblador."[73] Some observers believe that *pobladores* reject parties because partisan competition and directives from the top serve to create divisions within their organizations rather than to represent their needs (Petras 1988).

Partisan competition at the national level, meanwhile, has little relevance to the day-to-day concerns of *pobladores*. As long as political parties are more active in pursuing reforms at the central government level, even if they benefit *pobladores* in the long run, they will have little appeal to most *pobladores* and their functional organizations, which are much more concerned with issues such as employment, personal security, and problems of unemployed youth.[74] When the parties were instrumental in organizing the opposition to the Pinochet regime, they represented a cause with which *pobladores* could identify. Now that the parties are involved in more mundane political bargaining, this link has been weakened. For example, one *poblador dirigente* who had attended meetings of the various parties decided to run as an independent because she "wanted to do something for the community. . . . They [the party politicians] are all focused on getting posts at the municipal level."[75]

To be effective, at least in the near future, FOSIS will have to encourage the direct participation of *pobladores* and their functional organizations, as neither municipal governments nor political parties are well positioned to represent their concerns. In the longer term, though, political parties must adapt their strategies to incorporate local organizations and concerns. Otherwise, a significant majority will remain on the fringes of Chilean politics.

Conclusion

The Pinochet government leaves a mixed legacy in alleviating poverty. On the one hand, the government effectively provided for the basic needs of the poorest of the poor during a severe economic crisis, no small achievement considering the record of other countries in the region.

On the other hand, its narrow vision of social welfare policy, in conjunction with its disdain for participatory institutions, resulted in a safety net that also stigmatized the poorest. Those who participated in government programs became an underclass of sorts, dependent on government subsidies without improving their capacity to meet their own basic needs. This was complemented by a political context that prohibited participation by the poor in solving their own problems. When the poor were given that opportunity under the Aylwin regime, most of them — except a minority who are highly organized — were ill equipped to take advantage of it. In the words of a neighborhood *dirigente* in Villa El Cobre, "People are used to being told what to do."[76]

Improving the ability of the poor to help themselves may be an ambitious goal for any government program, but it is a realizable one, as shown by experiences such as that of Bolivia's Emergency Social Fund.

Unresolved conflicts at the local government level, in which newly introduced democratic practices, such as direct elections for neighborhood juntas, coexisted with remnants of the authoritarian regime, such as appointed mayors, made it difficult for the poor and inexperienced to begin participating in formulating the policies and projects that affect them. The poor have very weak links to intermediary institutions, such as political parties, which could help them formulate their demands more effectively vis-à-vis the state. In part this is a result of an extended period of authoritarian rule, yet it is also typical of the politics of the urban poor in most Latin countries.

As political parties gradually consolidate their position at the central government level, and as direct municipal elections and other municipal reforms are introduced, this situation will gradually change. Both parties and independent local organizations will take on increased importance. Presumably this will help the poor to participate in finding their own solutions. Particularly in the short term, though, FOSIS, with its focus on encouraging the poor to formulate and implement their own solutions as well as soliciting the state for resources, will be a critical institution.

FOSIS is well positioned to play a positive role in supporting the building of an institutional base that is suited to present-day economic and political realities as well as to the needs of the poor. It faces substantial challenges, however. At the central government level, avoiding partisan pressure is a constant concern. At the local level, FOSIS has to foster genuine participation among an inexperienced and largely unorganized population in a situation that remains partially dominated by authoritarian forces and deep divisions between left and right. Clearly, it is no easy task.

Poverty indeed exists in Chile. In absolute terms, however, it is much less severe than in most countries on the continent. Despite the severity of the economic crises of the late 1970s and early 1980s, steady progress was made in lowering the incidence of extreme poverty. This can be attributed to the preexisting social network and state experience with social welfare programs, as well as to the effective and focused policies of the military regime toward the poorest. Although the people at the margin of the poverty line lost access to a host of extremely valuable state services, this is gradually being reversed under the democratic regime. By eroding extreme poverty as well as implementing a far-reaching program of economic reform, the military government left its democratic successors a firm base upon which to build and the flexibility to implement a program as diverse and innovative as FOSIS.

The military performed more poorly on the political institutional front. This arena is often overlooked by those who implement antipoverty programs, but it is critical to their success, if success is gauged by the degree to which beneficiaries gain skills or resources necessary to help themselves. Because the military combined the objectives of authoritarian political control with those of alleviating poverty, it is no surprise that it failed to create mechanisms through which the poor can help themselves. This is where most work remains to be done.

Notes

1. The declining infant mortality rate (IMR) accelerated from 1965 to 1973, compared with its pace in the previous decade. The decline of the IMR then experienced another acceleration after 1976. Given the extreme economic crisis of the late 1970s, as well as the concurrent decrease in per capita public social welfare expenditure, this improvement in the IMR rate during this time needs further explanation. Raczynski identifies as the most important factor the traditional preference given to mother and child health by the Chilean state health system, which increased at this time. In addition, the period from 1964 to 1980 was one of relatively low population growth. The total population grew from 8.3 million to 11.1 million, but the population under age fifteen only grew from 3.2 million to 3.6 million (Raczynski and Oyarzo 1981). According to Bravo (1990), fluctuations in health indicators have a direct relation to short-term economic changes. Infant mortality is the health indicator most sensitive to changes in economic output and employment trends, with the employment rate having the strongest effects on fluctuations in the infant mortality rate.

2. See, for example, *World Development Report 1990: Poverty* (World Bank 1990), chap. 7; and Ribe and Carvalho 1990, 15–17.

3. The principle of targeting the poorest was an integral part of the "Chicago boys" philosophy. Its main proponent was Miguel Kast. His students effectively implemented the policy through the creation of the state planning agency, ODEPLAN, which was responsible for the municipal agency, SERPLAC. For details about Miguel Kast and the Fundación Miguel Kast, which advocates his philosophy as the basis for policies in the *poblaciones* (villages), see Chadwick and Ledermann (1990), 35–42. I would like to thank Philip O'Brien for bringing this point to my attention.

4. Manuel Marfan, Vice Minister of Economics, interview with the author in Santiago, January 17, 1992. The Aylwin government's economic strategy and its success at maintaining macroeconomic stability during and after the transition, in spite of the inflationary effects of substantial overheating of the economy by the Pinochet regime prior to the 1988 plebiscite, is detailed in Arriagada and Graham's "Chile: The Maintenance of Macroeconomic Stability During Democratic Transition" (forthcoming).

5. The education program was aimed at the nine hundred most disadvantaged schools in the country and then extended to an additional four hundred. For details on the education reforms, see de Kadt 1993. Details on the youth training program, which was extended to 100,000 youths, were obtained from the author's interviews with the head of the program, Juan Jose Rivas, Ministry of Labor, Santiago, January 21-22, 1992. The programs are also described in Arriagada and Graham (forthcoming).

6. See the studies reported in Hojman 1990.

7. Extreme poverty was defined as having a monthly income under 20,000 pesos, which would not be enough to meet basic subsistence needs (Vergara 1989, 64).

8. Chile's overall macroeconomic position vis-à-vis its neighbors also improved substantially after 1973, resulting in one of the strongest economies on the continent. See, for example, Graham 1991b.

9. In 1969 the poorest 10 percent of Chile's population had 1.3 percent of total income; by 1989 their relatively small share had dropped to 1.2 percent. During the same interval, the share of the wealthiest 10 percent increased from 39.0 percent to 41.6 percent (Program de Economía del Trabajo 1990).

10. Ninety percent of increases in social security payments during this time went to the *asignaciones familiares* (family quotas) and pensions for the poorest. By 1982, total spending in this field remained at only 28 percent of its 1970 levels (Vergara 1989, 44).

11. A detailed description of the pre-Pinochet social welfare system is beyond the scope of this paper. A comprehensive description can be found in Arrellano, *Políticas Sociales* (1985).

12. See Arrellano 1985, Castañeda 1990. Informal-sector or self-employed workers, along with agricultural laborers, were the bulk of the poorest sectors of the population in 1974. This sector represented 45 percent of the economically active population, earned on average the equivalent of the minimum wage or less, and received just over 14 percent of total national income. The vast majority (three-quarters or more) of workers in agriculture and services were in this sector, while only slightly over 40 percent of industrial workers were in this group. At the other end of the scale, approximately 9 percent of the population received over 35 percent of national income. The largest strata of the economically active population (46 percent) earned the equivalent of between one and four times the minimum wage and received approximately 50 percent of national income. This group was primarily composed of salaried employees — mostly in service industries — and manual industrial workers (Foxley and Muñoz 1974).

13. The system had slightly regressive tax effects as well, because social security contributions were tax deductible, and the highest paid workers paid the highest tax rates. In addition, it acted as a disincentive to employment by increasing the cost of hiring additional laborers (Foxley and Muñoz 1974). This phenomenon has occurred in other Latin American countries containing large informal sectors. When the countries introduced relatively advanced labor legislation, as in Peru in the mid-1970s, the legislation acted as a disincentive to hiring and increased the size of the informal sectors.

14. For example, the Fondo Común Municipal was established. All municipalities contributed to this fund, which distributed resources from rich to poor municipalities. This provided poor municipalities with independent resources, often for the first time.

15. Razcynski and Serrano 1988. See also Raczynski 1991.

16. Vergara 1989. The Inter-American Development Bank financed the lots with services, as it has done in several countries.

17. See, for example, Vergara 1989, 24–25.

18. This conclusion is based on the author's interviews in Santiago in November 1990 with central and municipal government officials who implemented the emergency employment programs, with people who participated in the programs, with community leaders in neighborhoods where the programs were implemented, and with several academics specializing in employment or poverty issues.

19. The programs were allocated over 5 billion pesos, or approximately $20 million, in the government's 1987 social spending budget of 274 billion pesos. The bulk of social spending (249 billion pesos) went to pensions, and a total of 20 billion pesos went to all social programs other than employment. In relative terms, therefore, 5 billion pesos was quite significant. The relative amount spent on employment programs at their height, in 1983, was much greater, as the programs employed approximately three times as many people in 1983 as in 1987 (data from SERPLAC Metropolitana 1990). In a study of four of Santiago's poorest municipalities, PEM and POJH resources accounted for 30–90 percent of the total.

20. PREALC 1988 and Graham 1990. Recent estimates of this figure are as high as 13 percent.

21. Jorge de la Fuente, former head of the Department of Development and Information, SERPLAC Metropolitana, interview with the author, Santiago, November 19, 1990.

22. In addition to the national training program, there was the Servicio Nacional de Capacitación y Empleo (SENCE), which was run by the Ministry of Labor. SENCE administered a variety of scholarship programs in conjunction with the private sector from the late 1970s on. The bulk of SENCE's activities, however, were concentrated in large private-sector firms, because it was difficult for smaller firms to participate in the subsidization system and the firms that presented proposals to SENCE tended to concentrate on training for executives and professionals. Thus the effect of SENCE on the poorest and least-skilled sector of the labor force was minimal, as was its coordination with the special employment programs (Echeverría 1990).

23. See, for example, Graham 1991a, and Ward and Chant 1987.

24. Jorge de la Fuente, interview with the author.

25. Many countries, including Panama, Peru, and Bolivia, found it necessary to implement employment programs in the early and mid-1980s. A comparison of the programs is beyond the scope of this paper, but it is relevant to note that the Chilean programs stand out in terms of decentralized administration, scale, and effective targeting of the poorest and most needy workers. See, for example, PREALC 1988.

26. Because such programs are designed to be temporary, it makes little sense to pay above-market wages. However, POJH and PEM wages clearly fell far short of meeting even minimum basic needs. PIMO and PEP had more realistic payment scales. If payment scales are too high, then there is little incentive to leave the program. In Peru, where the PAIT program paid the minimum wage, only 16 percent of workers were actively looking for other jobs. In contrast, 63 percent of PEM workers were actively seeking alternate employment (Graham 1991a).

27. Jorge de la Fuente, interview with the author. This was confirmed by several of the author's interviews with program officials and critics alike.

28. Roberto Urmaneta, PET, interview with the author, Santiago, November 22, 1990.

29. Dagmar Raczynski, CIEPLAN, interview with the author, Santiago, November 22, 1990.

30. Ivan Moreira Barros, mayor of La Cisterna, interview with the author, November 23, 1990.

31. Author's interview with the administrator of POJH in La Cisterna, November 23, 1990.

32. In an interview with the author Roberto Urmaneta cited the example of workers on the Pan American highway, who, although still resentful of the low wage levels, at least felt some satisfaction in participating in a project of national significance.

33. Karen Lashman, World Bank, Washington, D.C., interview with the author on November 13, 1990. Productive use of labor and good quality control are key factors in helping special program workers get reabsorbed into the labor force. The costs of establishing special employment programs are approximately the same, whether the program is productive or not. However, the main benefit to both workers and society from such programs is the productive input, both in training provided and in infrastructure created (Martens and Tomic 1983).

34. Scholnik and Teitelboim 1988; and author's interview with Isabel Vial, Chilean government official, Washington, D.C., December 3, 1990. Nongovernment sources usually provide a breakdown of employment figures that separates special employment programs from the overall figures.

35. Author's interviews with Jaime Ruiz Tagle, director, PET, Santiago, November 16, 1990; and with Tito Cordova, Vicaria Pastoral Obrero, and former POJH worker, Santiago, November 21, 1990.

36. This was confirmed by the author's interviews in November 1990 with former program workers, program officials, and community observers. It is also confirmed by the author's field research in Peru, where a similar program, PAIT, had similar effects on male-female relationships.

37. Official employment statistics described those who work as little as one hour a day as "employed." Thus, if official figures are examined more critically, the underemployment rate is higher. Although there is a great deal of differentiation in income levels in the informal sector, one means to gauge this rate is the size of this sector, defined as urban self-employed workers and domestic servants. In 1976, 35.1 percent of the economically active population was underemployed. In 1981, this figure was 34.4 percent. An analogous figure for 1989 — although not exactly the same — is that the informal sector in Santiago was 29.4 percent of the economically active population. Author's interview with Mariana Scholnik, MINEPLAN, Santiago, November 19, 1990; PET 1989; author's interview with Jorge de la Fuente; and Rivas 1987.

38. Author's interview with Jaime Ruiz Tagle.

39. Pedro Emilio Pérez of SENCE, former head of employment programs for the Quinta Normal region, interview with the author, Santiago, November 23, 1990.

40. Author's interview with Mariana Scholnik.

41. Author's interview with Pedro Emilio Pérez.

42. For details, see Hardy 1989, chap. 9.

43. See Graham 1991a.

44. Author's interviews with Señora Mercedes, Villa El Cobre resident, November 24, 1990; and Señora Leonor Romero, Maipu resident, November 21, 1990.

45. Interview with Mariana Scholnik; and Scholnik and Teitelboim 1988.

46. For experiences in Peru and Bolivia, see Graham 1991a and Graham 1991c.

47. Pedro Emilio Pérez, interview with the author. Pérez was forced to resign from his position in the program administration at this point.

48. Manuel Barrera, director, Center of Social Studies, interview with the author, Santiago, November 20, 1990.

49. The author interviewed several people involved with FOSIS in its early stages, including Molly Pollack, PREALC, Santiago, December 9, 1989; Lais Abramo, PREALC and Emergency Social Fund, La Paz, Bolivia, August 27, 1990; Dagmar Raczynski, CIEPLAN, Santiago, November 22, 1990; Nicolás Flaño, executive director, FOSIS, and alternate executive director of the World Bank, Santiago, November 22, 1990; Clarissa Hardy, FOSIS, Santiago, November 22, 1990; and Mariana Scholnik, MINEPLAN, Santiago, November 19, 1990.

50. Author's interview with Clarissa Hardy. Loans expected from the World Bank and the Inter-American Development Bank never materialized. Thus, much more will be expected from the government budget; this may jeopardize the operations of FOSIS in the future.

51. Author's visit to FOSIS and conversations with director and staff. For a critique of the Bolivian experience, see Graham 1991c.

52. Flaño 1990; and interview with author.

53. Jiménez 1990 and Echeverría 1990. Examples are SENCE's training scholarship program, which was implemented by private organizations after a process of public bidding, and the role played by CONIN — a private, nonprofit organization — in state nutrition policy.

54. The advisory board for FOSIS, composed of professionals and academics in the field, has been informally constituted but to date has not been called to meet (Dagmar Raczynski, advisory board member, interview with author in Santiago, November 22, 1990).

55. Author's interview with Clarissa Hardy.

56. See, for example, Arturo Valenzuela 1977 and Marcela Jiménez 1990. Since the 1800s, municipalities have been perceived more as an agent of the central government than anything else. The 1925 constitution and 1938 Popular Front government introduced a new kind of centralization based on state intervention and strong presidentialism. Under the Pinochet government, centralization was increased through authoritarianism and ideological control.

57. Three laws were the basis of this process: the Nueva Ley Orgánica Municipal of 1975, the Ley de Rentas Municipales of 1979, and Ley 3551 of 1981. Two important complementary laws were Ley 3000 of 1979 and Ley 1-3063 of 1980 (Castañeda 1990).

58. Author's conversations with PEM and POJH administrators, the mayor of La Cisterna, and Dagmar Raczynski. Also see Carlos Clavel 1990.

59. Author's interview with Dagmar Razcynski.

60. Raczynski and Serrano (1988) identify three types of mayors under the Pinochet regime: politicized (the ones with the strongest ties to the regime), technical-entrepreneurial (who tended to be young and skilled), and bureaucratic (who tended to be older and were the most difficult to categorize). The first were more likely to use the programs for political proselytizing, and the second for community improvements.

61. Author's interviews with Junta Vecinal directors Leonor Romero in Maipu (November 21, 1990) and Maria Inez Bravo in Villa El Cobre (November 17, 1990). Maria Inez Bravo recounted how she and her fellow directors were harassed and assaulted by the supporters of the former appointed junta directors.

62. This is confirmed by the author's conversations with Junta Vecinal directors in Villa El Cobre and Maipu, as well as with municipal officials in La Cisterna.

63. "El Municipio Actual: Características y Transición," Campaña Nacional de Capacitación para Líderes Locales y Vecinales (Party for Democracy 1990); and Jiménez 1990.

64. Author's interviews with Pedro Emilio Pérez and Dagmar Razcynski.

65. Author's interviews with Ivan Moreira Barros and Jorge de la Fuente.

66. There are now 5,010 Juntas Vecinales in Chile, of which 1,000 are in Santiago. From 1984 to 1987 alone, their number increased by 700.

67. During the first four years of their legal existence, there were nine thousand Centros de Madres. This number grew to as many as twenty thousand under the Allende government. This changed dramatically with the Pinochet government, which organized all juntas into the CEMA-Chile (Centros de Madres) under the directorship of Mrs. Pinochet. Yet women still participated, albeit on a lesser scale, because of the financial benefits they garnered from joint workshops and the social benefits that came from communal interaction. In 1987 there were 6,387 Centros de Madres, with approximately half in Santiago (Hardy 1989, 174–77).

68. Author's interview with Señora Mercedes, Villa El Cobre, November 17, 1990.

69. Author's interview with Maria Inez Bravo.

70. Leonor Romero, interview with the author. Neither Señora Leonor Romero nor any of her junta colleagues knew anything about FOSIS.

71. Author's interview with Maria Inez Bravo.

72. The one exception is the Communist party, which has, at various times, played an important organizational role in many *poblaciones*. Yet, given its proscription during the military years and its marginal position in the current government, its role in providing significant linkages to the state is limited.

73. Trade union leader quoted in Alan Angell, "Trade Unions in Chile in the 1980s," March 1989.

74. Author's interview with Dagmar Racynski.

75. Author's interview with Maria Inez Bravo.

76. Author's interview with Maria Inez Bravo.

References

Angell, Alan. 1989. "Trade Unions in Chile in the 1980s." Paper prepared for Conference on the Prospects for Democracy in Chile, held in March at the University of California at San Diego.

Arrellano, José Pablo. 1985. *Políticas Sociales y Desarrollo: Chile 1924–1984*. Santiago: CIEPLAN.

Arriagada, Genaro, and Carol Graham. 1994. "Chile: The Maintenance of Macroeconomic Stability During Democratic Transition." In *Voting for Reform: The Political Economy of Adjustment in New Democracies*, eds. Stephan Haggard and Steven B. Webb. Washington, D.C.: World Bank and Oxford University Press.

Bravo, Jorge. 1990. "Fluctuaciones en la Economía, El Empleo, y en los Indicadores de Salud: Chile 1960–1968." Working Paper 341. Santiago: PREALC.

Castañeda, Tarsicio. 1990. *Para Combatir La Pobreza: Política Social y Descentralización en Chile Durante Los '80*. Santiago: Centro de Estudios Públicos.

Chadwick, Margarita, and Cecilia Ledermann. 1990. "Centros Integrales de Desarrollo Comunitario: Una Contribución a las Estrategias de Desarrollo Social." In *Municipios y Organizaciones Privadas*, ed. Marcela Jiménez, 35-42. Santiago: Inter-American Foundation and Universidad Católica de Chile.

Clavel, Carlos, et al. 1990. "Estudio Sobre Los Programas Especiales de Empleo." Universidad de Chile, Department of Economics.

Echeverría, Christian. 1990. "El Estado y la Capacitación en Chile." Working paper. Santiago: SENCE.

Flaño, Nicolás. 1990. "El Fondo de Solaridad e Inversión Social: En Que Estamos Pensando." Paper prepared for PREALC Seminar on Fondos de Desarrollo Social, Santiago, 7-9 November.

Foxley, Alejandro, and Oscar Muñoz. 1974a. "Income Redistribution, Economic Growth and Social Structure: The Case of Chile." *Oxford Bulletin of Economics and Statistics* 56 (February).

Graham, Carol. 1990. "Recent Experiences with Employment Programs in Chile, Bolivia, and Peru." Memorandum, Inter-American Dialogue, Washington D.C. (March).

Graham, Carol. 1991a. "The APRA Government and the Urban Poor: The PAIT Program in Lima's Pueblos Jóvenes." *Journal of Latin American Studies* 24 (February): 91–130.

Graham, Carol. 1991b. "The Enterprise for the Americas Initiative: A Development Strategy for Latin America?" *Brookings Review* 9 (Fall): 22–27.

Graham, Carol. 1991c. "The Politics of Implementing Pro-Poor Measures During Adjustment: Bolivia's Emergency Social Fund." Brookings Institution, Foreign Policy Studies Program, June.

Graham, Carol. 1992. *Peru's APRA: Parties, Politics, and the Elusive Quest for Democracy in Peru.* Boulder, Colo.: Lynne Rienner.

Haindl, Erik, et al. 1989. *Gasto Social Efectivo.* Santiago: Universidad de Chile.

Hardy, Clarissa. 1989. *La Ciudad Escindida.* Santiago: PET.

Herrera, Nelson. 1989. "El Presupuesto Municipal: Estudio de Casos: La Florida, Peñalolen, Macul, San Joaquín, Puente Alto." Cuadernos de Trabajo 29. Santiago: Centro de Estudios Municipales.

Hojman, David E. 1990. "Chile after Pinochet: Aylwin's Christian Democrat Economic Policies for the 1990s." *Bulletin of Latin American Research* 9 (1) (1990): 25–48.

Jiménez, Marcela, ed. 1990. *Municipios y Organizaciones Privadas.* Santiago: Inter-American Foundation and Universidad Católica de Chile.

de Kadt, Emmanuel. 1993. "Poverty-Focused Policies: The Experience of Chile." Sussex, Institute for Development Studies, DS #319, January.

Lowden, Pamela. 1989. "Villa El Cobre: A Case Study of Santiago's Poor under Military Rule." M. Phil. thesis, University of Oxford.

Martens, Joost, and Blas Tomic. 1983. "Los Programas Especiales de Empleos: Algunas Lecciones de la Experiencia." Working paper 225. Santiago: PREALC.

Oxhorn, Philip David. 1989. "Democratic Transitions and the Democratization of Civil Society: Chilean Shantytown Organizations under the Authoritarian Rule," Ph.D. diss. Harvard University.

Party for Democracy. 1990. "El Municipio Actual: Características y Transición," Campaña Nacional de Capacitación para Líderes Locales y Vecinales."

PET. 1989. *Encuesta de Empleo.* Santiago: PET.

Petras, James. 1988. "The New Class Base of Chilean Politics." *New Left Review* 172 (November–December).

Politzer, Patricia. 1985. *Miedo en Chile.* Santiago.

PREALC. 1988. *Empleos de Emergencia.* Santiago: PREALC.

Program de Economía del Trabajo. 1990. *Encuestas de Empleo.* Santiago: PET.

Raczynski, Dagmar. 1991. "Descentralización y Políticas Sociales: Lecciones de la Experiencia Chilena y Tareas Pendientes." *Estudios CIEPLAN* (March): 141–52.

Raczynski, Dagmar, and César Oyarzo. 1981. "Porque Cae La Tasa de Mortalidad Infantil en Chile en Los Años 70?" Working paper. Santiago: CIEPLAN.

Razcynski, Dagmar, and Claudia Serrano. 1987. "Administración y Gestión Local: La Experiencia de Algunos Municipios en Santiago." Working paper 22. Santiago: CIEPLAN.

Razcynski, Dagmar, and Claudia Serrano. 1988. "Planificación Para El Desarrollo Local: La Experiencia de Algunos Municipios en Santiago." Working paper 24. Santiago: CIEPLAN.

Razeto, Luis, et al. 1990. *Las Organizaciones Económicas Populares 1973–1990.* Santiago: PET.

Ribe, Helena, and Soniya Carvalho. 1990. "Adjustment and the Poor." *Finance and Development* (September): 15–17.

Rivadeneira, Raúl. 1990. *Agresión Política.* La Paz: Editorial La Juventud.

Rivas, Gonzalo. 1987. "El Desempeño Empleador de la Economía Chilena Bajo El Régimen Militar." *Coyuntura Económica* 14 (April): 11–17.

Ruiz-Tagle, Jaime, and Roberto Urmaneta. 1984. *Los Trabajadores del Program de Empleo Mínimo.* Santiago: PET.

Scholnik, Mariana, and Berta Teitelboim. 1988. *Pobreza y Desempleo en Poblaciones.* Santiago: PET.

SERPLAC Metropolitana. 1990. "Memoria Departamento de Empleo, 1982–1990." Intendencia de Santiago.

Stallings, Barbara, and Robert Kaufman, eds. 1989. *Debt and Democracy in Latin America.* Boulder, Colo.: Westview.

Valenzuela, Arturo. 1977. *Political Power Brokers in Chile.* Duke University Press.

Vergara, Pilar. 1989. *Políticas Hacia La Extrema Pobreza en Chile: 1973–1988.* Santiago: FLACSO.

Ward, Peter, and Sylvia Chant. 1987. "Community Leadership and Self-Help Housing," *Progress in Planning* 27, pt. 2 (1987): 31–54.

World Bank. 1990. *World Development Report 1990: Poverty.* Washington: World Bank.

Political and Economic Reform in Argentina and Brazil: Contrasting Priorities, Contrasting Success

Margaret Sarles

Two South American giants — Argentina and Brazil — are in the process of fundamentally restructuring their political and economic systems. The changes taking place are the most radical since industrialization and urbanization began in the early twentieth century.

In the 1930s, Brazil and Argentina were led by military dictators who used a Mussolini model of government as the basic framework for political and economic development in the post-World War II period. Even under later, ostensibly democratic regimes, both countries retained many corporatist features. These, melded into agriculture-based patrimonial politics of the nineteenth century, led to large bureaucracies, government dominated economies with state-run labor unions, and personalistic politics. For large landowners and key industries, the line between the private and public sector and between private and public interests virtually disappeared.

In the 1980s, both countries emerged from new rounds of military dictatorships into a very different world. With the end of the Cold War, the threat of communism was no longer credible, and the authoritarian leadership lost its chief claim to international legitimacy as "democratic" defender against the vile specter of internal communist subversion. With the downfall of communism, U.S. foreign policy increasingly focused on supporting democratic governments.

Margaret Sarles is the chair of Latin American and Caribbean Studies of the School of Area Studies of the Foreign Service Institute in Arlington, Virginia.

Economically, the state-dominated model of development had failed. Argentina and Brazil, unable to adapt to new realities brought on by the oil crises of the early 1970s, acquired huge foreign debts. To pay their debts, both countries needed to increase their exports and become more competitive in world markets. Inflation reached new heights, the foreign debt soared, and both countries entered severe recessions.

The combination of international change and civilian leadership committed to democratic principles has impelled both Argentina and Brazil toward reform. Democratization and privatization have become the two banners of reform.

The economic and political reform processes have been intricately linked. In fact, although they are often described as two phenomena, both are basically one. Pushing away from regimes based on corporatist principles toward regimes based on pluralism and competitive principles, "democratization" is more than civilian rule and the formal procedures of democracy. Its reforms decrease the reach of the government, rebalancing the power between government and private sector, creating more political competition, diversity, and participation, and ultimately reversing a political culture based on authoritarianism and dependency. Similarly, "privatization" is more than the process of selling off government companies. Among other things, it means decreasing the economic control and dominance of the government and separating the "private sector" from the "public sector."

The old military dictatorships in Argentina and Brazil brought out the extremes of authoritarianism and corporatism in both societies, since no political or economic group was in a position to challenge seriously the dictatorships' power.

The Process of Political Transformation: Demilitarization

In 1976, all Central and South American countries except Costa Rica, Colombia, Venezuela, and Suriname were led by military dictators. Within ten years, nearly all military governments had been replaced by civilian ones. In Argentina and Brazil, virtually all sectors of society became repulsed by long-lived military regimes. Although both systems developed a strong commitment to civilian rule, the processes of demilitarization were quite different.

In Argentina, the military became completely discredited because of its rampant violations of human rights during the "dirty war" against suspected "subversives" and its abysmal performance in the Malvinas/Falkland Islands War against Great Britain. After seven years (1976-1983) in power, the generals were replaced by elected civilian President Raúl Alfonsín in 1983. The experience under the military dictatorship was a searing one for Argentines. Human rights activists and many ordinary citizens whose friends and relatives had been killed sought legal justice against the former military leaders. The processes of seeking justice and national reconciliation were among the most salient features of the Alfonsín government and helped create a sense of public outrage, of "Never again" toward military governments.

Political stability was not easily won. Three coup attempts failed. When Carlos Saúl Menem was elected as Alfonsín's successor, it was the first time in seventy-three years a civilian president from one party peacefully succeeded a president from an opposition party. Although Alfonsín left the presidency early, the principles of civilian leadership and orderly transfer of power were followed.

President Menem has succeeded in shifting the position of the military in Argentine politics, despite one coup attempt, and has continued to cut the military's budget. Altogether, between 1982 and 1992, military expenditures decreased from more than 6 percent to less than 2 percent of gross domestic product (GDP). Menem's government plans to reduce military personnel by 10 to 20 percent. In addition, Menem actively has sought a new role for the military, focusing it on international conflicts rather than on internal subversion. Sending troops attached to the United Nations to Iraq, Somalia, and other trouble spots not only moved the mission of military forces to another arena, it began the process of rehabilitating the military in the eyes of Argentines who had been thoroughly repulsed both by its internal excesses and its incompetence in the war with Britain.

The Brazilian military dictatorship was very mild by Argentine standards but lasted much longer. Brought into power in 1964 with the support of the traditional political parties, the military worked constantly with the Congress and political leadership even as it gradually dominated them. Human rights violations in Brazil, including torture and murder, occurred against labor, student, and leftist groups; however, altogether they amounted to a small fraction of similar violations in Argentina. As a result, in Brazil there was not the general outrage against the military that the Argentine population expressed against its military on human rights grounds.

Beginning in the mid-1970s, Brazil's military government committed itself to a gradual return to civilian rule, through a very long process that ended in 1985 when an electoral college selected the first civilian president in twenty-one years, José Sarney. The military's candidate lost out in the political maneuvering that preceded the election. The military was able to ensure, however, in spite of massive demonstrations demanding direct elections, control over the indirect process of selection.

During the years of President Sarney's administration (1985-1989), the military steadfastly remained out of politics. By 1989, with the first direct presidential elections since 1961, the military had no influence over the process except by its absence — its explicit commitment to no involvement. However, the military watched the process carefully, particularly as one of the two final candidates, Luís Inácio Lula da Silva, represented the labor groups repressed for so long by the military. But neither then, nor during the very disruptive impeachment process of President Fernando Collor de Mello in 1992, did the military act to influence the course of political events. Its major political activity has been to let all groups know that it would not get involved. Just as important, in the face of mounting economic crises and urban violence, there has been no serious call from civilian forces demanding a larger role for the military. The one exception to this was the United Nations Conference on the Environment (UNCED) in June 1992, when military troops in Rio de Janeiro were used to supplement police forces in decreasing petty crime for the thousands of visitors attending the conference. Their role in this instance was not political but, rather, emphasized the capacity of trained military to maintain order better than the police forces in a city where the fear of civil disorder continues to grow.

At present in Argentina and Brazil, military forces are not direct players in national politics, and in both countries contemporary political culture is averse to them assuming a governmental role. This "bottom line" of democratization has been reached in both countries.

The Military and the Economy

In the 1980s, the military governments of Argentina and Brazil were unable to adapt their economies to changing world conditions in spite of their authoritarian control. The primary reason was that corporatist models of development were very firmly in place. Businesses were accustomed to being protected from outside competition and were closely linked to politicians who continued to protect them.

In Argentina, organized labor, particularly in the public sector, enjoyed the privileges of a close relationship to the government. In Brazil, while some sectors of organized labor in the private sector (particularly in automobiles) fought for independence from the military, most workers continued to see the government as a necessary "protector" against exploitation and as a provider of the social services first set up by Getúlio Vargas in the 1940s. In the public sector, workers were often linked to political party leaders who controlled and expanded public sector employment and contracts as a partisan benefit. Both countries had developed cultures based on government economic dominance as investor, protector, and leader of "the engine of growth."

The second reason for both countries' militaries failure to adapt was intrinsic to the authoritarian and nationalist nature of the military regimes. Both national militaries were unhappy with the prospect of foreign interests owning natural resources or major industries — in spite of the need for serious foreign investment in the country. Embedded in the military's own ideology of protecting national sovereignty was a fierce reluctance to turn away from an import-substitution model and open up the economy to outside competition. As institutions, they were comfortable with large public sector enterprises they could easily control. In addition, as the military leadership lost all political support, it was unable to forge any consensus within society toward fundamental change. In both countries, when the militaries left power, their economies were in serious trouble. Both military regimes passed on economic legacies of debt, inflation, and government intervention.

The New Civilian Regimes: Politics Before Economics

During the first years of civilian government, neither Argentine nor Brazilian leaders were seriously able to reform their economies. The years after the return to constitutional democracy during the Alfonsín administration (1983-1989) in Argentina and the Sarney administration (1985-1989) in Brazil were dedicated to political consolidation.

In Argentina, the country focused on ridding the political system not only of military leadership but of military influence, a task of formidable proportions. President Alfonsín used the civilian court system to try the military for human rights abuses after military tribunals proved unwilling to undertake serious investigations and prosecutions. He even put key generals on trial for their abuses. This was a strong signal of his commitment to civilian control of the armed forces.

For Brazil, after twenty-one years of direct military rule, the burning question was how to restructure the political system: constitutional reform was the process chosen. During a painfully slow, nineteen-month process, the entire Congress acted as a constitutional convention, hammering out in intricate detail the rules for governing. The process brought new groups into the political process, reactivated old ones, and was a positive step in developing democratic processes. The final Constitution, however, was more an amalgam of interest group politics than an enduring document of political will. It took Brazil back to where it had been politically before the military stepped in, rather than moving it ahead to consolidate and deepen democratic institutions.

President Sarney, who came from a poor, politically conservative, northeastern state, was not the leader to build a new political coalition outside the old patrimonial political system. He wasted political capital on a costly fight over the length of his own tenure as president and opposed budget reform that might decrease the government's patronage power. For the government, it was back to "politics as usual," with mounting state corruption and deficits.

With the emphasis on civilian politics, economic reform was not successful during either transition. Argentina was put through four major stabilization programs but made little headway toward ending inflation and renewed economic growth. In fact, as the Alfonsín administration wore on, inflation became progressively worse, and each stabilization program broke down in ever greater inflationary surges. By 1989, the system collapsed. The Argentine government could find no sources of finance other than the printing press.

The international commercial banks refused to continue refinancing the foreign debt, and the government suspended interest payments in 1988. From January 1989 through the presidential elections in June 1989, Argentina's economy skyrocketed into hyperinflation — and then spiraled into depression.

In contrast, Brazil limped along with very high inflation but was saved from hyperinflation primarily by its practice of indexing the economy so that wages kept apace of prices. Brazil, like Argentina, tried an economic stabilization program, but it was unsuccessful.

Overall, President Sarney was not committed to serious economic reform. By his last year in office, he had given up, admitting that his ministers lacked the credibility to impose a workable economic policy and that they could not solve the foreign debt problem. He submitted economic proposals for tax reform and ending subsidies but refused to fight for them vigorously in the Congress and even repudiated parts of his reforms when challenged by business.

The Sarney regime illustrated that in Brazil "free competition" was a myth. A report issued by the Fundação Getúlio Vargas in 1989 noted that more than half of Brazil's industrial market was controlled by only 1.7 percent of the companies registered in the country, including government companies. Oligopolies in each sector fixed prices; "market prices" could not even be determined. Recognizing this, President Sarney tried to work with big businesses in each sector to set monthly prices as a way of decreasing inflation, through "sectoral chamber," a direct throwback to traditional corporatist organizations.

In the battle against inflation, Sarney was not successful. Inflation crept up month by month. By September 1989, it reached 36 percent per month; by November 1989, when Brazilians voted for a new president, inflation had reached 53 percent for the month.

Sarney's commitment to privatization was tepid. In early 1989, he proposed that sixty state-owned companies be sold. By August, the draft legislation he sent to the Congress included only sixteen firms. Three of these were profitable subsidiaries of Siderugia Brasileira, SA (SIDERBRÁS). SIDERBRÁS, a government steel holding company, was singly responsible for half the government's US$5 billion losses in 1988. By the end of Sarney's administration, the government had sold eighteen public enterprises for about $.5 billion, mostly to government pension funds.

By the end of the Alfonsín and Sarney regimes, both Argentina and Brazil were in serious economic crisis. Alfonsín's presidency ended in hyperinflation and economic panic, with monthly inflation at 200 percent. In Brazil, the situation was not quite so bad, merely terrible. Sarney left the presidency with monthly inflation at 73 percent, hyperinflation by most country's standards, but considered only an "imminent peril" in Brazil, the land of indexation.

Neither president exercised the political courage nor gained the political support necessary to cut expenditures and reform the state sector. Both presidents focused on strengthening their own political bases, instead of pushing for economic reform. Neither leader had the political strength or interest to advocate a strong privatization program.

Presidents Menem and Collor: Coming to Grips with Economic Reforms

President Carlos Menem of Argentina and President Fernando Collor de Mello of Brazil, successors respectively of Alfonsín and Sarney, took office only months apart, with both countries' economies in desperate straits. But two factors, one economic and one political, led the two countries along very different paths.

The economic difference was hyperinflation — Argentina went through it; Brazil did not. As a result, Argentine leadership and Argentine voters were shocked into support for a radical overhaul of the economy. Brazilian support for radical action was, in comparison, tepid and fragmented.

The political difference was party support, particularly in Congress: Argentina's Menem came in as standard-bearer of a powerful party, while Brazil's Collor invented his own small party (Partido de Recontrução Nacional (PRN) - National Reconstruction Party) to get elected and came into office with virtually no institutional support. As a result, Menem had political clout, and his political courage was backed by organization. Collor had only the force of his personality. He needed to negotiate each initiative personally with a highly fragmented Congress that offered no natural base of support to him.

Argentina's Menem came in with the strongest possible mandate to enact whatever necessary economic reforms, however unpalatable, to end hyperinflation and pull the country out of its malaise. He seized the moment, realizing that for the country to move forward it would have to dismantle the basic corporatist structure that had maintained it. In a shocking political move, he broke with the basic corporatist ideals of the Peronist party (Partido Justicialista) that elected him and began to disassemble the government behemoth that had dominated the Argentine economy for fifty years.

As the head of the major party which had traditionally reaped the benefits of non-competition and state dominance, he was in an excellent position to organize structural reform. To generate more income, tax collections were improved, loopholes advantageous to industry and agriculture were closed, the urban middle and upper classes were taxed, and movie stars were thrown into jail when they broke the law — all to symbolize the seriousness of the government's efforts.

Privatization of public enterprises was the mainstay of the economic transformation. Government-controlled companies, known to be snake pits of subsidies, monopoly pricing, and non-competitive management, were rapidly auctioned off. The money generated was used to pay government liabilities to pensioners and the foreign banks in exchange for a deal to reduce debt service. Airlines, telecommunications, railways, power, and oil concessions were sold. Even industries controlled by the military — petrochemicals, steel, and munitions — were sold. Empresa Nacional de Telecomunicaciones (Entel), the Argentine telecommunications company, was sold in 1990 to two consortia, both headed by foreign firms, for about US$5 billion, the largest sale to date. In the same year, Aerolineas Argentinas was sold for about $200 million. The railroads, traditionally Argentina's biggest money loser, have been partially sold, and even the subway system is being partially privatized. Water and energy industries have also been put on the auction block. Yacimientos Petrolíferos Fiscales Sociedad del Estado (YPF), the government oil company, was partially sold.

Privatization in Argentina decreased the number of government employees and eroded the patronage power of the old elite. It created a more level playing field for new economic competitors. Labor unions, whose fortunes were closely tied to huge public enterprises, were weakened as their numbers decreased and their privileges ended. At the same time, however, the unions were forced to become more autonomous and less dependent upon the government. Domestic manufacturers, once highly protected, found themselves facing stiff international competition for the first time. All these elements undermined the basic structure of corporatist Argentina.

These changes had their own repercussions, creating a sort of vicious circle. Because recession in Argentina had dampened internal demand, some domestic manufacturers had already made forays into the export market. To compete internationally, these firms were forced to become more efficient. They began to support tariff reform and trade liberalization to lower their own import costs and began to look skeptically at inefficient government companies. Government companies supplied many of the domestic manufacturers' inputs at high prices but at the same time supported privatizing these firms as a way of lowering their own input costs. Hyperinflation was the final shock leading to the realization that the alternative to economic reform with its higher taxes, lessened subsidies, and foreign competition was a continuation of economic stagnation and uncontrollable inflation.

Menem's policies brought inflation down to international levels and led to three years of economic expansion and substantial reductions in absolute poverty. His success has changed Argentina's economic ideology, which now favors market pricing, export-led growth, and an economy led by the private sector. While much remains to be done before corporatism is buried, Argentina's successes in developing political and economic pluralism and autonomy have given it a new vision of its development path.

The same cannot be said for Brazil. Brazil went through only a small part of this process. In spite of spiraling inflation and high debt, the Brazilian presidential election focused almost exclusively on politics.

First, a protracted electoral campaign mesmerized Brazil. The electorate had grown by 400 percent since the last presidential elections twenty-nine years earlier. No one under 49 years of age had ever cast a ballot for president. The campaign was exciting and its outcome uncertain. Both second-round candidates ran campaigns based on improving the lives of the poor, offering clear alternatives to the voters. Workers' Party candidate Luís Inácio Lula da Silva, a respected labor leader from the modern sector in São Paulo, gained support through extensive party organization.

In contrast, Fernando Collor de Mello, the scion of a wealthy political family from the poor northeast, created his own small party to run in the elections. He bypassed party organization, appealing directly to voters on the basis of his youthful dynamism. To most Brazilians, the election itself was enormously important as proof that Brazil had returned to democracy and civilian rule.

Without the pressure of hyperinflation, Brazilian voters focused on political and personal issues rather than economics. President Sarney's previous administration had reeked of corruption and clientelism. He had been unable to make his hard economic programs stick because they conflicted with the political elite's reliance on subsidies, employment patronage, and public works. The blur between "public" and "private" remained intact. How could economic reform occur without first dealing with corruption?

Candidate Collor milked this theme successfully, railing against the political "maharajahs" in state legislatures who gave themselves salaries and benefits worth more than $100,000. This resonated strongly among voters in poor northeastern states where most people earned less than one half of one percent of that figure. Voters even saw Collor's lack of traditional political party support as evidence that he was unencumbered with the clientelist obligations of his predecessor.

In November 1989, Fernando Collor de Mello was elected president, with a mandate to modernize the economy and clean up politics. Within a day of his inauguration in March 1990, he took action. He issued a series of presidential decrees to end inflation, reform the public sector, and privatize in sectors "not indispensable to the state." His shock therapy went further than any previous Brazilian effort.

Collor froze savings accounts, declared a moratorium on internal debt payments, issued a new currency, announced a tax reform policy, posted "for sale" signs on one hundred eighty-eight government companies, and set a preliminary target of dismissing eighty thousand to seven hundred thousand national government workers. He abolished the linkage between wage increases and the inflation rate, effectively ending the practice of indexation.

Experts compared Collor's decrees to Germany's anti-inflation program of 1948 and to "nuclear war" against inflation. Opponents labeled it flagrantly unconstitutional. Polls showed high levels of popular approval. Finance ministers, investment bankers, and political leaders around the world applauded. Inflation fell from 84.3 percent in March 1990 to 3.2 percent in April 1990. For a brief moment, Brazil seemed committed to the trailblazing road of economic reform opened by Chile, Mexico, and Argentina.

Like Menem, Collor opposed the corporatist rationale of government domination of the economy. He argued that Brazil's future economic health did not depend on the sheer size of its industry and on economies of scale but on its ability to compete internationally. He contended that the large state monopolies in basic industries, mining, communications, and transportation systems were drags on the economy. He and his economy minister also forcefully attacked the protected private sector, declaring a "war" on cartels and oligopolistic practices. He cut import taxes on all products made in Brazil by monopolies and sent anti-trust legislation to the Congress. Collor also asked for an early revision of the 1988 Constitution that gave the government a monopoly in the oil industry, restricted foreign capital, and guaranteed government employees job security. Collor bought squarely into the premise that the Brazilian economy needed a healthy dose of competition, including foreign competition.

President Collor's greatest real success was in trade liberalization and export promotion. Here, businessmen concerned with export markets followed the path of their Argentine counterparts. They became political supporters of the president's efforts to lower their input costs through privatization. Brazilian exporters worked closely with the administration through a Competitiveness Council to suggest regulatory and trade regime changes that would encourage greater exports. Average import duties declined to about 17 percent and continue to diminish.

In contrast to its trade liberalization, the process of privatization in Brazil was slow, mired in technical problems, politics, fear of foreign competition, and corruption. Technically, the administration first set its "destatization" program up in a way guaranteed to cause dissension and antagonism. Banks, pension funds, and brokerage houses were forced to purchase Privatization Certifications, which could only be used to purchase state companies. Similarly, public pension funds were required to use 25 percent of their reserves on certificates. Hence, groups were essentially forced to become buyers, at discounted prices, whether or not they wanted to participate.

Law suits were filed, effectively postponing the program, and eventually the pension groups and private firms won. There were other problems. The government had trouble setting a price for its companies. The Constitution limited the program's scope, particularly its restrictions on foreign firms. Congress did not see the program as a priority and postponed voting on it for many months. Eduardo Modiani, Collor's privatization czar, was forced to delay the start of the program from August 1990 to October, then to December 1990, then to late January 1991.

Modiani announced that Latin America's biggest steel producer, Minas Gerais Iron and Steel Mills, Inc. (USIMINAS), would be the first public firm to hit the auction block, expected to raise US$18 billion. All groups, both in favor of and against privatization, began to mobilize their forces over this test case. Many politicians, particularly those on the left, directly opposed the USIMINAS sale. The governor of Rio de Janeiro, who also led a labor party, openly opposed it. Federal deputies from Minas Gerais, working with the Confederação General dos Trabalhadores, were able to delay the sale. Demonstrations and violence outside the Rio stock exchange forced another month's delay, to October 24, 1991. On that day, USIMINAS was finally sold.

The results did not seem to merit the turmoil. Those who worried about foreigners buying a huge "national resource" were wrong. Less than 6 percent of the shares were bought by foreign investors. A consortium of Brazilian-owned companies bought the largest share, about 38 percent. Government-related groups bought up other huge chunks of the company. The Companhia Vale do Rio Doce (CVRD), a government holding company, bought about 15 percent of the shares, while USIMINAS employees were allocated 10 percent.

The USIMINAS sale broke open the privatization process, but the pace was still slow. In January 1992, Modiani announced that six companies had been sold and that the government had earned a total of US$1.7 billion through privatization — a much lower amount than originally anticipated. He earmarked twenty-two other companies for sale, estimating possible earnings of about US$3.4 billion, down from earlier estimates of US$18 billion.

Collor's government wanted to privatize Petróleo Brasileiro, SA (PETROBRÁS), Brazil's huge national petroleum company, but the Constitution forbade it. However, PETROBRÁS had spawned a group of profitable petro-chemical subsidiaries, and these the government could sell off. It began to dismantle PETROBRÁS. Opposition forces vigorously defended state control. Nationalists began an "O petróleo e nosso" ("The oil is ours.") campaign, echoing the themes sounded so successfully since Vargas first nationalized the oil industry. The Petrobrás Engineers Association led the effort.

Public Sector Employment — Same Delays and Lack of Action

These privatization efforts in Brazil took place in an economic environment of recession, mounting inflation and unemployment, and growing popular distrust of the president's program. Iraq's invasion of Kuwait raised oil prices in Brazil, severely straining Brazil's economy and import bill. Brazil had been exporting billions of dollars of arms to Iraq; this abruptly ended. The country was plunged into recession and was unable to pay its debt. Inflation crept back up steadily through 1990, and GDP fell by 4 percent.

Collor tried a second adjustment plan in February 1991, but within a short time it also proved unsuccessful, and the recession continued. In August, the Congress rejected, by an overwhelming margin, Collor's "provisional measure" granting pay increases to the military and public sector employees. High inflation persisted, reaching over 22 percent by October 1991. A pervasive sense that Collor had lost complete control of the economy led to calls for his impeachment. Polls showed that most Brazilians considered 1991 the worst year for them in over a decade.

Brazil's economic situation in 1991 was not at all the case in Argentina; the contrast could not have been greater. By 1991, Argentina's recession had ended, and the economy had grown a healthy 6 percent. What accounted for the difference? Primarily two variables, one economic and one political.

In Argentina hyperinflation had sobered all political groups, as they realized that economic disaster would continue unless they cooperated to support a strong reform program and stopped jockeying for special benefits. Menem therefore encountered political groups much more willing to nego-tiate toward a common goal than Collor did. Furthermore, Menem was the political leader of the Peronistas and had a strong political organization to help push forward his program in the Congress and among interest groups.

In Brazil, President Collor had neither the shock of hyperinflation nor the organized political support of his Argentine counterpart. The labor movement had supported his opponent. Public sector workers bitterly fought his efforts to cut the bureaucracy and sell off large chunks of it. Many leaders in the military and public enterprises zealously resisted foreign investment and privatization efforts. In short, no consensus developed over the need for basic reform or the direction it should take.

Collor's support in Congress was minuscule and uncertain. While the Constitution allowed him to begin his reform program by issuing decrees, these "provisional measures" had to be ratified in short order by the Congress. His National Reconstruction Party held very few seats in Congress. He was therefore forced to negotiate and compromise separately with every political interest to get any legislation through on his program.

To get political support Collor attempted several strategies. Throughout 1990 and 1991 he courted the Partido da Social Democracia Brasileira (PSDB), a widely respected but very small center-left party with leaders who favored his economic reform goals. The October 1990 legislative and gubernatorial elections were disturbing for him. The key to his legislative success lay with the governors, who generally controlled their state congressional delegations. In important states, including São Paulo, his gubernatorial candidates lost. After the elections, the governors began organizing against his recessionary economic policies. Partly through their influence, Congress re-imposed indexation in December 1990, undermining a cornerstone of Collor's stabilization program.

The governors also directly controlled government resources and increased spending dramatically in their states, particularly just before the elections. The 1988 Constitution developed immense new resources for the states, giving them greater influence over total public sector spending than they had ever had. Their own spending programs, therefore, became as important as the national government programs in determining the success of economic reform.

Collor understood that he needed the political and economic power of the newly elected governors. Without their support his program could not succeed. In February 1991 he reversed one important policy, approving US$3 billion in loans to state-owned banks in the four largest states: São Paulo, Minas Gerais, Rio de Janeiro, and Rio Grande do Sul. In return, Collor hoped to get these powerful governors to influence Congress in support of his economic plan.

Some of the governors supported Collor's efforts to speed up constitutional reform and to form a "social pact," but they rebuffed his attempts to link their congressional influence directly to state or federal finance policy. In late August, they specifically rejected his plan to roll over US$57 billion owed by the states to the central government in return for getting Congress to vote for his proposed constitutional amendments. This was a major political setback for the president.

Collor's strategy to link up directly with the PSDB to develop a stronger party base in Congress failed. His strategy of co-opting governors failed. He also attempted to use his cabinet appointments in 1991 to develop political support but with no greater success. He tried going over the heads of politicians "directly to the people" through television broadcasts. Nothing worked. The president's authoritarian, charge-ahead style was an empty shell. There was no political organization behind him.

The final nail in the coffin of Brazil's economic reform was political corruption. In the Latin American democracies of the 1980s, there has been a strong linkage in voters' minds between corruption and reform. The short-term impact of liberalizing the economy and cutting deficits is recessionary, with rising poverty and unemployment. Popular support for this painful process rests on a common belief in the need for reform and a sense of shared sacrifice.

Fernando Collor came into office as "Mr. Clean." His support rested solely on his personal image. He had no reserves of party or other organizational supporters. His popularity depended on his maintaining an image of honesty. Any weakening of his image would put his entire economic program in jeopardy.

This clean image began to dissipate shortly after Collor became president. Many of the accusations were tied closely to the reform process itself. Soon after Collor announced his first reforms in March 1990, there were rumors of special treatment in "defrosting" frozen bank accounts. In November 1990, the former president of PETROBRÁS accused the presidential palace of pressuring him to loan PETROBRÁS funds illegally to a group trying to buy Viação Aérea São Paulo, SA (VASP), a major airline being privatized by São Paulo. In the same month, Collor was connected to electoral fraud in his home state of Alagoas. In May 1991, departing Economy Minister Zelia Cardoso de Mello (not related to the president) accused President Collor of "bending rules" to help his brother.

The corruption charges began to center around a small political group informally dubbed the "Republic of Alagoas," an inner circle of Collor friends and advisors widely accused of influence-peddling. The president, aware of the importance of retaining an aura of honesty, tried to cut his losses. He removed his wife Rosane Malta de Collor — a powerful political figure in Alagoas — from the presidency of the Legião Brasileira de Assistencia (LBA). The LBA was a state-owned charitable organization with about 9,400 employees and a US$1 billion budget used as a political slush fund by many administrations. In Rosane Collor's hands the funds were disbursed to relatives and electoral campaigns until she was forced to resign. The president fired his education minister and his social action minister, old political cronies who used the school building program and social action programs for political patronage and payoffs.

By May 1992, the charges of corruption reached the president himself. His brother, Pedro Collor de Mello, accused the president and Paulo César "P.C." Farias, Collor's former campaign manager and a central figure in Alagoan politics, of tax evasion, illicit enrichment, and influence peddling. Week after week, the press uncovered a widening web of kickbacks, money laundering, payoffs, and corruption soon dubbed "Collorgate."

Under these circumstances, economic reform froze. The Congress and the entire population focused solely on the scandal and the subsequent effort to impeach the president. Collor fought fiercely, both by using through the legal system and by attempting to use promises of federal funds to congressmen and governors who supported him. He lost badly.

The Chamber of Deputies voted 434 to 38 to send the impeachment forward to the Senate. On October 2, 1992, Collor was suspended from the presidency for one hundred eighty days. In December 1992, the Senate convicted him, and Vice-President Itamar Franco became president of Brazil.

The impeachment illustrated how far the democratization of Brazil had come. Viewed one way, the impeachment of the first popularly elected president in decades was a tragic event, a testament of the fragility of political institutions.

Brazilians saw it otherwise. To most it showed two positive aspects: the strength of democratic institutions and a profound shift in political culture. Government institutions and the press set high standards for professionalism, probity, and competence. The court system, the congressional investigation committees, and the banking, police, and administrative offices involved in the investigation performed well. The press acted independently and competently. Congressmen who might otherwise have been swayed by Collor's financial promises were keenly aware of watchful voters. For this process, Brazilian political institutions showed their capacity to govern well under pressure.

Culturally, the common practice of patronage politics came under serious attack. The impeachment was a warning to public officials long accustomed to political immunity from abusing the public trust. It set a new standard for separating public and private interests. The "No" to Collor was a "No" to the traditional politics practiced by the Brazilian elite for much of the country's history.

Itamar Franco stepped into the presidency with his successor's economic program in tatters. He concentrated first on developing a political coalition in the Congress to put through a program, a goal that constantly had eluded Collor. He expanded his cabinet from fifteen to twenty-five members, using the appointments primarily as a means of furthering his congressional goals. Every new minister explicitly promised to support Franco's fiscal reform package.

Privatization was probably the most controversial item on the agenda for President Franco. He had firmly opposed the sale of USIMINAS in 1990, by far the largest privatization under President Collor, and he was thought to be less sympathetic to continuing the basic reform program set in place by Collor and his economic team.

In his first months as president, Franco halted privatizations to "clean up" the program, arguing that the $3.64 billion in companies sold had yielded almost no cash to the government. He removed the government leaders in charge of privatization and canceled the sale of Ultrafertil, a fertilizer company. This was followed by postponement of the sale of Brazil's largest steel mill, Companhia Siderúrgica Nacional (CSN), and thirty-five other government companies.

CSN was the first national steel mill, built in 1941 by the Vargas government to end dependence on foreign steel during the war. It had symbolized government economic leadership in the post-war period, and its sale was viewed as a milestone in the government's commitment to privatization. The postponement of the sale was equally symbolic of Franco's skepticism about the privatization program and led to great uncertainty about his economic program.

The uncertainty was partially resolved on January 19, 1993, when President Franco signed a decree centralizing control of privatization in the presidency and modifying its procedures. To "privatize" the privatizations, the president no longer permitted pension funds of public enterprises (estimated at $25 billion) to purchase state companies. He eased restrictions on foreign capital, with Congress and himself as final arbiters.

Finally, President Franco added some social protection to the process. The decree gave workers a right to participate in setting the auction prices, provided for retraining programs, and directly allocated some of the profits of privatization to health, education, and scientific and technological projects. This was the first effort in Brazil to link social welfare directly to privatizations — a procedure first undertaken in Mexico that had proved very popular.

Economic reform continues slowly in Brazil, still overshadowed by 1993's political events. In April 1993, a plebiscite determined that the presidential system should stay in place and not be replaced by a parliamentary system or a monarchy. Congressional elections are slated for October 1994. The 1988 Constitution set 1993 as the year for constitutional revision. All of these factors, particularly the constitutional reforms, will have an impact on the economic system. Until these issues are resolved, however, more definitive economic change remains hostage to politics in Brazil.

Argentina's Progress from Insolvency to Recovery

Richard S. Newfarmer

After four decades of relative decline, culminating in poverty-increasing recession and pernicious hyperinflation in the last half of the 1980s, Argentina in 1990 began its longest sustained period of economic growth since the golden 1920s. Inflation, woven into the socioeconomic fabric of Argentina with seeming permanence, abruptly receded to international rates, and the economy soared with growth rates above 5 percent annually. Investment poured into the country from abroad. Even the rival Chileans, normally skeptical of their neighbor's prospects, suddenly began to look for investment opportunities on the other side of the Andes.

Much of the success has been attributed to the March 1991 Convertibility Law, which fixed the domestic currency against the U.S. dollar and pledged international reserves to back it. In mid-1992, for example, *The Economist* wrote: "The turn-round began in April 1991, when Mr. Menem's fourth economics minister, Domingo Cavallo, fixed the exchange rate of the Argentine currency against the dollar, and banned the government from printing money to pay its deficits" (1992, 42). In fact, the reform effort began much earlier, was much deeper than exchange rate management, and was of necessity concentrated on public finance. Behind the veil of financial chaos that prevailed in Argentina in 1989-1991, and through two hyperinflations, three ministers of economy and six Central Bank presidents, authorities struggled to push the public sector down a path of profound economic reorganization. The new optimism in Argentina rests on these changes — as well as the clear vision of policy articulated by Minister Cavallo.

Richard S. Newfarmer is division chief in the Industry and Energy Operations Division of the World Bank.

Carlos Menem Assumes Office

Carlos Menem assumed the office of president of Argentina in July 1989 under the worst of economic conditions: Inflation had reached 200 percent monthly, and the economy was in deep recession. Decades of subsidies and economic privileges to Argentina's corporatist special-interest groups had made Argentina's economy one of the most distorted outside the Soviet bloc. Besides channeling investment into unproductive activities, this maze of subsidies produced an intractable public deficit that led to chronic inflation. Inflation drove Argentine savings abroad, and by the end of the 1980s, savings and investment were at half the levels of the 1970s.

At the center of the economic hurricane was public finance. The deficit exceeded 10 percent of gross domestic product (GDP). Tax evasion, the breakdown of tax administration, and loopholes — as well as inflation itself through the Tanzi effect — had driven tax collections in the second quarter of 1989 to their lowest levels in history. Frozen prices of public enterprises during hyperinflation drove enterprise balances further into the red.[1] The government, having suspended payment to commercial banks fifteen months before and in arrears to international financial institutions, had virtually no sources of external finance. Central Bank liquid reserves were approaching zero. With the *austral* money base at less than 1.5 percent of GDP — US$800 million — money emission could not close the fiscal accounts as the private sector reduced its holdings of financial assets to avoid the inflation tax — igniting the fires of hyperinflation.[2] With liabilities far exceeding assets, a large deficit, and no sources of finance, the Argentine government was effectively insolvent.

Although Menem enacted two stabilization programs, these soon broke down in new waves of high inflation. In hindsight, the enduring legacy of his first two years was not price stability, but a progressive recasting of the foundations of public finance. The government undertook difficult-to-reverse reforms in the legal framework, institutions, and policies. This process, not unlike a bankruptcy procedure, was characterized by three sets of actions. First, the government improved *revenue mobilization* to increase the quantity and quality of federal revenues. Second, it enacted *expenditure reforms* to reduce the scope and size of government through administrative reforms that reduced public employment, privatizations to ensure a permanent end to subsidies through public entities, and fiscal decentralization. Finally, the government began *restructuring its liabilities with domestic and foreign creditors* to adjust them to serviceable levels.

Revenue Mobilization

By the end of the 1980s, Argentines had virtually stopped paying taxes. Although the Argentine tax system had been fairly sophisticated in the late 1970s, increasing exemptions and the lack of political resolve in enforcing tax laws progressively eroded tax revenues. Taxes, which reached 19.5 percent of GDP in 1980, fell to low of 9.4 percent during the second quarter of 1989. More worrisome, the composition of revenues shifted as low collections of potentially efficient taxes compelled the government to rely on "tax handles" — export taxes, taxes on bank checks, and excessive energy taxes — and these discouraged productive investment. The value added tax (VAT) became riddled with exemptions, and the income tax withered because of improper inflation accounting and exemptions for income from capital. Tax incentives to subsidize industry in particular regions and sectors, beginning in 1977, were particularly pernicious; the cost of promotion schemes to the Treasury was estimated to have reached over 1.5 percent of GDP in 1989. The tax benefits at one time were so perverse that producers in Tierra del Fuego, the island just north of Antarctica, found it profitable to buy video machines in Japan, disassemble them in Panama, and then reassemble them on the island for sale in Buenos Aires, fifteen hundred miles to the north.

Tax administration eroded along with tax policy. The sharp deterioration in public sector salaries after 1984 drove tax inspectors into the employ of large taxpayers; tax rolls were not up-dated, and they vanished over the decade. By 1989, the General Tax Office (DGI) had virtually no tax roll, a low rate of inspections and audits, and a low rate of collection per audit; an audit costing the DGI US$800 produced US$35 in new cash revenues.

The Menem administration undertook a major effort to improve revenues through implementation of a much-broadened and uniform VAT, first on goods in February 1990, and extended to services in November 1990. Then the Cavallo package of February 1991 increased the tax on bank checks but made these deductible from the income and VAT taxes. At the same time, the government progressively eliminated export taxes during 1990 and early 1991, and removed several minor taxes — so the quality of the revenue mobilization effort improved substantially in 1992.

Revenue improvements would not have been possible without the strengthening of tax administration, begun in 1989. The government established a computerized control system for the largest taxpayers, rebuilt the tax rolls in 1989-1990, and modified labor agreements to "de-privatize" its internal revenue service through the dismissal of corrupt inspectors. The government hired some three thousand students during the Argentine summer of 1989-1990 to make more than 400,000 site inspections for VAT compliance. It also improved enforcement, enacting severe penalties for tax evasion in 1990, indicting a few popular television stars in well-publicized tax evasion cases, and closing over eight thousand businesses for VAT violations in 1991, up from five hundred in 1990 and zero the year before. Tax audits and indictments for tax fraud were doubled in 1990 and quadrupled in 1991. The president and his ministers played leading roles in changing public expectations about tax compliance with public speeches, decrees, and even advertisements. To encourage consumers to ask for VAT receipts, the Argentine internal revenue service established a televised national lottery based on consumer submissions of numbered VAT receipts from stores. These efforts, together with price stability, cumulatively produced dramatic rises in tax collections in 1992.[3]

Expenditure Reduction and Restructuring

The state-led, corporatist model of economic development had led to a steady expansion of Argentine public expenditures in the post-war period. Government expenditures had increased from a level of slightly less than 20 percent in 1966-1970 to a peak of nearly 40 percent in 1980-1982. Subsequent stop-go cycles of austerity and inflation after 1983 drove expenditures down more than 10 percentage points of GDP in 1989. These declines did not occur through any rational reduction in the scope and functions of government, but through compression of wages and investment. Expenditures had to be compressed further to make room for an increase in interest payments on the foreign debt taken over by the government in the early 1980s. The expenditure reduction effort has been built upon the triad of administrative reform, public enterprise privatization, and fiscal federalism.

Administrative Reform. The federal government had increased employment by 22 percent in 1981-1990 to about 600,000 workers, at a time when GDP was stagnant and the federal wage bill was contracting.[4] By 1990, average real wages in the civil service had fallen to under 35 percent of their January 1984 levels. The ratio of the highest-paid worker to the lowest had fallen to less than two-to-one in March 1990. The president of Argentina — the highest paid civil servant in the country — made the equivalent of US$700 per month. Salaries were so low that not one federal employee earned the minimum necessary to require payment of income taxes. At the same time, spending on materials fell to next to nothing, so teachers went without texts and hospitals suffered without supplies. The situation became so acute that in mid-1990 a group of businessmen began organizing a private corporate foundation to do something to improve public administration.

Confronted with a precarious cash flow in the second hyperinflation of February 1990, then-Minister Erman Gonzalez decided to reduce the size of the federal bureaucracy. The president in November 1990 launched a sweeping civil service reform that reduced federal employment by 90,000 in 1991 and is on track for a further decline of 30,000 in 1992. In addition, 130,000 teachers and health workers were transferred to the provincial governments in 1992. The reform also entailed a ministerial reorganization to concentrate federal activities on core objectives and on improvements in the civil service system through an improved salary structure and efficiency measures. These efforts allowed the government to reduce its wage expenditures about 10 percent in dollar terms in 1992 and at the same time increase average salaries, a combination that has probably never occurred in post-war Argentina.

However, the civil service reform was only one step to controlling expenditures. The government submitted to Congress in late 1990 a Law of Public Financial Management to revamp national fiscal accounting, establish modern auditing systems for all public expenditures, and require Congress to authorize annual debt ceilings. The government improved its programming and control of public expenditures in earnest beginning in February 1991. Then, in a little-noticed decree building upon the Law of Convertibility (1823/91), the government effectively indexed expenditures to revenues and granted the executive branch the legal authority to withhold spending. In 1992, the executive sent the federal budget to Congress on time, and Congress approved it *before* the beginning of the fiscal year — for only the second time in twenty-six years.

Public Enterprises. The hyperinflation of 1989 galvanized public opinion around the need to restructure radically public enterprises to free them from the clutches of private interests — including consumers enjoying uneconomic prices, labor groups benefiting from high wages and excess staffing, and industrialists selling to the state, often at huge mark-ups. The Alfonsín administration had tried to privatize several companies during 1988-1989, but these efforts stalled. In July 1989, under pressure from the economic crisis, Congress adopted the new administration's emergency timetable for divestiture of nearly all its enterprises. The government sold two television stations, the telephone company, and Aerolineas Argentinas; it also granted highway and railroad concessions to the private sector. The reorganization of the railways, including the privatization of long distance cargo lines and revamping of intra-urban service, was expected to phase down subsidies of US$1 million per day in 1991. Most important, the government launched a comprehensive restructuring of the petroleum industry — the first in Latin America — auctioning off the areas formerly monopolized by the state oil company (YPF), selling equity blocks in Yacimientos Petrolíferos Fiscales Sociedad del Estado (YPF), and creating a new pricing and investment regime that permitted world prices and private investment. The government intends to sell majority shareholdings in virtually all remaining public enterprises, including the defense industries, electricity distribution, ports and maritime transport, reinsurance, and eventually the entire power sector.

This program removed price setting from politics in the vast segment of the economy formerly covered by these enterprises. Also, the institutional change in these sectors cut off public subsidies to interest groups and opened up the possibility for enormous productivity gains over time. It also freed up capital and human resources for productive purposes. Asset sales also provided the macroeconomic program with a source of transitional finance — more than

US$1.5 billion to help close fiscal accounts in 1991 and 1992 — and the sales will help finance a debt reduction deal with commercial banks and pensioners.

Decentralization. The government also sought to restructure fiscal relationships with the provinces. Building on the "coparticipation law" of 1988, which fixed the share of federal revenues automatically transferred to the provinces at 58 percent, the government sought to limit macro instability arising from deficits in the provinces. This entailed limiting the resources provincial governments could access from their provincial banks by progressively terminating Central Bank lending to provincial banks. It also meant reducing extra-coparticipation transfers through the budget. Finally, it meant transferring classes of expenditures to provincial administration in 1992, notably secondary education and hospitals.

Thus, revenues jumped sharply beginning in 1991, on the basis of reforms enacted in 1990 and continued improvements thereafter. Expenditures fell sharply after 1988, and the quality began improving after 1989.

Restructuring Domestic and Foreign Debt

The government's final step in dealing with its insolvency involved restructuring its financing obligations. The government had financed its deficit through borrowing from the financial system (US$3.5 billion) and by accumulating arrears to external creditors (US$7 billion), social security pensioners, and others. Each of these required major initiatives.

Quasifiscal Deficit and Debt with the Financial System. Subsidies through the Central Bank were massive during the 1980s — in the form of rediscounts to housing and industry, guaranteed rates on foreign exchange purchases, costly bailouts to depositors in failed banks, and subsidies to the social security system. Roque Fernández, the Central Bank president, estimated Central Bank losses at US$48 billion during the 1980s. Even so, to pay for subsidies and financing to the Treasury, the Central Bank had to absorb funds through ever-higher legal reserve requirements and "compulsory investments" from the banking system.

Although the government ended new rediscounts to housing and industrial banks as well as liberal rediscounts to provincial banks in 1988, the Central Bank continued money emission to finance the Treasury as well as its own deficit. In 1988 and 1989, the rising interest bill of the Central Bank drove up the domestic interest bill, much as foreign interest payments had widened the deficit in the 1980s. This occurred even though the noninterest balance of the fiscal accounts was gradually improving. In late December 1989, faced with an exploding interest bill, rising Central Bank deficits, and the renewed threat of hyperinflation, the government took the drastic action of converting the domestic, short-term (mainly seven-day), interest-bearing obligations of the Central Bank into US$3.5 billion in ten-year external Treasury bonds

(BONEX). This virtually eliminated the Central Bank's quasifiscal deficit and the monetary emission necessary to finance it — at the cost of penalizing savers and erasing confidence in the financial system.

External Debt. In April 1988, the government suspended payment on its external debt to commercial creditors. By 1992, it had accumulated US$8 billion in arrears as part of a US$33-billion medium-term commercial bank debt. Public external debt was US$61 billion. The government reinitiated partial payments in June 1990 and has established a consistent track record of paying about 25 percent of interest due. At the same time, it allowed external debt to be used in exchange for the sale of assets, which reduced the debt stock by US$7 billion.

Progressive improvement in fiscal fundamentals in 1990-1991 allowed the government to negotiate with commercial banks on a debt reduction deal. In December 1992, the government signed an agreement with banks to reduce debt service. The agreement converted arrears in a twelve-year uncollateralized bond at LIBOR (London interbank offered rate) with a three-year grace, after a US$700 million down payment; it would exchange existing debt for either a collateralized par bond with a fixed interest rate (beginning at 4 percent and rising to 6 percent by the sixth year), or a collateralized *discount bond* at 65 percent of face value at LIBOR; new collateralized bonds would have a twelve-month rolling interest guarantee. The agreement, although increasing the cash payment, will end the accumulation of arrears and provide for a debt reduction similar to that of Mexico.

Arrears to Pensioners and Others. For the last decade, the government has paid only about half the legally mandated pension owed to social security recipients. Arrearages were not recorded in the fiscal accounts. The government accumulated arrears in 1990 with suppliers through the formal suspension of payment on goods and services already provided. In addition, the health funds have arrears with their service providers which will also result in new debt. Finally, the government, as part of its income tax reform, suspended the poorly designed loss-carry forward deductions for the corporate income tax, with the agreement to issue some US$4 billion in compensatory bonds. To settle these claims, Congress authorized the government to issue consolidation bonds (BOCONs) that will have terms of ten or sixteen years (with shorter terms for social security recipients) and a five-year grace on principal and interest. This may result in new debt of up to US$15-18 billion.

Policies Toward the Private Sector: Trade and Deregulation

Trade Regime. By 1989, Argentina's closed trade regime — among other things — made it the world's largest producer of 1968 Ford Falcons, each with a price tag of US$21,000. Argentina exported commodities and imported non-competing intermediate and capital goods. The government had begun opening the economy to import competition after October 1988, and the Menem administration accelerated these efforts after July 1989. Quantitative restrictions (QRs) over 30 percent of domestic production coverage in 1988 to 4 percent by late 1990. The ad valorem tariff band was narrowed to zero to 22 percent, with an average rate of about 18 percent; the Cavallo team virtually eliminated export taxes in 1991.

Deregulation. Heavy market regulation interacted with industrial concentration to dull competition. In October 1991, the government issued an omnibus deregulation decree which removed the market-impeding, last vestiges of the corporatist state built on special privileges. Stores were allowed to sell when they wished, grain and beef boards were dissolved, sugar and tobacco funds were abolished, and, in subsequent decrees, import privileges granted to local producers of medicines were abrogated. While it will take time for the market system to become more competitive, a new law of antitrust competition is under preparation to accelerate the process.

Back to the Future: The Convertibility Program

Because of these structural reforms, the February 1991 Convertibility Program began with the most favorable initial conditions of any program during the 1980s: The nonfinancial public sector, though still with serious problems, had a lower structural deficit, and the primary balance in the preceding two quarters was higher than for any program in the 1980s. The Central Bank's external quasi-fiscal deficit was virtually eliminated in January 1990.

Exceptional revenues from asset sales through the privatization program were also becoming available to finance the transition, the political debate having been won in the two previous years. Reserves were higher than for any program in the previous decade because of the free-floating exchange rate regime in 1990 and the use of the inflation tax to accumulate reserves. In addition, the public at large, after two hyperinflations, supported nearly all of the government's reform agenda by a wide margin because it understood the need to avoid monetary emission.

Minister Cavallo has articulated a vision of a modern state that takes Argentina back to the policy regime of 1898-1930, when fiscal conservatism, decentralized federalism in public services, and convertibility produced three decades of growth at more than 5 percent. Reserves in June 1992 surpassed US$8 billion. The positive cycle can continue as long as capital inflows continue and domestic prices converge soon to international prices.

However, Argentina is not yet free of its post-war past. The government has submitted to Congress an ambitious policy agenda of controversial reforms that would completely dismantle the remnants of the post-war corporatist order — including reforms of the social security system, reforms in union-controlled health insurance funds, labor legislation, and antitrust laws.

The government must complete ongoing initiatives in 1992-1993, including reform of the defense complex, the completion of the civil service reform, continued partial divestitures of public enterprises, and reform of the financial sector through downsizing the public banking sector. It must also improve public financial administration in the provinces — since they are to deliver most public services. Thus, the next three years will be as important for Argentina as the last three.

Poverty Reduction Efforts

In the ongoing process, the government must pay special attention to the plight of low-income groups in order to legitimize the program and harness the full potential of Argentine society. During the 1980s, the number of absolute poor — though still among the lowest poverty rates in the hemisphere — increased because of stagnant employment growth, the highly regressive impact of inflation on the real wage of those not able to bargain effectively with employers, and deterioration in social services.

The new program has already reversed some of these trends. Price stability has made the tax burden incalculably more equitable — since the inflation tax, which routinely averaged from 4 percent to 6 percent of GDP annually during the 1980s, was replaced by efficient taxes whose incidence falls proportionately greater on the wealthier segments of society. New investment has already increased the demand for low-skilled labor in construction in many urban areas. While open unemployment is still high at 6.9 percent, it has fallen somewhat from its peak of nearly 8 percent in 1989, while at the same time incorporating nearly 150,000 new workers into the labor force. Maintaining economic growth based on a low inflation tax is essential for poverty alleviation, as is the reconstitution of badly eroded social services.

Neglect of basic health services and the lack of social assistance targeting have stalled progress in reducing maternal and infant mortality and malnutrition, particularly in the poverty belts surrounding the cities of Buenos Aires and Rosario and in the less developed northern provinces. The government's general approach to improving these services is through decentralization of responsibility to the provincial level. To be successful in enhancing service delivery, however, the provinces must improve management of these social programs. The government is developing a program in conjunction with the provinces to improve maternal and child health care, and this kind of effort might well be expanded.

Perhaps more important, the government has prepared a draft law that would break the monopoly of unions on the supply of mandatory health insurance. The unions have been administering 3.5 percent of GDP from a compulsory wage tax with minimal public supervision. Reform of the health system would allow affiliates to choose their insurance companies, permit new competition, and mandate a minimum benefit package for a uniform premium. It would also establish universal access to a national health insurance program. To reduce the high cost of drugs, the government will need to follow up on import liberalization to open distribution channels to importers.

In education, the authorities are preparing to introduce a major reform to the financing of universities. This would involve implementation of tuition charges and student loans for low-income students. This is needed to improve financing available to the universities and reduce implicit subsidies to the educated middle class (some 1.7 percent of GDP); it would also free resources for strengthening the social safety net.

The Promise and Uncertainties of the Future

The most important uncertainties lie outside the control of government and involve, ironically, the private sector and markets. The private sector, long accustomed to easy profits from government financial instruments, may require time to relearn how to invest in productive activities. Also, the market mechanism has been dysfunctional for decades because of rigid rules governing labor markets, oligopolistic pricing by producers, and mark-up pricing by retailers; it may take some time for competition to discipline price and wage-setting.

For the convertibility model to work, competition must drive domestic prices into line with international prices. If market competition does not drive price convergence, recession may result, along with pressures to abandon convertibility. This process is already made difficult by the "overhang" of domestic savings held abroad by domestic residents, the product of years of capital flight; the repatriation of earnings on this capital (estimated at US$45 to $60 billion) tended to appreciate the exchange rate, creating a macroeconomic problem that the government has limited ability to influence. If pressures on the exchange rate do emerge, they could create strains on the still-unreformed banking system and on finances in the provinces.

These problems may portend some temporary setbacks. However, the Argentine effort to change public institutions — and the conduct of public finance — has brought the country back from the abyss of hyperinflation and insolvency. Argentines have shown real persistence in revamping economic institutions since 1989. The accelerating pace of policy reform in 1991-1992 makes it likely that Argentina has at last begun to realize its formidable economic potential.

Notes

1.   Institutionalizing reliance on the inflation tax during the 1980s eventually made the fiscal deficit endogenous — and explosive. The causal chain of fiscal deficits to inflation developed a strong feedback from inflation to deficits. The first channel was through the well-known Oliveira-Tanzi effect; inflation eroded real revenue collections because of the lags in collections, a phenomenon which worsened at the higher average inflation rates of the late 1980s because evasion became easier as the currency lost meaning and became less transparent.

A second channel was through tariffs of public enterprise, which were frozen at the beginning of the several stabilization attempts during the period, and rarely maintained real value; increases in the general prices level after the initiation of the stabilization program almost always erased initial gains in net revenue and led to increased deficits toward the end of the stabilization episode.

A third channel was the quasi-fiscal deficit of the Central Bank. Towards the end of the 1988 and 1989 stabilization episodes, as inflation accelerated and remonetization slowed, nominal interest rates rose, increasing the interest payments on the liabilities of the Central Bank. This more than offset interest receipts on assets, most of which had fixed interest rates or were otherwise unlinked to domestic market rates. Finally, financial markets, leery of inflation surges, responded to indicators of future inflation — notably movements in the exchange rate, increases in public enterprise prices, and fiscal deficits — with rapid portfolio shifts against the austral that could reduce the money base by 50 percent in a matter of days. By the end of the decade, only professional market players dominated the market, and the heightened responsiveness of financial markets to key indicators of future inflation interacted with the withered size of monetary aggregates to make the macroeconomy highly susceptible even to minor shocks.

2.   Rudiger Dornbusch and Juan Carlos de Pablo formalized these relationships in a model designed to show the relationship between inflation, growth, the budget deficit, and money creation under differing macroeconomic and financial conditions. The model states:

$$\pi = (\text{\ss}g\text{-}y)/(1\text{-}\text{\ss}); \ 1\text{---}g$$

where π is inflation, $\text{\ss}$ is the velocity of money under noninflationary circumstances, g is the rate of growth, and — is the response of velocity to the rate of inflation. While inflation is a function of money creation associated with the deficit, actual rates can differ enormously according to the rate of growth and financial conditions. Generally, this equation states that (1) inflation will be less the higher the rate of growth because growth generates a demand for money; (2) inflation will be greater the larger the budget deficit; and (3) the rate of inflation depends on the parameters for velocity; the higher the velocity of money (say, associated with dollarization), the greater will be inflation associated with any level of deficit; similarly, the higher the responsiveness of financial markets and velocity of money to inflation, the greater will be inflation.

See Chapter 4 of *Deuda Externa e Inestabilidad Macroeconómica en la Argentina* (Buenos Aires: Editorial Sudamericana, 1988) especially pages 77-79 and Appendix II.

3. Bank staff estimate that about 30 percent of the revenue gains in 1991 were attributable to the Oliveira-Tanzi effect of diminishing inflation on real revenues; the remainder was due to tax effort.

4. In addition, employment in public enterprises is about 300,000; in official banks, about 33,000; employment in the provincial governments is estimated at about 1 million (excluding nonconsolidated municipalities and provincial corporations). Also, the military has enlisted personnel of 86,000, paid through the national budget.

References

Dornbusch, Rudiger, and Juan Carlos de Pablo. 1988. *Deuda Externa e Inestabilidad Macroeconómica en la Argentina*. Buenos Aires: Editorial Sudamericana.

The Economist. 1992. "Which Menem?" 323(June 6-12):7762.

Public Policies in Conflict: Structural Adjustment Versus Alternative Development in Bolivia

Kevin Healy

During the second half of the 1980s, two high-profile public policies, structural adjustment and anti-narcotics, called special attention to Bolivia. These policies have influenced Bolivia's patterns of social and economic change in important ways.

The World Bank and the International Monetary Fund (IMF) have singled out Bolivia as a model for their radical free market adjustment program. The IMF Structural Adjustment and Stabilization Program of 1985, called the New Economic Policy (NEP), represented a radical departure from a state capitalist model practiced by successive Bolivian governments since the 1950s. From Washington, the Reagan and Bush administrations endorsed this IMF economic restructuring by placing it, together with democracy and drugs, among their priority concerns in U.S.-Bolivian policy.

At the same time, the Bolivian state pursued a combined law enforcement and alternative development strategy to eliminate coca leaf production for the drug industry. Alternative development is necessary to enable peasant farmers to shift away from coca leaf production toward viable small farm development with cash crops. This supply-side strategy acquired greater importance by the middle of the decade as drug trafficking became a high priority concern among Western Hemisphere nations.

Kevin Healy is a grant officer at the Inter-American Foundation. Dr. Healy is serving as visiting faculty fellow at the Kellogg Institute of the University of Notre Dame for the 1994-1995 academic year.

Analysts of the relationships between the national economy and the illegal industry tend to show how the coca-cocaine economy influences stabilization and economic recovery. This literature shows the illegal drug-driven economy's favorable impact on foreign exchange (Lee 1990), employment (Lee 1990, Healy 1986), small farmer incomes, and consumer prices (Henkel 1990). Published works which cast a negative light on economic effects of this illegal industry point to the "Dutch disease" aspects which inflate factors such as wages and export prices (Horton 1989) and the detrimental environmental effects (Healy 1986, Lee 1990). Here, however, it is argued that the NEP program increases the coca-cocaine expansion, a phenomenon which in turn undermines the success of the U.S.-Bolivia drug policy.

The Clinton administration should reexamine the relationship between these two leading policies. They should take into account the peculiarities of Bolivia, a relatively small, landlocked country with a large peasant population (42 percent). Without peasant development in Bolivia, national development is a myth. Indeed, there exist policy options which would support peasant purchasing power, income, and employment. A mix of state intervention and open markets would be more conducive to attaining U.S.-Bolivia anti-narcotics policy goals.

After a brief introduction to the NEP program and its impact, the discussion focuses on the general conditions of peasant agriculture, the performance of several key commercial crops including coca, and the national agricultural credit and investment policies. The next section examines the peasant *sindicato* political behavior in relation both to the NEP program and the official coca-reduction, alternative development efforts. The basic question of this chapter is whether the two mentioned public policies are working in concert or in conflict.

Background and Advent of Structural Adjustment

The NEP program in Bolivia instituted policy changes to reverse a process of economic deterioration which had continued uninterrupted during the decade of the 1980s. After record-breaking hyperinflation and four years of negative growth rates, the shattered 1985 Bolivian economy bordered on the edge of collapse. According to the World Bank, "Official estimates show a fall in GDP of over 10 percent from 1980-1985, 24 percent in per capita income terms. Per capita consumption is estimated to have dropped by a total of 16 percent over the period. Private fixed investment averaged about 3 percent of GDP in 1983-1985, compared to over 7 percent in 1980" (World Bank 1990, 25).

Other economic analysts show that under the Unidad Democrática Popular (UDP) government (1982-1985), open unemployment more than doubled, from 105,000 to 250,000, and real wages dropped by 30 percent. Bolivia's record-setting hyperinflation rose to the highest levels for the twentieth century. The failing economy triggered frequent strikes, road blockades, and other widespread protest by disgruntled social groups. The UDP government ultimately conceded to the political pressures by leaving office a year early in 1985.

The subsequent government of the Movimiento Nacional Revolucionario (MNR) (1985), headed by Victor Paz Estensorro, moved quickly to announce the NEP program, a radical departure both from UDP policies and the state-based economic model created by Bolivia's social revolution in 1952. The new NEP decrees ushered in closure of inefficient state mines, devaluation of the exchange rate, removal of price controls and public subsidies, curtailments of public expenditures in areas such as education and health, major tax reform, and a lowering of tariff barriers through trade liberalization. The new macroeconomic plan also established new fiscal incentives to bolster export production.

After an additional year of decline, the economy began its turnaround by rebounding to annual rates of growth of 2.5 percent from 1987 through 1990. Despite the economic gains, the new rates of positive economic growth were still lower than the population growth rate. The most dramatic change, however, was the elimination of hyperinflation within the first few weeks. Non-traditional exports increased sixfold during this period, from $34.3 million in 1985 to $206.6 million in 1989.

However, high social costs for the majority of the Bolivian population were also evident. The closures of mining enterprises and bankruptcies of factories threw tens of thousands of Bolivian workers out of work and into the urban informal sector and the expanding drug industry. The increase in national products such as soft drink beverages, beer, and illicit drugs and a decrease in shoes, clothing, and food revealed some of the distortions in the new patterns of production (Iriarte 1983, 330). Unemployment rates climbed once again from 15.5 percent to 21.5 percent of the labor force (Iriarte 1983, 420).

Peasant Agriculture in Bolivia

Before analyzing agricultural performance under the NEP program, it is important to make some introductory remarks about peasant agriculture in Bolivia. The role of Bolivian peasant small-plot agriculture is greater in national food and other commercial crop production than other nations in South America. In addition, some of the best physical resource and climatic conditions in Latin America for agricultural development are in Bolivia. Despite being denied access to public and private formal agricultural credit institutions, and receiving only minimal technical assistance through public agencies, peasants produce 80 percent of the value of national agricultural production.

The peasants also have the disadvantages of a high-cost transport system in the mountainous and tropical terrain, with only 37 percent of the national road surface open year round. Some 68 percent of the land units are under five hectares in size, and 40 percent of peasant-controlled lands suffer from serious soil erosion (MACA-FAO-PNUD 1990, XIII). According to a comprehensive study of the agrarian sector conducted by the international organization Fondo Internacional Desarrollo Agrícola (FIDA), between 1960 and 1985 anti-peasant public policies caused a net transfer of resources from the rural to the urban sectors. The tremendous amount of foreign aid flowing to Bolivia, the highest in the world after Israel, did little to alter the decapitalization in the peasant sector.

National Agricultural Progress Under the NEP

Various informed studies coincide in their conclusions that peasant agriculture has been on the wane since 1985. A Bolivian social research center, Centro des Estudios para el Desarrollo Laboral y Agrario (CEDLA) found that without coca, agricultural production increased at the annual rate of only 1.4 percent between 1985 and 1988 (CEDLA 1990, 18). However, if other export crops such as soybeans and coffee were excluded, production of food for national markets would have fallen to minus 4.1 percent between 1985 and 1988. A World Bank report states that "both volume and value added of the goods produced by the poor have decreased, indicating a fall in welfare. This has resulted in a decline in real prices and quantity of agricultural products" (World Bank 1990, 32). The report shows that the production of corn, wheat, potatoes, onions, sugar cane, and alfalfa remain considerably below the average for the period 1980-1985. Total agricultural production fell by 17 percent from 1985 to 1988 in volume terms and in 1988 remained 15 percent below the 1980-1985 average (World Bank 1990, 32). Another source indicates that between 1988 and 1989, national production of basic food declined from 5.5 to 4.9 million tons, which in per capita terms represented a drop of 698 kilos to 800 kilos per habitant (Sanabria 1991, 3).

Other indicators of the decline in Bolivian peasant agriculture include agriculture's drop in percentage of gross national product and the worsening of terms of trade for traditional peasant crops since 1986. The World Bank reported that "a price index of agricultural products declined by 29 percent from the stabilization to the end of 1988 relative to overall consumer prices."

Bolivian analysts offer several explanations for this NEP-caused stagnation in peasant agriculture. Various analysts point to the trade liberalization component of the NEP program, which represents a flat, low tariff rate on imported products. That tariff change, coupled with an overvalued exchange rate (from the inflow of drug dollars), has increased Bolivian agricultural imports. In 1989, food imports valued at $101 million were almost ten times the value of food exports ($11 million). Bolivia's expanding non-traditional agricultural exports of soybeans and coffee ($50 million in 1989) are not able to close this agricultural deficit.

Drug-dollar laundering in Bolivian cities and contraband trade among the increasing ranks of the unemployed and underemployed also brought more agricultural imports to Bolivia. A study by Econométrica, a Bolivian research center, argues that subsidized agro-industrial products from neighboring countries have 30 percent lower prices (Econométrica 1990, 18). The NEP's removal of fuel subsidies caused increased transportation costs, putting Bolivia at a competitive disadvantage with neighboring countries.

The agricultural production technologies, scientific research facilities, and transportation infrastructure in neighboring countries of Chile, Argentina, Peru, and Brazil create difficult foreign competition for Bolivia under these liberalized trade arrangements. Examples of their competitive agricultural products include Peruvian potatoes, barley, carrots, onions, and tomatoes; Chilean fruits, jams, and dairy products; Brazilian rice and corn; and Argentine potatoes. With social conditions more comparable to Africa than to South America, Bolivia must compete with these semi-industrial neighboring economies.

The contraction of national markets under NEP austerity also adversely affected the markets for highland agricultural products. Peasant communities supplying grains and fruits to the workforce of the state mining corporation, COMIBOL, lost their market when state enterprises closed, resulting in the dismissal of thousands of miners.

Non-Traditional Export Push: Soybeans and Coffee

Other than coca, to find examples of agricultural success under the NEP one must examine the performance of non-traditional agricultural exports. Soybeans are the strongest example, as demonstrated by productivity improvements and expanded acreage during the last half of the 1980s. Soybeans are the only industrial crop (cotton fiber, sugar cane, peanuts, and tobacco are others) to demonstrate positive production tendencies. Soybeans benefited from favorable world market prices and export incentives provided by the NEP to increase production from 223 metric tons in 1985, to 649 metric tons by 1989 (CEDLA 1990, 18). With a tariff rebate incentive of 10 percent, soybean producers add to their export price. Soybeans' international earnings increased fivefold in the latter half of the 1980s, ascending from $8.5 million in 1985 to $42 million for 1989.

However, most of the expansion of soybeans has occurred on non-peasant farms run by medium- and large-scale commercial producers such as Mennonite immigrants and agro-businesses. Soybean production requires capital equipment such as harvesters, which are inaccessible to most peasant households. Hence, only the most capitalized and well-organized groups among the peasantry have been able to participate in this export boom.

In terms of the coca-leaf expansion for the drug industry, soybean is not a substitution crop in that it does not grow in Bolivia's two coca-leaf growing zones of the Chapare and the Yungas, nor does it create significant new employment to draw agricultural workers from the coca zones. At the same time, it is not a crop for mountain regions, where production increases and profits would serve as a deterrent to the migrant peasant labor force for the drug industry. Thus its expansion under the NEP does not represent a net gain for the goals of illicit crop reduction and alternative rural development.

According to CEDLA's analysis, coffee is the other export crop demonstrating a positive, if modest, production trend during the period of the NEP program. Coffee increased from 114 metric tons to 128 metric tons between 1985 and 1988. Coffee is a more promising crop from the standpoint of CEDLA's central concern about the impact on coca. It is an export crop produced almost exclusively by peasant farmers on mountain plots in the coca growing Yungas region. Thus, coffee is a bonafide substitution crop since it is grown side by side with coca. The new production incentives for coffee might appear to coincide with the goal of crop substitution (or the prevention of coca expansion) in the Yungas area. This appears to be a case where the NEP export logic would work to the benefit of coca reduction and alternative development.

However, the price of coffee fell by 60 percent, plummeting export earnings from $25.6 million in 1985 to $12 million in 1989. Although the price for coca fell by the same percentage in the Yungas area, by comparison the two cash crops are not competitive. Note that under 1989 prices, one hectare of coca in the Yungas earns $823 while the same hectare of coffee is worth $286 (Econométrica 1990, 115). Peasants who participated in United Nations-sponsored alternative rural development programs were able to increase their productivity and gross income with coffee but were unable to repay the $2,000 per hectare value of their production loans. An important barrier to higher prices is that peasant farmers selling their coffee to local middlemen receive only 28 percent of the export price received by national trading companies in the capital city. Thus it appears that without internal empowerment of peasants within the national system of production and marketing and an "external structural adjustment" improving international prices for this non-traditional export, the NEP coffee expansion will continue at its slow pace and thus fail to replace much coca.

Potato Production

Another important Bolivian agricultural product to examine is the potato, which is perhaps, after coca, the cash crop most important to Bolivian society. Its importance for rural family consumption and cash crop production is highest in the highlands, where 70 percent of the rural inhabitants of the country reside. The Andean peasantry of Bolivia use between 25 and 45 percent of the land area in the highland departments for potato production, and 50 percent of the income of communities in this area is derived from potatoes (Godoy and Franco 1992, 35-36). The potato has the best profit structure among highland crops and is almost the only crop after coca enjoying margins of income gain which cover investments in imported, chemical fertilizers. Consumed three meals a day by Andean households, the potato is a mainstay of the rural diet.

Public policies and programs in agriculture have done little to improve the conditions of potato production, and, in some regions, yields are among the lowest in the world. Potato acreage and profitability have also declined over the past twenty-five years. Bolivia, for example, during this period has had poor communications and coordination with the International Potato Center in neighboring Peru, which has been able to develop new high-yielding varieties to increase yields and rural incomes for Peruvian peasants.

Potato earnings have declined during recent decades, suggesting that the NEP impact is simply continuing historical trends which were already in place. For example, between 1963 and 1976, potato prices declined by 50 percent (FIDA-CEDLA 1985, 405). Under the NEP, with the onset of market liberalization, it appears that once again a terms-of-trade squeeze undermines the economic incentives for potato producers.

Data from the highland valleys of the department of Cochabamba give evidence of this trend. The Cochabamba highlands supply peasant migrants to work in agricultural labor (sharecroppers, day laborers) as *pisadores* (stompers on the coca leaves in the coca paste-making pits), as members of families of Chapare smallholders, and as participants in trade, transport, and commerce linked to the coca-cocaine economic circuits. The economic fortunes of highland potato plots influence peasant decisions about migration to coca-growing and drug-processing areas.

In the western provinces of Misque and Aiquile, the Centro de Comunicación y Desarrollo Andino (CENDA), a non-governmental rural development organization, presented data for 1988-1989 showing that potato prices decreased by 9 percent while at the same time the value of chemical fertilizers, which are essential inputs for commercial potato production in Cochabamba, increased by 100 percent. Potato seed, another important commercial crop produced by peasant households in this micro-region, declined in price by 20.2 percent. In 1990, terms of trade for the potato improved temporarily because of a prolonged drought in the region.

To compensate for falling terms of trade, peasants expanded their production onto marginal land. This process led in turn to environmental decline through loss of soil, vegetation, and tree cover. This type of economic and environmental change invariably promises increased migration toward the coca-cocaine region for the future.

In another region, research findings of the Centro de Investigación y Promoción del Campesinado (CIPCA) on rural fairs in the Upper Cochabamba Valley between 1987 and 1989 showed the cost of transport increased by 33 percent, the dollar increased by 160 percent, and agricultural inputs (fertilizers, fungicides, insecticides, and seed) went up by 15 percent, while the price of the potato in dollar terms decreased by 49 percent. The winter crop of the miska potato fell in earnings from $1,000 to $650 per hectare.

The CIPCA study predicts that given the terms of trade trends under the NEP, potato production for the medium and long term will become unprofitable. These trends in the context of the NEP led to a drop in land area under potato production from 209,703 hectares in 1986 to 192,203 hectares in 1987 and 190,456 hectares in 1988.

Distribution of Agricultural Credit and Public Expenditure

The distribution of agricultural credit in Bolivia during the past three decades has been greatly skewed to benefit non-peasant commercial farmers, cattle ranchers, and agro-business groups. This outcome is especially true in the lowland Santa Cruz region. The NEP program in theory allows the market mechanism to achieve a more efficient allocation of financial capital within the national economy and among agricultural producer groups. Under the NEP program, interest rates reflect the free market price of capital instead of the subsidized amounts previously loaned by the national banks.

Agricultural credit policy is also an important state instrument for export promotion which lies at the heart of the NEP program. Part of the logic of export expansion within this NEP economic growth strategy is to generate needed foreign exchange when Bolivia's traditional mineral exports have plunged. This export bias in agricultural credit policy, however, has negative social consequences for the peasant majority.

Agricultural credit increased through both public and private banks between 1985 and 1989, from $29 million to $280 million. The Inter-American Development Bank loaned $199 million between 1987 and 1991, designated specifically for the establishment, expansion, diversification, and modernization of agricultural and agro-industrial enterprises, for the purposes of increasing the supply of products for internal consumption and encouraging the export of agricultural and agro-industrial production. The initial loan with the Central Bank of Bolivia supported 3,095 sub-loans, three-fourths of which were for Santa Cruz area and none of which went to peasant farmers (MACA-FAO-PNUD 1990, 28).

During the NEP's first four years, the only source (other than non-governmental organization credit programs) for formal agricultural loans to peasants was the Banco Agricola Boliviana (BAB). This bank never recovered from the delinquent loans of politically influential commercial agricultural groups from the Santa Cruz region. Their 1970s losses from cotton led to a loan delinquency representing 62 percent of the BAB's financial portfolio. The BAB thus became a relatively small financial player for agricultural development during the second half of the 1980s. During the recent final years prior to its closure, it channeled only 8 percent of the total amount available within the Bolivian banking system for agricultural loans. Since the peasantry achieved access to 53 percent of this amount, the small producers received 4 percent of the total national credit available for agriculture. Subsequently in 1991, the BAB closed its doors completely, thereby shutting off the peasantry's only source of public credit.

The expansion of non-peasant commercial farms and agro-industry takes place also through private banks for products such as soybeans and maize (for feed companies). This form of credit control led to Santa Cruz's expansion of crop production from 244,000 hectares in 1985-1986 to 559,000 hectares in 1991-1992. This pattern suggests the continuing power of the Santa Cruz agricultural elites within the NEP program period. Through institutions such as the Camara Agropecuaria, they continue to capture the lion's share of capital within the banking system. These elite have lost their credit subsidies of past years, but not their monopoly of access to this scarce resource. The NEP's logic is to continue to restrict the availability of credit to a privileged minority of agricultural producers.

The NEP program is also worsening the meager benefits received by the peasantry from the national agricultural budget. Between 1980 and 1985, the share of public investment for agriculture benefiting peasant producers averaged 31 percent. This percentage declined to 26 percent in 1986 and then fell to 16 percent in 1987 (Urioste 1990, 10). After evaluation of the share of each ministry's budget (agriculture, health, housing, infrastructure, energy, and so on) which benefits the peasant sector, this anti-peasant bias in state policy also is evident. The percentage average has gone from 7.8 percent in 1987 to 12.4 percent in 1988, then falling in 1989 and 1990 to 9.7 percent and 9.4 percent respectively.

Coca Leaf Expansion

The coca leaf, in contrast to the potato and other low performance crops, does not suffer negative impact from public policies of trade, credit, and investment. To the contrary, there seems to exist an inverse relationship between general agricultural decline and increased peasant migration from the highlands to the tropical lowlands for coca cultivation.[1] Coca leaf prices have fallen during the NEP period, yet connections to the illegal cocaine industry make it more attractive to peasant producers than other cash crops (Econométrica 1990, 30).[2] Coca leaf expansion on the heels of the NEP proceeded at a faster rate of increase (13.4 percent between 1985 and 1988) than other commercial crops. When including coca with twenty-two important agricultural products, the rate of growth of the agricultural sector jumps from 1.4 percent to 3.4 percent annually. According to official figures, coca in 1987 represented 28 percent of the national agricultural product, and in the major producer departments of La Paz and Cochabamba, the percentages were 33 percent and 66 percent respectively. As a logical extension of the open market concept, this production increase reveals Bolivia's comparative advantage over all its neighbors except Peru.

The expansion of coca production also reflects increased productivity from the use of chemical fertilizers on the comparatively high-yielding varieties of the Chapare. In light of the general agricultural decline in Bolivia, it is not surprising that even with lower prices, coca has continued its expansion during the NEP period.

To attain peasant grower participation in alternative rural development, U.S.-Bolivian interdiction policy has attempted to lower the price of coca. The major price decreases probably reflected overproduction of coca in Bolivia and the disruption of trafficking networks through effective law enforcement in Colombia.

Part of the explanation for continuing powerful economic incentives behind expanding leaf production in the face of falling prices is downstream integration into the industry. The production of coca paste has significantly increased earnings per hectare received by peasant growers and entrepreneurs. Some analysts suggest that productivity increases from technological innovation and development have resulted from substituting gasoline for kerosene in the peasant-managed paste-making pits of the drug industry.

The deterioration of highland peasant farms during the NEP period is a main factor propelling coca leaf expansion in Bolivia. Aside from some cases of exceptional grassroots development work by non-governmental development organizations, cash crop earnings, for both mountain and lowland regions, have not pulled many peasants away from planting and investing their labor in coca.[3]

The United States Agency for International Development (USAID), for example, dismantled its agricultural credit program for alternative development in the Chapare because of massive borrower delinquency.

The NEP-led closure of state mines and massive dismissal of workers not only had a negative impact on agricultural markets, but also led to miner migration to the Chapare to work as *pisadores* in coca paste-making and as new settlers for opening coca-leaf farming.

Peasant Sindicato Responses

The key opposition to the NEP program has come from Bolivia's principal labor groups of mine workers and peasants. The peasant *sindicatos* rallied to the support of the 23,000 mine workers dismissed from their jobs with the state-owned mining corporation. They participated in the dramatic 1985 "March for Life" protest between the cities of Oruro and La Paz. The peasant *sindicato* members themselves subsequently experienced the NEP's negative impact on food production, while their organizations became outspoken opponents of the neoliberal program. Yet their political capacity to mobilize had weakened because of political divisions, corruption, and clientelism among their leadership and disillusionment from a left-of-center government, the UDP (1982-1985).

Nonetheless, the peasant *sindicatos* frequently denounced the trade liberalization measures of the NEP program at congresses of the regional federations and the national confederation, the Confederación Unica Sindical de Trabajadores Campesinos (CSUTCB). The NEP critique became a center-piece of the national peasant agenda (*plataforma de lucha*) for change developed by delegates and their elected leaders. Thus, this opposition to the NEP bubbled up through a democratic structure tying the interests of local communities to advocacy positions taken by the national *sindicato* leaders.

While the CSUTCB's vocal protests have been unrelenting, the Bolivian state has failed to modify its trade liberalization measures. In response to hunger strikes and road blockades, the state offered concessions to the peasant *sindicatos* on issues other than trade liberalization.

The peasant *sindicatos* have been more successful, for example, in opposing the land tax reform of the NEP program. In 1986, the peasant *sindicatos* faced a Ley de Reforma Tributaria, imposing new taxes on peasant holdings regardless of size. Subsequently, the CSUTCB and the Central Obrero Boliviano (COB), the national trade union confederation, organized a referendum for the low-income sectors on the tax reform law and payment of the national foreign debt. The massive protest turnout gave a "no" vote on both issues. Demonstrations and rallies mobilizing tens of thousands of people further dampened the state's interest in the land tax reform. This widespread opposition, culminating in a 1989 hunger strike by peasant leaders, led to the tax law's repeal. New agreements have abolished the article in the Ley de Reforma Tributaria which taxed indigenous communal properties.

204 *Privatization Amidst Poverty*

During the second half of the 1980s, another struggle has taken place, over terms of the crop-reduction and alternative development programs, between the Chapare *sindicato* federations and the state. Efforts at coca reduction in 1985 galvanized the Chapare federations into nonviolent actions protesting joint U.S.-Bolivia policies (Healy 1988, 1991). This state-peasantry conflict over coca has been a tug of war in which the federations defend their economic interests and press for greater political influence in the formulation and implementation of policies and programs.

The peasant coca protests often focus on the negative effects on their markets of trade liberalization for alternative crops produced in coca-growing zones. As allies with other *sindicatos* opposed to the NEP program, the Chapare federations exchange support for other causes to obtain assistance in pushing their own agenda.

Peasant mobilizations in 1987 forced the Bolivian state to sign negotiated agreements for alternative development plans to include greater peasant participation in decision making. The *Plan Integral de Desarrollo y Sustitución* (PIDYS) established councils for peasant participation in local and national state decision making. When the state failed to put the council in operation within the Ministry of Agriculture and Peasant Affairs, the peasant *sindicatos* used a national road blockade in 1990 to force negotiation of new agreements for state compliance with the earlier accords.

Conclusions

Bolivia's peasant agricultural crisis did not begin with the advent of the NEP program. Long-established social and economic trends, and colonial and neo-colonial political structures, have undermined Bolivian peasant agriculture over centuries. The NEP program is the latest policy package offered by international political and economic planners which, in practice, would have a negative impact on the peasant population. The NEP program takes on added significance in Bolivia's case since two major multi-lateral financial institutions, the International Monetary Fund and the World Bank, have advocated it as a quasi-official doctrine of economic recovery and sustainable development for Third World countries.

Peasant agricultural production since 1985 shows similar patterns to earlier national agricultural policies. Currently, the high social costs for the peasantry take place under the guise of "structural reform". Bolivia's historical trends of deepening social and economic inequality and concomitant rural poverty have actually accelerated via the NEP program. Given its ostensible anti-peasant bias, the NEP program appears to work at cross purposes with the US-Bolivian drug policy. The NEP program has stimulated increased agricultural imports and the growth of a large labor force for the Chapare. This only undermines the state-led alternative development programs for peasant coca producers.

Bolivia's structural adjustment has led to widespread stagnation of agricultural food production and worsening terms of trade for important peasant crops such as potatoes. These trends increase internal migration to the Chapare micro-region, as well as to the major cities of La Paz, Cochabamba, and Santa Cruz.

The NEP-driven agricultural export expansion generates needed foreign exchange, but provides only minimal economic benefits to the peasant sector, especially to those peasant groups seeking alternatives to coca growing. The export of coffee from the Yungas area collapsed in the face of falling international prices. The peasantry's poor access to the Bolivian banking system, together with diminishing public investment and expenditure in rural communities, further increases rural poverty, thus spurring more migration to the coca growing areas.

National economic policy in Bolivia has tended to discriminate socially, squeeze economically, and exclude the peasantry politically. Simultaneously, those who benefit are urban and commercial sectors and a minority of better-off, non-peasant agricultural producers. This skewing was true even during the 1950s years of revolutionary upheaval, when the lion's share of economic and financial resources continued to flow to commercial farmers rather than the newly enfranchised peasant majority.

Cumulatively, the IMF policy in Bolivia thus results in preference for 1) export crops over national food crops, 2) large- and medium-sized producers over small-plot producers, 3) environmentally fragile lowland areas over agriculturally stable highland areas, 4) increased agricultural imports and needed food aid over domestic self-sufficiency and greater self-reliance, 5) urban interests over rural interests, and finally, as a result, 6) production of coca over other cash crops.

In view of these socially discriminatory preferences, successful peasant resistance to land tax reform should not come as a surprise. The Chapare *sindicato* mobilization reflected more than the state's efforts at crop reduction and alternative development. It was also a statement about the extremely difficult regional and national context for legal agricultural products.

Coca is one of the few crops in Bolivia which has buoyed the peasant economy amidst the national agricultural decline of the 1980s. In response to increased cocaine markets and attractive prices in the United States and Western Europe, peasant farmers have become dynamic economic actors by expanding production and surviving in an extremely harsh context. Peasant farmers have migrated from every highland region to the lower Chapare and Yungas areas to pursue income-generating opportunities.

Bolivia possesses comparative advantages over other southern South American countries for producing coca. Bolivia has a long historical experience in commercial coca-leaf production, a substantial domestic consumer market, important religious, medicinal, and societal roles for coca, and high-yielding coca varieties. These comparative advantages place Bolivia in a favorable position for international competition. On the other hand, state policies during the past four decades have weakened the position of peasants with other crops vis-à-vis agricultural producers in neighboring nations. With the Southern Cone's lowest per capita agricultural output, Bolivian peasants are in a precarious historical predicament for competing.

Within this reality, coca emerges as Bolivia's leading cash crop, a natural extension of the textbook application of structural adjustment programs. The Bolivian state itself recently began advocating the legal export of a tea-like product, *maté de coca*, and other legal industrial derivatives as a new economic development strategy. The NEP program, similar to past national agrarian policies, has left many peasant farmers, and perhaps the Bolivian state itself, with few attractive choices other than coca production within the rural economic reality of the 1980s and 1990s. Thus, prevailing national economic conditions place NEP and the drug-related alternative development programs in conflict with one another.

The Clinton administration has had to reconsider various aspects of its position on the Mexican NAFTA proposals in response to issues presented by environmental and labor groups in the United States. The administration may have to do the same with respect to its drug policy in Bolivia, given the difficulties in current agricultural conditions and related peasant opposition.

In particular, the Clinton administration should promote the role of peasant *sindicatos* in national policymaking, greater peasant access to affordable agricultural credit, and investments in highland transport and communications infrastructure and in industries with rural linkages. They also should provide temporary tariff protection for peasant producers to modify existing trade liberalization policies. Bolivia's national peasant *sindicato* movement would welcome a change from the Republican style "war on drugs" to a focus on sustainable, people-centered development.

Notes

1. Urban migration from agricultural deterioration, however, is greater than migration to the Chapare. Bolivia's city of El Alto has had some of the highest migration rates of any municipal area in Latin America in recent years.

2. Coca leaf prices averaged US$1.50 per kilo between 1985 and 1990, while the value for the first half of the decade averaged US$6 per kilo.

3. Lowland agriculture such as that of the Chapare also has been negatively affected by the NEP. Complaints by the peasant organizations of the lack of markets for alternative crops to coca have increased under the NEP. Incipient efforts with the export of pineapples and bananas sponsored by U.S. AID benefit only a small percentage of the Chapare's peasant coca producers.

References

Centro de Estudios Para el Desarrollo Laboral y Agrario (CEDLA). 1990. *CPE: Recesión Económica*. La Paz: CEDLA.

Econométrica. 1990. *Análisis de los Impactos Del Proyecto Agro-Yungas*. Vols. 1 and 2. La Paz: Econométrica.

Fondo Internacional Desarrollo Agrícola-Centro de Estudios Para el Desarrollo Laboral Agrario (FIDA-CEDLA). 1985. *Propuesta Para Una Estrategia de Desarrollo Rural de Base Campesino, Informe Especial de Programación de la República de Bolivia*. Vols. 1 and 2. La Paz: CEDLA.

Godoy, Ricardo, and Mario Franco. 1992. "Neglect and Bias in Bolivia's Agricultural Research." Manuscript. Cambridge: Harvard Institute for International Development.

Healy, Kevin. 1986. "The Boom Within the Crisis: Some Recent Effects of Foreign Cocaine Markets on Bolivian Rural Society and Economy." In *Coca and Cocaine: Effects on People and Policy in Latin America*, eds. Deborah Pacini and Christine Franquemont. Cambridge: Cornell University and Cultural Survival.

Healy, Kevin. 1988. "Coca, the State and the Peasantry in Bolivia, 1982-99." *Journal of Interamerican Studies and World Affairs* 30 (2 and 3) (Summer/Fall).

Healy, Kevin. 1991. "Political Ascent of Bolivia's Coca Leaf Producers." *Journal of Interamerican Studies and World Affairs* 33 (1) (Spring).

Henkel, Ray. 1990. "The Cocaine Problem." Tempe: Arizona State University. Unpublished manuscript.

Horton, Susan. 1989. "Labor Markets in an Era of Adjustment: Bolivia." Toronto. Unpublished manuscript.

Iriarte, Gregorio. 1983. *Analisis Crítico de la Realidad Esquemas de Interpretación*. La Paz: Secretariado Nacional de Pastoral Social (SENPAS-CEB).

Lee, Rensselaer. 1990. *The White Labyrinth: Cocaine and Political Power*. New Brunswick, New Jersey: Transaction Press.

Ministerio de Agricultural y Asuntos Campesinos (MACA-FAO-PNUD). 1990. "Lineamientos de Política Agropecuaria." Manuscript. La Paz: MACA-FAO-PNUD.

Sanabria, Fernando Camacho. 1991. "La Huella De La Desalimentación." *El Diario*. La Paz, Bolivia.

Urioste, Miguel. 1990. Development project proposal by Tierra. Unpublished manuscript.

World Bank. 1990. *Bolivia Poverty Report*. Internal document. Report No. 8646.

Critical Issues and Themes

Poverty, the Environment, and Women in the Work Force

Marguerite S. Berger

There is an old proverb that says, "Women hold up half the sky." As individuals and as North Americans concerned about the future of the developing countries of Latin America and the Caribbean, we can't afford to ignore or overlook this part of the population holding up half the sky. In particular, we need to keep in mind that the role women can play in reducing poverty in the region is extremely important.

As we in the Inter-American Development Bank (IDB) begin to implement a new mandate from our member countries that defines the priority areas for IDB investments in the 1990s and beyond, we are consciously seeking ways to support women's contributions to poverty alleviation and reduction. The Clinton administration also needs to strengthen women's participation in development, both at home and abroad. In order to do this, we must all face up to the new reality confronting everyone in the development process.

The way that women "hold up their share of the sky" has changed dramatically in just one generation in Latin America and the Caribbean. In the United States, the changes in women's economic participation have been quite evident and much discussed. Similar changes have been occurring in Latin America and the Caribbean. We need to take a look at these changes because they create a very different situation for development policy and programs, involving a new kind of labor force with new types of workers, new issues for social programs, new political and legislative agendas, and an added dynamism in the business community, especially in the region's small business sector.

Marguerite S. Berger is chief of the Women in Development Unit at the Inter-American Development Bank.

In discussing these changes and the issues they involve, it is useful to examine the reality of women in Latin America and the Caribbean. Specifically, this paper will outline their contributions to economic development in the region, discuss how this has changed in recent years, and point out some of the constraints that women face in trying to provide a better life for themselves and their families. It will conclude with some ideas about what we can do to assist women in the region and to strengthen their role in development.

It is very difficult to generalize about the situation of women in Latin America and the Caribbean. The Caribbean has English-speaking, Spanish-speaking, and French-speaking groups. Central America, the Andean countries, and the Southern Cone all represent very different cultural situations which affect the condition of women in those countries as well. Nonetheless, one thing is a fact in the 1990s: the economic emergence of women is a trend that has been growing and has become generalized across the region.

For better-off women in urban areas, the problem of this double burden has a solution. These women are able to buy their way out of some of their household responsibilities by hiring domestic servants. Poor women don't have that option, however, and are caught between the constraints of work and family.

As a series of articles in *The Washington Post* (February 14-18, 1993) pointed out, despite improvements in the overall living conditions of women in Latin America, many poor women still face desperate conditions. Statistics show huge variations among countries, regions, and income levels within the same country — for example, variations that range up to twenty years in female life expectancy and up to five births per woman. The impact of development has been uneven in the region, and the progress made has been insufficient to lift out of poverty the significant numbers of women still facing high birthrates, high risks of dying in childbirth, and low literacy and education levels.

Furthermore, across the board in Latin America — and throughout the world — women still earn much less than men, and women's political clout is limited. Given this situation, what can we do to assist women in Latin America and the Caribbean to make their lives better, their work more productive, and their families better off?

It is true that women have always contributed to production in the region, but until recently their contributions have mainly been within the family economy in the rural areas. Now, there is a massive increase in the number of women in the labor market outside of the home economy. Women now account for nearly 30 percent of the region's labor force. This figure may not seem like much relative to the United States, where women account for 40 percent of the labor market, or compared to regions like Africa, where women are highly visible in economic roles. However, this represents a huge leap for Latin America where, in the 1960s, women accounted for only 15 percent of the labor force. There has been a dramatic change in the region, although women's rates of participation in the labor force vary considerably across the region, ranging from a low of 16 percent in Guatemala to 68 percent in Jamaica. To get some sense of how the genders relate, men's rates of participation in the labor force in these regions are in the 60 to 80 percent range. The labor force participation rate for women has been growing at rates of between 3 to 6 percent per year in the past two decades, double the growth rate for men. This is a trend that is projected to continue into the next century.

As these figures indicate, women are making a strong contribution to the economies of the region. Even these figures, however, may underestimate the role of women because they are based on surveys which ask women, "What is your primary activity?" and many women still answer, "I am a housewife." Recently I was in northeastern Brazil, interviewing some farmers with a team from the United Nations. With my male colleagues I talked to a group of male farmers, asking them, "What do your wives do to contribute to agricultural production here?" They answered, "Nothing, they are housewives." Later, I asked the women themselves the same question. They said, "We are just housewives." However, after my colleagues had gone off to visit some irrigation ditches nearby and I had stayed behind, I talked with these women some more. They began telling me that their crop hadn't been very good the past year, that they had gotten a very bad price for the crop, how they were applying pesticides to their tomatoes, and similar sorts of stories. One woman even told me that she owned her family's land. She had divided it up with her husband, and they each farmed a different part of the land. She complained because this year she had a hard time finding people to work with her on her land, and she had to stay there far into the night during the peak season in order to harvest her crop herself. Yet this woman called herself "a housewife." I found that this situation was not uncommon for many rural women in Latin America, especially in small farm households.

What are the factors that have contributed to the change in women's situations in the region over the past generation? It is important to understand that the process of women's growing entrance into the work force is a process that is being reinforced by other changes occurring in the region's economies. There have been significant declines in fertility rates in the region while levels of education for the population as a whole have increased, but for women in particular, increasing urbanization, rising poverty, and changes in the demand for labor have had significant effects on their lives.

In Latin America and the Caribbean in the 1950s and 1960s, each woman had an average of seven children. Today this number is down to between four and five in most countries of the region. There are several countries in the Caribbean and the Southern Cone which have reduced fertility rates to three or fewer children per woman — numbers comparable to rates in the United States. Contraceptive use varies widely over the entire region, but on average it is estimated that about 50 percent of women of childbearing age use contraceptives, compared to 68 percent in the United States.

Today in the Latin American region as a whole, for the first time there is near parity in education for boys and girls. This extends, in most of these countries, all the way to the university level. In several countries, women outnumber men in university education, as is also the case in the United States. In general, the labor force in the region is much better educated, and women are much better qualified to contribute, not only through participation and production in the labor force, but also through their involvement in better child nutrition, child health and child survival, and to the betterment of their families in general. However, there are still some areas with serious problems in terms of female education, for example, the rural areas in countries such as Bolivia, Guatemala, and Haiti, where a high proportion of women remain illiterate, which limits their chances of improving their lives.

Urbanization is another important trend throughout Latin America in the past thirty years. Today, the region is approximately two-thirds urban, and some countries are as much as 75 percent urbanized. This has led to a greater role in the labor force for women. Small farm production has been constrained. As the ability of poor rural families to support themselves by farming has declined, there has been an increase in the migration of women to urban areas. In Latin America today, unlike other regions of the developing world, there is a higher proportion of female migration to urban areas than there is male. Women, particularly the young, go to urban areas in search of work as domestic servants, clerks in retail trade, and unskilled laborers in other service sectors. They also go to urban areas in search of better services for their families, particularly for their children. Urbanization has meant changes for families who migrate together, especially in terms of women's economic contribution. In rural areas, women are traditionally responsible for providing their families with food and clothing. In urban areas, they are now fulfilling that role by bringing an income into the household.

Perhaps the single most important factor increasing the labor force participation of women in the 1980s and 1990s is poverty. The process of economic adjustment in Latin America, consisting of changes in policy to open up the economies and attempts to control runaway inflation and government deficits, has resulted in serious declines in government services, real incomes, and employment. These declines were occurring even in the absence of economic adjustment measures but, in many cases, have been aggravated by new government policies. As a result, the incomes that women can bring into their families, especially poor families, is increasingly important. In some countries, this has resulted in dramatic changes in women's work patterns. In

Lima, Peru, for example, there was a 20 percent growth in women's participation in the labor force during 1990, a year of extreme hardships. Women desperate to bring an income to their families are looking for any kind of work.

The economic adjustment process has forced an invisible adjustment process within the household, with women bearing a disproportionate share of the burden for adjustment. They are taking on work, producing things in their homes that they previously were able to buy, substituting for services such as health care, education, and other social services by, for example, providing food in groups. In Peru a group of women have formed popular soup kitchens, called *comedores populares.* Women from poor neighborhoods band together, soliciting donations from different organizations, such as the church. With the money they receive, they purchase the food in bulk, prepare meals together, and serve their families in a central place. This is an example of the kinds of strategies women are pursuing to confront and overcome poverty.

Increasing poverty has also been associated with changes in the family structure, with women heading as many as 30 percent of the households in Latin America and over 40 percent in the Caribbean. In the United States, this figure has also reached 30 percent. In these households, women are the primary economic support for their families — on their own, with children, or assisted by lower earning household members. The households headed by women tend to be concentrated among the poorest sectors of the economy, since women tend to be lower wage earners and have fewer other income earners in their families.

The past generation has also witnessed great changes in the demand for labor. As the region's economies have become more service and export production oriented, there has been a growing demand for female labor, particularly for light assembly operations and packaging for agribusiness. With so many women in the labor force, the role of women can no longer be regarded as primarily that of child care and family; it also includes responsibilities and contributions outside the home in the labor market. The entrance of women into the labor force has given them greater opportunities and a greater voice in household decisions; however, their new role has presented them with quite a few new problems.

Many of these new problems relate to women's work tending to be concentrated in the urban informal sectors of the economy — the business sector outside the governments' regulatory framework. These businesses tend to be very small, with low levels of capitalization and very rudimentary technologies. They typically do not follow the labor laws and other regulations and include activities such as street vending, home-based manufacturing shops for shoes and clothing, informal restaurants, and other kinds of services.

Many of the informal sector jobs have been created by women who have not been able to find a job somewhere else.

Not too long ago, I ran into a friend from graduate school I hadn't seen in years at a conference of Latin American women's bureaus. I mentioned to her that I was very interested in working with women in these informal sector businesses. She asked, "How can you do that? Women don't want to work in that kind of situation. They want a steady job, not their own businesses. They don't want to be petty capitalists." I thought about this for awhile, and I had to admit that in a way, she was right. Many of these women, given a choice, would prefer to work in a factory, despite tough working conditions, job instability, and low pay. In rural areas, the women would prefer to work for agribusiness, even though they might be exposed to chemicals, the pay is low, and the work is seasonal. Many would prefer working under these conditions rather than risk working in their own businesses where they could lose everything from one day to the next, the conditions are extremely hard, the hours are long, the pay is low, and there is tremendous instability. Women who work on their own in the informal sector but who would prefer the stability of a more conventional, yet lower-paying job are "reluctant entrepreneurs." The lack of other alternatives has led them to create their own businesses.

Why aren't other types of jobs available to these women? Unemployment rates in most Latin American and Caribbean countries are very high, and unemployment rates for women tend to be higher than for men. Women tend to have less training in certain skill areas, and the wages that they could receive, even if they were able to find a job, are very low. One woman I met in Quito, Ecuador, was a hand knitter who had a business delivering hand-knitted clothing to different stores and other clients. She also sold children's knitted wear in the market or on the street corner near the market. She took a loan from a credit program in order to expand her operations, so that she could buy a stock of raw materials to expand her client network. She was always running out of material and would have to sell some of her product in order to purchase more raw material, interrupting the production process. After she received the loan, before she could invest it, her husband, who had been drinking, took the money away from her and spent it on something for himself. Soon after this, I found out that he had left her. She was alone, taking care of her young son, and still had to pay off that debt. The next time I visited her I found that she wasn't working in her own business and asked her why she abandoned the business when she was just starting to get out of debt and things seemed to be going well. She said she had found a job in a little factory, a sweat shop, actually, and preferred it because it was relatively steady work, and the owner of the factory lent her the money to pay off her loan. This woman was lucky because she was able to find a job. But her experience — both moving in and out of self-employment and having marital problems — is very common.

There is another reason why women become "reluctant entrepreneurs" in the informal sector, besides not having other opportunities, and that is their responsibility for the household. Women's work in Latin America and the Caribbean is not the same throughout the whole region but, in general, involves daily shopping for foodstuffs due to lack of refrigerators and food storage facilities, the preparation of all meals using time-consuming techniques, and caring for the children. Providing health care for the children often means going to a clinic, waiting all day to be seen, and perhaps being sent somewhere else where there is another half day wait to get medicine. In addition, women are responsible for negotiating for basic services on a continuing basis, such as their children's access to schools, and the family's access to a water supply and waste disposal. Women's household responsibilities place an incredible burden on their time. Therefore, they need work that is flexible, allowing them to be able to take care of the household while earning an income. Consequently, they often opt for their own businesses.

In rural areas, in small-scale agriculture, the role of women is very important. The smaller the farm, the more women tend to participate. With smaller farms, there is a pattern of male migration in search of seasonal work, which leaves women behind to take care of the home and the farm during those periods. Women also may have a vegetable garden, small animals to care for, handicrafts, and other types of income-producing activities, in addition to having to get water and firewood and caring for the children. In this situation, women with little access to agricultural extension services or credit have a difficult time making their work more productive.

In urban areas, this double role is not as much of a problem for women in middle class or wealthier families because they are able to buy their way out of some of their household responsibilities by hiring domestic servants. Poor women, however, don't have this option and are caught between the constraints of work and family.

How can we assist women in Latin America and the Caribbean to make their lives better, their work more productive, and their families better off?

First, we can support improvements in education. Although education levels are near parity for young men and women in most of the region, both the quality and type of education need improvement. The types of occupations that women are being trained for need to be improved to get them into more productive areas of the economy where there are higher paying jobs.

Health care services should be targeted, along with financing mechanisms that are more sustainable and more reliable. The focus of health care needs to be changed, placing more emphasis on preventive care, maternal and child health, reproductive health, and access to family planning. Efforts should be made to increase outreach to fathers as well as mothers, so that family health is not seen as the responsibility of women alone.

Improvements are urgently needed in basic infrastructure in Latin America, especially in the areas of water and sanitation. Access to water and adequate sanitation facilities is one of the main problems for women, even in urban areas. Women have to go in search of water, negotiate with water tank trucks for delivery, or fetch it from a common tap. The provision of clean, safe water supplies is very important for better child health. Access to fuel for cooking and heating, particularly in areas where deforestation has become a problem and women are forced to look farther and farther for fuel wood, is also a major area for action.

Child development and day care, although they are not specifically women's issues, have a major impact on women and are areas needing improvement. Poor women who have children are often faced with the problem of balancing their home and work place responsibilities. They are forced to choose between trying to earn money to feed their children or staying at home to care for them. Often this means leaving the children at home with other siblings or alone. Child care could ease that painful decision for women and help children at the same time. In Colombia, for example, there is a national project that has been going on for some time which establishes child day care centers in poor neighborhoods. A mother in the neighborhood is chosen by a group of other mothers. She is given assistance to improve her house and begin training in child development and nutrition in order to provide day care for five to ten children from the neighborhood, with the help of others in the neighborhood. The other mothers pay a small amount of money for the care of their children during the day. This is proving to be a very low cost, very effective solution now being tried in other countries.

Women in the region also need training and credit for their micro-enterprises. In other words, they need direct assistance to make their economic roles more effective. Generally, women don't hold titles to property or other assets required from banks as guarantees for traditional loans. In Latin America and the Caribbean, there have been several innovative programs which have sprung up to overcome this problem. One example is the Prodem Credit Program in Bolivia, which now has almost ten thousand beneficiaries, all receiving small loans without any physical guarantees. By using a mechanism relying on personal guarantees called "solidarity groups," each member guarantees the others' payments. These programs have been able to achieve a level of over 50 percent participation by women among their clientele. Women also need access to agricultural extensions and training on food crop production and export agriculture. They need support for formal sector employment both through placement and vocational training and through legal reforms that could open up more opportunities for them. Policy changes supporting employment creation will benefit women in the work force by creating a greater demand for their labor.

Finally, it is important to think about how we can strengthen women's grass roots and community organizations. These organizations get women together for projects such as the *comedores populares* or projects that improve the urban environment: school feeding programs, micro-enterprise support, organizing garbage collection, and other activities. Participation in these activities contributes to greater self-esteem and elevates their community standing, eventually translating into greater political participation and influence over the government, where they can make the needs of women heard.

Essentially, we know that women in Latin America and the Caribbean are contributing to regional economic and social development in many ways. Their role is vital to development, especially as they help to bring their families out of poverty. Poor women face many formidable obstacles to fulfilling their potential to make these contributions, but there are many things that can be done to help strengthen their role, such as improved general and child development education, health care, water and sanitation systems, as well as direct assistance for their economic roles and for strengthening their grass roots organizations. Women have always held up half the sky. Now it is time to give them the recognition and the help they deserve.

Development Banks, NAFTA, and the Enterprise for the Americas Initiative

Muni Figueres de Jiménez

The Enterprise for the Americas Initiative (EAI), launched in June 1991, is an open-ended U.S. policy proposal presenting a common goal that all countries in this hemisphere can work toward. It has three main components. The first is trade. The Initiative proposed, without a specific deadline, the formation of a hemispheric free trade zone which would involve all the countries of Latin America and the Caribbean, as well as the United States and Canada.

The second component is debt. In the EAI the Bush administration proposed a series of debt reduction or debt restructuring schemes under different categories, with different treatment for balances owed by Latin America and the Caribbean to the United States. An important point is that the debt reduction schemes were tied directly to the availability of resources for environmental development programs within these countries — especially small-scale, community-based environmental programs or environmental protection and natural resource development programs.

This debt portion of the EAI was to trigger complicated congressional chess-playing, involving two phases of the budgetary process in Congress. The first concerned the authorization, and the second the appropriation of funds.

Investment is the third component of the EAI. The first step, which directly involves the U.S. government and its budgetary process, is the formation of a fund called the Multilateral Investment Fund, to which the

Muni Figueres de Jiménez is the advisor of the Office of External Relations at the Inter-American Development Bank. She previously served in the Integration and Trade Development Division of the IDB and as minister of foreign trade for Costa Rica.

United States would commit $100 million per year over a five-year period. The Europeans, if they respond to the call, would contribute an additional $100 million over a five-year period, and the Japanese would contribute a third portion of $100 million over a five-year period. This would then create a package of $1.5 billion that would be used on a grant basis to assist countries in carrying out reforms to create a more attractive investment environment.

The second aspect of the investment component of the EAI is the development within the Inter-American Development Bank (IDB) of a program of investment sector loans. These are loans that the bank would make to countries in order to encourage macroeconomic policy decisions for the creation of an attractive investment climate.

These three pillars — trade, debt, and investment — represent the first comprehensive approach to the major economic problems in Latin America and the Caribbean by a United States administration. We have gone through ten years of nearly obsessive preoccupation with the Latin American and Caribbean debt problem. Yet, up to now, there has been no holistic approach capable of regenerating economic activity, renegotiating a country's debt, and reorienting its foreign financial relations in general, while simultaneously creating a strategy for attracting fresh capital.

The Enterprise for the Americas Initiative is based on the premise that the countries of the hemisphere are going to go through substantive economic reform. This involves making extremely painful political and social decisions within each country in the short run. It also involves a large reallocation of public resources and, therefore, a great many frustrations. This will mean taking a leap of faith because in Latin America and the Caribbean there is only one country that successfully has gone through an "economic reform" process, and that is Chile.

The "Chilean model" is often cited as the way that the countries of Latin America and the Caribbean could or should go to modernize their economies and become regenerated partners in the economic world. One problem with the Chilean reform process is that it was implemented under a nondemocratic political system. Therefore, it was able to draw on resources for implementation of its policies which newly democratic Latin American and Caribbean countries do not have access to.

The big question now in Latin America and the Caribbean is: Will these countries be able to go through the major economic reform that everyone recognizes is necessary? Will Mexico, which appears to be the next model country for economic reform, be able to undergo reform under democratic structures which are in themselves very tentative and which emphasize peaceful negotiating processes as opposed to confrontational ones?

Latin America has been going through a profound democratization process since the end of the Cold War. The previous emphasis on security and the military aspects of government has been reduced severely. At the same time, the region's societies are experiencing extremely profound transformations in the way power is established, the way power is used, and the way consensus is built.

The emphasis on government agendas has now switched to such political issues as building democracy and extending economic content to that democracy, both so that living conditions will improve and so that democratic systems can then be consolidated.

Trying to balance all of these goals simultaneously is a challenging undertaking. Attempting to build a democracy and simultaneously reforming an economy that in turn transforms the society is an extremely difficult challenge — not only for political leaders and nongovernmental sectors, but for all of society.

However, the EAI came at a time when the countries in Latin America and the Caribbean had more or less decided that they would have to commit to these changes and that they would commit to carrying out the economic reforms democratically. The EAI added additional pressure for them to move in that direction.

The Inter-American Development Bank would be a financial agent for many of the activities that would fall under the Enterprise for the Americas Initiative as proposed. In practice, it would serve to turn many of the decisions that governments are making into banking operations. It would also manage the Multilateral Investment Fund, and it would seek to use those monies to help the implementing countries cover the cost of some reforms. Thus, the Inter-American Development Bank would act as a fulcrum between the EAI and the countries that would carry out the series of changes contemplated in the Initiative.

The most visible area of change in the region may be that involving trade. Latin America and the Caribbean are, in fact, part of a worldwide movement to change the world trading system. There are tensions in several areas. Some countries or groups of countries want to retain a closed, protected market, and others want a more open trading system.

The United States is a country that faces momentous decisions in the area of trade. The southern region of the United States, in particular, is beginning to experience very close at hand the anticipated effects of trade liberalization under the North American Free Trade Agreement (NAFTA) negotiated with Mexico and Canada. Southerners are probably even more sensitive than people in other areas of the country to the possible consequences for them of NAFTA trade liberalization.

In Latin America and the Caribbean, various blocs of countries are being formed to create sub-regional schemes. Thirteen Caribbean nations, comprising the Caribbean Community and Common Market (CARICOM), are all seeking to integrate their economies and their markets into an economic whole that will be more competitive because it is bigger and stronger than the single countries in the world market. CARICOM represents a small grouping of 5.5 million people. With an export trade of $470 billion, as a bloc they are not a major player in the trade world, but they are very much aware of world trends and want to survive.

The six Central American countries, including Panama, represent the next layer in the sub-regional scheme. They have a total population of approximately 35 million, and their external trade is approximately ten times larger than that of the Caribbean countries.

The next sub-regional group is comprised of the five Andean bloc countries: Bolivia, Peru, Ecuador, Colombia, and Venezuela. This group is trying to form a number of trade accords in order to compete more efficiently in the international market.

Finally, the largest sub-group in Latin America is the Southern Cone Common Market, MERCOSUR, comprised of Argentina, Brazil, Uruguay, and Paraguay, with a total population of 186 million. Seventy percent of the economic power of those four countries is vested in Brazil alone, so these countries are facing tremendous challenges in forming trade partnerships between very small countries like Uruguay, with a population of 3.5 million, and very large countries like Brazil, with a population of 140 million.

The biggest integration scheme currently being negotiated in the hemisphere is the North American Free Trade Agreement — roughly a $6 trillion market. Therefore, the dimensions of NAFTA — which includes Mexico, the United States, and Canada — substantially exceed even those of MERCOSUR. The initial reaction of the Latin American countries and the Caribbean was very optimistic about the outcome of the Enterprise for the Americas Initiative because the countries have received this as a signal from the United States government that it wants to form a hemispheric solidarity vis-à-vis the rest of the world, a world which is going through many difficult transformations, where international relations are being redefined. But the Latin American and Caribbean countries are also watching how NAFTA develops with extreme caution, as the outcome may well serve as a model for what they also will have to negotiate later. They are going to be extremely attentive to the case of Canada, which has had two years now to go through its own Free Trade Agreement with the United States. The Latin American and Caribbean countries are beginning to wonder if there are lessons to be learned from the Canadian experience.

Undoubtedly, a new kind of hemispheric economic reality is evolving. Its initial effects and mechanisms are still mysterious and chaotic because many countries are also negotiating bilaterally. In spite of the current chaos, the tendency seems to be toward the formation of a hemispheric economic unity of some kind. Although we do not know exactly how it will be defined, the region's economic power, with respect to the rest of the world, will obviously be significantly greater than the individual power of any of these countries, both economically and politically.

Finally, there is one very big question for Latin America and the Caribbean which perhaps will be partially answered with the ultimate outcome of the North American Free Trade Agreement negotiations: How willing are the United States and Canada to implement their own economic reforms? If Latin American countries are withdrawing protective barriers from industries, does that mean that there will be symmetrical liberalization of sensitive industries within the United States and Canada? The social cost of this process is immensely high, as is the political cost for the public officials who are responsible for the decision making. But these processes and decisions will affect the quality of life throughout the hemisphere. It is incumbent upon us not only to hope for the best, but to work together now to make sure it is for the best.

The Evolving Concept of Environment and Sustainable Development

Barbara J. Bramble

The National Wildlife Federation (NWF) engages in both domestic and international programs. The domestic program, 90 percent of what we do, revolves around issues such as toxic waste, acid rain, and forest management policies. In the United States, the NWF is trying to get the government out of the business of subsidizing timber production from public lands at way below the cost of operation. We are attempting to do the same thing with grazing land, energy production, irrigation, and power schemes in the West. We are involved in a relatively new program that examines the potential dangers of the biotechnology industry; there continue to be many doubts and risks associated with the inadvertent release of artificially produced organisms that may affect their wild relatives.

Internationally, the NWF focuses on the interface of environmental and economic issues, to promote sustainable development. We attempt to understand what "sustainable development" really means and see how it can be identified if it already exists or promoted where it does not. The NWF International Division was begun in the early 1980s to determine how tax dollars were being spent by government agencies such as the U.S. Agency for International Development (U.S. AID), or indirectly, through the multilateral banks such as the Inter-American Development Bank or the World Bank,

Barbara Bramble is director, International Division of the National Wildlife Federation, Washington, D.C. This chapter is taken from remarks delivered at the Challenges to Hemispheric Development conference held at the Southern Center for International Studies, Atlanta, October 29, 1991.

which were not accountable to the public. In those days, projects were shrouded in secrecy. We discovered projects with disastrous effects, not just on the environment but on people's lives. What we found, from information given to us by colleague organizations, fledgling environmental groups all over the world, was that in some areas people were being made worse off instead of better off by many of these projects. There were quite a few specific cases where hundreds of thousands of people were displaced by dams without compensation. Yet the energy produced by the dams was meant for export or to serve a distant city, not the local inhabitants. A clear decision had been made that these people did not count; they were the ones who suffered, and yet no one thought about the consequences for them or for the land.

In 1983, the National Wildlife Federation started a campaign for environmental and social reforms of multilateral development banks (MDBs) based on pioneering work done by other groups studying U.S. AID. Many changes have been made in the MDBs as a result, such as their hiring of environmental experts as staff and adoption of new policies to conserve natural resources and consult local people. Those of us who work on this, as well as many people within the banks, would agree that quite a few changes are still needed in several important areas, such as access to information and public accountability. Although one could say that these reforms so far remain at the "rhetoric level" and have not yet affected the implementation of projects, there are some wonderful new things going on within the MDBs. The campaign itself and the way it was waged are interesting topics for discussion, as they have led to some remarkable developments in the worldwide environmental movement.

In the early 1980s, the National Wildlife Federation investigated a number of projects funded by multilateral development banks that had severe detrimental environmental and social impacts on local people. Evidence was gathered from the people affected, and opportunities were created to allow them to speak for themselves directly to those who were making the decisions affecting their lives. This personal approach, as opposed to the "issue a report" approach, depended on the credible testimony of the people affected by the projects. It had a very strong impact, producing an almost emotional response in some decisionmakers who heard the evidence. The first targets in that introduction process were not actually the banks themselves, but the U.S. Congress, because Congress approves the money for the U.S. contribution to the banks. We helped several congressional committees hold a series of hearings in which our organization and others brought people from various countries to serve as witnesses. Later, as this process gradually achieved access, we took the witnesses to see people at the U.S. Department of the Treasury, then to the MDBs themselves. We saw higher and higher levels of officials at the banks to the point that now meetings with the presidents of the MDBs are not at all unusual.

This has been a decade-long process of gaining access for local people as well as for ourselves. One of the interesting and important aspects of this process has been that the status of those witnesses we brought here to speak about their experiences seems to have been greatly enhanced after they returned home. Seemingly powerless, isolated, unimportant people, whose low status enabled the authorities to foist destructive projects off onto them, suddenly went home as international celebrities. This phenomenon has had a remarkable effect on the relationships of these people within their own countries. In some cases, it has even led to their own proposals for alternative development projects being listened to by their governments. This is an important development, since proposals that make sense in the context of a particular country, that are thought of, proposed, and promoted within that country, have a much greater likelihood of being appropriate and successful than something that is imposed from outside.

For example, in the 1980s, the World Bank funded a program in Brazil called Polonoroeste, designed to colonize the Western Amazon region. (At the same time, there was a similar World Bank-funded program to colonize the outer islands of Indonesia.) In Brazil, the basic idea was to provide land to poor migrant workers from other parts of the country and to exert sovereignty over the wilderness and the area's mineral wealth that the government feared could be claimed by a neighboring country. The central components of the Polonoroeste project were the paving of a thousand kilometer road and titling plots of land to the immigrants in rigid grid patterns unsuitable to rational use of the rainforest. In Indonesia, the plan was to bring people to the islands by boat, but then similarly to mark off the forest in plots for rice cultivation. In both cases, the rationale was the desperate need for poor people to have a place to farm. Nothing could have been less appropriate, since much of the land in these areas is entirely unsuitable for typical farming practices. These major projects, promoted by military governments, were basically accepted by the World Bank, which lent hundreds of millions of dollars to pave roads into pristine tropical forest areas, for the purpose of clearing and burning the forest, without concern for the people who already lived there, the indigenous tribal people. In Brazil, this population also included rubber tappers.

The road paving in Brazil was accompanied by massive publicity promoting migration to these areas. Across the country, Brazilian television carried the theme that this was "A Land Without People, For a People Without Land." The campaign succeeded in luring to the Amazon poverty-stricken families, many from the southern part of the country. Ironically, many of these people had been displaced by earlier projects financed by the MDBs to promote highly mechanized soybean production for export. Several states in Western Amazonia were inundated with hundreds of thousands of people looking for a piece of land to call their own, to raise some crops and take care of their families. Essentially a homesteading program, the plan was relatively simple. Unfortunately, the soils and climate of the area selected for the program were unsuitable. On top of the most controversial aspects of the project, such as the invasion of indigenous lands, the exploitation of the misery of the already displaced people from the South, and the cutting of tropical rain forest, the basic problem was that the colonists were left with pieces of land that were not cultivatible. The project was a tremendous subsidy for destruction, for no good reason except the military government's obsession with colonizing the area. Much of the land that was burned is now abandoned, and the people live in the Amazonia's growing urban slums.

In Brazil, the NWF worked very closely with indigenous groups and rubber tappers, bringing a number of them to Washington over a period of several years. Many of these people became famous. Our critics called them "jet-set environmentalists," "Eco-Indians," and "reborn environmentalists" because they suspected that these people really had no reason to be concerned about the environment. In fact, while these indigenous people were not technically "environmentalists," they cared and continued to care about saving the forests.

Chico Mendes, probably the most famous of them all and a hero now in many parts of the world, was assassinated in December 1988, in the culmination of his campaign to save the forests of his people. He was a rural union leader and an avowed leftist, the product of training by a very hard-line communist who traveled through Western Amazonia about forty years ago. In 1985, Chico had this marvelous idea that the rubber tappers of that region, who actually lived in harmony with the forest — deriving their product from natural rubber trees and able to produce a fairly reasonable income for a family if combined with gardening, hunting, and Brazil nut collection — could help to save the Amazon if the government would draw lines around the areas where they lived, creating "extractive reserves." This was our first example of what came to be called "sustainable development."

As the Polonoroeste project lumbered ahead in the mid-1980s, the environmental pressures on the area grew. Hundreds of thousands of people migrated to Rondonia State and cleared and burned land, producing smoke so thick that local airplane flights were grounded for weeks on end. The leaders of the indigenous movement and the leaders of the rubber tappers movement got together and created an Alliance of the Peoples of the Forest.

At about the same time, the Inter-American Development Bank (IDB) decided to fund the completion of the last one-fourth of the road, supplementing the World Bank's financing. (This is not a move the IDB would make today.) The ensuing controversy over completion of the road, including one year in which the United States cut off its contribution to the IDB, finally created an opening for positive proposals. The alliance of indigenous people and rubber tappers, along with their Brazilian and international supporters, went to the government of Brazil and to the MDBs with their extractive reserve proposal. Legal counsel was hired, legislation and regulations drafted, and eventually the Brazilian Congress and the environmental agency put the program into law.

The extractive reserve concept is now a part of the Brazilian legal system. It is a land-use type, similar to national parks, the fish and wildlife refuge system, or a national forest. The rules of the game are basically that land traditionally used by rubber tappers and other "extractivists" can be expropriated from whoever is trying to claim it: Compensation must be paid to the claimants to the land, and a land-use plan is to be developed with the participation of the residents of the reserve. Once legal status is established, it is then set aside for the people who live there as long as they agree to operate within the constraints of the land-use plan. This is a very interesting concept that originated from the people, not an outside organization.

The NWF has been working with the rubber tappers and indigenous groups in Brazil since 1986. Their problems after Chico Mendes' assassination continue, better in some ways and worse in others. The rubber tappers are famous now. They receive grants from the Ford Foundation, have an office and a facsimile machine, and have a known and established organization. However, they are under more pressure than ever from the ranchers and loggers. There have been more assassinations, and the shootings continue. The ranchers use the legal system to raise the compensation requirements and slow down establishment of reserves. They have hired environmental impact assessors to count the number of valuable trees on the land, hoping to prove that the mahogany or other timber on the land is so valuable that the nation cannot afford to condemn the land to rubber tapper use. The Collor de Mello government cut off the traditional price support for native rubber with no transition period to allow the tappers to develop alternative non-timber products.

Though the problems continue, the struggle is no longer a hidden or secret one. The individuals involved in the campaign are now on the international stage, speaking to government officials from around the world, negotiating with the English, Dutch, and Swedish on aid programs. This is due to their access to foreign media, World Bank officials in Washington, and individual members of Congress who, after meeting them, have been willing to write letters, visit Brazil, and make pleas for consideration of these ideas on their behalf.

To illustrate another type of campaign, the NWF also works on the link between trade and environment. We have been involved in negotiations of the General Agreement on Tariffs and Trade (GATT). We have been trying to persuade the administration in the United States and, together with our colleagues in Mexico, the government of Mexico that there are major environmental and social ramifications of the North American Free Trade Agreement (NAFTA).

The potential consequences of NAFTA must be analyzed and predicted where possible. If the problems likely to arise are pinpointed and analyzed in advance, then measures can be taken to avoid or reduce them. We have been working with colleagues from Mexico, setting up personal visits to Congress and the office of the U.S. Trade Representative, explaining that these are real problems that will not go away.

We have asked the U.S. Congress to put the administration on notice that certain stipulations must appear in the agreement, social and environmental safeguards. In addition, we have requested preparation of an adequate environmental impact assessment of the treaty. We want them to look at the quantity of investment that is likely to flow in one direction or another, leading to, if their rosy prognostications are correct, a huge increase in industrial investment in Mexico. If this comes about, then who is going to be responsible for the negative environmental effects — water pollution, soil erosion, and toxic waste dumps — that may occur in Mexico and the border areas, affecting people's health and the potential for future development? The Bush administration has prepared an action plan to look at some of these issues. They put several members of environmental organizations on some of the different committees assisting in the negotiation process. We have made great progress in a very short period of time, in pointing the public spotlight on the environmental aspects of trade agreements, but the needed safeguards are not yet included in the agreement.

The NWF is asking that a small percentage of the income and other taxes raised from NAFTA's expected trade and investment growth be devoted specifically to cleaning up the resultant pollution and to capacity building in Mexico's environmental agencies, for regulatory equipment, standard setting, and enforcement of rules and regulations. Mexico, as it turns out, has on its books a tremendous set of laws on many environmental subjects, but a very limited capacity to enforce them. We are quite convinced that it is completely irresponsible for the United States to put the burden of monitoring an enormous flood of new investment onto another country and then to claim we have no responsibility to help Mexico figure out the implications, especially the environmental and social consequences, of these plans.

To tie these environmental issues in with the issues confronting women and development in Latin America and the Caribbean, the common denominator of most of the problems facing women in the region today is poverty. Women have to deal with the environment in a very direct way. They are the ones who suffer most directly from environmental problems that are a direct consequence of the failed development strategies that have been undertaken up until now.

In Mexico, there is an air pollution problem associated with poverty which is a direct result of the amount of human excrement that is lying in the streets. When the weather is dry and the wind blows, this airborne, dried waste causes respiratory disease. Women are contaminated by pesticides in much of their work in the fields, and all the people eat vegetation that has been affected by downwind spray from airborne pesticide application. Meat also is contaminated by the animals' ingestion of pesticide-affected vegetation. There has been measured during the 1980s an historic level of pesticide contamination in mother's milk in Central America. Additionally, women are clearly affected by the loss of forest cover and the drying up of streams, as they usually are designated in poor families as the gatherers of fuel and water. They must search farther and farther for wood and water, adding to already heavy burdens of daily work.

In urban areas, the situation is, if anything, worse. Water contamination exists in all urban areas to the point that people are being made ill in vast numbers. Toxic contamination is at record levels in most of the megalopolises of Latin America. This is true of lead poisoning, particularly from the lead content of gasoline, which is affecting millions of children. Up until recently, the situation was similar in the United States, where eventually the public outcry forced even the Reagan administration to reduce lead levels in gasoline.

Women are not just victims of pollution and other environmental problems but are major managers of resources, either in farming or harvesting fuel wood and other non-timber products out of the forests, such as Brazil nuts and palm. Women also play a third role. They can be quite articulate advocates for change. My hope is that the groups we work with are gaining a platform that will allow them (primarily because of the harmful effects of pollution on their children) to become the voice that eventually will have an impact on government decisionmaking.

Finally, allow me a warning about "free trade." My sense is that we are now on a dangerous free trade bandwagon. It is almost a new ideology, or an abstract ideal that has been accepted by many as a goal, even though there are no examples of completely unfettered trade to analyze and assess the consequences. The way people talk about it today reminds me of how people in the 1920s and in the 1930s used to talk about communism. If communism had ever really been put into practice anywhere, it might have been quite nice — people wouldn't be selfish; they would produce for the common good; everybody would be taken care of. Lovely idea, but it never happened.

I think free trade can be placed in the same category. It is a concept that is being held up around the world as a solution to all problems. Obviously, people need trade, and people need freer trade than we have seen in most parts of the world, particularly the former Soviet Union and Eastern Europe. However, trade itself is not the goal; the goal is creating sustainable livelihoods while improving the quality of people's lives. Free trade should be seen as a means toward achieving that goal, toward attaining sustainable development.

Although there is a need for freer trade and economic activities more reliant on people's entrepreneurial instincts, this does not mean that trade should take place without basic decisions by societies about the rules of the marketplace. These would include regulations to protect human health and the environment, ban child labor, assure product information to consumers and labor's rights to organize, and correct other market failures. Many of the industrial leaders I have talked to in Europe understand this perfectly, but many U.S. policymakers do not appear to. They have promoted the concept of "free and unfettered" trade everywhere, among the multilateral lending institutions and in the negotiations for the United Nations Conference on Environment and Development.

The United States for several years has sent the message that it will not support more financial resources to help developing countries carry out the new agreements being made to improve environmental quality and reduce poverty. Many free trade advocates are not going to help pay for poverty reduction programs because they believe all social problems will be solved by the creation of a free market. This short-sighted ideology is probably as dangerous as the Cold War ever was, and we may have a new domino effect. What is needed is a sense of responsibility for our children and the future of our planet.

The U.S. and the Caribbean: The Power of the Whirlpool

Robert A. Pastor

Abstract: The Spanish-American War heralded the beginning of America's global role and its preoccupation with the Caribbean area. There are a host of theories to explain U.S. involvement in the Caribbean, but over time, the whirlpool pattern of intense involvement followed by disinterest suggests that security considerations have remained paramount. U.S. policy in the twentieth century can be divided into three periods: the protectorate era (1898-1933); the Good Neighbor Policy (1933-1953); and the Cold War (1953-1990). Whether the United States will be able to escape the unproductive and erratic relationships of the past depends on whether it uses the post-Cold War era to develop a collective defense of democracy and a social safety net for the poor people in the countries of the region.

On January 29, 1981, at his first press conference as president, Ronald Reagan was asked whether his meeting with Jamaican Prime Minister Edward Seaga encouraged him to develop a policy toward the Caribbean. He replied that Seaga's electoral victory — four days before his own — represented a "great reverse in the Caribbean situation.... The turn-around of a nation that had gone certainly in the direction of the Communist movement.... This opens the door," Reagan concluded, bringing his answer back to the question, "for us to have a policy in the Mediterranean."[1]

Robert A. Pastor is professor of political science at Emory University and director of the Latin American and Caribbean Program at Emory's Carter Center. He is the author of ten books; the most recent are *Integration with Mexico: Options for U.S. Policy* (Twentieth Century Fund, 1993) and *Whirlpool: U.S. Foreign Policy Toward Latin America and the Caribbean* (Princeton, 1992). He was director of Latin American Affairs on the National Security Council from 1977 to 1981.

This chapter appeared in *ANNALS* of the American Academy of Political and Social Sciences, 533, May 1994. Reprinted by permission of Sage Publications, Inc.

Sigmund Freud could have explained Reagan's slip; so could Alfred T. Mahan, an influential naval strategist, who wrote at the turn of the century that the time had come for the United States to act as if the Caribbean were "America's Mediterranean Sea." What Mahan meant was that for the United States to be a world power, it would need a naval strategy comparable to England's. Drawing explicit comparisons, Mahan argued that Malta is to Egypt, the Suez Canal, and the route to India for Great Britain what Puerto Rico "is to Cuba, to the future of the Isthmian Canal, and to our Pacific Coast." The Caribbean, Mahan wrote, was "now intrinsically unimportant." Its significance would rise in proportion to the power and ambition of the United States.[2]

The Spanish-American War not only divided the nineteenth from the twentieth centuries, it also represented a watershed in U.S. relations with its nearest neighbors and the world. In the nineteenth century, the United States concentrated on development and continental expansion and paid little or no attention to the chronic instability in the Caribbean. After the war, the United States became almost obsessed with instability in its neighbors. The politics of these countries had not changed; what had changed was the United States.

Scholars of inter-American relations have spent much time trying to locate the motive for U.S. involvement in the internal affairs of its neighbors. Instead of a single answer, they have amassed a collection of explanations that range from security (keep out rivals, maintain stability), political or ideological (promote democracy, prevent revolution, communism, or "alien" ideologies), economic (imperialism, secure access to investment or trade), to psychological (an impulse to dominate, a fear of insecurity, misperception). A particular explanation might be cogent for a given case, but in trying to understand what moves the United States over time, one needs to look for patterns in the history of U.S. relations with the region.

One pattern that stands out is the way in which U.S. attention to the region fluctuates between obsession and disinterest. I have referred to this pattern as a "whirlpool,"[3] a whirling eddy which occasionally sucks the United States into a vortex of crisis where it becomes preoccupied by small Caribbean nations or their leaders. U.S. presidents react to the crises with security, political, and economic programs that have historical antecedents even if the policymakers of the time are not aware of them. Then, almost as suddenly, U.S. interest and resources shift away from the region, and many Americans can hardly recall either their nemesis or the reason for their intervention. Americans then feel they have escaped the whirlpool, but history suggests that they are on the rim, only to be pulled into the vortex with the next crisis.

Although the history of U.S. relations with the Caribbean is replete with examples of America's drive to extract resources, uproot seemingly alien ideologies, implant a political philosophy, or prescribe an economic orthodoxy, this whirlpool pattern suggests that the dominant motive has been U.S.

security. From Mahan's guiding vision to Reagan's Freudian slip, the United States has been motivated not so much to control the region but to keep things from veering out of control where they could be exploited by others viewed as hostile. The line separating a policy of control, and a need to keep things from veering out of control, is not always easy to find during crises. But if control were the motive, the United States would retain a presence after the crisis, and that has seldom been the case.

The nations in the region are too small and poor to constitute a direct threat to the United States; the threat that moves the United States is that more powerful adversaries from Europe or Asia could forge a relationship with one of the small nations that would permit the more powerful one to use it as a base to attack or harass the United States or its neighbors. When the threat diminishes, so does U.S. interest. That accounts for the apparent cycle between preoccupation at moments of intense geopolitical rivalry and neglect at times of geopolitical calm.

The end of the Cold War raises, once again, the question as to whether the United States has escaped the whirlpool of unproductive relations or whether it is just at its rim. Interest in the Caribbean has declined, but is the decline permanent? That question can only be addressed satisfactorily after we review the history of U.S. policy toward the Caribbean and examine the changes that have occurred in the last two decades.

A Survey of U.S. Policy

U.S. foreign policy toward the Caribbean has been the sum of the answers to questions as to whether the United States ought to have a "special relationship" with the region and what that means. This broad question has led to many others, including how to preclude instability; discourage foreign penetration; defeat anti-American revolutionaries; promote peaceful political change; foment economic development; defend human rights; reinforce democracy; gain respect for U.S. investment, the American flag, and U.S. citizens; and maintain good relations with our neighbors. Answers to these questions have differed from one administration to the next, and particularly when there is a change in the party in power. But the differences have never been as great as the administration claims at its beginning, nor as little as it suggests when its power is waning or its policy is wanting, and it seeks strength by asserting continuity or bipartisanship. Nevertheless, in identifying the threads of continuity that have tied presidents as different as Carter and Reagan, one can better appreciate the elusive concept of national interest. In discerning the changes in policy toward similar problems, we might better establish the boundaries of real choice.

In the twentieth century, U.S. foreign policy toward the Caribbean can be divided into three periods: 1) the protectorate era, 1898-1933; 2) the Good

Neighbor Policy, 1933-1953; and 3) the Cold War, 1953-1990. We shall discuss the post-Cold War era after a survey of the history.

The Protectorate Era

The United States has always been of two minds — realistic and idealistic — on how to relate to the Caribbean. It has aimed to prevent foreign rivals from getting a foothold, but it has also sought ways to translate its idealism into policy. The tension between these two sides was captured in two congressional amendments passed within three years of each other. The Teller Amendment to the Declaration of War against Spain in 1898 declared that the United States would not annex Cuba, the main prize of the war. In an age of imperialism, this was an unusual act of self-denial, and some leaders, notably Theodore Roosevelt, took pride in the amendment as proof that U.S. motives were different from and purer than those of Europe's imperialists.

The Platt Amendment was passed in 1901 to grant the United States rights to intervene in Cuba's internal affairs to protect lives and property or preserve Cuban independence. This amendment not only appears self-contradictory — how can U.S. intervention preserve Cuban independence? — but it also appears to negate the Teller Amendment. In actuality, the amendments represented the two sides of the American perspective on Cuba and, more broadly, the Caribbean. The United States wanted Cuba to be free, but it feared that too much freedom could cause instability and foreign — that is, non-U.S. — intervention, and so it imposed limits.

Those limits were enunciated in President Theodore Roosevelt's "Corollary to the Monroe Doctrine," a message to Congress in December 1904. Roosevelt wrote that "chronic wrongdoing, or an impotence which results in a general loosening of ties of civilized society...may force the United States, however reluctantly, ...to the exercise of an international police power."[4] Just three years before, Roosevelt allowed three European governments to intervene to collect debts from Venezuela provided no territory was acquired. His position evolved for several reasons, including the negative reaction by the American public to the European bombing of Venezuela and his growing fear of German machinations in the Dominican Republic.

During the protectorate period, U.S. Marines intervened more than twenty times in the Caribbean area. Like all nations, the United States is moved by fears more than by hopes. The fear of Germany's gaining a foothold in Hispaniola in 1915 led U.S. policymakers to invade the island. "Though it [the United States] did not need and did not want such a coaling station [in Haiti], it could not permit a European government to secure one," wrote a former Secretary of State to a Senate Committee investigating the intervention. "The indications were that Germany intended to obtain one unless she was prevented from doing so by the United States."[5]

The construction of the Panama Canal — with an investment equivalent to one-third of the U.S. budget in 1914 — was a sign of U.S. expansion and a motive for widening its arc of defense. U.S. presidents became preoccupied with protecting this strategic asset from the region's instability and other foreign powers — to the extent that some historians referred to our entire policy toward the Caribbean Basin as "the Panama policy."[6]

Still, there were many different ways to defend the Canal and U.S. interests in Latin America during the twentieth century. Theodore Roosevelt and Elihu Root, his Secretary of State, tried to preclude revolution by international treaties. William Howard Taft used marines, dollars, and customs receiverships to help the countries remain solvent and stable. Woodrow Wilson replaced "dollar diplomacy" with the promotion of liberty, but, like his predecessors, he continued to use the marines.

On the eve of World War I, U.S. fears of German activities in the region intensified. On July 29, 1915, President Wilson ordered U.S. Marines to occupy Haiti. During the next year, the United States occupied the Dominican Republic, and on March 8, 1917, one month before the U.S. declared war against Germany, American forces intervened again to prevent civil war in Cuba. The stated cause of these interventions was instability in each country, and the declared good was to promote democracy, but the sense of urgency in the United States related more to events in Europe than in the Caribbean.

If the Spanish-American War heralded the arrival of the United States as the preeminent power in the Caribbean Basin, then the end of World War I signaled that the United States had become the leading power in the entire world. The European powers, preoccupied with their own recovery, withdrew or sharply reduced their already limited economic and diplomatic presence in the Caribbean. No power stood in the way of the United States. Realist theories would argue that the United States would maintain and expand its presence in the Caribbean and around the world, but the opposite happened. Woodrow Wilson led the peace negotiations in Europe, but the U.S. Senate rejected involvement in the institutions that he helped construct.

The yearning for normalcy and isolation that led the Senate to block the Treaty of Versailles impelled the U.S. government to disengage gradually from the Caribbean. In addition, the United States wanted to end its interventions in the region because they were proving more costly and less effective than expected. This was not due to a loss of will in the United States but rather to the strengthening of national leaders and institutions in the affected countries.

Just as the interventions tended to follow a similar pattern, so, too, did the exits. U.S. economic advisers set up customs relationships, whereby they managed government expenditures and revenues and ensured that the nations would remain solvent. The marines then helped establish a military guard, which they hoped would be nonpartisan. Then, with some difficulty and military assistance, U.S. diplomats supervised elections that were intended to legitimize a new government. Most U.S. diplomats recognized the shallowness of the new democracies and the threats that the new armies might try to seize power. Nonetheless, Washington decided to withdraw the marines, and with one momentary reversal — in Nicaragua in 1925 — U.S. soldiers went home, beginning in 1921 and ending in 1934.

The Good Neighbor Policy

In an article in *Foreign Affairs* in 1928, Franklin D. Roosevelt criticized the interventions of the previous decades: "By what right...other than the right of main force, does the United States arrogate unto itself the privilege of intervening alone in the internal affairs of another sovereign Republic?...Single-handed intervention by us in the internal affairs of other nations must end."[7] Elected president four years later, Roosevelt used his inaugural address to repeat his promise to Latin America that he would dismantle the old protectorate system and replace it with a new "good neighbor" policy.

In practice, Roosevelt's policy had three components.[8] First, he pledged nonintervention in the internal affairs of Latin America. He withdrew the marines from the remaining countries in which they were still based and repealed the dreaded Platt Treaties. Although Secretary of State Cordell Hull's statement on nonintervention at the Montevideo Conference often is cited as the beginning of the policy, the real test was passed by Hull and Roosevelt in 1933 when they rejected at three different times the recommendation of U.S. Ambassador to Havana Sumner Welles to land marines in Cuba, allegedly to protect American citizens but really to control political events.[9] One of the consequences of accepting the principle of nonintervention, however, was that it removed the principal impediment — the United States — from the path to power by military dictators, like Anastasio Somoza of Nicaragua, Fulgencio Batista of Cuba, and Rafael Trujillo of the Dominican Republic.

The second element of the policy was freer trade by Reciprocal Trade Agreements. As congressman and senator, Cordell Hull had been a vigorous advocate of free trade for many years, and he gave it highest priority when appointed Secretary of State. With much of the world divided into trading blocs, the one region with the most countries eligible for such agreements was Latin America, and as a result, by 1945, 16 of the 22 bilateral trade agreements signed by the United States were with hemispheric governments.

The third element of the Good Neighbor Policy was a systematic effort by the United States to consult with its Latin neighbors. Even before the storm clouds of war gathered over Europe, Roosevelt and Hull took the inter-American conferences seriously. The investment paid off when war began. Except Argentina, the region gave virtually complete support to U.S. war aims.

After Roosevelt died and the war ended, the broad outlines of the Good Neighbor Policy were maintained by President Harry Truman. Truman made a few changes — for example, experimenting with a more active policy to promote democracy and distance itself from dictators — but the major change was the new agenda of Latin America. The region wanted loans preferably at subsidized rates for economic development. At the Bogotá Conference in 1948 to establish the Organization of American States, the region's foreign ministers asked Secretary of State George Marshall for a "Marshall Plan for Latin America." He explained that Europe's recovery was urgent. He promised to convey their concerns to Truman, who later launched his Point IV Technical Assistance Program for Latin America and the developing world, although the magnitude of the aid was trivial as compared to the Marshall Plan.

The Cold War

While some U.S. government officials were concerned about the spread of communism in Latin America in the 1940s, the first serious intrusion of the Cold War occurred in Guatemala, where the U.S. government covertly tried to unseat the leftist Arbenz government in June 1954. As a colonel in the army, Jacobo Arbenz and several of his colleagues overthrew dictator Jorge Ubico in 1944. A free election brought Juan José Arevalo to power as president, and he undertook a program of reforms that unsettled the conservative establishment in the country. Arbenz was elected in 1951, and with the support of the Communist Party, he accelerated reforms into ever more sensitive areas, including the inequitable land-tenure system.

The Eisenhower administration was worried about Communist influence and urged Arbenz to dismiss party members from his government. Dependent on them for ideas and political support, Arbenz refused.[10] The United States imposed an embargo on arms sales to the regime, and when it discovered a shipload of arms was sailing to Guatemala from Eastern Europe, Eisenhower authorized a covert action plan. The plan failed to overthrow Arbenz, but it catalyzed the Guatemalan military, already suspicious and alienated from the president, to take action against him.

The coup's significance was the message it conveyed across Latin America that the United States would not tolerate leftists even if they came to power by free elections and that it would work closely with right wing dictators like Somoza and Guatemala's Carlos Castillo Armas in order to stop communism. This had the unfortunate effect of reducing the political space for democrats, encouraging leftists to revolt, and inviting rightists to suppress dissent.

Fidel Castro learned another lesson from Guatemala, one that Allen Dulles, director of the Central Intelligence Agency, failed to grasp until the failure of the Bay of Pigs. After coming to power, Castro replaced the military with his own guerrilla force. Dulles executed a strategy against Castro similar to the one he used against Arbenz, but he failed in Cuba because Castro's military was ready to defend him.

Nonetheless, the fear of "more Cubas" led President Eisenhower and then President Kennedy to propose Marshall Plan-type schemes to facilitate the region's development. After resisting the idea of international commodity agreements and the establishment of an Inter-American Development Bank, Eisenhower finally accepted both in his last year in office. Kennedy's bold 10-year, $10 billion foreign aid program to Latin America, the Alliance for Progress, was aimed to foster development, social and land reforms, and reinforce democracy. While it did not achieve its high expectations, it did energize the region in important ways.

The fear of communism also led President Kennedy to try to remove Cuba's dictatorial neighbors. In Haiti, "Papa Doc" Duvalier outlasted President Kennedy. In the Dominican Republic, the Central Intelligence Agency supported conspirators who assassinated Rafael Trujillo in May 1961. Within a year, an election was held, but the new president, Juan Bosch, was overthrown seven months later. In April 1965, civil war broke out as Bosch's followers tried to retake power. President Johnson sent 22,000 soldiers. While the Dominican Republic did not become another Cuba, most scholars of the intervention conclude that this was never likely; the only outcome with a high probability was that U.S. intervention would severely damage U.S. relations with Latin America, as it did.[11]

Within a year of the intervention, and for more than a decade, American attention was diverted away from the Caribbean to war in Vietnam and the Middle East and détente with the Soviet Union. By 1977, the United States could no longer ignore the resentment in Panama over obsolete Canal treaties, and Jimmy Carter took the unpopular decision of revising those treaties and modernizing U.S. relations with that small country.[12] Carter also reoriented U.S. relations with the Third World to put a high priority on human rights. The policy saved lives in Haiti; freed political prisoners in Argentina, Central America, and Cuba; and helped democratic trends in Peru, Ecuador, Brazil, and the Dominican Republic, among others. An attempt to engage the Cuban government made some progress but ultimately foundered on Cuba's expansionist ambitions in Africa.

The most significant initiative of the Carter administration in the Caribbean was aimed at the newly independent English-speaking Caribbean. Beginning in 1962 and continuing through the 1980s, twelve small English-speaking islands or territories in or on the Caribbean became independent. The new nations became a critical mass, distinct from the old Latin Caribbean and intent on appropriating the term "Caribbean" to apply to their community. To respond to the development problems of these micro-states, Carter launched the Caribbean Group for Cooperation in Economic Development under the auspices of the World Bank. The Caribbean Group was composed of thirty nations and fifteen international institutions, and within four years it quadrupled the aid given to the region and coordinated it to encourage integration.

In 1979, two leftist revolutions occurred, one on the small island of Grenada and the other in the Central American country of Nicaragua. Together with other events in the world — the Iranian Revolution and the taking of American diplomats as hostages, the Soviet invasion of Afghanistan, and the Soviet-Cuban intervention in Ethiopia — these two Caribbean revolutions made some Americans uneasy. No one articulated the apprehension and frustration better than Ronald Reagan in his presidential campaign in 1980.

The change in policies toward the Caribbean from Carter to Reagan was as dramatic a shift as the United States had seen between two presidents in the twentieth century. While the Carter administration started with an interest in promoting economic development in the Caribbean but eventually returned to a concern for national security, the Reagan administration, reflecting a more traditional approach, made the same journey in the opposite direction. But this understates the different points of departure of the two presidents.

Carter believed that the United States should work with small nations on a shared agenda of human rights and development on the basis of mutual respect and multilateral cooperation. President Reagan believed that the East-West struggle was paramount, and the small nations were important only to the extent that they were allies or enemies in this wider struggle. Reagan viewed instability as being inflicted on some countries in the Caribbean by Cuba and the Soviet Union. As he told the *Wall Street Journal* in 1980, "The Soviet Union underlies all the unrest that is going on. If they weren't engaged in this game of dominoes, there wouldn't be any hot spots in the world."[13]

Reagan adopted a very confrontational approach to Grenada, and in October 1983, when one faction of the revolutionary government attacked another, he joined with six Caribbean nations to invade the island, arrest the revolutionaries, and restore a democratic government to power. The centerpiece of his East-West strategy in the region was his support for the Salvadoran government and the Nicaraguan contras. As with President Kennedy, however, Reagan was sensitive to criticism that his anti-Communist strategy lacked a positive component, and so he fashioned a development program and institutions to promote democracy. His Caribbean Basin Initiative allowed one-way free trade for certain products from the region's small nations in order to promote development.

George Bush adopted a less ideological and belligerent approach than his predecessor, although he also intervened with military force in the area — in Panama in December 1989. That was actually the first unilateral military intervention in Latin America in 65 years. Bush promoted democratization in Haiti by supporting election-monitoring efforts by the United Nations, the

Organization of American States, and a council of presidents, the latter led by Jimmy Carter. These efforts culminated with the election of December 1990 and the victory of a priest, Father Jean-Bertrand Aristide, who had established a reputation for resisting the Duvaliers. Within seven months of his inauguration, however, he was overthrown by the military. The Organization of American States condemned the coup and recommended an embargo and diplomatic isolation, but Aristide remained locked out of the country. The Bush administration initially supported the efforts to restore Aristide, but it seemed to lose interest after stemming the flow of refugees.

Similarly, the United States, Canada, and Great Britain supported efforts by Carter's Council of Freely Elected Heads of Government to mediate electoral reforms in Guyana, and these permitted free, fair, and accepted elections on October 5, 1992 — the first in 28 years. The opposition leader, Dr. Cheddi Jagan, won the election, and, with that election, the entire English-speaking Caribbean became democratic.

Perhaps the most far-reaching of Bush's initiatives in the area was in trade. First, he made the Caribbean Basin Initiative permanent, and then, at the request of the President of Mexico and, subsequently, the Prime Minister of Canada, he negotiated and, on December 17, 1992, signed the North American Free Trade Agreement (NAFTA). In response to requests from throughout the region to join the regional trading area, Bush proposed the Enterprise for the Americas Initiative in May 1990.

President Bill Clinton modified NAFTA to include side agreements on the environment and labor standards, and he promised to extend the agreement throughout the hemisphere after Congress approved it.

The Caribbean in the Post-Cold War Era

The three nations that emerged as world powers at the dawn of the twentieth century are the same three that stand the tallest as the century nears its end: Germany, Japan, and the United States. Germany is the pivot of a wide and deep European Community; Japan increasingly looks to Asia as a base for a modern co-prosperity sphere; and the United States is the center of a North American trade area that could eventually include the entire hemisphere.

This reorganization of world economic and political power has profound implications for the Caribbean. Thirty-five years ago, there were only three independent countries in the Caribbean, and all three were trying to rid themselves of dictatorship. Only one — the Dominican Republic — succeeded. Haiti continues to struggle under an oppressive dictatorship, having experienced only a seven-month democratic interlude in 1991. Cuba remains controlled by an aging revolutionary and a repressive one-party system.

In the meantime, twelve English-speaking parliamentary democracies became independent. These new nations are much smaller, more stable politically, more advanced socially, and more vulnerable economically than the old Latin Caribbean. The advantage and disadvantage of the entire area stem from its proximity to the United States, which is the principal destination for the region's products and a highly unequal competitor for its skilled population. The United States is, therefore, both a solution and a problem, a source of aid and a rival, an outlet for unskilled labor and a magnet for the region's talent. Caribbean nations all confront a vexing strategic dilemma: how to retain autonomy while seeking regional integration, how to elude the dominance of the United States while securing improved access to its market.

While states ponder these difficult questions, people have begun to answer them with their feet. Migration has created a powerful new bond connecting the region and the United States. At least 10 percent of the population of each of the nations of the Caribbean live in the United States, and the second-largest city of most of the nations is either in New York or Florida. This human union will decisively reshape U.S.-Caribbean relations in the post-Cold War era in both a positive and a negative way.

Positively, immigrants help both the sending and the receiving nations understand that their differences are less than each had thought and that their cross-national stereotypes fail to capture the dynamism of human potential. With an expanding Caribbean population within the United States, the region looks less distant and foreign from the U.S. perspective, and the United States looks less Anglo-Saxon, white, and imperious from the Caribbean.

At the same time, the human traffic does generate social tensions and fears, particularly of large numbers of illegal aliens descending on U.S. shores. Perhaps the principal motive behind the Clinton administration's drive to restore President Jean-Bertrand Aristide to power in Haiti was the desire to stop Haitian refugees. As the Haitian military proved uncooperative and refugee flows continued, President Clinton faced an agonizing dilemma. The fear of refugees may replace the fear of communism in the post-Cold War era as the principal concern of the United States in the region.

No nation in the Caribbean has felt the impact of the end of the Cold War more severely than Cuba. With its subsidies and trade with the Soviet bloc cut or ended, Cuba found itself untethered, and its economy plummeted. With meager rations of oil, the country's traffic slowly came to a halt. Castro proclaimed an opening for foreign investment and heralded each new investor from Europe or Latin America, but the United States tightened the embargo. Both Washington and Havana froze into Cold War hostility even as some countries in the hemisphere called for a thaw.

The Caribbean protested the isolating of Cuba, but not so vehemently as to cause problems in their relations with the United States or competition against their own tourist industries. As the Caribbean began to contemplate the low-cost tourist and manufacturing potential of the region's largest island, many began to realize that a capitalist Cuba would pose a far more serious threat than a Communist Cuba ever did. Moreover, the transition toward a more open society might be violent, creating pressures internationally, and especially in the United States, to intervene.

Nonetheless, both the Cuban predicament and the Haitian nightmare remain isolated from the broader challenges that the rest of the Caribbean faces — how to relate to an expanding North American free trade area and how to secure the region's democracies. These twin challenges are distinct but related to each other. To the extent that the region enters into NAFTA, the prospect for securing their democracies is enhanced.

The Caribbean Community and Common Market (CARICOM) has begun to struggle with these implications. The massive report Time for Action, of the West Indian Commission, chaired by Sir Shridath Ramphal, is a clarion call for accelerating and deepening West Indian integration as a first step toward building new trading relationships with the rest of the world. While the report recommends widening CARICOM to include other nations in the Caribbean Basin and enhancing relations with Europe, Brazil, and Latin America in an almost laundry-list approach to international relations, it concludes by recommending "as a matter of high priority and with a sense of urgency, the possibility of negotiating as a group a common position for entry into NAFTA."[14]

The United States and its North American partners need to decide how NAFTA should be expanded.[15] Certainly, the small, vulnerable nations of the Caribbean Basin would prefer to join the club on more favorable terms than the three big North American countries. A more delayed and graduated transition should be considered. New security arrangements to defend democracies in the area should also be reviewed, either as part of an expanded NAFTA or in parallel arrangements.

The Ebbs and Flows of the Whirlpool

During the twentieth century, U.S. policies toward the Caribbean have been anchored to a set of interests that have changed much less than the strategies formulated to pursue them. The motive for U.S. engagement sometimes has been altruistic — to promote democracy or development — but more often it has been fear, a disproportionate fear for such a large power in such a small sea, but a fear nonetheless that events could turn hostile to U.S. interests. It follows that American foreign policy in the Caribbean always has seemed to err on the anxious side. In the nineteenth century, the United States was anxious to prevent "another Haiti," an independent black republic. In the early twentieth century, the United States was anxious to prevent governments in the region from defaulting to European creditors lest that be used as a pretext for European intervention. During World War II, the United States was anxious to keep out Nazi Germany and, after that, Soviet Russia. After the Soviets turned up ninety miles off-shore, the U.S. became anxious to avoid "another Cuba."

Beyond this elemental security interest, the United States has also tried, at different times, to promote human rights, democracy, social reforms, and economic development. U.S. national interests are not immutable; they have changed over time, although sometimes so slowly as not to be perceptible. For example, the Panama Canal is no longer a vital asset to the United States, although it remains vital for Panama. With the advent of aircraft carriers, which are too large to transit the Canal, U.S. interests in the Canal changed from being strategic to being primarily economic — from permitting the U.S. fleet to move rapidly between oceans to providing a marginal economic advantage in the shipment of supplies.

U.S. interests do not change radically from one administration to the next, but the value and priority that each administration attaches to these interests often changes quite markedly. Both Carter and Reagan, for example, promoted U.S. interests in human rights, but Carter gave them a much higher priority than did Reagan. Both wanted to prevent Communist inroads into the hemisphere, but Reagan saw the threat as so dire that he was willing to support armies that committed atrocities.

Franklin D. Roosevelt, Harry Truman, and Jimmy Carter pledged nonintervention and meant it. Dwight D. Eisenhower, John F. Kennedy, Lyndon Johnson, Richard Nixon, Ronald Reagan, and George Bush violated their pledges of nonintervention because they perceived serious threats to U.S. security. Kennedy, Carter, Reagan, and Bush all proposed development programs in the area, although none had enough of an impact to lift the region up to the level of sustainable development.

Presidents defined U.S. interests differently; they also chose different means to defend them. Carter and Bush were more willing to consider multilateral approaches than Reagan was, while Bush and Reagan gave more emphasis to military aid, invasions, and covert actions than Carter did.

With the end of the Cold War, the United States and the nations of the Caribbean have an opportunity to swim free of the whirlpool that has captured the entire region since the turn of the century. To succeed, however, it is necessary to understand that the whirlpool's force was not a function of the East-West conflict; more than anything, it was due to the chronic instability and vulnerability of the small nations of the region. If a group felt that its access to power was blocked, it would almost always seek support from outside. That meant either the United States or if it were already supporting the government, then its enemy. Thus internal strife was connected to international intervention.

Many condemned Washington, Moscow, or Havana for this predicament, but the real culprit was the absence of a framework for securing peaceful political change and the lack of resources to help nations improve the lives of their people. The way to untie the Gordian knot connecting internal conflict with international intervention is by forging a new collective defense of democracy within a broader arrangement that will assist the process of development and the pursuit of social justice. If governments in the region do not realize they are currently on the rim of the whirlpool, then they will find themselves recaptured someday. If they develop a strategy to preserve democracy and sustain development, then they can escape to a truly new world.

Notes

1. "The President's News Conference, January 29, 1981," in *Public Papers of the Presidents of the United States: Ronald Reagan, 1981,* (Washington, D.C.: Government Printing Office, 1982), 59.

2. These quotes come from Mahan's book, *Lessons of the War with Spain,* cited in Samuel Flagg Bemis, 1943, *Latin American Policy of the United States: An Historical Interpretation,* (New York: Harcourt, Brace), 408n.

3. Robert A. Pastor, 1993, *Whirlpool: U.S. Foreign Policy toward Latin America and the Caribbean* (Princeton, N.J.: Princeton University Press).

4. Theodore Roosevelt, "Annual Message from President Theodore Roosevelt to the United States Congress, December 6, 1904," reprinted in *The Evolution of Our Latin American Policy: A Documentary Record,* ed. James W. Gantenbein, (New York: Octagon, 1971), 361-62.

5. Letter from Robert Lansing, former Secretary of State, to Senator Medill McCormick, Chairman of the U.S. Senate Select Committee on Haiti and Santo Domingo, May 4, 1922, in *Evolution of Our Latin American Policy,* ed. James W. Gantenbein, 636.

6. Bemis, *Latin American Policy of the United States,* 185-89.

7. Franklin D. Roosevelt, 1928, "Our Foreign Policy: A Democratic View," *Foreign Affairs,* 6: 584-85 (July).

8. See Irwin F. Gellman, 1979, *Good Neighbor Diplomacy: United States Policies in Latin America, 1933-1945,* (Baltimore, Md.: Johns Hopkins University Press); Bryce Wood, 1961, *The Making of the Good Neighbor Policy* (New York: Colombia University Press).

9. For an excellent account of U.S. policy toward Cuba when Welles was ambassador, see Wood, *Making of the Good Neighbor Policy,* chaps. 2,3.

10. The literature on the Guatemalan revolution is diverse in interpretation. The best recent book that incorporates much of the evidence of the previous works is by Piero Gleijeses, 1991, *Shattered Hope: The Guatemalan Revolution and the United States, 1944-1954* (Princeton, N.J.: Princeton University Press).

11. See Abraham F. Lowenthal, 1972, *The Dominican Intervention* (Cambridge, Mass.: Harvard University Press).

12. For an analysis of the Carter, Reagan, and Bush administrations, see Pastor, *Whirlpool,* chaps. 3-5.

13. Quoted in Ronnie Dugger, 1983, *On Reagan: The Man and His Presidency* (New York: McGraw-Hill), 353.

14. *Time for Action: The Report of the West Indian Commission,* 1992, (Barbados: West Indian Commission), 457-58.

15. For a strategy for both the United States and the Caribbean, see Robert A. Pastor and Richard Fletcher, 1993, "Twenty-First Century Challenges for the Caribbean and the United States: Toward a New Horizon," in *Democracy in the Caribbean: Political, Economic, and Social Perspectives,* 1993, ed. Jorge I. Domínguez, Robert A. Pastor, and Delisle Worrell (Baltimore, Md.: Johns Hopkins University Press), 255-76.

The Evolving Japanese Perspective on the North American Free Trade Agreement

Kanako Yamaoka

The Japanese private sector regards the North American Free Trade Agreement (NAFTA) with both anticipation and anxiety. Japanese firms are concerned with the buildup of any economic bloc in North America, but many also believe that NAFTA may provide 1) opportunities for macro-level economic development of the region, which would also benefit the businesses of Japanese investors already established in Mexico, and 2) for Japanese investors and firms considering new investments, more opportunities and increased access in Mexico. At present, however, most of the Japanese private sector has not yet committed to further Mexican investment. They are carefully observing and evaluating the confirmation of NAFTA after completion of negotiations by the Salinas, Clinton, and Campbell administrations and their respective legislatures.

The Dramatic Increase of Japanese Foreign Investment in the 1980s

In the last half of the 1980s, Japanese worldwide foreign direct investment (FDI) increased dramatically. The reasons for this increase of Japanese FDI are 1) a sharp appreciation of the Japanese yen against the U.S. dollar, triggered by the September 1985 Plaza Agreement, 2) protectionism and regionalism in developed country markets, and 3) new investment opportunities arising from increased liberalization and economic development in developing countries.

Kanako Yamaoka is a research fellow at the Institute of Developing Economies in Tokyo, Japan, and a visiting scholar at the Centro de Estudios sobre Asia y Oceanía in Havana, Cuba. For this chapter, Ms. Yamaoka received many suggestions from colleagues at the Institute, especially Drs. Akira Hirata and Yumiko Okamoto.

The principal effect of the appreciation of the Japanese yen against the U.S. dollar was, logically, that it became much more difficult for a Japanese firm to export its manufactured goods at internationally competitive prices, while imports of course became even easier. Japan, unlike Latin America, had developed its economy through a strategy of imports of natural resources and exports of finished goods. This was an inevitable strategy for Japanese industrial development as Japan has few raw materials and needs to import them. However, this dramatic shift in foreign exchange rates made Japan reconsider its economic development strategy. In order to maintain foreign product markets, many Japanese firms increased FDI in both developed and developing countries.

The Plaza Agreement was the catalyst triggering Japan into this shift, but such indirect factors as those referred to above also played a very important role in this change. The Japanese FDI to developed countries came after the formation of the European Community's trade bloc, with the predictable escalation of trade conflicts with the United States and the European Community (EC) countries. Japanese FDI in developing countries was made because of their low production costs, new economic liberalization policies, and increased economic development. Japanese production in developing countries was mainly for re-export to Japan and to third countries, while production in developed countries was destined for the domestic market to avoid disadvantages from the established trade bloc.

Therefore, the Japanese FDI flow into both developed and developing countries increased tremendously. In 1989, annual flow of Japanese FDI exceeded the $50 billion level, five times that of 1985. As a result of the increase of FDI, the overseas production ratio (the share of overseas production in total production) of Japanese firms also increased, especially in the industrial machinery sector. In 1988, the overseas production ratio was especially high in the subsectors of precision instruments (13.9 percent), electrical machinery (10.6 percent), and transport machinery (9.4 percent). The reason for this high overseas production was that many of these products are under various import restrictions by developed countries, and it is relatively easy to separate machinery from its production process and to transfer some of the sub-processes to developing countries (Yamazawa and Hirata 1990-1991).

At the same time, the Japanese government encouraged domestic consumption in order to maintain the growth of the Japanese economy. This shift in Japan's economic policy is an historical change made after thirty-five years of "export-oriented" economic policy. As a consequence, Japan developed a system of importing goods produced by overseas subsidiaries. By 1988, Japan's importation of manufactured goods as a percentage of real GDP had doubled within a three-year period. Specifically, electric machinery and clothes showed a significant increase in imports. This increase is due both to that policy and to active private investment (Yamazawa and Hirata 1989-1990).

The Japanese Private Sector and NAFTA

In the expansion process of Japan's FDI, regions that received the lion's share of Japanese investment were North America and Asia (Japan External Trade Organization 1991; see Figure 1).

Figure 1
Japan's Foreign Direct Investment by Region

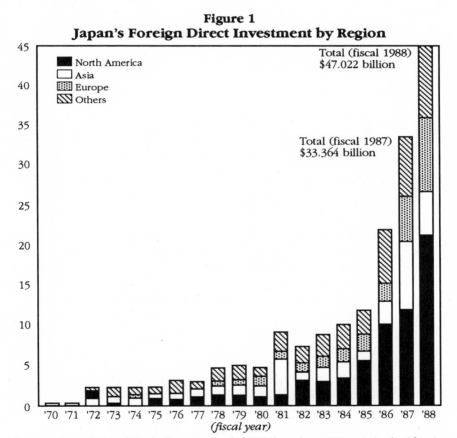

Source: Japan External Trade Organization (JETRO), based on MOF statistics (notification basis).

In these regions, the United States and Southeast Asia played the most important role. Mexico did not fare especially well in this expansion, although total Japanese FDI to Mexico has been increasing. As a consequence, the ratio of Japanese firms in Mexico has been decreasing and is relatively small (Banco de Mexico 1991; see Table 1).

Table 1
Cumulative Direct Foreign Investment
By Country of Origin
(Millions of dollars)

	1982	1983	1984	1985	1986	1987	1988	1989	1990p/
United States	7334.8	7601.4	8513.4	9840.2	11046.6	13716.2	14957.8	16771.7	19079.7
W. Germany	862.9	972.9	1125.4	1180.8	1399.4	1446.3	1583.0	1667.7	1955.9
Japan	776.6	780.4	816.0	895.3	1037.5	1170.3	1319.1	1334.8	1455.6
Switzerland	571.7	587.9	647.7	788.9	823.0	918.2	1004.5	1198.9	1346.9
Spain	345.2	357.9	369.6	383.6	477.3	603.1	637.2	681.2	692.0
U.K.	302.0	351.2	395.5	451.9	558.2	987.1	1754.7	1799.4	1913.8
France	118.6	228.5	237.3	248.0	564.9	596.1	748.5	765.0	946.0
Sweden	140.2	169.3	230.4	235.9	280.5	297.2	329.7	336.6	349.9
Canada	140.2	162.3	194.8	229.7	270.3	289.6	323.5	360.9	417.0
Italy	32.4	33.4	33.9	34.5	38.5	41.3	41.3	47.9	52.5
Others	161.8	224.8	335.9	340.1	578.9	864.9	1388.1	1623.0	2100.2
TOTAL	10786.4	11470.1	12899.9	14628.9	17053.1	20930.3	24087.4	26587.1	30309.5

Note: It should be noted that actual foreign investment as shown by the balance of payment figures is lower than new foreign investment registered due to lags between authorization and actual investments and because some authorized investments are not made.

Source: Dirección General de Inversión Extranjera. SECOFI.

Research data show that most of the increase of Japanese FDI in Mexico derives from electric and automotive companies, particularly through *maquiladoras* along the Mexican-U.S. border.

Since the U.S. and Mexican governments launched negotiations for NAFTA, little new investment from Japanese firms has been made in Mexico, as compared to that from other countries, particularly the United States and Germany. One reason is that the Japanese market demands excessively high quality overall, so much so that in many cases the priority of quality exceeds even that of price. So far, Japanese private investors are not convinced that their subsidiaries could reach such high quality levels in their finished production. Another reason is that Japanese firms are concerned with conditions which could be added in the NAFTA negotiations by the United States and Canada, such as requirements for local contents.

Thus, under NAFTA, Japanese FDI could be most effectively made when a Japanese subsidiary established in Mexico becomes a production base for the U.S. and Canadian markets, as the Japanese Mission for Promotion of Economic Exchange with Mexico stated recently. Under this marketing strategy, subsidiaries of some Japanese firms already established in the United States may well be poised to move into Mexico for two reasons: 1) their geographical proximity will give them an advantage to produce "low value-added and high transportation cost" goods, and 2) the higher price elasticity in the U.S. market can be expected to absorb relatively low-quality goods. This type of investment may be statistically invisible, since the actions of Japanese subsidiaries in the United States cannot be seen in most data which show the total increase of U.S. investment in Mexico.

It is difficult to predict whether Japanese firms will see more opportunities or more obstacles with NAFTA. A recent survey made by the Japanese-Mexican Chamber of Commerce of sixty-six Japanese subsidiaries in Mexico is interesting in this regard. Unless economic performance in Mexico is drastically changed, this research data will be useful to foresee possible problems which future Japanese subsidiaries could have. While over 90 percent of these sixty-six Japanese companies consider NAFTA a policy action aimed at the eventual formation of an economic bloc, over 70 percent of them also consider NAFTA to be necessary for the revitalization of the Mexican economy. Some 30.6 percent believe that NAFTA could be beneficial to their businesses, while only 14.5 percent consider that it would be negative. The logic of the pro-NAFTA plurality is that they expect indirect effects to come from the increase of total investment in Mexico, contributing to the subsequent increase in domestic demand.

As for the local contents issue, Japanese private investors see that 1) it would be difficult to reach a higher percentage of local parts in their products, and, therefore, 2) it is urgent to develop a Mexican parts industry accompanied by technological transfer.

Furthermore, as many as 80 percent of these Japanese firms consider that even under NAFTA, local producers in the Mexican economy will still need a considerable period of time before they can realize or fully use any expected benefits from any such new agreement.

The Japanese Government Perspective: Interest and Suspicion

The Japanese government has not issued any official statement on NAFTA. They are closely observing all developments with interest and, frankly, with some suspicion. Certainly, they do not welcome the creation of any new trade bloc. Yet they have kept themselves from commenting on NAFTA where Japan has no direct participation.

In private conversations with Japanese colleagues, the staff of the Ministry of International Trade and Industry (MITI) implied that they are not yet ready to form an economic bloc among Asian countries as a counter balance to two possible foreign blocs, one in the European Community and the other in the Western Hemisphere. The Japanese government's official position continues to be that it commits itself to maintaining a free trade system among nations in the context of the rules, norms, and treaties of the present global framework, which they have come to know well.

Conclusion

As overall Japanese FDI increases, the possibility of Japanese investment into new locations also increases. Some firms, particularly those in the automotive and electrical industries, are the most likely to invest in Mexico under NAFTA, as some of the same sectors have already done in the *maquiladoras*. Japanese subsidiaries located in the United States and Canada would also be likely to consider moving to Mexico, in order to produce their products destined for the U.S. and Canadian markets more economically.

However, it is unlikely that those Japanese firms with investments already in Asia would move their operations to Mexico because of NAFTA. Their reluctance comes from uncertainty about the development of the Mexican economy, not only from the point of view of Mexico's balance of payments problems, but also from the perspective of comprehensive economic structures such as infrastructure and basic industries. It is vital that the Mexican economy first become more stabilized and more diversified.

Eventual effects of NAFTA on Japan's private sector will not appear as significant in the immediate or short terms. However, be sure that Japan is very interested in NAFTA and is observing with great interest the negotiations among the Canadian, Mexican, and U.S. administrations, as well as the respective congressional debates.

Appendices

Expanding Trade and Creating American Jobs

Governor Bill Clinton
North Carolina State University
Raleigh, North Carolina

October 4, 1992

Ladies and gentlemen, I came to North Carolina today to talk about a difficult and important issue for our country. I wanted to come here because I think of North Carolina as a mixture of the best in America's economy, its traditional industries, and farms, and its modern, hi-tech future. I came here today to tell you why I support the North American Free Trade Agreement.

If it is done right, it will create jobs in the United States and in Mexico, and if it is done right and is part of a larger economic strategy, we can raise our incomes and reverse the awful trend of now more than a decade in which most Americans are working harder for less money.

If it is not done right, however, the blessings of the agreement are far less clear, and the burdens can be significant. I'm convinced that I will do it right. I am equally convinced that Mr. [former President George] Bush won't.

We live in a world that has been revolutionized almost beyond comprehension. We have seen in the last few years the Soviet Union disintegrate, the Berlin Wall, freedom fighters released from their prisons in Eastern Europe and South Africa, the Cold War end. That was the era in which I was born and in which Mr. Bush came of age, and over the last generation, less obviously but no less dramatically, we have seen unbelievable changes transforming the global economy, which have had their impact here at home.

A little more than a generation ago, international trade and investment were a seemingly insignificant portion of our nation's income, but today our exports and imports of goods and services amount to about a quarter of our entire economy.

A little more than a generation ago, American workers, consumers, and companies lived almost entirely within the American economy. Today, we live within the world economy, and foreign trade accounts for almost as high a proportion of our economic activity as it does in Japan and Western Europe.

A little more than a generation ago, we were virtually unchallenged in the world marketplace, but today we are challenged as never before, not only by Japan and Western Europe, but by other countries as well.

A little more than a generation ago, the world was a far simpler place. We could support free trade and open markets and still maintain a high-wage economy because we were the only economic superpower, and our capacity to control our destiny was largely totally within our own hands.

Now, because money and management and production are mobile and can cross national borders quickly, we face unprecedented competition from developing countries, as well as wealthy ones.

You know that in North Carolina, and so do I. A textile worker in Carolina has to compete against a textile worker in Singapore, perhaps, to sell sweaters in Germany.

It's also hard to tell who the players are. An American car may have more foreign parts in it than a foreign car that happens to be made in an American assembly plant.

This, in other words, is not a simple debate. The world is changing in complex ways. The choices before us are difficult, and it is imperative that at least we understand what is going on and that we have an honest and forthright discussion of all the forces at play.

For a high-wage country like ours, the blessings of more trade can be offset, at least in part, by the loss of income and jobs as more and more multinational corporations take advantage of their ability to move money, management, and production away from a high-wage country to a low-wage country.

We can also lose incomes because those companies that stay at home can use the threat of moving to depress wages, as many do today. Other countries like Germany and Japan have, quite frankly, managed this problem much better than we have. How have they done it? First of all, by maintaining a more highly skilled work force not just among their university graduates, but up and down the line among all their workers. Second, by investing more in modern plant and equipment and in research and development and developing better systems of moving ideas from the laboratory to the marketplace, so that if they lose one kind of manufacturing job, there are always other kinds opening up — in contrast to what you often have here, where when people lose their manufacturing jobs, they look around until their unemployment runs out and then eventually take a job making half what they used to make.

Third, these countries do a better job of controlling their external costs like health care and energy. The average German factory produces the same amount of output as the average American one for one-half the energy input. And our country spends 30 percent more of our income on health care than any other nation with which we compete.

Next, other countries do a better job of exporting more and of continuously increasing productivity by working together more closely — business and labor, government and education. But also, let's be frank, Germany and Japan have policies that are tougher in keeping high-wage jobs at home, at least for the home market. The Europeans have an absolute ban on foreign car sales that exceed 16 percent of the market now in Western Europe. The Japanese distribution system means that only 3 percent of the cars sold in Japan are not Japanese. We have an auto parts export surplus of $4 billion with every country in the world, but when you add Japan in, we have a $9 billion deficit.

For some time now — as you see, this is a very complicated thing — for some time, I have felt that one of the most difficult problems in modern politics, and therefore in this presidential election, is the simplistic and superficial labeling of complex issues.

As network news sound bites have shrunk — by one study they're down to less than nine seconds now — public discussions of important issues have gotten the short shrift. On perhaps no other issue has the decline of discourse been more pronounced than on the issue of trade, an issue of great impact to you here in North Carolina in positive and negative ways, on farmers and textile workers, furniture makers, engineers, and scientists in the research triangle. Too much is at stake here to avoid the real issues, and, yet, time and again, that is what we do.

The issue here is not whether we should support free trade or open markets. Of course, we should. The real issue is whether or not we will have a national economic strategy to make sure we reap the benefits, and the answer today is, we don't.

Too many Republicans would say that it's a simple issue: free trade always equals economic growth. Well, it can, but only if we have a comprehensive national strategy to promote that kind of growth. Some Democrats would say that free trade today always equals exporting jobs and lowering wages. Well, it sure can if you don't have a comprehensive economic strategy to maintain a high-wage, high-growth economy.

It is in that context that we have to look at this North American Free Trade Agreement. Is it good for Americans? Will it help us to develop a high-wage, high-growth economy here at home? Or, by opening Mexico to more U.S. and foreign investment, will it simply encourage more United States companies to abandon their workers and communities here and move to Mexico? Will it depress wages of those who are left here, and will they even have, ironically, less money to buy the products that Mexico will send back to this country?

If you look at the experience of the *maquiladora* plants, those that have moved to Mexico right across the border, there is certainly cause for concern. We can see clearly there that labor standards have been regularly violated, that environmental standards are often ignored, and that many people who have those jobs live in conditions which are still pretty dismal, not just by our standards, but theirs.

So there is some reason to fear that there are people in this world and in our country who would take advantage of any provisions insuring more investment opportunities simply to look for lower wages without regard to the human impact of their decisions.

Still, you must look at the other side of the coin. Changes in Mexico under President Salinas have ballooned our two-way trade with them and have eliminated the trade deficit we once had with Mexico thus creating jobs here in America even as our investment policies have cost them.

I can also say, based on my own experience, that a good economic policy can grow manufacturing jobs even in tough global competition. In our state, thanks to highly productive workers and creative business leaders, good cooperation between the government and private sector, good incentives and aggressive support for educating workers, promoting quality management, and marketing more products, we have grown manufacturing jobs at ten times the national average for several years now. You heard Governor Hunt say that we now rank first in the country in private sector job growth. There are many and complex reasons for this, but we did have a definite strategy that involved partnerships with a deliberate decision not to give up our manufacturing base. That is very important.

In the United States of America today, only about 16.5 percent of the work force is in manufacturing. In my state, it's 22 percent. In this state, I think it's still about 28 percent, the largest in the United States. I want to make it very clear I am committed to maintaining a strong manufacturing base in this country.

My granddaddy used to say that in the Depression, people were so poor, they took in one another's washing for a living. That would be the equivalent of an economy that was only a service economy, where nobody in America ever made anything. The great economic powers in this world are the people who make things. We have 16.5 percent of our work force in manufacturing, Japan has 28 percent, and Germany has 32 percent. We must do better, and we can.

I believe NAFTA can contribute to this effort, not undermine it, as long as we move aggressively to address the serious omissions from the agreement. I believe we have to do more for our own workers. And we have to protect the environment on both sides of the border, both because it's good for the environment and because if they don't do it, it will further lower their cost of production, to promote prosperity on both sides of the border.

If we do these things and, again, if we develop a serious economic policy at home, then NAFTA can be a very good thing for the United States.

We simply cannot go backwards when the rest of the world is going forward into a more integrated economy. We cannot go inward when our opportunities are so often outward. For all our history, America has moved ahead and reached out, colonizing a wilderness, exploring a continent, always seeking what President Kennedy called the New Frontier.

And today we must forge ahead again. As president, I will seek to address the deficiencies of the North American Free Trade Agreement through supplemental agreements with the Canadian and the Mexican governments and by taking several key steps here at home. I will not sign legislation implementing the North American Free Trade Agreement until we have reached additional agreements to protect America's vital interests. But I believe we can address these issues without renegotiating the basic agreement.

This agreement, however, is only one piece of a larger puzzle. Even the present negotiations recognize that, as there are other issues being discussed all along. We need not only to reduce trade barriers, but to prepare our entire work force not only to compete in the global economy, but to live with the changes in it and to make sure nobody gets left behind.

I remain convinced that the North American Free Trade Agreement will generate jobs and growth on both sides of the border if and only if it's part of a broad-based strategy, and if and only if we address the issues still to be addressed. If we don't do these things, we can kill NAFTA, but we'll still lose jobs. And that's the important point I want to make. I have been governor of a state that has seen jobs go on a fast track to Mexico and to other countries. If we do nothing on this agreement and we don't address the serious worker retraining and economic investment issues in this country and we don't change our economic policy, we will still lose jobs because money, production, and management are mobile, and there are people, unfortunately, in this world who would rather move for cheap wages than stay and work for productivity.

We have got to face the bigger issue. We cannot overload NAFTA and make it the symbol of either all our hopes, as Mr. Bush has done, or all our fears, as some of the opponents have done. We have got to see this as a part of a real big effort to rebuild the American economy from the ground up. This is not an abstract question. It has real consequences for real people.

For more than a decade, our country has been led by yesterday's men, who were out of touch, out of ideas, and out of step with the developments in the global economy, who refused to recognize not only new opportunities, but new challenges and new responsibilities.

Americans have paid a terrible price for their policies. Trickle-down economics have given us a weakened economy, declining wages for more than two-thirds of our workers, longer work weeks, lost jobs, greater inequality, greater poverty, one in ten Americans on food stamps today, a hundred thousand Americans a month losing their health insurance, and the real sense that we may be raising the first generation of Americans to do worse than their parents.

Without a national economic strategy, this country has been allowed to drift. Meanwhile, our competitors have organized themselves around clear national goals to save, promote, and enhance high-wage, high-growth jobs.

In a Clinton administration, we will approach trade and every other issue with single-minded focus, to do what is best for ordinary Americans who are willing to work hard to get ahead. But that focus must also recognize the new rules of the global economy. When Japan discovers a way just to make cars a little better, or when the European Community closes its markets to American pork, or when our president refuses to issue export credits and European farmers take away a Russian market that was meant to be for us, or when a country in South Asia or South America violates copyright standards for software, the impact is felt in factories and farms and families all across America.

But when people line up in Paris to watch an American movie, when families around the world eat American food, when a jet made in Seattle lands or takes off from an airport in Seoul, American jobs and paychecks are more secure. Our prospects and our prosperity depend upon our ability to win in this kind of environment, an environment in which what we earn depends on what we can learn, in which Americans who only finish high school and have no further education and training face far grimmer futures than their parents, an America in which, if we do not equal our competitors in research and development and our skill in bringing ideas into manufacturing jobs here at home, unless we have a conversion plan to take all the money by which we reduce defense and invest it in an American economy for the twenty-first century — in transportation, communication, and environmental cleanup technologies, in biotechnology, in the new frontiers that will provide tens of thousands, indeed, hundreds of thousands of high-wage jobs if we seize the opportunities, unless we do that, whatever we do on this trade agreement will not guarantee or undermine the future we are otherwise going to have.

We've got to understand what the big rules are and start following them. Our competitors know it. The Germans and the Japanese do more with education, from public school to apprenticeships to training in the work force, than we do. The average German factory spends five times as much money retraining its workers as the average American employer on an annual basis. They do more on research and development than we do. They spend a higher percentage of their income.

But when our companies do have well-trained workers and competitive products and services and high levels of cooperation and productivity, they do very well indeed. We still have some of the finest companies in the world that dominate their marketplaces in spite of the fact that they live in a country that doesn't encourage investment in new plants over investment in new Maseratis or third or fourth homes. They do well in spite of the fact that they live in a country which won't control health care costs and in spite of the fact that they live in a country which doesn't guarantee that workers will always have the opportunity to have high, high, high levels of education and training.

But no matter what we do in preparing our workers and investing money, we've still got to have markets for our products. As much as we export, the Germans export a far higher percentage per capita than we do. We need more markets. And today, regional economic blocs are emerging, very formally in Western Europe and less formally, but still surely, in Asia, organized by Japan and Japanese investment.

It is too early to say whether the integration of Western Europe will be a plus or minus for America. If they keep opening trade, well, that's good.

We now have a $17 billion surplus with Europe. But they also limit car imports to 16 percent, and they recently restricted imports of American agricultural products on the flimsiest of excuses.

So while we don't know what will happen with these other regional trading blocs, we know enough to know that we need stronger ties to our neighbors both for positive opportunities and to protect us in the event that other countries become more protectionist.

We can only do that with Canada, which is already at roughly our standard of living, and with Mexico, which is way below our standard of living, if we find a way to grow our economies together in ways that are good for all of us.

So I advocate this treaty as a beginning of that process. I hope that one day we'll have a global agreement for the General Agreement on Tariffs and Trade which will be fairer to our country and which will open markets around the world. But in the meantime, we need to do more in our own region.

If we can make this agreement work with Canada and Mexico, then we can reach down into the other market-oriented economies of Central and South America to expand even further. But these three economies together will give us, in terms of population, the largest trading market in the world today.

It will provide more jobs through exports. It will challenge us to become more competitive. It will certainly help Mexico to develop, but still, that is also in our interest: A wealthier Mexico will buy more American products; as incomes rise there, that will reduce pressure for immigration across the border into the United States, which depresses wages here.

President Salinas has taken some important steps. He's privatized corporations, he's reduced his debt, he's tamed inflation, and he's brought down trade barriers. As I said, the unilateral initiative of the Mexicans has led to a huge increase in the products we sell there and the evaporation of the trade deficit. They also encouraged us to enter these negotiations.

Now, what we have to do, I will say again, is to have a new kind of leadership to make this work. We have to have an overall trade policy that says to our trading partners, particularly our wealthy ones, if you want access to our market, you've got to give us access to yours.

When the president [Bush] went to Japan, it was sort of sad. He took the auto company executives and pleaded with the Japanese to buy cars. But his United States trade representative had given him a report that said that if Japanese markets were as open as American markets, they would buy $10 billion more products from us every year, everything from agriculture to auto parts to electronics, in ways that would create three hundred thousand high-wage jobs in America.

So we had to say trading blocs are not enough. We need fair treatment in other countries if we are giving them fair treatment in ours.

But let me get back to this agreement. Although it is unpopular with some people and organizations I admire and who represent the very Americans I am fighting so hard for in this election, I think we should go forward with it because it advances our interests, the interests of ordinary Americans, more than it undermines them if we also do the other things needed to deal with the deficiencies in this agreement and if we have a good new economic policy.

The agreement reduces and eventually eliminates trade barriers in place, especially in Mexico, against a number of major American exports. It opens up larger markets for our goods and services. It will phase out virtually all tariffs between the United States and Mexico over the next fifteen years, with some of the most sensitive products being given the longest transitions.

Yet, as I said, there are critical issues which remain unaddressed, from workers' rights to farmers' needs to environmental protection. Despite the promises he made to really address these in a forthright way, Mr. Bush has failed, most important, to provide adequate assistance to our workers, those most likely to be hurt by economic integration with Mexico.

American farmers could also suffer without stronger safeguards for their interests. And the environmental provisions are still too weak. This agreement does nothing to reaffirm our right to insist that the Mexicans follow their own labor standard, now frequently violated — this is a very important issue — and not aggravate the wage differentials which already exist.

As we move toward free trade, we must always remember why we're doing it to help the working men and women of America. We should not do things that are not in the interest of our people over the long run.

There are apparel workers, fruit and vegetable farmers, electronic workers, and auto workers who are at risk not only of short-term dislocation, but of permanent damage if this agreement is not strengthened and improved. Industries that have already been hard hit by the flow of jobs to Mexico will continue to be hurt unless we negotiate tougher measures to protect them and to make ourselves more competitive.

The shortcomings in the agreement are really a reflection, however, of the shortcomings in the Bush economic policy as a whole, not just in his approach to trade with Mexico or to world trade, but in the whole approach to the economy and the environment.

This agreement underscores the core of the differences between me and Mr. Bush. From the national economic recession to the dislocations caused by defense cutbacks, his attitude has been that we should have trickle-down economics and let the market have its way, keep taxes lowest on the wealthiest Americans, then get out of the way. He seems to be saying, "So what if some workers get hurt or some farmers get hurt or some environmental damage is done? So what? Sooner or later, it'll all come out in the wash." Well, a lot of Americans are being washed away by that economic philosophy.

I want America to go forward with expanded trade with our neighbors. I also want an America that has a national economic strategy that makes sense. And I believe there are some things we need to do to make this agreement stronger, but I think they can be addressed [apart from] the basic free trade agreement.

As president, I will ensure adequate measures are taken, however, before Congress acts to implement the free trade agreement. I don't want to give up all our leverage to help our workers and to make sure our environment is protected by basically ratifying the agreement through legislation. I think that we don't have to reopen the agreement, but we do have to insist that protection for our workers and for the environment proceed on parallel tracks. We should do it all at once.

President Bush has many tools at his disposal to protect our interests, in addition to the things that ought to be done to the agreement. But he has failed to use them. As president, I will aggressively pursue the remedies available in our current trade laws and in the proposed agreement to protect our jobs, our businesses, our farmers, and our environment from unfair practices. In addition, I think there are five unilateral steps we should take, and there are three supplemental agreements we should negotiate with Canada and Mexico to achieve an acceptable package. Here they are. First, what we have to do: We've got to address the long-neglected needs of our working people, both skilled and unskilled, who are on the front lines of new economic conditions and who may be displaced. The most glaring omission in the president's package is its lack of meaningful assistance to vulnerable workers and communities.

For those who need training, we must provide it. Mr. Bush's record on these issues is not a good one. In the last three budgets, he has proposed totally eliminating the training assistance that goes to people whose jobs are displaced by foreign competition.

In his 1993 budget, he cut employment and training programs by $40 million. In a cynical election-year ploy, his Labor Department proposed some more money for job training and other trade assistance to Michigan workers who have lost their jobs. It amounted to about $4.60 a worker.

In our administration, the Clinton/Gore administration, we won't play politics with the lives of working men and women.

We will give you real programs to deal with real problems: trade adjustment assistance that includes training, health care benefits, income supports, and assistance to communities to create jobs. You can train people all you want, but if they don't have anything to do, it will be like being all dressed up with no place to go.

While Mr. Bush has, in the eleventh hour, made a proposal more generous than anything he has said before, it is still way too little too late. I will do more; it will be better. The American working people will be proud of it. It will ensure dignity and the opportunity to continue to be a productive member of the American work force.

The second thing we have to do is move to protect our environment. The Bush administration on this score is so bad that Mr. Bush's own cabinet secretary sent a memo to all of his employees saying what a bad job the president had done at the Earth Summit. And he's even stopped calling himself the environmental president. It's not surprising that they did little to deal with this issue in the [NAFTA] negotiations. Before we implement this, we have to be sure first that there will be environmental cleanup and infrastructure investments in our country sufficient to do what we have to do.

The third thing we have to do is to make sure we do something for the farmers who are at risk here. I am convinced, having read this agreement with some care, that some of the farmers will do better under it than they fear that they will and that the losses in some sectors have been somewhat exaggerated. However, there will certainly be some dislocation. Assistance should be provided to farmers who are threatened. We can assist them first by strict application of American pesticide requirements to imported food. We should help some growers shift to alternative crops, and those who may lose out to competition should be just as eligible for transition assistance as workers in businesses and communities are.

Fourth, we ought to make sure that NAFTA, the trade agreement, doesn't override the democratic process. For example, in the provisions on the environment, the current agreement contains no mechanism for public participation in defending challenges to American laws if we apply our environmental laws against Mexican products or in bringing challenges to the practices of other parties. I think the new Congress should pass legislation to provide for public participation in crafting our position in ongoing disputes and to give citizens the right to challenge objectionable environmental practices by the Mexicans or the Canadians.

Fifth, I think we have to make sure this agreement's provisions allowing foreign workers to cross our borders are properly implemented. We have to assure that certain professional workers aren't brought in here as strikebreakers. The recent experience where Canadian workers were brought into the country to break our nurses' strike by American nurses is an example of this. That should never be repeated. As president, I have said repeatedly, I would support a law to outlaw the use of permanent replacement workers, and I certainly will negotiate to stop the use of replacement workers from Canada and Mexico.

I want to note this agreement allows Mexican truckers to drive in the United States without having to satisfy all the U.S. safety and training standards. That troubles me, and I think that you have to say that we must do everything we can under the agreement, and there are some things we can do, to assure there is adherence to U.S. standards through tough inspections.

There are several areas now where we have to negotiate supplemental agreements which I would want to present together with the agreement that's already been negotiated. Before implementing the agreement, we must establish an environmental protection commission with substantial powers and resources to prevent and clean up water pollution. The commission should also encourage the enforcement of the country's own environmental laws through education, training, and commitment of resources and provide a forum to hear complaints. Such a commission would have the power to provide remedies, including money damages and the legal power to stop pollution. As a last resort, a country could even be allowed to withdraw.

If we don't have the power to enforce the laws that are on the books, what good is the agreement? We must have some assurances on this. This is a major economic as well as environmental issue. Best of all, I'm going to ask Senator Gore to take charge of ensuring that an effective commission is established and that it does work to protect the environment.

The Bush administration has talked about setting up a commission, but it's too little, too late. It won't even be up for final discussion until next year. By then, the incentives the other countries have to do anything meaningful will have evaporated if the agreement is already adopted. This is unacceptable. Al Gore and I will ensure that the environmental protection commission is up and running when the free trade agreement is up and running.

A second commission with similar powers should be established for worker standards and safety. It, too, should have extensive powers to educate, train, develop minimum standards, and have similar dispute resolution powers and remedies. We have got to do this. This is a big deal.

Perhaps the toughest issue of all is how to obtain better enforcement of laws already on the books on the environment and worker standards. It's interesting that the agreement negotiated by the Bush team goes a long way to do this in protecting intellectual property rights and the right to invest in Mexico but is silent with respect to labor laws and the environment.

I want to remedy that. I'm interested in the impact of this agreement on the rest of the people, not just those investing in Mexico, but the rest of the people in this country and the rest of the people in their country.

So we need a supplemental agreement which would require each country to enforce its own environmental and worker standards. Each agreement should contain a wide variety of procedural safeguards and remedies that we take for granted here in our country, such as easy access to the courts, public hearings, the right to present evidence, streamlined procedures, and effective remedies. I will negotiate an agreement among the three parties that permits citizens of each country to bring suit in their own courts when they believe their domestic environmental protections and worker standards aren't being enforced.

Finally, I want to ask Congress to grant the authority to the president to continue negotiations on the impact of this treaty. What if we have a global agreement? How will that impact this? And most important, what happens if there is an unexpected surge in imports in one sector or another that displaces huge numbers of people in this economy?

We have in our present trade law, believe it or not — a lot of people don't know this — we have in our present trade law the capacity to protect our own workers if there is, quote, "an unexpected surge in exports" — or imports into our country in some sectors of the economy where the displacement is too great for us to manage, too great for us to retrain, too great for us to put people to work in other sectors. That provision is contained for automobiles only in the North American Free Trade Agreement, and the remedy is weakened substantially.

I believe we should negotiate a parallel agreement that deals with the fact that neither the Mexicans nor the Americans know what the full consequences of this agreement are going to be. You can't get anybody to agree on how many jobs we're going to lose or how many jobs we're going to gain out of this. And I think it's fair to say that we don't want to do anything that's unnecessarily crippling to them, and they shouldn't want to do anything that's unnecessarily crippling to us. So I will ask the Congress to give me extended authority to negotiate another agreement to deal with the ability of both countries to move in the event there is an unexpected and overwhelming surge in imports into either country which would dislocate a whole sector of the economy so quickly that there's nothing we could do about it to overcome the economic impact.

Now, I want to say one more time, none of this will make a difference unless we have a new economic policy. This administration has no strategy to create and preserve jobs in middle America, but they offer job training, low cost loans, and technical assistance to companies that'll move to Central America. I know that most of you saw or now have heard the television show which documented the fact that the United States Agency for International Development has spent at least $298 million for programs to encourage American businesses to shut down here and move to Central America and the Caribbean. In fact, your tax dollars paid for this advertisement. And I quote — you paid for this: "Rosa Martinez produced apparel for the U.S. markets on her sewing machine in El Salvador. You can hire her for fifty-seven cents an hour."

How do you feel about paying for that? You paid for low-interest loans to a plant in Tennessee to shut down in Tennessee, put 304 people on the street, and move to Central America. But that fellow running that plant couldn't get the same low-interest loan to modernize plant and equipment in Tennessee to keep those people working.

You paid for an employee of the United States government who was photographed in an interview saying that the workers in the country he was working in were more reliable than the workers in Miami, Florida. You paid for that. It is no wonder that the American working people are so frightened of having this [Bush] administration implement this trade agreement.

We've got to stop using our own taxpayers' money to export their own jobs. And it's unbelievable to me that we have actually spent more money under the Bush administration last year to train workers in Central America than we spent to train people in middle America who had lost their jobs because of foreign competition.

Now, those are their priorities. But let me say again, it's not enough just to stop what they are doing wrong. We have to do some new things right. And let me reel them off quickly:

We've got to change the tax system in this country. We should give people more incentives if they invest in new plants, new equipment, new small businesses, research and development, housing, the kinds of things that put the American people to work and we should remove from the tax code the incentives to shut plants down here and move them overseas. That's what we should do.

This is entirely consistent with what the other wealthy countries do. This is the only country — you look at Germany and Japan, look at their tax code — that would say we're not going to give you an investment tax credit to modernize your equipment and your plant, but shut your plant down, move it overseas, we'll give you a tax deduction for shutting the plant down, we'll give you loss carried forward for the losses in the earlier years. Keep your money down there, and you'll never have to pay income tax on it in America.

It's all backward. We need a tax system that's an investment, job-oriented tax system that says, we want people to make money in America, but we want them to make it the old-fashioned way — make millionaires by putting other Americans to work. That's very, very important.

I mentioned this once before, and you clapped so I know you got it, but we've got to have a conversion strategy to do something with the defense money. The defense budget is going to be cut no matter who wins this election. But look what has happened. What has happened under the present administration is all that money is going to the S&L [savings and loan] bailout and higher health care costs. I want to put it into jobs for Americans. It's important.

We have got to finally join the other advanced nations and have a national system to bring health costs in line with inflation and provide basic health care to all Americans, one that preserves the strengths of our system but deals with the problems.

We've got to bring energy usage into competitive lines with more efficiency and alternative uses of energy, more use of cheap American natural gas, renewable energy sources, and efficiency. If we could be as efficient in every factory and office building as our foreign competitors, it would free up billions of dollars to reinvest in this economy.

If we could bring health care costs in line with inflation, it would save the average American family $1,200 a year and hundreds of billions of dollars for this economy, which could be reinvested for new jobs by the end of this decade, hundreds of billions of dollars. And let me point out, that is why our campaign has been getting such broad-based support. The Teamsters endorsed the Clinton-Gore ticket, the first Democratic ticket they had endorsed in two decades. In the hi-tech center of America, Silicon Valley, twenty-one computer and electronic executives endorsed our ticket; two-thirds of them were Republicans. In Chicago the other day, four hundred business executives endorsed our campaign; a third of them were Republicans because they know that what's going on now is not working.

On the health care issue, Mr. Bush keeps dumping on me, but the Nurses' Association endorsed our campaign, the first time they ever had. The American College of Physicians, seventy-seven thousand doctors, issued a health care plan very similar to mine, and last week people who had been executives in both the Republican and Democratic administrations said that Bush's health care plan would not control costs that mine would save the average family nearly $1,200 a year by the year 2000 — and that we would cover everybody, and his plan would still leave 27 million people uncovered. There is a reason why this kind of support is being generated for this ticket.

For all of its complexities, the debate over this treaty [NAFTA] comes down to this: It's clear what the benefits of trade are. It's clear what the hazards of investment across national lines are, and the issue you have to face is: Who do you trust to protect our workers, our communities, and our environment? George Bush, whose administration encourages American corporations to move to other countries with low wages and lax environmental laws, and even spends your tax money to finance it, or Bill Clinton and Al Gore who have a long record of fighting for good jobs and a healthy environment?

Do you trust George Bush, who has amassed the worst economic record in fifty years, the first decline in manufacturing, two-thirds of the working people with their wages going down, one in ten Americans on food stamps, quadrupled the debt in the last twelve years with our investment in the future going down and no strategy for the future? Or a different kind of Democrat who believes we can have both open markets and a strong domestic economy?

In the end, whether the North America Free Trade Agreement is a good thing for America is not a question of foreign policy. It is a question of domestic policy. If we are not strong at home, we will inevitably be weaker abroad. We have to build a new economy in which incomes and employment are rising and companies are growing, a society in which opportunity is expanding and hope comes alive again.

And so I say to you, my fellow Americans, we have to have the courage to change, and a part of that change should involve a closer relationship with Mexico, now under better leadership than ever in my lifetime. If we have the determination to reject failed policies and the old labels of the past, if we have the vision to see and work toward a better tomorrow, then we need not fear the future. If we seize this day and shape this change, we can make our great country what it was meant to be. Thank you very much.

Statement by
President-elect Clinton

On the Signing of the
North American Free Trade Agreement

December 17, 1992

Today, the leaders of the United States, Canada, and Mexico take an important step toward the economic integration of North America. In signing the North America Free Trade Agreement (NAFTA), President Bush, President Salinas and Prime Minister Mulroney bring our nations closer to the goal of free trade and economic prosperity.

I want to reaffirm my support for this agreement and underscore my commitment to work with the American people and our neighbors to the north and south to ensure NAFTA is properly implemented. The goal of free trade is one I support, but NAFTA is only one piece of the strategy necessary to ensure that we move wisely toward an integrated region.

If implemented as part of a comprehensive economic growth strategy, NAFTA will create the largest market in the world, spur more American jobs, and promote growth in Mexico and Canada. Our economy will benefit from eliminating Mexico's higher tariffs, from reducing barriers to trade in services, and by better protecting intellectual property rights.

A successful NAFTA, however, must be coupled with a plan to protect our environment and to prepare our entire work force to compete in the global economy. During the campaign, I laid out in detail the three supplemental agreements we must have before proceeding with the implementing legislation, involving the environment, workers, and special safeguards for unexpected surges in imports. I also indicated five areas the United States can address unilaterally as we move to implement NAFTA. These areas include worker assistance, the environment, farmers, greater public participation, and closing loopholes for foreign workers. I believe these steps do not require renegotiation of NAFTA.

I intend to work closely with the governments of Mexico and Canada as well as with the leadership in Congress to ensure these important goals are met. I believe they are achievable and essential to advancing our common goal of prosperity for all the people of our nations. I look forward to early meetings with President Salinas and with Prime Minister Mulroney to move this process forward.

Statement of Principles on Participatory Development

J. Brian Atwood

There is nothing more basic to the development process than participation. That is a lesson we have learned over the years, but it is one that we have not fully appreciated in all of its implications.

First, broad access by people to their country's economy and participation in their society's decision-making processes are results we seek to support; they are fundamental to sustained development; and

Second, our support is more likely to lead to these results if the development programs are relevant to people's needs, and for this there needs to be broad participation by people in defining development priorities and approaches.

Participation, therefore, describes both the end and the means: both the kind of results we seek and the way that we, as providers of development and humanitarian assistance, must nurture those results.

The ends and the means are closely related. For our scarce funds to contribute meaningfully to the goal of sustainable development — to development that broadens economic, social, and political access and enables a society to keep improving the quality of life for its people — the development approaches themselves must be sustainable. They must be consistent with the priorities and values of those who will have to sustain the effort after the donor has left. This is true for a village-level project, and it is true for a national-level program. It applies to policy reforms as well. The policy changes that may be needed to open up economies to innovation and local investment must be supported by sufficient social consensus and a sense of shared sacrifice, or they will not be sustained.

J. Brian Atwood is the director of the U.S. Agency for International Development. This Statement of Principles was delivered by Mr. Atwood on November 16, 1993.

Development assistance works best when it contributes to efforts that people in the recipient society are already attempting to carry out, and when it fully takes into account the priorities and values of affected groups.

The efficiency of this approach has been shown repeatedly, whether we look at the local level of water-user association, or consider the degree of social consensus that a national government must count on to carry out and sustain changes in policy or social and economic programs.

Studies have shown this. Our experience at USAID has demonstrated it, through both the successes and failures of our efforts. Private foundations, the Inter-American and African Development Foundations, and private development assistance organizations around the world have learned it. Other bilateral and multilateral donors are learning it.

How are we to know whether such consensus exists, or can perhaps be brought about, or whether a given program truly matches local priorities and values? The answer is, we must build opportunities for participation into the development processes in which we are involved.

We sometimes do this very well, particularly at the community level, for example, by using participative planning techniques in rural development programs. We will do this more consistently.

We will now build opportunities for participation into development processes at all levels — from community-level projects to the design of USAID's country strategies.

In short, democratizing the development process will be the cornerstone of our approach.

The fact is, unless development assistance is informed by local realities and the people who experience them daily, it will very rarely succeed. Unless policy reforms and other major national commitments are perceived as serving a broad national interest, they will be difficult to sustain.

The reason for this is quite simple. It is their country, not ours. It is their community, not ours. We can advise, we can assist, and we can choose not to assist, but the decisions about development priorities and policies must be reached by that society at large, not by us. It is they who bear the risk; they must make the commitment. Providers of development assistance — whether a well-meaning private voluntary group inadvertently imposing an inappropriate cultural style, or whether a panel of prestigious international experts prescribing policy changes from a vantage point far removed from the particular political and social environment — fail if we forget that it is their country, not ours.

Let us start with that basic truth, therefore, as we construct a development approach based on participation — one that democratizes the development process. Our approach will be oriented by these guiding principles:

One. We will listen to the voices of ordinary people — especially to people whose voices tend to be stifled by more powerful groups in their societies — as we try to discern national and local priorities. This will mean encouraging governments to consult affected populations and to provide them "seats at the table" so that these groups might represent local reality and their own interests during the course of a development program. It will also mean developing and maintaining direct channels of communication between USAID and groups representing a wide range of views and interests in the society.

Two. In defining our strategies at a country level and in pursuit of our global objectives, we will aim to support the initiatives of indigenous communities and organizations. We will seek to understand what is already happening, what particular opportunities exist for USAID to contribute to development processes for which there is well-rooted local support. Our assistance — whether directed in support of national programs or channeled to specific local projects — will aim to complement the "social energies" and commitments shown by the "recipient society."

That does not mean our aid cannot support new ideas, or ideas that are new to a given society. It does mean that we must first strive to ensure that the new idea is fully "owned" by legitimate indigenous institutions and that people who will be affected have a voice in how it is applied.

Nor does it mean that USAID should not have its own priorities. We must and we do: our priorities are set forth in the strategy documents for our four areas of concentration, and our severely limited resources will prevent us from supporting many worthy endeavors. It does mean, however, that we will seek to understand local priorities independently of our own priorities, capabilities, and resources.

Three. We will cast widely for expertise. The technical expertise available to USAID in many areas is world-class, and our technical assistance is often of greater value to recipient countries than the material resources we can offer. However, we will not be satisfied with our technical analysis until we have opened it to debate by a range of experts in the universities and research institutions of the recipient country and by other qualified experts in donor agencies.

Moreover, we will routinely and systematically test our expert analysis against the reality experienced by affected populations. To this end, we will develop appropriate ways in each country context to consult with organizations representing the interests of small-scale farmers and businesspeople, slum dwellers, fishing communities, tribal groups, poor women, professional associations, environmental, charitable, and development PVOs, and other people whose experience provides a needed reality check on the assumptions and prescriptions of outside experts.

This does not mean than we will expect to find harmony among the views of local experts. We will sometimes find more conflict than consensus among the perspectives of indigenous communities and interest groups. We will, however, recognize that competition among a plethora of interests lies at the heart of the democratic process. To the extent appropriate to our role as an outsider, we will strive to make that competition more open and fair, and thereby create as broad a view of the national interest as possible.

Four. We will assure that USAID projects and programs are accountable to the end user. That will mean, for example, that a health sector project under which municipal governments receive training materials, family planning services, and other support from U.S. private agencies will have some mechanism to permit the "clients" — in this case, the municipal governments — to tell USAID whether the services received from these PVOs meet their needs. It will also mean that the woman receiving the family planning service has some say over the way these services are delivered in her community.

Five. We will ensure that projects we support strengthen the capacity of the poor to take the next steps in their own and their community's development. That is, in all our efforts — not just those aimed explicitly to promote our "democracy" objective — we will seek to empower the poor to sustain the development process. Sometimes this will be as simple as, for example, in a project aimed at training village health workers, providing opportunities for these health workers to meet, get to know each other, and thereby begin to identify common concerns and, perhaps, to initiate further efforts to improve local sanitation and health conditions.

Six. To overcome the tendency of projects to benefit only local elites, we will use gender analysis and techniques for data collection and consensus building such as participative rural appraisal (PRA). PRA is a development planning methodology that helps the different groups and institutions in a given community to agree on a common course of action and to take an active role in organizing the inputs of the various outside agencies.

Seven. We will find ways to streamline our procedures for approving and amending projects so as to allow the local reality to drive our programs, rather than to have our procedures drive our definition of local reality. Too often in the past, we in the development business have acquired a stake in a project we have designed and our procedures make it difficult to modify. Sustainable development means that the local recipients have the only stake that counts.

Eight. We will keep our focus on results — on the results experienced by real people in the recipient societies — rather than merely on tracking the material inputs to projects and our adherence to our procedures. We will not lessen our commitment to accountability for the taxpayers' dollars nor our adherence to legal requirements. However, we must satisfy our need for accountability in ways that do not prevent us from achieving the results that will affect people.

Nine. We will practice a respectful partnership with indigenous and American or international private organizations, ranging from non-profit development institutions to professional associations and businesses, that collaborate with us in providing development and humanitarian assistance. We will work with those that are committed to strengthening institutions and empowering people in the recipient society. Our partnership means that we will listen to our partners' views and will work together in ways that reflect our complementary strengths. We recognize the uniquely American values and experience that U.S. PVOs offer, as well as their considerable range of skills and expertise. At the same time, we will not lose sight of the objective of strengthening indigenous institutions and capabilities and will seek ways to expand our support to indigenous organizations and to facilitate the sharing of experience and expertise among them.

Ten. We will take the measures necessary to equip ourselves to make good on these principles. This will not be easy. We will need, for example, to find ways for Mission staff to spend more time out of the capital cities and more time in meaningful dialogue with a wide range of local groups. This will mean streamlining our procedures so as to relieve already overburdened staff of some of the work they currently do.

We will seek ways to empower USAID's own personnel, in the Missions as well as at AID/W, unleashing their innovation and creativity in finding better ways to serve our "clients" in the recipient societies.

We will strengthen relevant skills and aptitudes in our staff and contractors — stronger language and cultural skills, skills in discerning social processes, gender analysis and other techniques to enhance participation, skills in dealing with conflicting interests and, where possible, in enhancing awareness by local groups of a broader national interest. We will find ways to address this need in our personnel policies and practices.

We will consider realistically the costs of applying a participatory approach to our work. Many measures will involve little or no cost, and some may save money and mobilize larger amounts of local resources. Nevertheless, it takes time and resources to consult broadly, and the consultative process can sometimes be slow. We will ensure that these costs are outweighed by the benefits of focusing our development resources more securely on the priorities of the recipient society.

I have asked the Bureau of Policy and Program Coordination to make these principles central to their work in defining the Agency's priorities and procedures. We will enlist the help of many interested staff from all Bureaus, as well as from the Missions, in helping to develop guidelines for the implementation of these principles. Your assistance will be needed in finding ways to overcome the obstacles to participation, both in the field and in USAID's own procedures.

The principles I have outlined will place USAID squarely on the cutting edge of change. This is where I and, I believe, the American people want us to be. We will have learned the lessons that development professionals around the world are learning: development is a people process, and our efforts must aim to support the efforts of local people. That way we will show real, lasting results.

Contributors

Marguerite S. Berger is chief of the Women in Development Unit of the Inter-American Development Bank. Previously, she was senior associate of the Futures Group and director of research for the firm's project on Gender in Economic and Social Systems, funded by the United States Agency for International Development, and an economist with the International Center for Research on Women. She is an author and editor of the book *Women's Ventures*.

Barbara J. Bramble is the director of the International Division at the National Wildlife Federation in Washington, D.C., a program she established at the nation's largest conservation organization. The program concentrates on the interconnections between sustainable management of natural resources and long-term economic development. Ms. Bramble is an environmental lawyer who has represented national and local conservation groups in a range of cases involving energy, land use, and pollution issues.

Richard E. Feinberg serves as special assistant to President Clinton and senior director, Inter-American Affairs, National Security Council. Previously, he was president of Inter-American Dialogue and, from 1982 to 1991, executive vice president of the Overseas Development Council and director of studies from 1977 to 1979. Feinberg served as a member of the Policy Planning Staff, Office of Secretary, Department of State. From 1969 to 1971, he served as a Peace Corps volunteer in Chile. Feinberg has published numerous articles and books, including *The Intemperate Zone: The Third World Challenge to U.S. Foreign Policy* and *Subsidizing Success: The Export-Import Bank in the U.S. Economy.*

Richard D. Fletcher has been deputy manager of the Plans and Programs Department of the Inter-American Development Bank since July 1985. From 1980 to 1985, he served as deputy manager for Integration in the Economic and Social Development Department of the bank. Mr. Fletcher, a Jamaican national and former Rhodes Scholar, came to the bank after serving in international organizations and, from 1977 to 1980, as minister of state for finance and planning in Jamaica.

Carol Graham is a visiting fellow in the Vice Presidency for Human Resources at the World Bank and professorial lecturer in Latin American Studies at Johns Hopkins University School of Advanced International Studies. She is the author of several articles on the political economy of compensation during reform in journals including the *Journal of Latin American Studies, World Development, SAIS Review,* and the *Journal of Interamerican Studies and World Affairs.* She is the author of *Peru's APRA: Parties, Politics, and the Elusive Quest for Democracy* (Lynne Rienner, 1992) and *Safety Nets, Politics, and the Poor: Transitions to Market Economies* (Brookings, 1994). She has served as a consultant to the World Bank and to the Inter-American Development Bank on the design of safety net programs in Latin America, Africa, and Eastern Europe. Her research on safety nets was supported by an award from the John D. and Catherine T. MacArthur Foundation's Research and Writing Competition and by the Brookings Institution.

Kevin Healy has been a grant officer for the Inter-American Foundation for the Andean region since 1978. He has published a book on rural development in Bolivia and numerous articles on peasant and indigenous social movements, grass roots development, the impact of the coca-cocaine economy in the Andes, and Andean efforts toward cultural revitalization. He has also been a professorial lecturer at the School of Advanced International Studies of The Johns Hopkins University. Dr. Healy is serving as visiting faculty fellow at the Kellogg Institute of the University of Notre Dame for the 1994-1995 academic year.

Muni Figueres de Jiménez is the advisor of the Office of External Relations at the Inter-American Development Bank. She previously served as chief of the Integration and Trade Development Division in the Economic and Social Development Department of the IDB. Mrs. Figueres was Costa Rica's first minister of foreign trade, from 1986 to 1988, where her main responsibility was to establish a new foreign trade policy within the framework of the country's economic adjustment process. From 1988 to 1990, she served as special presidential trade representative to the United States.

Felipe Larraín B. is professor of economics at the Universidad Católica de Chile. He has worked as economic advisor to several governments in Latin America and the Caribbean, including Bolivia, Ecuador, Jamaica, Mexico, Paraguay, Peru, and Venezuela. He has also been a consultant to the Government of Canada, the Inter-American Development Bank, the International Monetary Fund, the United Nations, and the World Bank. Professor Larraín has published over fifty articles and seven books in Latin America, the

United States, and Europe. His latest book is *Macroeconomics in the Global Economy*, coauthored with Jeffrey Sachs and now in translation into ten languages.

Jorge A. Lawton, a former permanent resident of Chile, has worked and lived, since 1967, throughout the hemisphere: in Brazil, Mexico, the Caribbean, in addition to Chile and the United States. Dr. Lawton is Human Rights and Human Development Fellow at Emory University's Center for Ethics in Public Policy and the Professions. In 1993, he served as an officer with the UN civilian mission in Haiti. He pursued his graduate studies in Chile (FLACSO), France, and Washington, D.C. (Johns Hopkins University, PhD). He has served on the staff of The Brookings Institution, the U.S. Senate, and (as consultant) the World Bank. In addition to books and scholarly articles, Dr. Lawton has published in *The Financial Times* (London), *The Washington Post, Opinão* (Brazil), *Uno Mas Uno* (Mexico), *The New Republic,* and *Le Monde Diplomatique,* among others.

Nora Lustig is a senior fellow in the Foreign Policy Studies program at The Brookings Institution. Since 1975, she has been a professor of economics with El Colegio de Mexico's Center of Economic Studies in Mexico City. Among her publications in Spanish and English are *Mexico: The Remaking of an Economy* and *Distribución del Ingreso y Crecimiento en México: Un Análisis de Ideas Estructuralistas.* She coedited *North American Free Trade: Assessing the Impact* and has published articles in many academic journals. Dr. Lustig's current research focuses on income distribution and poverty in Latin America.

Moisés Naím is a senior associate at the Carnegie Endowment for International Peace in Washington, D.C., and is also a professor at The Johns Hopkins University School of Advanced International Studies and at IESA, a business school and research center in Caracas. He holds a doctorate from the Massachusetts Institute of Technology. Dr. Naím served as Venezuela's minister of industry from 1989 until the end of 1990, when he became an executive director at the World Bank. He is a member of the U.S. Academy of Science/National Research Council Committee on Economic Reform and Democratization, the Editorial Board of the *Latin American Research Review*, the World Bank's Latin American Advisory Board, and a fellow of the World Economic Forum in Geneva.

Richard S. Newfarmer is division chief in the Industry and Energy Operations Division of the World Bank. For five years previously, he was the World Bank's principal economist for Argentina. Before joining the World Bank, Dr. Newfarmer worked at the Overseas Development Council and on the economics faculty at the University of Notre Dame.

Robert A. Pastor is professor of political science at Emory University and director of the Latin American and Caribbean Program at Emory's Carter Center. He has authored books, monographs, and many articles on U.S. foreign policy, Latin America and the Caribbean, and international political and economic issues. Dr. Pastor served as the director of Latin American and Caribbean Affairs on the National Security Council from 1977 to 1981.

Margaret Sarles is the chair of Latin American and Caribbean Studies of the School of Area Studies at the Foreign Service Institute in Arlington, Virginia. She teaches a regional seminar on Latin America and the Caribbean and the advanced area studies course on Brazil for U.S. diplomats assigned to Latin America. Prior to this, she worked for five years as a senior analyst for the Agency for International Development, Bureau for Latin America and the Caribbean, in the Office of Agriculture and Rural Development.

Kanako Yamaoka is a research fellow at the Institute of Developing Economies of Japan. She has published articles and chapters on the region, especially on Cuba. She is currently staying in Cuba as a visiting scholar at the Centro de Estudios sobre Asia y Oceanía, in order to work on economic relations between Japan and Cuba.

Index

A

AD (Acción Democrática) 43, 47
ad valorem tariff band 186
adjustment 69, 71, 73, 75, 174
  cost 71, 85
  economic programs 20, 56
  living standards 71
  process 69, 71, 73, 77
  structural 112, 193, 198, 205
Administrative Reform 182
advisory communal development
  councils 146
Aerolineas Argentinas 170, 183
Afghanistan, Soviet invasion 243
AFP (pension fund administrators) 116
Africa 13, 20, 197, 242
agriculture 25, 71, 72, 75, 76, 83,
  111, 113, 114, 196, 197, 198, 199
  credit 76, 194, 195, 200, 202, 206
  deficit 197
  development 195
  economic hardship 76
  employment 75, 77
  food production 205
  imports 196, 197
  investment policies 194
  non-traditional exports 197
  output 75, 76, 83, 85
  patrimonial politics 163
agro-business 197, 200, 201
aid programs 135, 231
AID/W 281
airlines 112, 116, 170, 176

Alfonsín, Raúl 164, 165, 169
  administration 165, 167, 168,
    169, 183
Allende, Salvador 27, 122
  administration 122, 127, 148
Alliance for Progress 29, 242
Alliance of the Peoples of the
  Forest 230
aluminum 46, 50
Amazonia 230
Andean countries 212, 224
Andean Pact 4
antipoverty 121, 131, 139, 143
antisystem populists 150
antitrust
  competition 186
  laws 187
  legislation 172
Arbenz, Jacobo (Guatemala) 27,
  241
Arevalo, Juan José (Guatemala) 241
Argentina 2, 4, 11, 46, 64, 112, 163,
  164, 165, 166, 167, 168, 172, 179,
  180, 186, 187, 197, 224, 240, 242
  closed trade regime 185
  "coparticipation law" 184
Aristide, Jean-Bertrand 244, 245
armed forces 54, 55, 167
Asia 7, 13, 237, 244, 253, 255, 256,
  265
Asian Tigers 2, 7, 10
Aspe, Pedro 4
assistentialism 146
auctions 59, 115, 116, 183

austral money base 180
authoritarian
control 166
leadership 163
"mobilization" 27
authoritarianism 164
automobile industry 11, 13
avitaminosis 72, 81
Aylwin, Patricio 125, 146
administration 124, 140, 141,
144, 145, 146, 147, 151
Christian and Social
Democrats 122

B

Bahamas 10
balance of payments 5, 57, 70
Banco Agricola Boliviana
(BAB) 201
Banco del Estado 114
bankruptcies 195
banks 173, 175, 184, 188, 201,
205, 228
foreign 57, 170
public sector downsizing 187
reprivatization 74
Barbados 10, 11
Batista, Fulgencio 240
Bay of Pigs 241
Bogotá Conference, 1948 241
Bolivia 51, 141, 143, 150, 193, 194,
200, 224
Emergency Social Fund 142,
143, 151
Bosch, Juan (Dominican Republic) 27, 242
boundaries
economic 13
ideological 112
international 13
Brady Plan 12

Brazil 2, 4, 11, 27, 163, 164, 165,
166, 167, 168, 169, 171, 174, 197,
213, 224, 229, 231, 242, 246
"Republic of Alagoas" 176
"social pact" 175
Bretton Woods
institutions 4
System 29
brokerage houses 173
Bureau of Policy and Program
Coordination 281
Bush, George 12, 243, 244, 247,
259, 264, 266, 267, 268, 273, 275
administration 193, 221, 232,
244, 270, 272
economic policy 267

C

Canada 12, 221, 224, 244, 254,
256, 265, 266, 268, 269, 275, 276
capital 3, 6, 82, 85, 167
flight 3, 10, 42, 46, 84, 188
foreign 51, 172, 178
inflows 3, 5, 6, 7, 186
investment abroad 71
markets 3, 5, 115
shortage 2, 7
capitalism 116
Cardoso de Mello, Zelia 176
Caribbean 10, 17, 22, 211, 213, 221,
222, 235, 236, 238, 239, 242, 243,
244, 245, 246, 271
Basin Initiative 243, 244
Common Market 4
Economic Development
Group 242, 243
English-speaking 212, 242, 244,
245
European creditors 246
French-speaking 212
manufacturing 246
regional integration 245

Caribbean *continued*
  Spanish-speaking 212
CARICOM (Caribbean Community
  and Common Market) 224, 246
cartels 172
Carter, Jimmy 237, 242, 243, 244,
  247
  administration 242, 243
  human rights 247
CAS (Comités Comunes de Acción
  Social) 129, 130, 145
CASEN (socioeconomic
  characteristics survey) 130
Castillo Armas, Carlos 241
Castro, Fidel 27, 241, 245
  military 242
  regime 27
cattle ranchers 200
Cavallo, Domingo 4, 179, 181, 186
CEDLA 198
Central America 64, 212, 224, 271,
  272
  Common Market 4
Central Bank 3, 6, 7, 179, 180,
  184, 185, 186, 200
Central Intelligence Agency 241,
  242
Central Obrero Boliviano
  (COB) 203
Centro des Estudios para el
  Desarrollo Laboral y
  Agrario 196
Centros de Madres (Mothers'
  Centers) 148
"Chicago school" 122
child care 218
child development 218, 219
Chile 2, 3, 4, 6, 21, 27, 46, 64, 111,
  112, 113, 114, 117, 122, 125, 126,
  128, 132, 139, 140, 142, 143, 144,
  147, 149, 150, 151, 152, 172, 179, 197
  assets 113, 114, 115, 116

Chile *continued*
  democracy 121
  economic policy 122
  employment programs 136
  growth rate 121
  military regime 113, 132
  nongovernmental organiza-
    tions 143
  open election 122
  poverty 121, 125
  privatization 115
  social welfare 122, 127
"Chilean model" 222
China 23
cholera 9
Christian and Social Democrats 122
Christian Democrat 43, 122, 127,
  144
church groups 143
civil
  disobedience 44
  disorder 166
  service 182, 183
civilian
  forces 166
  governments 164, 165, 167, 168,
    171
clientelism 171, 203
Clinton, Bill 244, 245, 273
  administration 12, 29, 194, 206,
    211, 245, 251, 264, 268
coca 194, 196, 197, 198, 199, 201,
  202, 204, 205, 206
  expansion 198
  growing 198, 199, 204, 205
  paste 202, 203
  production 193, 202, 203, 206
  reduction 194, 198, 204
  zones 198

coca-cocaine
  economic circuits   199
  economy   194
  expansion   194
  industry   202
  region   200
CODECO (Community Development
  Council)   145, 146
coercion   74
Cold War   5, 12, 15, 22, 23, 24, 25,
  26, 28, 163, 223, 234, 235, 237,
  238, 241, 245, 247, 259
Collor de Mello, Fernando   4, 166,
  169, 171, 172, 174, 175, 176, 177,
  178
  administration   173, 231
  "Collorgate"   177
  electoral fraud   176
  impeachment   174, 177
  PRN   169
Collor de Mello, Pedro   176
Colombia   4, 6, 10, 13, 22, 64, 72,
  164, 218, 224
comedores populares   215, 219
COMIBOL   197
communal kitchens   149
communications   114, 172
communism   23, 24, 26, 28, 163,
  233, 235, 236, 241, 245, 246
Communist Party   241
community
  development activities   145
  initiative   30
  organizations   139, 146
  participation   146
  services   131
Companhia Siderúrgica Nacional
  (CSN) 178
Companhia Vale do Rio Doce
  (CVRD) 173
compensation programs   141

competition   13, 61
  foreign   61, 171, 173
competitive principles   164
Competitiveness Council   172
CONASUPO (National Commission
  for Popular Subsistence)   80
Confederação General dos
  Trabalhadores 173
Confederación Unica Sindical de
  Trabajadores Campesinos   203
conglomerates   115
CONIN (Corporación de Nutrición
  Infantil) 131
consolidation bonds
  (BOCONs)   185
constitutional reform   175
consumer
  demand   7
  goods   44, 46
  price index   71
consumption   70, 74, 75, 81, 82, 194
Convertibility
  Law   179, 183
  model   188
  Program   186
cooptation   74
Coordinación General del Plan
  Nacional de Zonas Deprimidas y
  Grupos Marginados
  (COPLAMAR)   78
copper   111, 127
CORFO (Chilean Development
  Corporation) 114, 115
Corporación de Reforma Agraria
  (CORA) 113
corporatist   164, 169, 170, 171, 172
  ideals   169
  models   166, 182
  order   186
  organizations   168
  principles   164
  special-interest groups   180

corruption 10, 58, 59, 60, 61, 62, 171, 176, 181, 203
Costa Rica 11, 164
Council of Freely Elected Heads of Government 244
credit 43, 115, 180
 foreign 115
 markets 112
crime 50, 56, 81
Cuba 11, 22, 236, 238, 239, 240, 242, 243, 244, 245, 246
 Platt Amendment 238
 Teller Amendment 238
currency 70, 172, 179
 convertibility 48
 domestic 70
 foreign reserves 3, 43

D

dams 42
debt 6, 12, 42, 51, 77, 114, 115, 167, 171, 174, 221, 222
 annual ceilings 183
 commercial banks 185
 crisis 3, 12, 46
 external 77, 185
 foreign 16, 42, 46, 48, 112, 164, 168, 182, 203
 international 40
 payments 172
 reduction 184, 185, 221
 renegotiation 50, 51
 restructuring 184, 221
 service 3, 6, 170
decentralization 129, 145, 146, 184, 187
 federalism 186
decision-making process 30
deficit 43, 77, 180
deforestation 218
demilitarization processes 164

democracy 5, 28, 121, 164, 171, 193, 223, 236, 237, 239, 242, 247, 248
democratization 29, 30, 164, 166, 177
depression 1, 115, 168
deregulation 60, 61, 186
devaluation 2, 48, 49, 70, 75, 85
development 9, 11, 12, 13, 15, 16, 17, 18, 20, 21, 22, 23, 24, 25, 29, 30, 40, 116, 171, 232, 243, 247, 248
 alternative 31, 193, 194, 198, 229
 capital 23
 community-level 31
 economic 13, 17, 19
 hemispheric 28
 human 16
 indicators 30
 indices 26
 initiatives 22, 23
 methodologies 20
 national 194
 overproduction 18
 peasant 194
 policy 211
 political 12, 25
 port facilities 23
 process 17, 28, 30, 277, 278
 rural 198
 state-dominated model 164
 strategies 5, 11, 15, 16, 20, 21, 22, 31, 232
  post-Cold War 28
 sustainable 230, 234, 277
 top-down attitudes 30, 148
 women 211, 212
divestiture 116, 183, 187
Dominican Republic 23, 27, 238, 239, 240, 242, 244

drugs   193, 195
  dollar laundering   197
  dollars   196
  illicit crop reduction   198
  industry   193, 195, 198, 202
  policy   206
    U.S.-Bolivia   194, 204
  processing areas   199
  related alternative development
    programs   206
"Dutch disease" (Bolivia)   194
duties   46
Duvalier, "Papa Doc"   242

E

Earth Summit   269
East Asia   10, 11, 12
Eastern Europe   111, 112, 117, 233,
  241, 259
"Eco-Indians"   230
economic
  activity   63, 222
  adjustment   214, 215
  bloc   251
  central formulae   17
  change   4, 200
  competitor   170
  consequences   60
  crisis   122, 130, 132, 136, 140, 183
  deregulation   64
  deterioration   194
  development   206, 237, 243, 247,
    251
  disaster   174
  growth   171, 179, 187, 195, 261
  ideology   171
  indexing   19, 168
  indicators   15
  inefficiencies   43
  liberalization   39, 40, 112
  model   19, 195

economic   *continued*
  modernization   65
  nationalism   13
  neoclassical theory   19
  organizations   149
  panic   169
  performance   76
  pluralism   171
  policy   4, 5, 62, 111, 122, 168
  power   59
  privileges   180
  productivity   42
  programs   178, 236
  progress   6
  prosperity   275
  recession   133, 175
  recovery   194
  reform   168, 170, 172, 175, 176,
    178, 222, 223, 225
  reorganization   179, 193
  stabilization program   168
  stagnation   9, 10, 171
  strategy   10
  structure   17
  superpower   260
  surplus   18
  survival   82
  system   178
  universal problem   19
  world order   10
Economic Solidarity Pact   73, 76
economy
  illegal drug-driven   194
  international   124
  state-centered   60
Ecuador   224, 242
education   7, 10, 16, 20, 46, 56, 72,
  78, 79, 81, 124, 126, 127, 130,
  134, 141, 184, 188, 195, 213, 214,
  217, 265

education *continued*
  budget 130
  economic 63
  expenditures 78, 79
  women 214
egalitarian revolution 26
Eisenhower, Dwight D. 25, 241,
  242, 247
  administration 241
El Gran Viraje 47
El Salvador 271
elections 40, 146, 165, 244
electoral
  college 165
  politics 140
employment 72, 73, 75, 76, 77, 130,
  134, 138, 139, 140, 141, 142, 150,
  180, 182, 194, 214
  crisis 133
  emergency programs 124, 132, 137,
    140
  formal 77, 140
  informal 77
  programs 21, 126, 129, 132, 133,
    135, 136, 137, 138, 139, 140,
    141, 145
Empresa Nacional de
  Telecomunicaciones (Entel) 170
Enterprise for the Americas Initiative (EAI) 221, 222, 223, 224,
  244
environment 194, 200, 211, 233,
  269
  agencies 232
  development programs 221
  impact assessors 231
  issues 232
  practices 269
  protection 221, 267, 270
  trade agreements 232
  worldwide movement 228

environmentalists 230
Ethiopia, Soviet-Cuban
  intervention 243
Europe 11, 12, 23, 222, 237, 238,
  239, 240, 245, 246
European Community (EC) 244,
  252, 255, 264
European Recovery Program 24
exchange rate 43, 48, 59, 179, 186,
  188, 195, 196
expansionary policy 70
expenditures 70, 78, 82, 124, 180,
  182, 183, 184
  public 80, 182, 195
  reduction 70, 71
  social 72, 78, 124
export 3, 4, 5, 6, 7, 11, 12, 16, 40,
  43, 46, 48, 50, 52, 59, 164, 172,
  195, 196, 197, 198, 200, 252, 261
  armaments 11, 174
  coffee 198, 205
  markets 170, 172
  non-oil 46, 50
  non-traditional 50, 195
  oil 40, 46
  prices 194, 197
  taxes 181, 186
external
  finance 180
  sector 52
extractive reserve concept 230, 231

F

factor payments 71
families 215, 217, 233
Far East 11
Farias, Paulo César "P.C." 176
farming 200, 229
Fernández, Eduardo 43
Fernández, Max 150
fertility 16, 19, 213

Ficha (social stratification measurement system)   129, 130, 145
fiscal
   conservatism   186
   crises   3, 62
   decentralization   180
   deficit   2, 43, 64, 70, 77
   federalism   182
Florida   245
Fondo Internacional Desarrollo Agrícola (FIDA)   196
food costs   80
Ford Foundation   231
foreign
   competition   197
   deposits   6
   donations   142
   earnings   41
   economic policy   22
   exchange   1, 16, 40, 41, 43, 46, 55, 62, 184, 194, 200
   interest payments   184
Foreign Assistance Act   25
forest management policies   227
formal sector   73, 76
"Fortress Latin America"   13
FOSIS (Fund for Solidarity and Social Investment)   124, 125, 141, 142, 143, 144, 146, 147, 148, 149, 150, 151, 152
Foxley, Alejandro   4, 5
France   23, 112
Franco, Itamar   177, 178
free trade   4, 5, 7, 12, 193, 200, 221, 233, 234, 240, 255, 260, 261, 267, 275
freedom of expression   63
Frei, Eduardo   122, 130
   administration   124, 127, 148
Fujimori, Alberto   150
Fundo Común Municipal (common municipal fund)   144

G

GATT (General Agreement on Tariffs and Trade)   48, 231, 266
Gaviria, César (Colombia)   64
GDP (Gross Domestic Product)   1, 2, 7, 9, 16, 42, 43, 46, 47, 49, 114, 165, 174, 180, 181, 182, 188, 194
   compulsory wage tax   187
   deflator   78, 79
   fiscal deficit   77
   inflation tax   187
   Japan   252
   Mexico   71
   per capita   25, 85
   taxes   181
General Tax Office (DGI) (Argentina)   181
Germany   238, 239, 244, 247, 260, 261, 263, 265, 272
   anti-inflation program, 1948   172
gini coefficient   30
global
   economy   259, 275
   marketplace   13, 21
GNP (Gross National Product)   16, 20, 127, 128, 196
Gonzalez, Felipe   112
Gore, Al   270, 273
Goulart, João (Brazil)   27
government   74
   controlled companies   170
   controls   59
   credits   59
   deficit   214
   expenditures   77
   intervention   167
   liabilities   170
   mismanagement   10
   pension funds   169
   policies   214

government *continued*
  revenue 40
  services 78, 214
  spending 69, 77, 78
  technocrats 1, 4, 47
  technopols 1, 4, 5, 7
Great Britain 23, 164, 165, 244
Greece 23
Grenada 243
growth 9, 19, 42, 50, 69, 187
  agricultural 202
  Asian-style 7
  boom-and-bust syndrome 7
  capitalist 17
  consumption 7
  economic 18, 24, 28, 41, 57, 85
  export-led 12, 171
  long-term 124
  non-oil 50
  rates 16, 121, 194
Guantánamo naval base 22
Guatemala 27, 241
Gulf War 50
Guyana 27, 244

H

Haiti 23, 238, 239, 242, 243, 244,
  245, 246
HDI (Human Development Index) 19, 30
health 56, 78, 79, 81, 195, 214
  programs 48
  sector 79, 131
  services 139, 187
health care 19, 46, 72, 79, 131,
  134, 187, 217, 219, 273
  curative 126, 127
  preventive 126, 132, 217
  universal coverage 132

health insurance 123, 127, 132, 187,
  188, 264
  reforms 187
Herrera Campins, Luis 43
Hispaniola 238
Hong Kong 2, 10
housing 126, 131
human capital 3, 82, 132, 138
human rights 15, 21, 30, 165, 237,
  242, 243, 247
  abuses 122, 167
  violations 121, 164, 165
hyperinflation 1, 6, 47, 52, 58, 64,
  122, 168, 169, 170, 174, 179, 180,
  182, 183, 184, 186, 188, 194, 195

I

illiteracy 11, 72
IMF (International Monetary
  Fund) 4, 40, 48, 193, 204, 205
immigrants, Mennonite 197
imperialism 10
import 3, 10, 16, 43, 46, 48, 62,
  252
  capital 3
  consumer goods 3
  costs 170
  domestic markets 10
  duties 172
  government controls 59
  liberalization 52, 188
  luxury 57
  manufactured 48
  privileges 186
  quotas 42
  suppression 3
  taxes 172
IMSS (Mexican Institute of Social
  Insurance) 79, 80
income 9, 16, 21, 24, 46, 47, 49, 70,
  71, 72, 74, 75, 79, 82, 83, 84, 170,

income *continued*
  194, 214
  agriculture   71, 75, 76
  declining   72, 81
  distribution   30, 42, 69, 128
  earned   70, 73
  household   71, 74
  non-wage   71, 74, 75, 83
  per capita   16, 20, 42, 47
  real   70, 71, 72
  social   70, 71
  total   74, 75
Income and Expenditure Survey,
  1977   72
income tax   48, 181, 182, 185
Independent Democratic Union   140
indexation   172, 175
Indo-China   23
Indonesia   10, 229
industrialization   10
industries, foreign-owned   166
industry   114
infant mortality rate (IMR)   11, 16,
  47, 72, 81, 123, 125, 130, 153, 187
inflation   2, 7, 39, 40, 41, 42, 49,
  52, 53, 64, 70, 71, 74, 85, 121,
  164, 167, 168, 169, 171, 172, 174,
  179, 180, 181, 182, 187, 214
  rate   16, 172
  Tanzi effect   180
  tax   180, 186, 187
informal sector   72, 76
infrastructure   3, 46, 136, 137, 141,
  145, 218, 256, 269
insolvency   188
instability   239
institutional crisis   58
insurance companies   188
intendéncias (regional administrations) 135

Inter-American and African Development Foundations   278
Inter-American Development Bank
  (IDB) 4, 48, 200, 211, 222, 223,
  227, 230, 242
inter-American relations   236
interest payments   3, 48, 71, 168, 182
interest rates   2, 3, 6, 43, 45, 48,
  49, 77, 78, 114, 115
  global   3, 6
  government controls   59
internal revenue service   181
international
  commercial banks   168
  financial accounts   6
  financial community   5
  financial institutions   16
  market   224
  reserves   43
International Potato Center   199
interventionist state governments   13
investment   7, 43, 74, 76, 79, 112,
  116, 121, 124, 143, 180, 182, 221,
  222
  foreign   40, 41, 51, 167, 174, 262
  human capital   132, 138
  industrial   232
  opportunities   58, 179
  public   70, 77, 116
  tax credit, United States   272
investor confidence   6, 56
investors   116
  foreign   40, 56, 61, 112, 117, 173
Iranian Revolution   243
Iraq   165, 174
iron ore   41
irrational politics   6
ISI (import-substitution policy) 11,
  21, 41
  industrialization strategy   11
  model   10, 11, 167

ISSSTE (Health and Social Security Institute for State Employees) 79, 81
Italy 23

J

Jagan, Cheddi (Guyana) 27, 244
Japan 13, 222, 244, 251, 252, 260, 261, 263, 264, 265, 272
  automobile manufacturing (in U.S.) 13
  investment 251, 253, 254, 256
  Mexican investment 251
  NAFTA (North American Free Trade Agreement) 255
  private sector 251, 256
  yen 251, 252
Japanese FDI (worldwide foreign direct investment) 251, 252, 253, 254, 256
Japanese Mission for Promotion of Economic Exchange 254
Japanese-Mexican Chamber of Commerce 255
jobs 267
Johnson, Lyndon B. 17, 25, 26, 242, 247
  administration 26
judicial system 59
JUNJI (National Association of Child Care Centers) 130
Junta Nacional de Auxilio Escolar 126
Junta Vecinal 145, 146, 147, 148, 149

K

Kennedy, John F. 25, 26, 27, 242, 243, 247, 263
  administration 26, 29
Keynesian revolution 16
Korea 2, 10, 23
Kuwait 174

L

labor 70, 75, 76, 85, 124, 126, 129, 133, 137, 166, 174, 187
  force 6, 77, 126, 132, 137, 195, 211, 214
  males 213
  markets 137, 188
  non-remunerated family 76, 77
  organized 128, 166
  standards 244, 262
  unions 122, 163, 170
land tax reform 203, 205
land-tenure system 241
Latin America 221
Latin Caribbean 242
law enforcement 193
layoffs 74, 76
Legião Brasileira de Assistencia (LBA) 176
Ley de Reforma Tributaria 203
liberalized trade arrangements 197
liberation movements 23
LIBOR (London interbank offered rate) 185
life expectancy 11, 16
linear development perspective 22
literacy 16, 20, 148
living
  conditions 223
  standards 69
low birth weight 72
Lusinchi, Jaime 43

M

macroeconomic
  balance 2
  distortions 40
  equilibrium 124
  management 2
  policy decisions 222

Malaysia 10, 11, 13
malnutrition 9, 72, 81, 125, 130, 187
Malta de Collor, Rosane 176
Malvinas/Falkland Islands War 164
Manifest Destiny 29
manufacturing jobs 74, 261, 262
maquiladoras 73, 254, 256, 262
market 12
   competition 188
   domestic 10, 70
   economy 16, 39, 65, 121
   financial 4, 51, 116
   forces 71
   global commodity 4
   industrial 168
   international capital 5
   liberalization 199
   open 13, 202, 260
   pricing 168, 171
   reforms 39
   system 186
market-oriented
   approach 58
   economies 266
Marshall Plan 29, 241, 242
Martí, Jose 22
maté de coca 206
media 62, 63, 64, 231
Mediterranean 235
Mendes, Chico 230, 231
Menem, Carlos Saúl 64, 165, 169, 171, 172, 174, 179, 180
   administration 181, 186
   Peronist party (Partido Justicialista) 169, 174
MERCOSUR 4, 224
Mexican National Accounts 71, 73, 76, 77

Mexico 2, 4, 6, 12, 13, 42, 46, 64, 69, 70, 71, 72, 73, 74, 75, 76, 78, 81, 83, 85, 111, 112, 172, 178, 222, 224, 231, 232, 244, 251, 253, 256, 259, 262, 263, 266, 268, 269, 274, 275, 276
   balance of payments crisis, 1982 69
   employment practices 74
   fiscal
      cutbacks 70, 72
      deficit 70, 77
      surplus 77
   income 70, 71, 73, 75, 76, 80, 82, 83, 84
      distribution 84, 85
      non-wage 72, 73, 74, 75, 83, 84
      social 70, 77
      total 70, 82, 83, 84
      wage 73, 74, 83
   labor laws 74
   living
      conditions 72
      standards 71, 72
middle class 127
Middle East 242
middle-income sectors 75, 82, 84
migrant workers 229
migration 18, 19, 20, 199, 200, 229, 245
   families 214
   internal 205
   male 217
   return 75
   United States 75, 82, 84
military 54, 64, 166, 167, 223
military coup, Peru 1968 111
military governments 39, 64, 122, 124, 126, 128, 130, 131, 133, 138, 141, 144, 145, 163, 164, 165, 166, 167, 229, 230, 240, 244

Minas Gerais Iron and Steel Mills, Inc. (USIMINAS)   173, 177
MINEPLAN   141
mineral wealth   229
minimum wage   72, 73, 75, 80, 81, 130, 134, 139
mining   111, 113, 114, 172, 195, 197
Ministry of Agriculture and Peasant Affairs 204
Ministry of Health   79, 80
Ministry of International Trade and Industry (MITI)   255
Miterrand, François   112
monetary
   emission   7, 185, 186
   restraint   74
monopolies   112, 117, 170
Monroe Doctrine   22, 238
Montevideo Conference   240
mortality rates   19
Movimiento Nacional Revolucionario (MNR)   195
multilateral development banks (MDBs) 228, 229, 231
Multilateral Investment Fund   221, 223
municipal reform   144, 145, 146, 147
Mussolini model of government   163

National Mining Enterprise (ENAMI)   113
National Reconstruction Party   175
National Renovation   140
nationalism   24, 112
nationalization   111, 113
natural resource development programs 221
natural resources   166, 228
neoliberal economic philosophy   121, 122, 124, 128
neoliberal program   203
New Economic Policy (NEP)   193, 194, 195, 196, 197, 198, 199, 200, 201, 202, 203, 204, 205, 206
New Frontier   263
Nicaragua   23, 240, 243
Nixon, Richard   247
non-competitive management   170
non-tariff barriers   48
nongovernmental organizations   143, 144, 147, 148, 149
North America   10, 11
North American free trade area   246
nutrition 16, 19, 72, 81, 126, 131, 214, 218
NWF (National Wildlife Federation)   227, 228, 230, 231, 232

N

NAFTA (North American Free Trade Agreement)   1, 6, 7, 12, 206, 221, 223, 224, 225, 232, 244, 246, 251, 253, 254, 255, 256, 259, 262, 263, 264, 267, 269, 270, 271, 273, 275, 276
National Consumers Institute (INCO)   81
National Fund for Regional and Municipal Development   146
national health system   130
National Institute of Nutrition   72

O

OAS (Organization of American States) 241, 244
ODEPLAN (National Planning Office) 129, 141
OECD nations   127
officials de confianza   147
oil   12, 40, 41, 58, 76, 111, 172, 174
   companies   111, 170
   concessions   170
   crises   164
   exploitation   41

oil *continued*
  exports   40, 46
  GDP   50
  income   42, 50
  market   41
  prices   39, 41, 42, 50, 52, 174
  revenues   39, 42, 43, 46, 49, 50,
    59, 61
  "shock"   42
oligopolies   54, 60, 63, 168, 172
open trading system   223
output   70, 71, 75, 76, 78
Overseas Development Council   30
  QLI (Quality of Life Index)   30

P

Palenque, "Compadre"   150
Panama   22, 72, 181, 224, 247
Panama Canal   22, 239, 247
  treaties   242
Panama policy   239
  Caribbean Basin   239
Paraguay   4, 224
participative rural appraisal
  (PRA)   280
Partido da Social Democracia
  Brasileira (PSDB)   175
patronage   13, 21, 177
Pax Americana   23, 29
pay increases   174
Paz Estensorro, Victor   195
peasant   199
  agricultural crisis   204
  agriculture   194, 195, 196
  coca producers   205
  coca protests   204
  controlled lands   196
  employment   194
  income   194
  labor force   198

peasant *continued*
  public policies   196
  purchasing power   194
  sindicato   194
  transport system   196
PEM (minimum employment
  program)   132, 133, 134, 135, 136,
  137, 138, 139, 145, 148
pension   127, 132, 170, 184, 185
  funds   116, 173, 178
PEP (expansion program for professionals)   133, 135
Pérez, Carlos Andrés   5, 39, 40, 43,
  44, 47, 64, 65
  administration   40, 47, 48, 50,
    58, 59, 60, 65, 111
  political adversaries   40
Peronist party (Partido Justicialista)
  (Argentina)   169
Peru   3, 111, 139, 150, 197, 199,
  224, 242
PETROBRÁS (Petróleo Brasileiro,
  SA)   173, 174, 176
Petrobrás Engineers Association   174
petroleum industry   183
PIMO (labor-intensive pro-
  gram)   133, 134, 135, 137
Pinochet, Augusto   122, 148
  administration   122, 123, 127, 135,
    136, 140, 145, 146, 148, 149,
    150, 151
  UDI members   147
  Independent Democratic Union
    Party   140
Pinochet marches, Chile   139
pisadores   199, 203
Plan Integral de Desarrollo y
  Sustitución (PIDYS)   204
plataforma de lucha   203
Platt Amendment   22, 238
Platt, Orville   22
Platt Treaties   240

Plaza Agreement, September 1985 251
plebiscite, Brazil 1993 178
plebiscite, Chile 1988 122, 140, 147
pluralism 164
PNAC (national complementary feeding program) 130
benefits 130
poblaciones 137, 150
pobladores 144, 147, 148, 149, 150
dirigente 150
Point IV Technical Assistance Program 241
POJH (occupational program for heads of household) 132, 134, 135, 136, 137, 138, 139, 145, 148
policies 47, 62, 70, 71, 74, 180, 204
agrarian 206
anti-narcotics, U.S.-Bolivia 194
decentralized 125
expansionary 69
fiscal 45, 52
income 73, 74
monetary 2, 45, 52
poor 125
productivity-enhancing 85
public 60, 199, 201
social 124, 138, 146
tax 128
wage 128
policy
decisions 73
design 21
reform 188, 278
policymakers 73
political
competition 164
consequences 60
crises 58
destabilization 133

political *continued*
ethics 59
instability 54, 61
institutions, formal 149
prisoners 242
unrest 74
Polonoroeste project 229, 230
poor 75, 80, 122, 129, 143, 151
agriculture 83
households 71, 72, 75, 83, 85
rural 72, 76
self-employed 83
urban 80, 85
popular economic organizations 148, 149
potatoes 198, 199, 200, 201
poverty 6, 9, 16, 17, 18, 20, 21, 28, 29, 31, 42, 47, 69, 71, 72, 80, 83, 85, 121, 124, 130, 176, 187, 211
alleviating 124, 125, 132, 139, 141, 142, 151, 187
Chile 121, 122, 123, 124, 126, 128, 129, 130, 141, 143
extreme 83, 125, 126, 132, 146, 152
index 129
"map" 143
reduction 171, 187, 234
social programs 47, 56
urban 83
women 211
power concessions 170
PPD (Party for Democracy) 147
Prebish, Raúl 10
prices 2, 4, 43, 45, 48, 62, 70, 77, 80, 168, 180, 183, 186, 188, 194, 196
agricultural goods 75
aluminum 50
coca 198, 202
coffee 198

prices *continued*
    controls   42, 74, 195
    deflator   71, 79
    fuel   46
    goods and services   74
    government controls   59
    international   186, 188, 198
    liberalization   48
    natural gas   46
    oil   43, 50, 52
    oligopolistic   188
    stability   2, 180, 182, 187
    world market   197
private-sector   16, 47, 50, 79, 111,
    113, 133, 137, 164, 171, 172, 188
privatization   3, 48, 59, 61, 111,
    112, 113, 114, 115, 116, 117, 164,
    168, 169, 170, 172, 173, 174, 178,
    180, 183, 186
    agriculture   114
    banking   114
    corruption   59
    process   29, 115, 116, 173
    public enterprise   170, 182
    social welfare   178
    state-owned enterprises   64
Privatization Certifications   173
privilege   13, 21
PRN (Partido de Recontrução
    Nacional)   169
Prodem Credit Program   218
profits   53, 70, 71, 74, 83
programs
    government   130
    stabilization   180
Promoción Popular (Popular
    Promotion)   148
PRONASOL (Programa Nacional de
    Solidaridad)   85
property rights   113
protection   13, 21, 251

protest   195. *See also* riots
PSDB, Brazil   175
public
    accountability   228
    credit   201
    deficit   180
    enterprises   169, 180
    expenditures   77
    finance   46, 115, 179, 180
    health   72, 148
    institutions   188
    investment   205
    sector   3, 7, 16, 47, 49, 59, 61,
        80, 112, 113, 164, 166, 167,
        172, 175
    services   48, 58, 112
    works   21, 133, 171
Public Financial Management
    Law   183
Puerto Rico   22, 236

Q

Quantitative restrictions (QRs)   186
quota limits   46

R

radicalism   26
railroads   127, 170
rain forest   230
Reagan, Ronald   235, 236, 237,
    243, 247
    administration   193, 233, 243
    Communist threat   247
    East-West strategy   243
RECADI (Regimen de Cambios
    Diferenciales)   43, 48
recession   64, 124, 164, 170, 174,
    179, 180
Reciprocal Trade Agreements   240
reforms   2, 50, 60, 64, 113, 164, 174,
    178, 180, 182, 184, 187, 188, 222

reforms *continued*
  economic   2, 5, 6, 39, 40, 51, 54, 63, 64, 164, 169, 187
  market-oriented   39, 40, 61, 122
  political   48, 164
  social   26, 53, 247
  structural   56, 170
  Venezuela   39, 47, 48, 49, 52, 57
regimes   4, 27, 59, 163, 164
  anti-communist   27
  dictatorial   27
regionalism   251
regulation   112
rents   74
reserves   186
  liquid   180
revenue mobilization   180
revenues   46, 180, 181, 186
  non-oil   46
  oil   46, 49, 50, 59, 61
  public   46, 77
revolution   236
riots   44, 50, 64, 165. *See also* protest
Rodríguez, Miguel   5
Roosevelt, Franklin D.   240, 241, 247
Roosevelt, Theodore   22, 23, 238, 239
  Rough Riders   22
rubber tappers   229, 230, 231

S

Salinas de Gortari, Carlos   5, 85, 262, 266, 275, 276
  administration   78, 85, 251
Sarney, José   165, 167, 168, 169, 171
  administration   165, 167, 168, 169
savings   74, 115, 116, 180
school   19, 72

school lunch program   130, 131, 139, 219
Seaga, Edward (Jamaica)   235
"sectoral chamber"   168
security   235, 236, 246
self-employed   71, 77
SERPLAC (Regional Secretariat for Coordination and Planning)   129, 135
SIDERBRAS (Siderugia Brasileira, SA)   168
da Silva, Luís Inácio Lula   166, 171
sindicatos   203, 204, 205, 206
Singapore   2, 10, 260
social
  assistance   143
  class relations   19
  conditions   9, 78
  improvements   11
  indicators   81
  indices   19
  insurance   79
  justice   248
  needs   126
  policy   48
  programs   47, 78, 211
  revolution   26
  rights   17
  sector   77, 78, 128
  structure   17
  tension   44
  unrest   74
social security   79, 127, 128, 131, 132, 184, 185, 187
  pensions   132, 184
social services   6, 47, 123, 166, 187
social welfare   122, 124, 125, 127, 128, 129, 142, 143, 178
  activities   142, 143
  expenditures   123, 127
  policy   121, 123, 124, 128, 143

social welfare *continued*
  spending   127, 138
Socialists   122, 147
Somalia   165
Somoza, Anastasio   240, 241
South Africa   259
South America   264
Southeast Asia   253, 264
Southern Cone   206, 212, 213
  Common Market   224
Soviet bloc   180, 245
Soviet Russia   247
Soviet Union   111, 117, 233, 242,
  243, 259
soybeans   197, 201, 229
Spain   22, 112
Spanish-American War   22, 235,
  236, 239
spending   78, 79, 183
  public   42, 43, 77
  social   48, 70, 71, 78, 128, 132,
    141
stabilization   73, 75, 77, 168, 175, 194
stagnation   10, 11, 12, 17, 29
state
  capitalist model   193
  controls   43
  owned enterprises   3, 47
steel mills   42
stock
  exchange   116
  market   40, 57, 61, 115, 116
  ownership   116
strikes   74, 122, 195
structural deficit   186
subsidies   6, 42, 44, 56, 70, 77, 80,
  128, 129, 131, 139, 140, 145, 168,
  170, 171, 180, 183, 184
  agriculture   76
  credit   116, 201

subsidies *continued*
  direct   53
  food   80, 81, 131
  fuel   197
  general   71, 80
  government   125, 151
  housing   131
  industry   181
  price   48, 80
  public   183, 195
  special-interest   3
  targeted   80
subway system   170
supply and demand   19
supply-side strategy   193
Suriname   164
Switzerland   10

T

Taft, William Howard   23, 239
Taiwan   2, 10
tariffs   4, 6, 46, 48, 275
  barriers   195
  change   196
  hikes   42
  rates   112, 196
  rebate incentive   197
  reform   170
tax   46, 77, 128, 170, 171, 180, 181,
  187
  break   116
  burden   187
  codes   3, 272
  collection   3, 46, 170, 180
  energy   181
  evasion   180, 181
  export   181
  fraud   181
  increase   70, 141
  laws   180

tax *continued*
 loopholes 42
 peasant holdings 203
 reform 46, 124, 168, 172, 195, 203
 system 141, 180, 272
technology 76
telecommunications 170
Teller Amendment 238
Thailand 11
The Enterprise for the Americas Initiative 12
Third World 10, 17, 18, 20, 24, 26, 27, 28, 29, 242
Tierra del Fuego 181
timber 227, 231
Title IX ("Utilization of Democratic Institutions in Development") 25
trade 4, 5, 7, 12, 48, 53, 70, 121, 222, 223, 224, 244
 foreign 16, 122, 260
 liberalization 4, 53, 64, 170, 172, 173, 195, 196, 203, 204, 206, 223
trading blocs 240, 265
training program 124, 135
 national 133, 135, 137, 138
transportation
 costs 197
 systems 172
Treasury bonds (BONEX)
 external, Argentina 184
Treaty of Versailles 239
Trujillo, Rafael 27, 240, 242
Truman Doctrine 29
Truman, Harry 241, 247
Turkey 23

U

U.S.-Bolivia policies 193, 202, 204
U.S.-Caribbean relations 245

U.S.-Latin American relations 12
Ubico, Jorge (Guatemala) 241
UDI (Independent Democratic Union) 147
UDP (Unidad Democrática Popular) 194, 195, 203
UN Economic Commission for Latin America (ECLA) 10
UNCED (United Nations Conference on the Environment) 166
underdevelopment 15, 16, 17, 18, 24, 31
underemployment 77, 138, 197
UNDP (United Nations Development Programme) 19
 HDI (Human Development Index) 30, 31
unemployment 49, 72, 74, 76, 77, 122, 124, 133, 137, 138, 140, 174, 176, 187, 194, 197
 compensation 48
 insurance benefits 76
 rate 76, 132, 140, 195
 women 216
 youth 150
unions 47
 monopoly 187
United Nations 6, 165, 198, 243
United Nations Conference on Environment and Development 234
United States 6, 12, 13, 17, 21, 22, 23, 26, 27, 28, 75, 82, 84, 221, 222, 223, 224, 231, 232, 234, 235, 236, 237, 238, 239, 241, 244, 245, 246, 247, 253, 256, 263, 269, 271, 275
 aid officials 15, 24
 aid programs 15
 anti-communism 26
 bank loans 23
 bilateral trade agreements 240
 business 22

United States *continued*
  Congress   25, 228
  customs houses   23
  customs receipts   23
  Department of State   26
  Department of the Treasury   228
  Depression   262
  development   21, 24, 25, 28
  diplomats   240
  dollar   179, 251, 252
  dominance   245
  economic policy   22, 263
  expansion   239
  foreign aid   242
  foreign policy   26, 163, 235, 237, 246
    Cold War   235, 238, 241
    Good Neighbor Policy   235, 237, 240, 241
    protectorate era   235, 237, 238, 240
  hemispheric
    hegemony   23
    initiatives   15
    policy   22
  history   25
  illegal workers   85
  investments   23
  jobs   259
  liberal tradition   28
  Marines   238, 239, 240
  naval forces   22
  officials   27
  policy   26, 27, 235
  policymakers   234
  political culture   28
  presidents   236, 239
  priorities   27
  PVOs   281
  relations   236

United States *continued*
  security   22, 236, 247
  Senate   239
  theorists   15
  Trade Representative   232
  war aims   240
  world influence   26
UP (Unidad Popular)   111, 114
urbanization   214
Uruguay   4, 224
USAID (U.S. Agency for International Development)   26, 29, 202, 227, 228, 271, 278, 279, 280, 281, 282

V

value added tax (VAT)   48, 181, 182
Vargas, Getúlio   166, 178
Velasco, Juan   111
Velázquez, Ramón J.   64
Venezuela   2, 4, 5, 39, 40, 41, 42, 43, 44, 45, 46, 47, 48, 50, 51, 53, 54, 55, 60, 61, 63, 64, 65, 111, 164, 224, 238
  autonomy   47
  corporations   51
  debt   51
  economy   40, 56, 58
  education   47
  February 1992 coup attempt   5
  fiscal balance   52
  fiscal crisis   55, 56
  government   48, 50
  guerrilla war   44
  military budget   55
  Ministry of Industry   45, 46
  Ministry of Public Finance   46
  new economic policies   58
  oil   41
  public sector   42
  violence   50

Viação Aérea São Paulo, SA (VASP) 176
Vietnam 26, 29, 242

W

wages 70, 71, 73, 74, 75, 76, 79, 82, 83, 84, 133, 137, 168, 182, 194
  agricultural 75, 83, 84
  earners 73, 76, 77, 83
  income 73, 74, 75, 77, 84, 85
  rural workers 75
  social 70
Washington, D.C. 23
wealthy 75, 84, 85
welfare 72, 128, 196
Western Europe 260, 261, 265
Wilson, Woodrow 23, 239
women 211, 212, 213, 214, 215, 218, 232, 233
  agribusiness 216
  agriculture 217
  birth rate 212
  child care 217, 218
  contraceptives 214
  development 211, 212, 219
  earnings 212
  economic
    contribution 214
    participation 211
  education 212, 214, 217
  environmental problems 233
  families 212, 214, 215
  health care 217
  home economy 212, 217
  housewives 213
  illiteracy 214
  income 214, 217
  income-producing activities 217
  informal sector 215, 216

women *continued*
  labor force 212, 213, 214, 215
  life expectancy 212
  living conditions 212
  lower wages 215
  migration 214
  opportunities 215
  organizations 219
  Peru 215
  political clout 212
  pollution 233
  poverty 211, 212, 214, 215, 232
  "reluctant entrepreneurs" 216, 217
  resource managers 233
  self-employment 216
  sexual abuse 139
  unemployment 216
  vocational training 218
  workers 137, 213
workers 127, 133, 134, 138, 139, 146, 166, 211
Workers' Party 171
working class 123
world
  economy 12, 13, 260
  markets 64, 70, 164
  trading system 223
World Bank 4, 16, 25, 48, 144, 193, 194, 196, 204, 227, 229, 230, 231, 243
World War I 239
World War II 9, 23, 29, 72, 163, 247

Y

Yacimientos Petrolíferos Fiscales Sociedad del Estado (YPF, Argentina) 170, 183
Yugoslavia 23

338.98   Privatization amidst
Pri   poverty.

DATE			
10/17/05			